HOW TO FORM A CORPORATION IN TEXAS

Karen Ann Rolcik

Mark Warda

Attorneys at Law

Third Edition

SPHINX® PUBLISHING

AN IMPRINT OF SOURCEBOOKS, INC.®
NAPERVILLE, ILLINOIS
www.SphinxLegal.com

Third edition, 2004

Published by: **Sphinx® Publishing, A Division of Sourcebooks, Inc.®**

<u>Naperville Office</u>
P.O. Box 4410
Naperville, Illinois 60567-4410
630-961-3900
Fax: 630-961-2168
www.sourcebooks.com
www.SphinxLegal.com

This publication is designed to provide accurate and authoritative information in regard to the subject matter covered. It is sold with the understanding that the publisher is not engaged in rendering legal, accounting, or other professional service. If legal advice or other expert assistance is required, the services of a competent professional person should be sought.

From a Declaration of Principles Jointly Adopted by a Committee of the
American Bar Association and a Committee of Publishers and Associations

This product is not a substitute for legal advice.

Disclaimer required by Texas statutes.

Library of Congress Cataloging in Publication Data
Rolcik, Karen Ann.
  How to form a corporation in Texas / by Karen Ann Rolcik and Mark Warda.--
3rd ed.
      p. cm.
  Includes index.
  ISBN 1-57248-470-5 (alk. paper)
  1. Incorporation--Texas--Popular works. I. Warda, Mark. II. Title.
KFT1413.5.Z9R65 2004
346.764'06622--dc22
                                    2004004731

Printed and Bound in the United States of America
VH — 10 9 8 7 6 5 4 3 2 1

Contents

USING SELF-HELP LAW BOOKS

Before using a self-help law book, you should realize the advantages and disadvantages of doing your own legal work and understand the challenges and diligence that this requires.

The Growing Trend

Rest assured that you won't be the first or only person handling your own legal matter. For example, in some states, more than seventy-five percent of the people in divorces and other cases represent themselves. Because of the high cost of legal services, this is a major trend and many courts are struggling to make it easier for people to represent themselves. However, some courts are not happy with people who do not use attorneys and refuse to help them in any way. For some, the attitude is, "Go to the law library and figure it out for yourself."

We write and publish self-help law books to give people an alternative to the often complicated and confusing legal books found in most law libraries. We have made the explanations of the law as simple and easy to understand as possible. Of course, unlike an attorney advising an individual client, we cannot cover every conceivable possibility.

Cost/Value Analysis

Whenever you shop for a product or service, you are faced with various levels of quality and price. In deciding what product or service to buy, you make a cost/value analysis on the basis of your willingness to pay and the quality you desire.

When buying a car, you decide whether you want transportation, comfort, status, or sex appeal. Accordingly, you decide among such choices as a Neon, a Lincoln, a Rolls Royce, or a Porsche. Before making a decision, you usually weigh the merits of each option against the cost.

When you get a headache, you can take a pain reliever (such as aspirin) or visit a medical specialist for a neurological examination. Given this choice, most people, of course, take a pain reliever, since it costs only pennies; whereas a medical examination costs hundreds of dollars and takes a lot of time. This is usually a logical choice because it is rare to need anything more than a pain reliever for a headache. But in some cases, a headache may indicate a brain tumor and failing to see a specialist right away can result in complications. Should everyone with a headache go to a specialist? Of course not, but people treating their own illnesses must realize that they are betting on the basis of their cost/value analysis of the situation. They are taking the most logical option.

The same cost/value analysis must be made when deciding to do one's own legal work. Many legal situations are very straight forward, requiring a simple form and no complicated analysis. Anyone with a little intelligence and a book of instructions can handle the matter without outside help.

But there is always the chance that complications are involved that only an attorney would notice. To simplify the law into a book like this, several legal cases often must be condensed into a single sentence or paragraph. Otherwise, the book would be several hundred pages long and too complicated for most people. However, this simplification necessarily leaves out many details and nuances that would apply to special or unusual situations. Also, there are many ways to interpret most legal questions. Your case may come before a judge who disagrees with the analysis of our authors.

Therefore, in deciding to use a self-help law book and to do your own legal work, you must realize that you are making a cost/value analysis. You have decided that the money you will save in doing it yourself outweighs the chance that your case will not turn out to your satisfaction. Most people handling their own simple legal matters never have a problem, but occasionally people find that it ended up costing them more to have an attorney straighten out the situation than it would have if they had hired an attorney in the beginning. Keep this in mind while handling your case, and be sure to consult an attorney if you feel you might need further guidance.

Local Rules

The next thing to remember is that a book which covers the law for the entire nation, or even for an entire state, cannot possibly include every procedural difference of every jurisdiction. Whenever possible, we provide the exact form needed; however, in some areas, each county, or even each judge, may require unique forms and procedures. In our state books, our forms usually cover the majority of counties in the state, or provide examples of the type of form which will be required. In our national books, our forms are sometimes even more general in nature but are designed to give a good idea of the type of form that will be needed in most locations. Nonetheless, keep in mind that your state, county, or judge may have a requirement, or use a form, that is not included in this book.

You should not necessarily expect to be able to get all of the information and resources you need solely from within the pages of this book. This book will serve as your guide, giving you specific information whenever possible and helping you to find out what else you will need to know. This is just like if you decided to build your own backyard deck. You might purchase a book on how to build decks. However, such a book would not include the building codes and permit requirements of every city, town, county, and township in the nation; nor would it include the lumber, nails, saws, hammers, and other materials and tools you would need to actually build the deck. You would use the book as your guide, and then do some work and research involving such matters as whether you need a permit of some kind, what type and grade of wood are available in your area, whether to use hand tools or power tools, and how to use those tools.

Before using the forms in a book like this, you should check with your court clerk to see if there are any local rules of which you should be aware, or local forms you will need to use. Often, such forms will require the same information as the forms in the book but are merely laid out differently or use slightly different language. They will sometimes require additional information.

Changes in the Law

Besides being subject to local rules and practices, the law is subject to change at any time. The courts and the legislatures of all fifty states are constantly revising the laws. It is possible that while you are reading this book, some aspect of the law is being changed.

In most cases, the change will be of minimal significance. A form will be redesigned, additional information will be required, or a waiting period will be extended. As a result, you might need to revise a form, file an extra form, or wait out a longer time period; these types of changes will not usually affect the outcome of your case. On the other hand, sometimes a major part of the law is changed, the entire law in a particular area is rewritten, or a case that was the basis of a central legal point is overruled. In such instances, your entire ability to pursue your case may be impaired.

INTRODUCTION

Each year hundreds of thousands of corporations are registered in this country, tens of thousands in Texas alone. The corporation is the preferred way of doing business for most people because it offers many advantages over partnerships and sole proprietorships. It is not a coincidence that the largest businesses in the world are corporations.

The main reason people incorporate is to avoid personal liability. While sole proprietors and partners have all of their personal assets at risk, corporate shareholders risk only what they paid for their stock. With so many people ready to sue for any reason or for no reason, the corporation is one of the few inexpensive protections left.

Creating a simple corporation is very easy and it is the purpose of this book to explain, in simple language, how you can do it yourself. A simple corporation as used in this book is one in which there are five or fewer shareholders and all of them are active in the business. If you plan to sell stock to someone who is not active in the business or to have six or more shareholders, you should seek the advice of an attorney. However, some guidance is provided throughout this book as to what some of the concerns will be in these circumstances.

If your situation is in any way complicated or involves factors not mentioned in this book, you should seek the advice of an attorney practicing corporate law. The cost of a short consultation can be a lot cheaper than the consequences of violating the law.

If you plan to sell stock to outside investors, you should consult with a lawyer who specializes in securities laws. Selling a few thousand shares of stock to friends and neighbors may sound like an easy way to raise capital for your business, but it is not! Since the stock market crash of the 1930s there have been federal laws regulating the sale of securities. There are harsh criminal penalties for violators and the laws do not have many loopholes. The basic rules are explained in Chapter 5.

This book also explains the basics of corporate taxation, but you should discuss your own particular situation with your accountant before deciding what is best for you. He or she can also set you up with an efficient system of bookkeeping, which can save both time and money.

Good luck with your new business!

I THE CORPORATE ENTITY

A *corporation* is an entity created under state law. Once recognized by the state, the corporation becomes a *legal person* that has certain rights and obligations, such as the right to do business and the obligation to pay taxes. Sometimes one hears of a law referring to *natural persons*. That term is used to differentiate them from corporations.

Business corporations were invented hundreds of years ago to promote risky ventures. Prior to the use of corporations, persons engaged in business faced the possibility of unlimited liability. By using a corporation, many people could put up a fixed sum of money for a new venture, such as a voyage to explore the new world. If the venture made money, they shared the profits. If the venture went into debt, the most they could lose was the initial investment they put up.

The reasons for having a corporation are the same today. They allow investors to put up money for new ventures without risk of further liability. While our legal system is making more and more people liable for more and more things, the corporation remains one of the few innovations that has not yet been abandoned.

Before forming a corporation, you should be familiar with the following common corporate terms that will be used in the text.

Shareholders
A *shareholder* is a person who owns stock in a corporation. In most small corporations the shareholders are the same as the officers and directors, but in large corporations most shareholders are not officers or directors. Sometimes small corporations have shareholders who are not officers, such as when the stock is in one spouse's name and the other spouse runs the business. Specific laws regarding issuance of shares and shareholders' rights are in the *Texas Business Corporation Act* (TBCA), Articles 2.12 through 2.30. (see Appendix B.) Articles of the TBCA will be referred to throughout the text like *TBCA art.* followed by a number (*e.g.*, TBCA art. 2.12).

Officers
Officers are usually the president, secretary, treasurer, and vice president of the corporation. These persons run the day-to-day affairs of the business. They are elected each year by a vote of the board of directors. In Texas, one person can hold all of the offices of a corporation.

Board of Directors
The *board of directors* is the controlling body of a corporation that makes major corporate decisions and elects the officers. It usually meets just once a year. A corporation can have one director (who can also hold all offices and own all the stock). In a small corporation, the board members are usually also officers.

Registered Agent
The *registered agent* is the person designated by the corporation to receive the legal papers that must be served on the corporation. The registered agent should be regularly available at the *registered office* of the corporation. The registered office can be the corporate office, the office of the corporation's attorney, or the office of another person who is the registered agent.

Articles of Incorporation
Articles of Incorporation is the name of the document that is filed with the Secretary of State to start the corporation. In most cases, it legally needs to contain only five basic statements. Some corporations have lengthy Articles of Incorporation, but this just makes it harder to make changes in the corporate structure. It is usually better to keep the Articles short and put the details in the bylaws.

Bylaws
Bylaws are the rules governing the structure and operation of the corporation. Typically the bylaws will set out rules for the board of directors, officers, shareholders, and corporate formalities.

The *Texas Business Corporation Act* contains most of Texas' laws regarding general corporate activities. For example, it lists all of the powers of corporations so they do not have to be recited again in the Articles of Incorporation or bylaws.

Legal definitions of other corporate terms are included in the TBCA art. 1.01. (see Appendix B.)

2 DECIDING TO INCORPORATE

Before forming a corporation, the business owner or prospective business owner should become familiar with the advantages and disadvantages of incorporating.

Advantages

The following are some of the advantages that a corporation has over other forms of businesses, such as sole proprietorships and partnerships.

Limited Liability   The main reason for forming a corporation is to limit the liability of the owners. In a sole proprietorship or partnership the owners are personally liable for the debts and liabilities of the business. Creditors can go after all of the owner's (or owners') assets to collect. If a corporation is formed and operated properly, the owners can be protected from all such liability.

Example: If several people are in partnership and one of them makes many large extravagant purchases in the name of the partnership, the other partners can be held liable for the full amount of all such purchases. The creditors can take the bank accounts, cars, real estate, and other property of any partner to pay the debts of the partnership. If only one partner has money, he or she may have to pay all of the debts accumulated by all the other partners.

With a corporation, only the corporation is liable for damages, and if there was not enough money to pay a claim, the owner cannot be touched. When doing business in the corporate form, the corporation may go bankrupt and the shareholders may lose their initial investment, but the creditors cannot touch the assets of the owners.

Example: One true example is a business owner who owned hundreds of taxis. He put one or two in each of hundreds of different corporations that he owned. Each corporation only had minimum insurance, and when one taxi was involved in an accident, the owner only lost the assets of that corporation.

Warning: If a corporate officer or shareholder does something negligent, signs a debt personally, or guarantees a corporate debt, the corporation form will not protect him or her from the consequences of his or her own act or from the debt.

Continuous Existence

A corporation may have a perpetual existence. When a sole proprietor or partner dies, the assets of the business may go to his or her heirs, but the business does not exist any longer. If the surviving spouse or other heirs of a business owner want to continue the business, they will be considered a new business even if they are using the assets of the old business. With a partnership, the death of one partner may cause a dissolution of the business.

Example 1: If a person dies owning a sole proprietorship, his or her spouse may want to continue the business. That person may inherit all of the assets but will have to start a new business. This means getting new licenses and tax numbers, registering the name, and establishing credit from scratch. With a corporation, the business continues with all of the same licenses, bank accounts, etc.

Example 2: If one partner dies, the partnership may be forced out of business. The heirs of the deceased partner can force the sale of their share of the assets of the partnership even if the surviving partner needs them to continue the business. If the surviving partner does not have the money to buy the heirs out, the business may have to be dissolved. With a corporation, the heirs would only inherit stock. With properly drawn documents, the business could continue.

Ease of Transferability

A corporation and all of its assets and accounts may be transferred by the simple assignment of a stock certificate. With a sole proprietorship or partnership, each of the individual assets must be transferred and the accounts, licenses, and permits must be individually transferred.

Example: If a sole proprietorship is sold, the new owner will have to get a new occupational license, set up his or her own bank account, and apply for a new taxpayer identification number. The title to any vehicles and real estate will have to be put in his or her name and all open accounts will have to be changed to his or her name. New credit applications will also probably have to be submitted.

With a corporation, all of these items remain in the same corporate name. As the new shareholder, he or she would elect him- or herself director, and, as director, he or she would elect him- or herself president, treasurer, and any other offices he or she wanted to hold.

NOTE: *In some cases, the new owners will have to submit personal applications for things such as credit lines or liquor licenses.*

Transfer of Ownership

By distributing stock, the owner of a business can share the profits of a business without giving up control. This is done by keeping a majority of stock or by issuing different classes of stock, with and without voting rights.

If a person wants to give his or her children some of the profits of the business, he or she can give them stock and pay dividends to them without giving them any control over the management. This would not be practical with a partnership or sole proprietorship.

Ease of Raising Capital

A corporation may raise capital by selling stock or borrowing money. A corporation does not pay taxes on money it raises by the sale of stock.

If a corporation wants to expand, the owners can sell off ten, fifty, or ninety percent of the stock and still remain in control of the business. The people putting up the money may be more willing to invest if they know they will have a piece of the action than if they were making a loan with a limited return. They may not want to become partners in a partnership.

NOTE: *There are strict rules about the sale of stock, with criminal penalties and monetary fines up to $100,000. (see Chapter 5.)*

Separate Record Keeping A corporation has its own bank accounts and records. A partner or sole proprietor may have trouble differentiating which expenses are for business and which are for personal items.

Tax Advantages There are some tax advantages that are available only to corporations. Some of these include the following.

- ✪ Medical insurance for your family may be fully deductible.

- ✪ A tax deferred trust can be set up for a retirement plan.

- ✪ Losses are fully deductible for a corporation whereas an individual must prove there was a profit motive before deducting losses.

Ease of Estate Planning With a corporation, shares of a company can be distributed more easily than with a partnership. Different heirs can be given different percentages, and control can be limited to those who are most capable.

Prestige The name of a corporation sounds more prestigious than the name of a sole proprietor to some people. John Smith d/b/a Acme Builders sounds like one lone guy. Acme Builders, Incorporated, sounds like it might be a large operation. No one needs to know that it is run out of a garage. One female writer on the subject has suggested that a woman who is president of a corporation looks more successful than one doing business in her own name. This probably applies to everyone.

Separate Credit Rating A corporation has its own credit rating, which can be better or worse than the owner's credit rating. A corporate business can go bankrupt while the owner's credit remains unaffected or an owner's credit may be bad but the corporation may maintain a good rating.

Disadvantages

There are, unfortunately, certain disadvantages to doing business in the corporate form of which you should be aware. These include some of the following.

Extra Tax Return   A corporation is required to file its own tax return. This is a bit longer and more complicated than the form required by a sole proprietorship and may entail additional expenses if the services of an accountant are required. A partnership must also file its own tax return, so there is no advantage or disadvantage over a partnership as far as tax returns are concerned.

Annual Report   A corporation must file a one-page *annual report* with the state (which lists names and addresses of officers and directors).

Separate Finances   The owners of a corporation must be careful to keep their personal business separate from the business of the corporation. The corporation must have its own records and have minutes of its meetings. Money must be kept separate. But in every business, records should be separate, so the corporate structure might make it easier to do so.

Extra Expenses   There are, of course, expenses in operating a corporation compared to not operating one. These expenses include additional start-up filing fees, additional attorney expenses for those using an attorney, and other expenses a corporation has to pay that a sole proprietor does not. For example, a corporation owner will have to pay unemployment compensation for him- or herself, which would not have to be paid if the owner were a sole proprietor.

Checking Accounts   Checks made out to a corporation cannot be cashed; they must be deposited into a corporate account. Some banks have higher fees just for businesses that are incorporated. (See pages 33–34 for tips on avoiding high bank fees.)

3

CHOOSING THE BEST TYPE OF CORPORATION FOR YOU

There are several types of corporation to choose from. Each has its own advantages and disadvantages depending on what your goals are. Each also has requirements that may prevent you from selecting a certain one.

Texas Corporation or Foreign Corporation

A person wishing to form a corporation must decide whether the corporation will be a Texas corporation or a *foreign* corporation. A foreign corporation is one incorporated in another state even though it does business in Texas.

Delaware Corporations
In the past there was some advantage to incorporating in Delaware, since that state had very liberal laws regarding corporations. Many national corporations are incorporated there. However, most states have liberalized their corporation laws in recent years—so today there is no advantage to incorporating in Delaware for most people.

Nevada Corporations   Nevada has liberalized its corporation laws recently to attract businesses. It allows bearer stock and other rules that allow more privacy to corporate participants. It also does not share information with the Internal Revenue Service and does not have a state income tax.

Texas Corporations   Today Texas has very favorable corporate laws so out-of-state laws are not an advantage. If you form a corporation in a state other than Texas, you will probably have to have an agent or an office in that state and will have to register as a foreign corporation doing business in Texas. This is more expensive and more complicated than just registering as a Texas corporation in the beginning. Also, if you are sued by someone who is not in your state, they can sue you in the state in which you are incorporated, which would probably be more expensive for you than a suit filed in your local court. In some states your corporation may be required to pay state income tax.

S Corporation or C Corporation

A corporation has a choice of how it wants to be taxed. It can make the election at the beginning of its existence or at the beginning of a new tax year. The choices are as follows.

S Corporation   Formerly called a *Subchapter S corporation*, an *S corporation* pays no income tax and may only be used for small businesses. All the income or losses of the corporation for the year are passed through to the shareholders who report them on their individual returns. At the end of each year the corporation files an *information return* listing all of its income, expenses, depreciation, etc. and sends to each shareholder a notice of his or her share as determined by percentage of stock ownership.

Advantages. Using this method avoids double taxation and allows pass-through of losses and depreciation. The business is treated like a partnership. Since many businesses have tax losses during the first years due to start-up costs, many businesses elect S status and switch over to C corporation status in later years. Once a corporation terminates its S status, there is a five-year waiting period before it can switch back.

Disadvantages. If stockholders are in high income brackets, their share of the profits will be taxed at those rates. Shareholders who do not *materially participate* in the business cannot deduct losses. Some fringe benefits such as health and life insurance may not be tax deductible in an S corporation.

Requirements. To qualify for S corporation status the corporation must:

- ✪ have no more than seventy-five shareholders (shares owned by a husband and wife jointly are considered owned by one shareholder), none of whom are nonresident aliens or corporations, all of whom consent to the election;

- ✪ have only one class of stock;

- ✪ not be a member of an *affiliated group*;

- ✪ generate at least twenty percent of its income in this country and have no more than twenty percent of its income from *passive* sources (interest, rents, dividends, royalties, securities transactions); and,

- ✪ file **FORM 2553** before the end of the fifteenth day of the third month of the tax year for which it is to be effective and have it approved by the IRS.

Multiple Corporations. The IRS has approved the use of two or more S corporations in partnership to increase the number of allowable investors in a venture. It may also be possible for an S corporation to form a partnership with a C corporation.

C Corporation   A *C corporation* pays taxes on its net earnings at corporate tax rates. Salaries of officers, directors, and employees are deducted from income, so are not taxed to the corporation, but money paid out in dividends is taxed twice. It is taxed at the corporation's rate as part of its profit and then the stockholders must include the amounts they receive as dividends in their income.

Advantages. If taxpayers are in a higher tax bracket than the corporation and the money will be left in the company for expansion, taxes are saved. Fringe benefits such as health, accident, and life insurance are deductible expenses.

Disadvantages. Double taxation of dividends by the federal government is the biggest problem with a C corporation. Also, Texas has a franchise tax that comes very close to being an income tax on corporations. The franchise tax is a combination of a tax imposed on *capital* and a tax imposed on *earned surplus* (a disguised income tax). The franchise tax on capital is imposed at a rate of 0.25%. The franchise tax on earned surplus is imposed at a rate of 4.5%. Franchise tax must be reported on the Texas Corporation Tax Report form and paid May 15th.

NOTE: *This tax does not apply to money taken out as salaries, and many small business owners take all profits out as salaries to avoid double taxation and the Texas franchise tax. But there are rules requiring that salaries be reasonable. If a shareholder's salary is deemed to be too high relative to his or her job, the salary may be considered dividends and subject to the double taxation.*

Requirements. None. All corporations are C corporations unless they specifically elect to become S corporations.

Closely Held Corporation Election

A closely held corporation election is beneficial for many small businesses. Its purpose is to place restrictions on the transferability of stock. Often it obligates a shareholder to offer to the corporation or other current shareholders the opportunity to purchase the stock before offering it to any outside purchaser. If the corporation and shareholders reject the offer, they typically must still consent to who the transferee (buyer) of the shares will be.

To elect to have these restrictions, they should be included in the bylaws, printed on the certificates, and in many states they must be included in the Articles of Incorporation.

Inc. or P.C.

Certain types of services can only be rendered by a corporation if it is a *Professional Corporation*. These are such businesses as attorneys, certified public accountants, veterinarians, architects, psychologists, licensed professional counselors, and licensed marriage and family therapists. A professional corporation comes under nearly all of the rules of the *Texas Business Corporation Act* regarding corporations in general unless they conflict with *Texas Professional Corporation Act* (TPCA). The

TPCA specifically governs professional corporations. It is found at Article 1528(e) of the *Texas Business Corporation Act*. The major differences between a corporation and a professional corporation are as follows.

Purpose   A professional service corporation must have one specific purpose spelled out in the Articles of Incorporation and that purpose must be to practice one of the professions. A professional service corporation may change its purpose to another legal purpose, but it will then no longer be a professional service corporation. (TPCA, Sec. 4.)

Name   The name of a professional corporation must contain the words *company*, *corporation*, *incorporated*, or any abbreviation of these, or the phrase *professional corporation* or the initials *P.C.* It may contain the name of some or all of the shareholders and may not contain the names of deceased or retired shareholders, provided the name is not contrary to the law or ethics regulating the practice of the professional service rendered through the professional corporation. (TPCA, Sec. 8.)

Shareholders   Only persons licensed to practice the profession may be shareholders of a professional corporation. A shareholder who loses his or her right to practice must immediately sever all employment with and financial interests in such corporation.

Merger   A professional corporation may not merge with any other corporation except a Texas professional corporation that is licensed to perform the same type of services.

Professional Associations

Individuals licensed to practice certain medical related professions, such as medicine, osteopathy, podiatry, dentistry, optometry, or chiropractics may render services in the form of a corporation if it is a *Professional Association*. A professional association comes under many of the rules of the *Texas Business Corporation Act* regarding corporations in general unless they conflict with Texas Revised Civil Statutes Annotated Article 1528f, commonly known as the *Texas Professional Association Act* (TPAA). The TPAA specifically governs professional associations. The major differences between a general corporation and a professional association include the following.

Purpose   A professional association must have one special purpose spelled out in the Articles of Association and that purpose must be to render any type of personal service to the public which requires that the person performing the service obtain a license. (Examples are doctors, osteopaths, dentists, and the like.) It may not engage in any other business, but it may invest its funds in real estate, mortgages, stocks, bonds, or other investments. (TPAA, Sec. 5(A).)

Name   The name of a professional association must include the word or words *associated*, *association*, *professional association*, or *and associates*, or the abbreviation *assoc.* or *P.A.* The name shall not be one that is contrary to or in conflict with any law or ethics regulating the practice or practitioners of any professional service rendered through or in connection with the professional association.

Shareholders   Only those persons licensed to perform the same type of professional service as that for which the professional association was formed may be shareholders.

Not-for-Profit Corporations

Not-for-profit corporations are usually used for social clubs, churches, and charities and are beyond the scope of this book. While they are similar to for-profit corporations in many aspects, such as limited liability and the required formalities, there are additional state and federal requirements that must be met.

In some cases, a business can be formed as a not-for-profit corporation. It would not be allowed to distribute profits to its founders but it could pay salaries and enjoy numerous tax advantages. For information on books dealing with not-for-profit corporations, check your local bookstore or library.

Start-Up Procedures

After deciding on the type of corporation that best suits your needs, you are ready to start the process of incorporating your business. There are several steps to take to accomplish this, but having everything in order from the beginning will help keep the business running smoothly.

Name Check

The very first thing to do before starting a corporation is to thoroughly check out the name you wish to use to be sure it is available. Many business have been forced to stop using their name after spending thousands of dollars promoting it.

Local Records   To check for other corporations using the name you want, you should call the corporate records office of the Secretary of State's office at 512-463-5555. If your name is too similar to another corporate name, then you will not be allowed to register it. You should also ask about *assumed names*. Assumed names are business names being used by individuals and corporations. There is no law saying that two people cannot use the same assumed name, so the Secretary of State allows anyone to file any name, even if a hundred other people have already registered it.

Assumed names are registered in the county in which the person is doing business or, if a corporation, in the county where the entity maintains its registered office. They are also registered with the Secretary of State. If you want to be sure that no one else has used your name, check the official records of your county and any other counties where you plan to do business.

Business Listings

Since some businesses neglect to properly register their name (yet still may have superior rights to the name), you should also check phone books and business directories. Many libraries have phone books from around the country as well as directories of trade names.

Internet

Use the Internet to search for the name you would like to use. You can search every yellow pages listing for free. You can select a state, enter your business name, and it will tell you if any other companies are listed with that name. One site that allows you to search all states at once is

www.infoseek.com.

Trademark Search

If you do not have access to a computer at home or work, you may be able to use one at your public library or have the search done at your library for a small fee.

To be sure that you are not violating a registered trademark, you should have a search done of the records of the United States Patent and Trademark Office. This can be done online at **www.uspto.gov**. You can also have a search done for a small fee at some libraries if they subscribe to Dialog Information Services or a similar service.

Another alternative is to order a search from a trademark search firm. This is usually the most thorough, but the cost can range from $100 to $500 or more. Some firms that do searches are:

Government Liaison Services, Inc.
3030 Clarendon Blvd., Suite 209
Arlington, VA 22210
800-642-6564

Thomson & Thomson
500 Victory Road
North Quincy, MA 02171-1545
800-692-8833

XL Corporate Service
62 White Street
New York, NY 10013
800-221-2972

Name Reservation

It is possible to reserve a name for a corporation for a period of 120 days for a fee of $40. However, this is usually pointless because it is just as easy to file the Articles of Incorporation as it is to reserve the name. One possible reason for reserving a name would be to hold it while waiting for a trademark name search to arrive.

Similar Names

Sometimes it seems like every good name is taken. But a name can often be modified slightly or used on a different type of goods. If there is a *TriCounty Painting, Inc.* in Dallas, it may be possible to use something like *TriCounty Painting of Austin, Inc.* if you are in a different part of the state. Try different variations if your favorite is taken. Another possibility is to give the corporation one name and then do business under an assumed name. (See "Assumed Names" on page 20.)

Example: If you want to use the name "Flowers by Freida" in Houston and there is already a "Flowers by Freida, Inc." in Fort Worth, you might incorporate under the name "Freida Jones, Inc." and then register the corporation as doing business under the fictitious name "Flowers by Freida." Unless "Flowers by Freida, Inc." has registered a trademark for the name either in Texas or nationally, you will probably be able to use the name.

NOTE: *You should realize that you might run into complications later, especially if you decide to expand into other areas of the state. One protection available would be to register the name as a trademark. This would give you exclusive use of the name anywhere that someone else was not already using it. (see p.18.)*

Forbidden Names

A corporation may not use certain words in its name if there would be a likelihood of confusion. There are state and federal laws that control the use of these words. In most cases, your application will be rejected if you use a forbidden word. Some of the words that may not be used without special licenses or registration are:

Accounting	Cooperative
Bank	Disney
Banker	Insurance
Banking	Olympic
Credit Union	Trust Company

Trademarks The name of a business cannot be registered as a trademark, but if the name is used in connection with goods or services it may be registered. Such registration will grant the holder exclusive rights to use that name except in areas where someone else has already used the name. A trademark may be registered either in Texas or in the entire country.

Each trademark is registered for a certain *class* of goods. If you want to sell *Zapata* chewing gum, it doesn't matter that someone has registered the name *Zapata* for use on shoes. If you want to register the mark for several types of goods or services, you must register it for each different class into which the goods or services fall and pay a separate fee for each category.

For protection within the state of Texas, the mark may be registered with the Texas Trademark Office of the Texas Secretary of State's office. The cost is about $50. Application forms and instructions are contained in the book *How to Start a Business in Texas*, published by Sourcebooks, Inc.® The forms can also be obtained by visiting the Texas Secretary of State at **www.sos.state.tx.us** and selecting *trademark form* under the *Business & Public Filing* drop down menu.

For protection across the entire United States, the mark can be registered with the United States Patent and Trademark Office. The cost is about $335. (The procedure for federal registration is more complicated than state registration and is explained in the book *How to Register Your Own Trademark* available from Sourcebooks, Inc.®)

Assumed Names A corporation may operate under an assumed name just as an individual can. This is done when a corporation wants to operate several businesses under different names or if the business name is not available as a corporate name. Assumed names used to be registered in each county, but they are now registered statewide with the Secretary of State. However, registering an assumed name does not give the registrant any rights to the name. While corporate names are carefully checked by the Secretary of State and disallowed if they are similar to others, assumed names are filed without checking and any number of people may register the same name. The cost of registering an assumed name is $25. Application forms and instructions are contained in the book *How to Start a Business in Texas*, published by Sourcebooks, Inc.® Forms can also be obtained from your local courthouse or online at **www.sos.state.tx.us** and selecting *Corporation Index of Forms* under the *Business & Public Filing* drop down menu.

NOTE: *When an assumed name is used by a corporation, the corporate name should also be used. If the public does not see that they are dealing with a corporation, they may be able to* pierce the corporate veil *and sue the stockholders individually.*

Articles of Incorporation

The act that creates the corporation is the filing of Articles of Incorporation with the Secretary of State. Some corporations have long, elaborate Articles that spell out numerous powers and functions, but most of this is unnecessary. The powers of corporations are spelled out in Texas law (see TBCA art. 2.02 in Appendix B) and do not have to be repeated. (In fact, the statute *says* that the powers do not have to be repeated in the Articles, but they often are. Attorneys can charge a lot more for Articles of Incorporation that are long and look complicated.) The main reason to keep the Articles of Incorporation short is to avoid having to amend them later. By putting all but the basics in the **BYLAWS** of the corporation, you can make changes in the corporate structure much more easily. The **ARTICLES OF INCORPORATION** included in this book (forms 2 and 3) are as simple as possible for this purpose.

Requirements   Texas law requires that only nine things be included in the Articles of Incorporation. Some things, such as the purpose of the corporation, regulations for the operation of the corporation, and a par value of the stock may be spelled out in the Articles of Incorporation, but this is not advisable since any changes would then require the complicated process of amending the Articles. It is better to spell these things out in the bylaws. The nine matters required to be contained in the Articles and a few of the optional provisions include the following.

Name of the corporation. The corporation name must include one of the following six words:

Incorporated	Inc.
Corporation	Corp.
Company	Co.

The reason is that persons dealing with the business will be on notice that it is a corporation. This is important in protecting the shareholders from liability. The last two choices, *company* and *co.*, are not as good as the others because they are not clear notice that the business is incorporated.

Address of the corporation. The address of the principal office and the mailing address of the corporation must be provided.

Duration. The duration of the corporation need not be mentioned if it is to be perpetual. If not, the duration must be in the Articles.

Professional Corporations. There are two additional requirements for corporations that will be professional corporations.

1. The purpose of the corporation must be stated and must be limited to the practice of one profession.

2. The name must contain the designation, *Professional Corporation* or *P.C.*

Purpose. The purpose or purposes for which the corporation is organized must be stated. Language you will want to use or at least include is:
> *to transact any and all lawful business for which corporations may*
> *be organized under the Texas Business Corporation Act.*

The number of shares of stock the corporation is authorized to issue. This is usually an even number such as 100, 1000, or 1,000,000. It does not matter what number you pick. A lot of people authorize 1,000,000 shares (with a par value of \$0.01 or 0.001) because it sounds impressive.

In some cases, it may be advantageous to issue different classes of stock such as common and preferred, or voting and nonvoting, but such matters should be discussed with an attorney or accountant.

If there are different classes of stock, the Articles of Incorporation must contain a designation of the classes and a statement of the preferences, limitations, and relative rights of each class. In addition, if there are to be any preferred or special shares issued in *series*, the Articles must explain the relative rights, preferences, and any authority of the board of directors to establish preferences. Any preemptive rights must also be outlined.

This book explains how to form a corporation with one class of stock. It is usually advisable to authorize double or quadruple the amount of stock that will be initially issued. The unissued stock can be issued later if more capital is contributed by a shareholder or by a new member of the business.

One important point to keep in mind when issuing stock is that the full par value must be paid for the shares. If this is not done then the shareholder can later be held liable for the full par value. (For more important information about issuing stock see Chapter 5.)

The name of the registered agent and the address of the registered office. Each corporation must have a registered agent and a registered office. The registered agent can be any individual or a corporation. The registered office can be the business office of the corporation if the registered agent works out of that office, it can be the office of another individual who is the registered agent (such as an attorney), or it may be a corporate registered agent's office. The business address of the registered agent is considered the registered office of the corporation. A post office box alone is not a sufficient address for the registered office.

Directors. The number of directors making up the initial board of directors and their names and addresses must be included in the Articles of Incorporation. The name of the city and state are a sufficient address for the directors.

The name and address of the incorporator of the corporation. The incorporator of the corporation may be any person, even if that person has no future interest in the corporation. For people who need to be incorporated quickly, there are companies in Austin that can, on a moment's notice, have someone run over to the Corporations Section of the Secretary of State's Office to file corporate Articles, which are later assigned to the real parties in interest. Only one incorporator is required, but every person who is listed as an incorporator must sign the documents. The incorporator does not have to be a resident of Texas.

Effective date. A specific effective date may be in the Articles but is not required. They are effective upon filing. If an effective date is specified it may not be more than ninety days after filing.

Execution   The Articles of Incorporation must be signed by each incorporator and dated. The Articles do not have to be notarized. Anyone over the age of eighteen can be the incorporator and there is no need to have more than one person sign. Rights of other parties can be spelled out at the incorporation meeting (also known as the organizational meeting).

Forms
Articles of Incorporation need not be on any certain form. They can be typed on blank paper or can be on a fill-in-the-blank form. In the back of this book are forms of **ARTICLES OF INCORPORATION** for both a regular corporation (see form 2, p.189) and a professional corporation (see form 3, p.191).

Filing
The Articles of Incorporation must be filed with the Secretary of State of Texas by sending them to:

Office of the Secretary of State
Corporations Section
Statutory Filings Division
P.O. Box 13697
Austin, TX 78711-3697

You should mail them along with a **TRANSMITTAL LETTER** (see form 1, p.187) and the filing fees. The fee is $300. If you wish to receive a certified copy of the Articles, the cost is $1 per page plus $10 for the certificate. This is an unnecessary expense since such certified copy is rarely, if ever, needed. The better alternative is to enclose a photocopy along with the Articles and ask that it be *stamped with the filing date* and returned.

The return time for the Articles is usually a week or two. If there is a need to have them back quickly they may be sent by a courier, such as FedEx, with prepaid return. In such cases they are filed the day received and returned shortly thereafter. The address for courier delivery is:

Office of the Secretary of State
Corporations Section
James Earl Rudder State Office Building
1019 Brazos
Austin, TX 78701

If you want the Articles to be reviewed or filed very quickly, you may request *special handling* or *expedited handling*. The fee for this service is $25 per document. The documents are sorted when received by the Secretary of State and those requesting special handling or expedited handling are processed prior to all other mail received that day. This $25 fee is also required for documents filed in person that are requested to be given special handling or expedited handling.

Shareholder Agreement

Whenever there are two or more shareholders in a corporation they should consider drawing up a *shareholder agreement*. This document spells out what is to happen in the event of a disagreement between the parties. In closely held corporations the minority shareholders have a risk of being locked into a long-term enterprise with little or no way to withdraw their capital.

A shareholder agreement is a fairly complicated document. You should consider having it drawn up by an attorney. This may be costly, but the expense should be weighed against the costs of lengthy litigation should the parties separate. A less expensive alternative is to obtain a few sample agreements from a law library and tailor one to fit your needs. Some of the things that should be addressed in such an agreement could include:

- ✪ veto by minority shareholder;

- ✪ greater than majority voting requirement;

- ✪ cumulative voting;

- ✪ deadlocks;

- ✪ arbitration;

- ✪ dissolution;

- ✪ compulsory buy-out;

- ✪ preemptive rights;

- ✪ restrictions on transfers of shares; and,

- ✪ refusal of a party to participate.

Organizational Paperwork

Every corporation must have bylaws and must maintain a set of minutes of its meetings. The bylaws must be adopted at the first meeting. The first minutes of the corporation will be the minutes of the organizational meeting.

Bylaws

The **BYLAWS** are the rules for organization and operation of the corporation. They are required by TBCA art. 2.23. Two sets of bylaws are included with this book. Form 11 is for simple corporations and form 12 is for professional corporations. To complete them, you should fill in the name of the corporation, the city of the main office of the corporation, the proposed date of the annual meeting (this can be varied each year as needed), and the number of directors to be on the board.

Waiver of Notice

Before a meeting of the incorporators, the board of directors, or the shareholders can be held to transact lawful business, formal notice must be given to the parties ahead of time. Since small corporations often need to have meetings on short notice and do not want to be bothered with formal notices, it is customary to have all parties sign written **WAIVERS OF NOTICE**. Texas law allows the waiver to be signed at any time, even after the meeting has taken place, for both shareholders (TBCA art. 9.10 (A)) and for directors (TBCA art. 9.10 (B)). **WAIVERS OF NOTICE** are included in this book for the organizational meeting (form 9) and for the annual and special meetings (forms 19, 21, 23, and 25).

Minutes

As part of the formal requirements of operating a corporation, minutes must be kept of the meetings of shareholders and the board of directors. Usually only one meeting of each is required per year (the annual meeting) unless there is some special need for a meeting in the interim (such as the resignation of an officer). The first minutes that will be needed are the minutes of the organizational meeting of the corporation. At this meeting the officers and directors are elected; the bylaws, corporate seal, and stock certificates are adopted; and other organizational decisions made. Most of the forms should be self-explanatory, but sample filled-in forms are in Appendix C of this book.

Resolutions

When the board of directors or shareholders make major decisions, it is usually done in the form of a resolution. The important **RESOLUTIONS** at the organizational meeting are those such as choosing a bank (see form 13, p.229) and adopting S corporation status (see form 18, p.243).

Consent in Lieu of Organizational Meeting

Texas law (TBCA arts. 3.06 and 9.10) allows the initial board of directors to execute incorporation papers without a meeting. However, it is better to have a formal meeting to prove to possible future creditors that you conduct the corporation in a formal manner.

Tax Forms

The IRS routinely offers seminars throughout the State of Texas. The IRS Small Business Tax Education Program is designed to assist small business owners in understanding the various tax reporting and tax paying obligations of a small business. There is no charge for these seminars. You can contact your local Small Business Development Center to find the times and locations of such seminars. You can also contact the IRS Taxpayer Education and Communication offices at:

Austin area: 512-499-5832 or email SBSE.TEC.Austin@irs.gov

Dallas area: 214-767-2421 or email SBSE.TEC.Dallas@irs.gov

Houston area: 713-209-3543 or email SBSE.TEC.Houston@irs.gov

The IRS or your accountant can help you to make sure you are filing all of the necessary tax reporting documents. However, there are certain forms you need to be aware of during the start-up of your corporation.

Form SS-4 (Employer Identification Number)

Prior to opening a bank account, the corporation must obtain a federal employer identification number, which is the corporate equivalent of a Social Security number. This is done by filing **FORM SS-4.** (see form 6, p.197.) This usually takes two or three weeks, so it should be filed early. Send the form to:

Internal Revenue Service Center
Austin, TX 73301

If you need the number quickly, you may be able to obtain the number by phone by calling the IRS at 512 462-7843 before 4:30 P.M. Be sure to have your **FORM SS-4** complete and in front of you before calling.

As an alternative, you may obtain your federal employer identification number online. **FORM SS-4** is available online at **www.irs.gov**. Select *Businesses* and then *Employer ID Numbers*.

When you apply for this number you will probably be put on the mailing list for other corporate tax forms. If you do not receive these, you should call your local IRS forms number and request the forms for new businesses. These include Circular E explaining the taxes due, the W-4 forms for each employee, the tax deposit coupons, and the Form 941 quarterly return for withholding.

Form 2553 (S Corporation)

If your corporation is to be taxed as an S corporation, you must file **FORM 2553** with the IRS within seventy-five days of incorporation. (see form 17, p.237.) A filled-in sample is shown in Appendix C. As a practical matter, you should sign and file this at your incorporation meeting; otherwise, you may forget. To make the S corporation status official, you should also adopt a corporate resolution electing to be taxed as an S corporation and keep it in your minute book.

Form AP157 (State Sales Tax Application)

If you will be selling or renting goods or services at retail, you must collect Texas Sales and Use Tax. Some services such as doctors' and lawyers' fees are not taxed, but most others are. If you have any doubt, check with the Comptroller of Public Accounts. First, you must obtain a tax number, which requires you to fill out a simple questionnaire. To obtain this form, you can call the Comptroller (your local office should be listed in the beginning of your phone book under Texas State Government Offices/Comptroller of Public Accounts), or you can write to the Comptroller of Public Accounts, State of Texas, Austin, TX 78774. This form is also included in our book *How to Start a Business in Texas*. After you obtain your tax number, you will be required to collect sales tax on all purchases. Tax returns must be filed quarterly. After a year, if your taxes are low, you may be allowed to file only annually.

Corporate Supplies

A corporation needs to keep a permanent record of its legal affairs. This includes the original charter; minutes of all meetings; records of the stock issued, transferred, and cancelled; fictitious names registered; and any other legal matters. The records are usually kept in a ring binder. Any ring binder will do, but it is possible to purchase a specially prepared *corporate kit* that has the name of the corporation printed on it and usually contains forms such as minutes, stock certificates, etc. Most of these items are included with this book, so purchasing such a kit is unnecessary unless you want to have a fancy leather binder or specially printed stock certificates.

Some sources for corporate kits are:

Excelsior-Legal, Inc.
610 Magic Mile
P.O. Box 5683
Arlington, TX 76005
800-221-2972

Texas Corporation Supplies, Inc.
P.O. Box 12695
Houston, TX 77217
800-392-3720

Corpex
480 Canal Street
New York, NY 10013
800-221-8181

Corporate Seal

One thing that is not included with this book is a *corporate seal*. This must be specially made for each corporation. Most corporations use a metal seal like a notary's seal to emboss the paper. These can be ordered from many office supply companies. In recent years, many corporations have been using rubber stamps for corporate seals. These are cheaper, lighter, and easier to read. Rubber stamp seals can also be ordered from office supply stores, printers, and specialized rubber stamp companies. The corporate seal should contain the full, exact name of the corporation, the word *SEAL*, and the year of incorporation. It may be round or rectangular. The more common practice in the State of Texas, however, is that a corporation not adopt a seal.

Stock Certificates and Offers to Purchase Stock (TBCA art. 2.19)

Texas corporations are no longer required to issue stock certificates to represent shares of ownership. However, as a practical matter it is a good idea to do so. This shows some formality and gives each person tangible evidence of ownership. If you do issue shares, the face of each certificate must show:

✪ the corporate name;

✪ that the corporation was organized under Texas law;

✪ the name of the shareholder(s); and,

✪ the number, class, and series of the stock.

The certificate must be signed by one or more officers designated by the bylaws or the board of directors.

If there are two or more classes or series of stock, the front or back of the certificate must contain:

✪ a full statement of all designations, preferences, limitations, and relative rights of each class or series or

✪ a statement that the Articles of Incorporation contain the designations, preferences, limitations, and relative rights of each class or series.

The certificate must also state that the corporation will make available such a statement to the certificate holder without charge.

The stock certificates can be fancy, with engraved eagles, or they can be typed or even handwritten. Several blank **STOCK CERTIFICATE** forms are included in Appendix D. (see form 35, p.279.) For professional corporations, the following statement should be typed on the certificate:

The transfer of the shares represented by this certificate is restricted by the bylaws of the corporation.

Before any stock is issued, the purchaser should submit an **OFFER TO PURCHASE STOCK**. (see form 14, p.231.) The offer states that it is made pursuant to IRS Code Section 1244. The advantage of this section is that in the event the business fails or the value of the stock drops, the shareholder can write off up to $50,000 ($100,000 for married couples) of the loss as ordinary income, rather than as a long-term capital loss that would be limited to $3,000 a year. This can provide tremendous tax savings in the event of a loss in value of the business.

Some thought should be given to the way in which the ownership of the stock will be held. Stock owned in one person's name alone is subject to probate upon death. Making two persons joint owners of the stock (joint tenants with full rights of survivorship) would avoid probate upon the death of one of them. However, taking a joint owner's name off in the event of a disagreement (such as divorce) could be troublesome. When a couple jointly operates a business, joint ownership would be best. But when one person is the sole party involved in the business, the desire to avoid probate should be weighed against the risk of losing half the business in a divorce. Another way to avoid probate is to put ownership of the stock in a living trust.

In Texas, stock owned in one spouse's name alone is considered community property, and the nonowner spouse is treated as having an ownership interest in one-half of the stock. If the stock is intended to be owned by one spouse alone, the stock certificate should contain language such as *John Doe, as his sole and separate property.*

Organizational Meeting

The real birth of the corporation takes place at the initial meeting of the incorporators and the initial board of directors. At this meeting, the stock is issued and the officers and board of directors are elected. Other business may also take place, such as opting for S corporation status or adopting employee benefit plans.

Usually minutes, stock certificates, and tax and other forms are prepared before the organizational meeting and used as a script for the meeting. They are then signed at the end of the meeting. Otherwise, they may be forgotten until it is too late.

The agenda for the initial meeting is usually as follows:

1. Signing the **WAIVER OF NOTICE OF ORGANIZATIONAL MEETING** (see form 9, p.213).

2. Noting persons present.

3. Presentation and acceptance of Articles of Incorporation (the copy returned by the Secretary of State).

4. Election of directors.

5. Adoption of **BYLAWS** (form 11 or form 12).

6. Election of officers.

7. Presentation and acceptance of corporate seal.

8. **BANKING RESOLUTION** (see form 13, p.229).

9. Acceptance of **Offers to Purchase Stock/Offers to Sell Stock** (see form 14, p.231). (Use form 16, **Bill of Sale**, if property is traded for stock.)

10. **Resolution to Reimburse Expenses** (see form 15, p.233).

11. Adoption of special resolutions such as **Form 2553** and **Resolution Adopting S Corporation Status** (forms 17 and 18).

12. Adjournment.

At the end of the meeting, the stock certificates are usually issued; but in some cases, such as when a prospective shareholder does not yet have money to pay for them, they are issued when full payment is received.

To issue the stock, the certificates at the end of this book should be completed by adding the name of the corporation, a statement that the corporation is organized under the laws of Texas, the number of shares the certificate represents, and the person to whom the certificate is issued. Each certificate should be numbered in order to keep track of them. A record of the stock issuance should be made on the **Stock Transfer Ledger** (see form 33, p.273) and on the **Stock Certificate Stubs** (see form 36, p.289). The stubs should be cut apart on the dotted lines, punched, and inserted in the ring binder.

Minute Book

After the organizational meeting, you should set up your minute book. As noted, this can be a fancy leather book or a simple ring binder. The minute book usually contains the following:

✪ a title page ("Corporate Records of _____");

✪ a table of contents;

✪ the letter from the Secretary of State acknowledging receipt and filing of the Articles of Incorporation;

✪ a copy of the Articles of Incorporation;

✪ a copy of any registered **ASSUMED NAME CERTIFICATE**;

✪ a copy of any trademark registration;

✪ the **WAIVER OF NOTICE OF ORGANIZATIONAL MEETING**;

✪ the **MINUTES OF ORGANIZATIONAL MEETING**;

✪ the **BYLAWS**;

✪ a **SAMPLE STOCK CERTIFICATE**;

✪ any **OFFERS TO PURCHASE STOCK**;

✪ any tax forms such as:

   • **FORM SS-4** and Employer Identification Number certificate;

   • **FORM 2553** and acceptance; and,

   • Form AP157 and state tax number certificate.

✪ **STOCK TRANSFER LEDGER**; and,

✪ **STOCK CERTIFICATE STUBS**.

Bank Accounts

A corporation must have a bank account. Checks payable to a corporation cannot be cashed; they must be deposited into an account.

Fees Unfortunately, many banks charge ridiculous rates to corporations for the right to put their money in the bank. You can tell how much extra a corporation is being charged when you compare a corporate account to a personal account with similar activity.

Example: For similar balance and activity, an individual might earn $6.00 interest for the month while a corporation pays $40.00 in bank fees. Surely the bank is not losing money on every personal account. Therefore, the corporate account is simply generating $46.00 more in profit for the bank.

Some banks have set up reasonable fees for small corporations, such as charging no fees if a balance of $1000 or $2500 is maintained. Because the fees can easily amount to hundreds of dollars a year, it pays to shop around. Even if the bank is relatively far from the business, using bank-by-mail can make the distance meaningless. But do not be surprised if a bank with low fees raises them.

Another way to save money in bank charges is to order checks from a private source rather than through the bank. These are usually much cheaper than those the bank offers because the bank makes a profit on the check printing. If the bank officer doesn't like the idea when you are opening the account, just wait until your first batch runs out and switch over without telling the bank. They probably will not even notice, as long as you get the checks printed correctly. While most *business checks* are large (and expensive), there is no reason you cannot use small *personal size* checks for your business. They are easier to carry around and work just as well (unless you want to impress people with the size of your check).

Paperwork All you should need to open a corporate bank account is a copy of your Articles of Incorporation and your federal tax identification number. Some banks, however, want more. If you have trouble opening the account, you can use a **Banking Resolution** to provide the bank with any additional documentation they may need. (see form 13, p.229.)

Licenses

Counties and municipalities are authorized to levy a license tax on the *privilege* of doing business. Before opening your business, you should obtain a county occupational license and if you will be working within a city, a city occupational license. Businesses that perform work in several cities, such as builders, must obtain a license from each city they work in. This does not have to be done until you actually begin a job in a particular city.

County occupational licenses can be obtained from the tax collector in the county courthouse. City licenses are usually available at city hall. Be sure to find out if zoning allows your type of business before buying or leasing property because the licensing departments will check the zoning before issuing your license.

Problems occasionally arise when persons attempt to start a business in their home. Small new businesses cannot afford to pay rent for commercial space and cities often try to forbid business in residential areas. Getting a county occupational license often gives notice to the city that a business is being conducted in a residential area.

Home Businesses

Some people avoid the problem by starting their businesses without occupational licenses, figuring that the penalties are nowhere near the cost of office space. Others get the county license and ignore the city rules. If a person has commercial trucks and equipment parked on his or her property, there will probably be complaints by neighbors and the city will most likely take legal action. But if a person's business consists merely of making phone calls out of the home and keeping supplies inside the house, the problem may never surface.

The best course of action is to keep a low profile. Using a post office box is sometimes helpful in diverting attention away from the residence. However, the Secretary of State and the occupational license administrator will want a street address. There should be no problem using a residential address and explaining to the city that it is merely the corporate address and that no business is conducted on the premises.

5

SELLING CORPORATE STOCK

When you start your new corporate business, you will probably issue stock to yourself and any other owner. However, if you sought other owners as initial investors or if in the future you want to sell stock to raise additional capital, you may be subject to some very complicated rules governing the sale of stock.

Securities Laws

The issuance of securities is subject to both federal and state securities laws. A *security* is stock in the company (common and preferred) and debt (notes, bonds, etc.). The laws covering securities are so broad that any instrument that represents an investment in an enterprise, when the investor is relying on the efforts of others for profit, is considered a security. Even a promissory note has been held to be a security. Once an investment is determined to involve a security, strict rules apply. If the rules are not followed, there can be criminal penalties imposed and civil damages awarded to purchasers.

The rules are designed to protect people who put up money as an investment in a business. In the stock market crash in the 1930s, many people lost their life savings in swindles. The government wants to be sure that it will not happen again. Unfortunately, the laws can also make it difficult to raise capital for many honest businesses.

The goal of the laws covering sales of securities is that investors be given full disclosure of the risks involved in an investment. To accomplish this, the law usually requires that the securities must either be registered with the federal Securities and Exchange Commission and/or a similar state regulatory body. Lengthy disclosure statements must be compiled and distributed.

The law is complicated and strict compliance is required. The penalties are harsh. You most likely would not be able to get through the registration process on your own. Seek out a lawyer with experience in securities law. But, like your decision to incorporate without a lawyer, you may wish to consider some alternatives when attempting to raise capital without a lawyer.

One alternative is to borrow the money as a personal loan from friends or relatives. The disadvantage with doing this is that you will have to pay them back personally if the business fails. However, you may have to do that anyway if they are close relatives or if you do not follow the securities laws.

Another option is to tailor your stock issuance to fall within the exemptions in the securities laws. There are some exemptions in the securities laws for small businesses that may apply to your transaction. (The antifraud provisions always apply, even if the transaction is exempt from registration.) Some exemptions are explained in the next section, but you should make at least one appointment with a securities lawyer to be sure you have covered everything and that there have not been any changes in the law. Often you can pay for an hour or so of a securities lawyer's time for $200 or $300 and just ask questions about your plans. He or she can tell you what not to do and what your options are. Then you can make an informed decision.

Federal Exemptions from Securities Laws

In most situations when one person, a husband and wife, or a few partners run a business and all parties are active in the enterprise, securities laws do not apply to their issuance of stock to themselves. These are the simple corporations that are the subject of this book. As a practical matter, if your father or aunt wants to put up some money for some stock in your business you probably will not get in trouble. They probably will not seek triple damages and criminal penalties if your business fails.

However, you may wish to obtain money from additional investors to enable your business to grow. This can be done in many circumstances as long as you follow the rules carefully. In some cases you do not have to file anything with the SEC, but in others you must file some sort of notice.

Federal Private Placement Exemption

If you sell your stock to a small group of people without any advertising you can fall into the private offering exemption. To do so all of the following conditions must be met.

- ✪ All persons to whom offers are made are financially astute, are participants in the business, or have a substantial net worth.

- ✪ No advertising or general solicitation is used to promote the stock.

- ✪ The number of persons to whom the offers are made is limited.

- ✪ The shares are purchased for investment and not for immediate resale.

- ✪ The persons to whom the stock is offered are given all relevant information (including financial information) regarding the issuance and the corporation.

There are numerous court cases explaining each aspect of these rules, including such questions as what is a *financially astute* person. If you have a question regarding any of these rules, consult an attorney or at least look for a court case explaining it. If you meet these rules, you must submit a filing claiming the exemption is made upon the United States Securities and Exchange Commission.

Federal Intrastate Offering Exemption

If you only offer your securities to residents of one state, you may be exempt from federal securities laws. This is because federal laws usually only apply to interstate commerce. *Intrastate* offerings are covered by SEC Rule 147. If it is followed carefully, your sale will be exempt from federal registration.

Federal Small Offerings Exemptions

In recent years the SEC has liberalized the rules in order to make it easier for businesses to grow. Under Regulation D, adopted by the Securities and Exchange Commission, there are three types of exemptions found under SEC rules 504, 505, and 506.

The offering of securities of up to $1,000,000 in a twelve-month period can be exempt under SEC Rule 504. Offers can be made to any number of persons, no specific information must be provided, and investors do not have to be sophisticated.

Under Rule 505, the offering of up to $5,000,000 can be made in a twelve-month period, but no public advertising may be used and only thirty-five nonaccredited investors may purchase stock. Any number of accredited investors may purchase stock.

Accredited investors are sophisticated individuals with high net worth or high income, large trusts or investment companies, or persons involved in the business.

Rule 506 has no limit on the amount of money that may be raised but, like Rule 505, does not allow advertising and limits nonaccredited investors to thirty-five.

Texas Securities Laws

Unfortunately, the simplification of federal requirements has not been accompanied by similar changes at the state level. Texas and most states still have much stricter requirements for the issuance of securities. There is a movement to change the laws, but for now the only way to avoid the Texas registration procedures is to qualify for the Texas limited offering.

Limited Offering Exemption

The most common *limited offering exemption* can apply if the following are true:

✪ there are thirty-five or fewer purchasers of shares and

✪ no advertising or general solicitation is used to promote the stock.

These rules may sound simple on the surface but there are many more rules, regulations, and court cases explaining each one in more detail. For example, what does *thirty-five persons* mean? Sounds simple, but it can mean more than thirty-five persons. Spouses, persons whose net worth exceeds a million dollars, and founders of the corporation may not be counted in some circumstances.

Other States
Under current law, you must be registered in a state in order to sell stock to its residents. If you are not registered in a state, you must turn down any residents from that state that want to buy your stock.

As you can see, the exemption does not give you much latitude in raising money. Therefore for most issuances you will have to register.

If you are going to sell stock in more than one state, in addition to the federal laws, each state has its own *blue sky* requirements and exemptions. If you are going to raise money from investors, check with a qualified securities lawyer.

Internet Stock Sales

With the advent of the Internet, promoters of stock have a new way of reaching large numbers of people, most of whom are financially able to afford investments in securities. However, all securities laws apply to the Internet, and they are being enforced. Recently, state attorney generals have issued cease and desist orders to promoters not registered in their states.

Payment for Shares

When issuing stock, it is important that full payment be made by the purchasers. If the shares have a par value and the payment is in cash, then the cash must not be less than the par value. In most states, promissory notes cannot be used in payment for shares. The shares must not be issued until the payment has been received by the corporation.

Trading Property for Shares
In many cases, organizers of a corporation have property they want to contribute for use in starting up the business. This is often the case when an ongoing business is incorporated. To avoid future problems, the property should be traded at a fair value for the shares. The directors should pass a resolution stating that they agree with the value of the property. When the stock certificate

is issued in exchange for the property, a bill of sale should be executed by the owner of the property detailing everything that is being exchanged for the stock.

Taxable Transactions

In cases where property is exchanged for something of value, such as stock, there is often income tax due as if there had been a sale of the property. Fortunately, Section 351 of the IRS Code allows tax-free exchange of property for stock if the persons receiving the stock for the property or for cash *end up owning* at least eighty percent of the voting and other stock in the corporation. If more than twenty percent of the stock is issued in exchange for services instead of property and cash, then the transfers of property will be taxable and treated as a sale for cash.

Trading Services for Shares

In some cases, the founders of a corporation wish to issue stock to one or more persons in exchange for their services to the corporation. It has always been possible to issue shares for services that have previously been performed. Some states make it unlawful to issue shares for promises to perform services in the future. In Texas, the TBCA art. 2.16A states that shares can be issued in exchange for a contract for services to be performed.

6 RUNNING A CORPORATION

There are not many differences between running a corporation and any other type of business. The most important point to remember is to keep the corporation separate from your personal affairs. Do not be continuously making loans to yourself from corporate funds and do not commingle funds.

Another important point to remember is to always refer to the corporation as a corporation. Always use the designation *Inc.* or *Corp.* on everything. Always sign corporate documents with your corporate title. If you do not, you may lose your protection from liability. There have been many cases when a person forgot to put the word *pres.* after his or her name and was held personally liable for a corporate debt!

Corporate Records

Texas law requires that a corporation keep accurate accounting records and a permanent record of *minutes of the proceedings of its shareholders, its board of directors, and each committee of the board of directors.* (TBCA art. 2.44.)

Additional corporate documents are required to be kept and Texas law prescribes the manner in which these records should be maintained and accessible by others.

Record of Shareholders

The corporation must keep a record of its shareholders including their names and addresses and the number, class, and series of shares of stock owned. (TBCA art. 2.44 (A).) This can be kept at the registered office, principal place of business, or office of its stock transfer agent (if any). The **STOCK TRANSFER LEDGER** can be used for this purpose. (see form 33, p.273.)

Corporate Documents

The corporation must maintain copies of the following:

- ❂ **ARTICLES OF INCORPORATION** and all amendments;

- ❂ **BYLAWS** and all amendments;

- ❂ resolutions regarding stockrights;

- ❂ minutes of shareholders' meetings and records of actions taken without a meeting for the last three years;

- ❂ written communications to all shareholders for the last three years;

- ❂ financial statements furnished to shareholders for the last three years;

- ❂ names and addresses of all current directors and officers; and,

- ❂ the most recent annual report.

Form of Records

The minutes may be in writing or in *any other form capable of being converted into written form within a reasonable time*. This would mean that they could be kept in a computer or possibly on a videotape. However, it is always best to keep at least one written copy. Accidents can easily erase magnetic media.

Examination of Records

Any shareholder of a corporation has the right to examine and copy the corporation's books and records after giving written notice at least five days before the date on which he or she wishes to inspect and copy them.

There are certain limitations to this right, but a corporation wrongfully refusing to honor a shareholders request to see the books can be liable for all the shareholder's expenses in enforcing his or her right. (TBCA art. 2.44(B)-(C).)

The shareholder may have his attorney or agent examine the records and may receive photocopies of the records. The corporation may charge a reasonable fee for making photocopies. If the records are not in written form, the corporation must convert them to written form. The corporation must bear the cost of converting the records.

Balance Sheets Upon written request from a shareholder, the corporation must furnish its annual statements for the last fiscal year showing in reasonable detail its assets, liabilities, and results of its operations. (TBCA art. 2.44 (F).)

Shareholder Meetings

The corporation must hold annual meetings of the shareholders. These meetings may be formal and held at a restaurant or they may be informal and held at a swimming pool. A sole officer and director can hold them in his or her mind without reciting all the verbiage or taking a formal vote. But the important thing is that the meetings are held and that minutes are kept. Regular minutes and meetings are evidence that the corporation is legitimate if the issue ever comes up in court. Minute forms for the annual meetings are included with this book. (see form 22, p.251.) You can use them as master copies to photocopy each year. All that needs to be changed is the date, unless you actually change officers or directors or need to take some other corporate action.

Special Meetings When important decisions must be made by the board of shareholders between the annual meetings, the corporation can hold special meetings. Form 26 provides a template that you can use to record the meetings.

Action without a Meeting Under the procedures of TBCA art. 9.10 (A), action may be taken by the shareholders without a formal meeting. However, for a small corporation it is best to use formal meetings in case someone later tries to pierce the corporate veil.

Notice of Meetings Under Texas law, shareholders with voting rights must be notified of the date, time, and place of annual and special meetings at least ten but not more than sixty days prior. (TBCA art. 2.25.) No description of the purpose of an annual meeting need be given, but the purpose for a special meeting must be stated in the notice. Use forms 21 or 25 to waive notice of the meeting.

Voting A shareholder may waive notice either before or after the meeting if done in writing and included in the minutes. Unless a shareholder objects, attendance at a meeting waives objection to the notice or lack thereof.

The following rules apply to voting at the shareholders' meeting.

- ✪ Unless otherwise provided in the Articles of Incorporation or bylaws, a quorum consists of a majority of the shares entitled to vote. (TBCA art. 2.28 (A).)

- ✪ Once a share is represented at a meeting for any purpose, it is deemed present for quorum purposes for the rest of the meeting. (TBCA art. 2.28 (A).)

- ✪ Holders of a majority of the shares represented may adjourn the meeting. (TBCA art. 2.28 (B).)

- ✪ The Articles of Incorporation may authorize a quorum of less than a majority, but it may not be less than one-third. (TBCA art. 2.28 (A)(2).)

Voting for Directors Unless otherwise provided in the Articles of Incorporation, directors are elected by a plurality of votes. Shareholders do not have a right to cumulative voting unless provided in the Articles.

Board of Directors Meetings

The corporation must hold annual meetings of the directors. These meetings also may be formal and held at a restaurant or they may be informal and held at a swimming pool. A sole officer and director can hold them in his or her mind without reciting all the verbiage or taking a formal vote. But the important thing, like with the shareholders, is that the meetings are held and that minutes are kept. Regular minutes and meetings are evidence that the corporation is legitimate if the issue ever comes up in court. Minute forms for the annual meetings are included with this book. (see form 20, p.247.) You can use them as master copies to photocopy each year. All that needs to be changed is the date, unless you actually change officers or directors or need to take some other corporate action.

Special Meetings   When important decisions must be made by the board of directors between the annual meetings, the corporation can hold special meetings. Form 24 provides a template that you can use to record these meetings.

Action without a Meeting   Under the procedures of TBCA art. 9.10 (B), action may be taken by the directors without a formal meeting. However, for a small corporation it is best to use formal meetings in case someone later tries to pierce the corporate veil.

Notice of Meetings   Under Texas law, regular meetings of the board of directors may be held without notice unless the Articles of Incorporation or bylaws provide otherwise. (TBCA art. 2.31.) Directors must be notified of the time, date, and place of special meetings within the time frame prescribed in the bylaws.

Voting   The following rules apply to voting at the directors' meeting.

✪   Unless otherwise provided in the Articles of Incorporation or bylaws, a quorum consists of a majority of the number of directors prescribed in the Articles or bylaws.

✪   The Articles of Incorporation may authorize a quorum of less than a majority, but it may not be less than one-third.

✪   If a quorum is present for a vote, a vote by a majority of those present constitutes an act of the board of directors unless otherwise provided in the Articles or bylaws.

Committees   Unless prohibited by the bylaws, the board of directors may designate a committee of its members that can exercise all authority of the board except that it may not:

✪   approve or recommend actions that by law must be approved by the shareholders;

✪   fill vacancies on the board or committees thereof;

✪   adopt, repeal, or amend the bylaws;

✪   propose reacquisition of shares; or,

✪   recommend a voluntary dissolution of the corporation.

Also, meeting rules of committees must comply with the rules for the board itself. Each committee must have at least two members and alternate members may be designated. Setting up a committee does not relieve a member of his or her duty to act in good faith in the best interests of the corporation.

Annual Reports

Every corporation must file an annual report. Fortunately, this is a simple one-page form that is sent to the corporation by the Secretary of State and usually merely has to be signed. It contains such information as the federal tax identification number, officers' and directors' names and addresses, the registered agent's name, and the address of the registered office. It must be signed and filed by May 15th.

Piercing the Corporate Veil

The major benefit of a corporation is the limited liability of its shareholders. However, if the formalities of running a corporation are not observed and documented in the records of the corporation, it is possible that courts will permit a creditor or person suing a corporation to bypass the corporation and collect from the personal assets of a shareholder. This is called *piercing the corporate veil.*

In some cases, a corporation is established but the owner runs the corporation just the same way as if he or she owned the business him- or herself. The owner may not follow the reporting requirements necessary for a corporation, may commingle personal funds or assets with the corporation's funds or assets, may ignore the rights of other shareholders, or may try to use the corporation as a fraudulent means to protect his or her personal assets from creditors.

It is very important that the corporation be run according to the law and that a detailed minute book be kept of the corporation's activities. Annual meetings of shareholders and directors should be held and minutes of these should be kept in a minute book. Recordkeeping is very important to prove the existence and operation of the corporation in accordance with the statutes. When a corporation is sued, one of the first documents that the plaintiff's attorney will ask to review is the corporation's minute book. If the attorney believes that the corporation has not been properly run, the attorney will often sue the individual shareholders as well.

A good explanation of Texas law on piercing the corporate veil is contained in the Texas Supreme Court case, *Castleberry v. Branscum,* 721 S.W.2d 270 (1986).

7 AMENDING CORPORATE DOCUMENTS

From time to time and as your business grows and changes, you may find it necessary to revise corporate documents. Some of these changes require formal amending procedures and filing with the Secretary of State. Follow the procedures outlined in this chapter to make your changes.

Articles of Incorporation

Because the **ARTICLES OF INCORPORATION** included in this book are so basic, they will rarely have to be amended. The only reasons for amending them would be to change the name or the number of shares of stock or to add some special clause, such as a higher than majority voting requirement for directors. If the amendment is made before any shares are issued, it may be done by the incorporator or directors by filing Articles of Amendment signed by the incorporators or director stating the name of the corporation, the amendment, the date adopted, and a statement that it is made before any shares were issued. If the amendment is made after shares have been issued, the Articles of Amendment must be signed by the president or vice president and the secretary or assistant secretary.

The Articles of Amendment must contain the name of the corporation, the amendments, the date of adoption by the shareholders, and, if the change affects the outstanding shares, a statement of how the change will occur. The Articles of Amendment must be filed with the Secretary of State along with the filing fee of $150. The procedure for amending corporate Articles depends upon who is doing the amending and at what point in time the amendment is adopted. For more information, you should refer to TBCA arts. 4.01 through 4.07. (see Appendix B.)

Bylaws

The shareholders may always amend the **BYLAWS**. The board of directors may amend the **BYLAWS** unless the Articles of Incorporation state otherwise or unless the shareholders provide that the **BYLAWS** may not be amended by the board. (TBCA art. 2.23.)

Registered Agent or Registered Office

To change the registered agent or registered office, a form must be sent to the Secretary of State with the fee of $15. (see form 32, p.271.) This form can be used to change both the registered agent and the registered office, or to just change one of them. If you are changing just one, such as the agent, then list the registered office as both the old address and the new address.

8 DISSOLVING A CORPORATION

There may come a time when you decide to stop doing business and dissolve the corporation. There are distinct procedures to follow depending on whether or not you have actually begun the operation of your business. The steps to take and the ability for the corporation to act after dissolution are discussed in this chapter.

A Corporation that *has not* Started Business

If a corporation has been formed but has not yet started to do business and has not issued shares of stock, the corporation may be dissolved by a vote of the majority of the incorporators or directors. Articles of Dissolution should be prepared and submitted to the Secretary of State in compliance with article 6.01 of the TBCA. All of the incorporators or directors must sign the Articles of Dissolution. You must file two copies of the form. (see form 27, p.261.) The filing fee for voluntary dissolution of a corporation under article 6.01 is $40.

In addition to the Articles of Dissolution, you must obtain from the Comptroller of Public Accounts a certificate that indicates all franchise taxes have been paid and the corporation is in good standing. This certificate must be attached to the Articles of Dissolution in order for the Secretary of State to process the dissolution.

Requests for certificates or questions on tax should be sent to:

Comptroller of Public Accounts
Tax Assistance Section
Austin, Texas 78774-0100
800-252-1381

When you request a certificate from the Comptroller, you should advise the Comptroller that the certificate will be submitted with a dissolution under Article 6.01. This should help to ensure that the certificate that you receive from the Comptroller will have the necessary statements for the dissolution. The certificate must also show that it is valid through the date of receipt and the filing of the dissolution by the Secretary of State.

A dissolution, like all other corporate documents, is filed as of the date the documents are received in correct form. Since the corporate franchise tax year runs from January 1 until December 31, a corporation that intends to dissolve and not incur liability for an additional year's franchise tax must be certain that complete and correct Articles of Dissolution, the appropriate tax certificate, and the fee are received by the Secretary of State on or before December 31 of that year.

A Corporation that *has* started Business

If a corporation has issued shares of stock or has started doing business, a voluntary dissolution of the corporation may be adopted by the written consent of all of the shareholders of the corporation or by an act of the corporation. (see form 29, p.265.) Dissolution by act of the corporation involves the adoption of a resolution to dissolve the corporation by the directors (see form 30, p.267) and the affirmative vote of at least two-thirds of the outstanding shares of the corporation. (TBCA art. 6.06.) If any class of stock is entitled to vote as a class, the resolution must receive the affirmative vote of two-thirds of the outstanding shares of such class as well as two-thirds of the total outstanding shares of the corporation. After the resolution has been adopted, the corporation must send, by registered or certified mail, written notice of its intention to dissolve to each person or entity that may have a claim against the corporation. The corporation must stop doing business, take all necessary steps to liquidate its business and finalize its affairs, and then file the **ARTICLES OF DISSOLUTION** with the Secretary of State. (see form 28, p.263.)

The corporation is required to obtain a certificate from the Comptroller stating that all taxes administered by the Comptroller have been paid, that the corporation is out of business, and that the corporation is in good standing with the Comptroller for purposes of dissolution.

Limited Survival of Corporation after Dissolution

After the certificate of dissolution has been issued by the Secretary of State, the existence of the corporation ceases. However, Article 7.12 of the TBCA provides that the corporation survives for limited purposes after dissolution. These purposes include lawsuits, other proceedings, and appropriate action by shareholders, directors, and officers, as well as other purposes listed in Article 7.12.

Bankruptcy

If your corporation is in debt beyond its means it can file for bankruptcy. There are two types of bankruptcy that a corporation may file for. Chapter 7 bankruptcy is for liquidation and Chapter 11 for reorganization of debts.

If the debts are small and there is little chance the creditors will pursue collection, then bankruptcy is unnecessary. You can allow the state to dissolve the corporation for failure to file the annual report. However, if the debts are large and you fear the creditors will attempt to collect the debt from the officers or directors, go through formal bankruptcy and/or dissolution. Such a scenario is beyond the scope of this book and you should consult an attorney or bankruptcy text for further guidance.

9 CORPORATE ALTERNATIVE: LIMITED LIABILITY COMPANY

During the past several years, a popular alternative to forming a corporation in Texas is to form a limited liability company. Limited liability companies were first recognized as entities by the Internal Revenue Service in 1988.

A limited liability company combines features of a corporation and a limited partnership. A limited liability company (commonly referred to as an LLC) is organized under the Texas Limited Liability Company Act (TLLCA, article 1528n of the Texas Business Corporation Act). A limited liability company has the same limited liability for its owners as a corporation and also provides the opportunity to be taxed as a partnership.

This chapter contains a brief overview of some of the characteristics of an LLC and some of the requirements to organize and operate an LLC.

Advantages of an LLC

The primary advantage of an LLC is that the personal liability of its owners is limited. The owners of an LLC are called *members*. Just as with shareholders of a corporation, the personal assets of the members are protected from the claims of business creditors of the LLC. The managers of the LLC (similar to directors of a corporation) as well as the officers of the LLC are also personally protected from the debts of the business.

In addition, double taxation is avoided. A corporation, unless it elects to be treated as an S corporation, must pay income tax on its profits. When these profits are distributed to the shareholders in the form of dividends, the shareholders must pay income tax on the amount of the dividends they receive. In contrast, an LLC is treated as a partnership for income tax purposes. That means that the earnings of the LLC are allocated among the members who pay income tax on their share of the earnings. The LLC does not pay income tax.

Management and ownership of the LLC is very flexible. The rights of the members to receive the benefit of the LLC's income and to participate in the management of the LLC can be varied according to the regulations or operating agreement of the LLC. Unlike most corporations, voting rights and income rights do not have to be directly related to the amount of the member's investment in the LLC.

Organizing a Limited Liability Company

Just like with a corporation, an LLC is formed when **ARTICLES OF ORGANIZATION** are filed with the Secretary of State. (see form 36, p.289.) You should first check to make certain the name you intend to use is available. (See Chapter 4 for a discussion of determining whether a name is available.)

Articles of Organization

Article 3.02 of the TLLCA requires that the Articles of Organization of an LLC contain the following:

- ✪   the name of the LLC;

- ✪   the period of the LLC's existence;

- ✪   the name and address of the registered agent of the LLC; and,

- ✪   the names and addresses of the initial managers of the LLC.

Name of Limited Liability Company. An LLC must contain one of the following in its name:

✪ Limited Liability Company;

✪ Limited Company;

✪ LLC;

✪ L.L.C.;

✪ LC; or,

✪ L.C.

Duration. The period of the LLC's existence must be specified in the Articles of Organization. The period of existence can be for a specified term of years or it can be perpetual in existence.

Regulations Although not required under Texas law, it is beneficial to have regulations or bylaws that set forth the operation and management of the LLC. (see form 37, p.291.) The regulations serve the same purpose as the bylaws of a corporation and contain many of the same types of provisions as do bylaws. Among these provisions are:

✪ requirements for admitting new members after the LLC is formed;

✪ who will manage the LLC;

✪ the different officers that may be elected by the managers to operate the LLC on a day-to-day basis;

✪ the manner in which income will be distributed and shared among the members; and,

✪ reasons to dissolve the LLC and the steps that will wind up the business of the LLC if it is dissolved.

Organizational Meeting

Just like with a corporation, the LLC really comes into being at the initial meeting of the members and managers. At this meeting, the managers will elect officers such as a president, secretary, and treasurer, designate a bank for the LLC, adopt the regulations of the LLC, and the like. See Chapter 4 for a listing of the various items that can be covered in an Organizational Meeting.

If a meeting is not held, all of the initial organization procedures for starting an LLC need to be followed. Form 10 will document these steps and act as a record for the actions you take.

Minute Book and Recordkeeping

Most LLCs keep a minute book similar to that of a corporation. The minute book usually contains the following:

✪   a title page (*Records of _____, a Texas Limited Liability Company*);

✪   a table of contents;

✪   the letter from the Secretary of State acknowledging receipt and filing of the **ARTICLES OF ORGANIZATION**;

✪   a copy of the **ARTICLES OF ORGANIZATION**;

✪   a copy of any **ASSUMED NAME CERTIFICATE**;

✪   a copy of any trademark registration;

✪   any **WAIVER OF NOTICE OF ORGANIZATIONAL MEETING**;

✪   the minutes of the organizational meeting;

✪   the **REGULATIONS**;

- ✪ a sample membership certificate;

- ✪ any offer to purchase membership interests;

- ✪ tax forms such as **FORM SS-4** and Employer Identification Number certificate; and,

- ✪ the ledger of members.

Bank Accounts and Licenses

An LLC must have a bank account. Checks payable to an LLC must be deposited and cannot be cashed. Some counties or cities may require a license to operate a business within its boundaries. Chapter 4 contains a detailed discussion of bank accounts and licenses for a corporation. That discussion applies to LLCs as well.

Running a Limited Liability Company

Because an LLC is very similar to a corporation, the rules for running an LLC on a day-to-day basis are the same. Chapter 6 contains a detailed discussion of how a corporation should be run and the recordkeeping requirements for a corporation. That discussion applies to LLCs as well.

One of the rules that needs to be followed is having an annual meeting. If you have a member-managed LLC, you can use form 39, **MINUTES OF THE ANNUAL MEETING OF THE MEMBERS**, to record and document the meeting. If you decide to have managers (much like a board of directors for a corporation) they will need to conduct an annual meeting as well. Form 40, **MINUTES OF THE ANNUAL MEETING OF THE MANAGERS**, can be used to record and document that meeting.

GLOSSARY

A

annual report. A document filed by a corporation or limited liability company each year usually listing the officers, directors, and registered agent.

articles of incorporation. The document that demonstrates the organization of a corporation. Also called *certificate of incorporation* in some states.

articles of organization. The document that demonstrates the organization of a limited liability company.

B

blue sky laws. Laws governing the sale of securities.

bylaws. Rules governing the conduct of affairs of a corporation.

C

C corporation. A corporation that pays taxes on its profits.

common stock. The basic ownership shares of a corporation.

contract. An agreement between two or more parties.

corporation. An organization, recognized as a person in the law, that is set up to conduct a business owned by shareholders and run by officers and directors.

D

distributions. Money paid out to owners of a corporation or a limited liability company.

E

employee. Person who works under another person's control and direction.

employer identification number (EIN). Number issued by the Internal Revenue Service to identify taxpayers who do not have Social Security numbers.

estate planning. Preparing documents such as a will, trust, and other arrangements to control the passing of one's property at death.

exemption. The ability to sell certain limited types of securities without full compliance with securities registration laws.

F

fictitious name. A name used by a business that is not its personal or legal name.

G

general partnership. A business that is owned by two or more persons.

I

intangible property. Personal property that does not have physical presence, such as the ownership interest in a corporation.

intellectual property. Legal rights to the products of the mind, such as writings, musical compositions, formulas, and designs.

L

liability. The legal responsibility to pay for an injury.

limited liability company. An entity recognized as a legal *person* that is set up to conduct a business owned and run by members.

M

membership agreement. A contract controlling the operation of a limited liability company in which the company is run by members.

management agreement. A contract controlling the operation of a limited liability company in which the company is run by its managers.

minutes. Records of the proceedings of corporate meetings.

N

nonprofit corporation. An entity recognized as a legal *person* that is set up to run an operation in which none of the profits are distributed to controlling members.

O

occupational license. A government-issued permit to transact business.

operating agreement. A contract among members of a limited liability company spelling out how the company is to be run.

option. The right to buy stock at a future date, usually at a predetermined price.

organizational meeting. The meeting of the founders of a corporation or limited liability company in which the company is structured and ready to begin business.

P

par value. A value given to newly-issued stock, which formerly had legal significance, but now usually does not relate to anything except taxation (in some states).

partnership. A business formed by two or more persons.

personal property. Any type of property other than land and the structures attached to it.

piercing the corporate veil. When a court ignores the structure of a corporation and holds its owners responsible for its debts or liabilities.

professional association. An entity recognized as a legal *person* that is set up to conduct a business of professionals, such as doctors and other health care professionals.

professional corporation. An entity recognized as a legal *person* that is set up to conduct a business of professionals, such as attorneys and other non-health care professionals.

promoters. Persons who start a business venture and usually offer interests for sale to investors.

proprietorship. A business that is owned by one person.

R

registered agent. The person authorized to accept legal papers for a corporation or limited liability company, sometimes called a resident agent.

resident agent. *See registered agent.*

S

S corporation. A corporation in which the profits are taxed to the shareholders.

securities. Interests in a business, such as stocks or bonds.

shareholder agreement. A contract among the owners of a corporation that spells out their rights.

shares. Units of stock in a corporation.

stock. Ownership interests in a corporation.

T

tangible property. Physical personal property, such as desks and tables.

trademark. A name or symbol used to identify the source of goods or services.

transferability. The ability to sell shares of stock in a corporation.

U

usury. Charging an interest rate higher than what is allowed by law.

W

withholding. Money taken out of an employee's salary and remitted to the government.

Z

zoning. Government regulation controlling the use of a piece of real property.

Appendix A:
Checklist
and Fee Schedule

The following checklist includes all steps necessary to form a simple for-profit corporation in Texas. The fee schedule details the fee amounts for organizational documents to be submitted to the Secretary of State.

Checklist for Forming a Texas Limited Liability Company

☐ Decide on company name

☐ Prepare and file **ARTICLES OF ORGANIZATION**

☐ Send for federal *Employer Identification Number* (**IRS FORM SS-4**)

☐ If necessary, prepare Members' Agreement

☐ Meet with accountant to discuss capitalization and tax planning

☐ If necessary, meet with securities lawyer regarding membership share sales

☐ Obtain ring binder for minutes

☐ Hold organizational meeting

    ☐ Complete regulations, waiver, minutes, offers to purchase membership shares

    ☐ Sign all documents and place in minute book

☐ Issue membership shares

    ☐ Be sure consideration is paid

    ☐ Complete **BILL OF SALE** if property is traded for membership shares

    ☐ Fill in **TRANSFER LEDGER**

☐ File **ASSUMED NAME CERTIFICATE** if one will be used

☐ If necessary, get city or county licenses

☐ Open bank account

Office of the Secretary of State
Corporations Section
P.O. Box 13697
Austin, Texas 78711-3697

FEE SCHEDULE

I. DOMESTIC BUSINESS CORPORATIONS
(Art. 10.01 TBCA; Art. 1302 – 7.05 TMCLA)

Reservation of Corporate Name	$40.00
Transfer of Reserved Name	15.00
Termination of Reserved Name	15.00
Articles of Incorporation	300.00
Articles of Amendment	150.00
Articles of Merger/Share Exchange	300.00
Articles of Conversion	300.00
Restated Articles of Incorporation	300.00
Change of Registered Agent and/or Registered Office	15.00
Change of Address of Registered Agent	15.00
Resignation of Registered Agent	no fee
Statement of Operation as a Close Corporation	15.00
Statement of Restriction on Transfer of Shares	15.00
Resolution Establishing Series of Shares	15.00
Cancellation of Redeemable Shares	15.00
Cancellation of Re-Acquired Shares	15.00
Reduction of Stated Capital	15.00
Articles of Dissolution	40.00
Articles of Revocation of Dissolution	15.00
Reinstatement following tax forfeiture	75.00
Reinstatement following non-tax forfeiture	50.00
Statement of Delayed Effective Condition	15.00
Articles of Correction	15.00
Any instrument for which no express fee provided	15.00
Expedited Processing fee per document	***25.00***

II. PROFESSIONAL CORPORATIONS
[Fees same as Business Corporations]
(Section 5 TPCA)

III. PROFESSIONAL ASSOCIATIONS
(Section 22 TPAA)

Articles of Association	$200.00
Annual Statement	35.00
Other fees are same as those for business corporations	

IV. FOREIGN BUSINESS CORPORATIONS
(Art. 10.01 TBCA)

Certificate of Authority	$750.00
Amended Certificate of Authority	150.00
Withdrawal of Certificate of Authority	15.00
Termination of Certificate of Authority	15.00
Registration/Renewal of	
Registration of Corporate Name	75.00
Expedited Processing fee per document	***25.00***

V. NON-PROFIT CORPORATIONS
(Art. 9.03 TNPCA)

Reservation of Corporate Name	$40.00
Transfer of Reserved Name	15.00
Termination of Reserved Name	15.00
Articles of Incorporation	25.00
Articles of Amendment	25.00
Articles of Merger or Consolidation	50.00
Restated Articles of Incorporation	50.00
Change of Registered Agent and/or Registered Office	5.00
Change of Address of Registered Agent	15.00
Resignation of Registered Agent	no fee
Reinstatement following tax forfeiture	no fee
Reinstatement following non-tax forfeiture	25.00
Articles of Dissolution	5.00
Articles of Revocation of Dissolution	5.00
Certificate of Authority	25.00
Amended Certificate of Authority	25.00
Withdrawal of Certificate of Authority	5.00
Statement of Delayed Effective Condition	5.00
Articles of Correction	15.00
Any instrument for which no express fee provided	5.00
Expedited Processing fee per document	***25.00***

VI. LIMITED PARTNERSHIPS
(Art. 12.01 TRLPA)

Reservation of Limited Partnership name	$50.00
Transfer of Reserved Name	50.00
Termination of Reserved Name	25.00
Registration/Renewal of Foreign LP name	75.00
Certificate of Limited Partnership	750.00
Certificate of Amendment	200.00
Registration as a Foreign Limited Partnership	750.00
Amended Registration of Foreign Limited Partnership	200.00
Restated Certificate of Limited Partnership	200.00
Certificate of Cancellation	200.00
Certificate of Correction	200.00
Change of Registered Agent and/or Registered Office	50.00
Change of Address of Registered Agent	50.00
Resignation of Registered Agent	no fee
Certificate of Merger or Conversion	200.00
Statements filed under Section 3.04 of the Act	25.00
Periodic Report	50.00
Late fee for periodic report $25.00 mo. not to exceed	100.00
Reinstatement Fee	100.00
Preclearance of any document for filing	50.00
Any instrument for which no express fee provided	25.00
Expedited Processing fee per document	***25.00***

VII. DOMESTIC AND FOREIGN LIMITED LIABILITY COMPANIES (Art. 9.01 TLLCA)

Reservation of Limited Liability Company Name	$25.00
Transfer of Reserved Name	10.00
Termination of Reserved Name	10.00
Registration/Renewal of Registration of Foreign Limited Liability Company Name	10.00
Articles of Organization	200.00
Articles of Amendment	100.00
**Articles of Merger	200.00
**Articles of Conversion	200.00
Articles of Share Exchange	10.00
Restated Articles of Organization	200.00
Change of Registered Agent and/or Registered Office	10.00
Change of Address of Registered Agent	10.00
Resignation of Registered Agent	no fee
Articles of Dissolution	25.00
Certificate of Authority	500.00
Amended Certificate of Authority	100.00
Withdrawal of Certificate of Authority	10.00
Termination of Certificate of Authority	10.00
Statement of Delayed Effective Condition	10.00
Reinstatement following tax forfeiture	75.00
Reinstatement following non-tax forfeiture-domestic	10.00
Reinstatement following non-tax forfeiture-foreign	50.00
Articles of Correction	15.00
Any instrument for which no express fee provided	10.00
Expedited Processing fee per document	*25.00*

**Any other filing fee paid under the corporation, partnership, or other entity statutes of this state for the filing of articles of merger or conversion with respect to entities organized under those statutes will be credited against the $200.00 filing fee.

VIII. REGISTRATION OF FINANCIAL INSTITUTIONS

Texas Probate Code §105A

Foreign Corporate Fiduciary	no fee

Texas Finance Code §201.102
BANK, SAVINGS & LOAN, SAVINGS BANK, TRUST COMPANY:

Application for Registration	$750.00
Amended Registration	150.00
Change of Registered Agent and/or Registered Office	15.00
Cancellation/Withdrawal of Registration	15.00
Expedited Processing fee per document	25.00

CREDIT UNION:

Application for Registration	$25.00
Amended Registration	25.00
Change of Registered Agent and/or Registered Office	5.00
Cancellation/Withdrawal of Registration	5.00
Expedited Processing fee per document	*25.00*

IX. DOMESTIC AND FOREIGN REGISTERED LIMITED LIABILITY PARTNERSHIPS (Section 3.08 (b) and Section 10.02, TRPA)

DOMESTIC:

Application for Registration	(each partner)	$200.00
Renewal of Registration	(each partner)	200.00
Amendment of Registration		10.00
Plus $200.00 for any partner added by the amendment		
Withdrawal of Registration		no fee
Expedited Processing fee per document		*25.00*

FOREIGN:

Statement of Foreign Qualification	
$200.00 per partner in Texas	
but not less than $200.00 or more than $750.00	
Renewal of Qualification	
$200.00 per partner in Texas	
but not less than $200.00 or more than $750.00	
Amendment/Correction of Qualification	$10.00 plus
$200.00 per partner in Texas added by amendment	
but not more than $750.00	
Withdrawal of Qualification	no fee
Change of Registered Agent and/or Registered Office	10.00
Change of Address of Registered Agent	10.00
Resignation of Registered Agent	no fee
Expedited Processing fee per document	*25.00*

X. APPOINTMENT OF AGENT (Section 12, Texas Uniform Unincorporated Nonprofit Association Act, and Section 201.103, Texas Finance Code)

Appointment of Agent	$25.00
Amendment of Appointment of Agent	5.00
Resignation of Agent	no fee
Cancellation of Appointment	5.00
Expedited Processing fee per document	*25.00*

XI. ASSUMED NAMES (Chapter 36, Texas Business & Commerce Code)

Assumed Name Certificate	$25.00
Abandonment of Assumed Name	10.00
Expedited Processing fee per document	*25.00*

XII. TRADEMARKS (Chapter 16, Texas Business & Commerce Code) *Expedited Processing Not Available for Trademark Documents*

Application for Registration	$50.00
Renewal of Registration	25.00
Assignment of Registration	10.00
Recordation of Instrument Relating to Title	10.00

XIII. COPIES AND CERTIFICATES

Certificates of Status and Other Certificates
 of Fact (per certificate) $10.00
Long Form Certificate   25.00
 (Status plus list of filings)
Certified Copies $1.00 per page/plus 10.00 per certificate
Uncertified Copies (50 pages or less)   per page .10
 more than 50 pages   per page .15
Fax transmission of Certificates, Copies,
 Acknowledgement of Filings, etc   per page 2.00
Expedited Processing Fee for Certificates and
 Copies (per certificate)   ***10.00***

XIV. CREDIT CARD PAYMENTS

Credit cards (MasterCard, Visa and Discover) are accepted in payment of fees. A 2.1% credit card processing cost will be assessed on the total fees to be paid by credit card.

XV. EXPEDITED PROCESSING

Document will be processed by close of business
on the business day following the day of receipt.
Per Document   ***$25.00***

XVI. FORMS

To obtain forms for making certain filings with the Corporations Section, call **1-900-263-0060**. Forms are available at this number by fax or by mail. There is a charge of $1.00 per minute for ordering forms. Forms are also available on the Internet at **www.sos.state.tx.us**

XVII. SOSDIRECT

Access to the business entity and UCC databases is available via the Internet through SOSDirect. For information call (512) 475-2755 or visit our web site at www.sos.state.tx.us.

Form No. 806
Revised 10/01

APPENDIX B:
TEXAS BUSINESS
CORPORATION ACT

Included in this appendix are the Texas corporation statutes that will be most useful in organizing your corporation or limited liability company. There are other statutes that cover things such as mergers, buyback of shares, share dividends, proxies, votings trusts, and other matters that might come up in the future.

This appendix includes Articles 1–13, which apply to corporations. It also contains Article 1528n, which applies to LLCs.

You can obtain a full copy of the statutes from the Secretary of State.

Business Corporation Act

Part 1.

Art. 1.01. Short Title, Captions, Parts, Articles, Sections, Subsections, and Paragraphs

A. This Act shall be known and may be cited as the "Texas Business Corporation Act."

B. The Division of this Act into Parts, Articles, Sections, Subsections and Paragraphs and the use of captions in connection therewith are solely for convenience and shall have no legal effect in construing the provisions of this Act.

C. This Act has been organized and subdivided in the following manner:

(1) The Act is divided into Parts, containing groups of related Articles. Parts are numbered consecutively with cardinal numbers.

(2) The Act is also divided into Articles, numbered consecutively with Arabic numerals.

(3) Articles are divided into Sections. The Sections within each Article are numbered consecutively with capital letters.

(4) Sections are divided into subsections. The subsections within each Section are numbered consecutively with Arabic numerals enclosed in parentheses.

(5) Subsections are divided into paragraphs. The paragraphs within each subsection are numbered consecutively with lower case letters enclosed in parentheses.

Art. 1.02. Definitions

A. As used in this Act, unless the context otherwise requires, the term:

(1) "Articles of incorporation" means the original or restated articles of incorporation and all amendments thereto.

(2) "Associate," when used to indicate a relationship with a person, means:

(a) a domestic or foreign corporation or other entity of which the person is an officer or partner or is the beneficial owner of 10 percent or more of a class of voting shares or similar securities of that corporation or other entity;

(b) a trust or estate in which the person has a substantial beneficial interest or as to which the person serves as trustee or in a similar fiduciary capacity; or

(c) a spouse of the person or a relative of the person, or of the person's spouse, who has the same home as the person or who is a director or officer of such person or any of its affiliates.

(3) "Authorized shares" means the shares of all classes which the corporation is authorized to issue.

(4) "Cancel" means to restore issued shares to the status of authorized but unissued shares.

(5) "Certificated shares" means shares represented by instruments in bearer or registered form.

(6) "Conspicuous" or "conspicuously," when prescribed for information appearing on a certificate for shares or other securities, means the location of such information or use of type of sufficient size, color, or character that a reasonable person against whom such information may operate should notice it. For example, a printed or typed statement in capitals, or boldface or underlined type, or in type that is larger than or that contrasts in color with that used for other statements on the same certificate, is "conspicuous."

(7) "Consuming assets corporation" means a corporation which is engaged in the business of exploiting assets subject to depletion or amortization and which elects to state in its articles of incorporation that it is a consuming assets corporation and includes as a part of its official corporate name the phrase "a consuming assets corporation," giving such phrase equal prominence with the rest of the corporate name on its financial statements and certificates representing shares. All its certificates representing shares shall also contain a further sentence: "This corporation is permitted by law to pay dividends out of reserves which may impair its stated capital."

(8) "Conversion" means:

(a) the continuance of a domestic corporation as, and in the organizational form of, a foreign corporation or other entity; or

(b) the continuance of a foreign corporation or other entity as, and in the organizational form of, a domestic corporation.

(9) "Converted entity" means any domestic or foreign corporation or other entity to which a converting entity has converted or intends to convert as permitted by Article 5.17 of this Act.

(10) "Converting entity" means any domestic or foreign corporation or other entity that has converted or intends to convert as permitted by Article 5.17 of this Act.

(11) "Corporation" or "domestic corporation" means a corporation for profit subject to the provisions of this Act, except a foreign corporation.

(12) "Disinterested," when used to indicate a director or other person is disinterested in a contract, transaction, or other matter for purposes of approval of a contract or transaction under Article 2.35-1 of this Act and for purposes of considering the disposition of a claim or challenge with respect to a particular contract or transaction or to particular conduct means the director or other person, or an associate of the director (other than the corporation and its associates) or other person, is not a party to the contract or transaction or is not materially involved in the conduct that is subject to the claim or challenge and does not otherwise have a material financial interest in the outcome of the contract or transaction or the disposition of the claim or challenge. A director or other person is not to be considered to be materially involved in conduct that is subject to a claim or challenge or to otherwise have a material financial interest in the outcome of a contract or transaction or the disposition of the claim or challenge solely by reason of the existence of one or more of the following circumstances:

(a) the person was nominated or elected as a director by persons who are interested in the contract or transaction or who are alleged to have engaged in the conduct that is subject to the claim or challenge;

(b) the person receives normal director's fees or similar customary compensation, expense reimbursement, and benefits as a director of the corporation;

(c) the person has a direct or indirect equity interest in the corporation;

(d) the corporation or its subsidiaries has an interest in the contract or transaction or was affected by the alleged conduct;

(e) the person or an associate or affiliate of the person receives ordinary and reasonable compensation for services rendered to review, make recommendations, or decide on the disposition of the claim or challenge; or

(f) in the case of a review by the person of alleged conduct that is subject to a claim or challenge:

(i) the person is named as a defendant in the derivative proceeding with respect to such matter or as a person who engaged in the alleged conduct; or

(ii) the person approved of, voted for, or acquiesced in, as a director, the act being challenged if the act resulted in no material personal or financial benefit to the person and the challenging party fails to allege with particularity facts that, if true, raise a significant prospect that the director would be adjudged liable to the corporation or its shareholders by reason of that conduct.

(13) "Distribution" means a transfer of money or other property (except its own shares or rights to acquire its own shares), or issuance of indebtedness, by a corporation to its shareholders in the form of:

(a) a dividend on any class or series of the corporation's outstanding shares;

(b) a purchase, redemption, or other acquisition by the corporation, directly or indirectly, of any of its own shares; or

(c) a payment by the corporation in liquidation of all or a portion of its assets.

(14) "Foreign corporation" means a corporation for profit organized under laws other than the laws of this State.

(15) "Independent," when used to indicate a director or other person is independent for purposes of considering the disposition of a claim or challenge with respect to a particular contract or transaction or to particular conduct or alleged conduct means:

(a) the director or other person is disinterested;

(b) the director or other person is not an associate (other than by reason of being a director of the corporation or one more of its subsidiaries or associates) or member of the immediate family of a party to the contract or transaction that is the subject of the claim or challenge or that is alleged to have engaged in the conduct that is subject to the claim or challenge;

(c) the director or other person, or an associate or member of the immediate family of the director or other person, does not have a business, financial, or familial relationship with a party to the contract or transaction that is the subject of the claim or challenge or that is alleged to have engaged in conduct that is subject to the claim or challenge, which, in each case, could reasonably be expected to materially and adversely affect the director's or other person's judgment with respect to the consideration of the disposition of the matter subject to the claim or challenge in the interests of the corporation; and

(d) the director or other person is not otherwise shown, by a preponderance of the evidence by the person challenging the independence of the director or other person, to be under the controlling influence of a party to the contract or transaction that is the subject of the claim or challenge or that is alleged to have engaged in conduct that is subject to the claim or challenge.

A director or other person is not considered to have a relationship that could be expected to materially and adversely affect the director's or other person's judgment with respect to the consideration of the disposition of a matter subject to a claim or challenge or to otherwise be under the controlling influence of a party to a contract or transaction that is the subject of the claim or challenge or that is alleged to have engaged in conduct that is subject to a claim or challenge solely by reason of the existence of one or more of the following circumstances:

(a) the person has been nominated or elected as a director by persons who are interested in the contract or transaction or who are alleged to have engaged in the conduct that is subject to the claim or challenge;

(b) the person receives normal director's fees or similar customary compensation, expense reimbursement, and benefits as a director of the corporation;

(c) the person has a direct or indirect equity interest in the corporation;

(d) the corporation or its subsidiaries have an interest in the contract or transaction or were affected by the alleged conduct;

(e) the person or an associate or affiliate of such person receives ordinary and reasonable compensation for services rendered to review, make recommendations, or decide on the disposition of the claim or challenge; or

(f) the person or an associate (other than the corporation and its associates), immediate family, member or affiliate of the person has an ongoing business relationship with the corporation that is not material to that person, associate, family member, or affiliate.

(16) "Insolvency" means inability of a corporation to pay its debts as they become due in the usual course of its business.

(17) "Investment Company Act" means the Investment Company Act of 1940 (15 U.S.C. Sec. 80a-1 et seq.);

(18) "Merger" means (a) the division of a domestic corporation into two or more new domestic corporations or into a surviving corporation and one or more new domestic or foreign corporations or other entities, or (b) the combination of one or more domestic corporations with one or more domestic or foreign corporations or other entities resulting in (i) one or more surviving domestic or foreign corporations or other entities, (ii) the creation of one or more new domestic or foreign corporations or other entities, or (iii) one or more surviving domestic or foreign corporations or other entities and the creation of one or more new domestic or foreign corporations or other entities.

(19) "Net assets" means the amount by which the total assets of a corporation exceed the total debts of the corporation.

(20) "Other entity" means any entity, whether organized for profit or not, that is a corporation (other than a domestic or foreign corporation), limited or general partnership, limited liability company, real estate investment trust, joint venture, joint stock company, cooperative, association, bank, trust, insurance company or other legal entity organized pursuant to the laws of this state or any other state or country.

(21) "Share dividend" means a dividend by a corporation that is payable in its own authorized but unissued shares or in treasury shares. An amendment to a corporation's articles of incorporation to change the shares of any class or series, whether with or without par value, into the same or a different number of shares, either with or without par value, of the same class or series or another class or series does not constitute a share dividend.

(22) "Shareholder" or "holder of shares" means the person in whose name shares issued by a corporation are registered at the relevant time in the share transfer records maintained by the corporation pursuant to Article 2.44 of this Act.

(23) "Shares" means the units into which the proprietary interests in a corporation are divided, whether certificated or uncertificated shares.

(24) "Stated capital" means, at any particular time, the sum of:

(a) the par value of all shares of the corporation having a par value that have been issued;

(b) the consideration fixed by the corporation in the manner provided by Article 2.15 of this Act for all shares of the corporation without par value that have been issued, except such part of the consideration that is actually received therefor (which part must be less than all of that consideration) that the board by resolution adopted no later than sixty (60) days after the issuance of those shares may have allocated to surplus; and

(c) such amounts not included in paragraphs (a) and (b) of this subsection as have been transferred to stated capital of the corporation, whether upon the payment of a share dividend or upon adoption by the board of directors of a resolution directing that all or part of surplus be transferred to stated capital, minus all reductions from such sum as have been effected in a manner permitted by law.

(25) "Subscriber" means the offeror in a subscription.

(26) "Subscription" means a memorandum in writing, executed before or after incorporation, wherein an offer is made to purchase and pay for a specified number of theretofore unissued shares of a corporation.

(27) "Surplus" means the excess of the net assets of a corporation over its stated capital.

(28) "Treasury shares" means shares of a corporation which have been issued, have been subsequently acquired by and belong to the corporation, and have not been canceled and restored to the status of authorized but unissued shares. Treasury shares do not include shares held by a corporation, either directly or through a trust or similar arrangement, in a fiduciary capacity. Treasury shares shall be deemed to be "issued" shares but not "outstanding" shares, and shall not be included in the total assets of a corporation for purposes of determining its "net assets."

(29) "Uncertificated shares" means shares not represented by instruments and the transfers of which are registered upon books maintained for that purpose by or on behalf of the issuing corporation.

(30) "Electronic transmission" means a form of communication that:

(a) does not directly involve the physical transmission of paper;

(b) creates a record that may be retained, retrieved, and reviewed by the recipient; and

(c) may be directly reproduced in paper form by the recipient through an automated process.

B. Part Twelve of this Act provides definitions of terms used in the Texas Close Corporation Law.

C. A reference in this Act to another statute is a reference to that statute as amended.

Business Corporation Act
Part 2.
Art. 2.01. Purposes

A. Except as hereinafter in this Article excluded herefrom, corporations for profit may be organized under this Act for any lawful purpose or purposes. Corporations for the purpose of operating nonprofit institutions, including but not limited to those devoted to charitable, benevolent, religious, patriotic, civic, cultural, missionary, educational, scientific, social, fraternal, athletic, or aesthetic purposes, may not adopt or be organized under this Act.

B. No corporation may adopt this Act or be organized under this Act or obtain authority to transact business in this State under this Act:

(1) If any one or more of its purposes for the transaction of business in this State is expressly prohibited by any law of this State.

(2) If any one or more of its purposes for the transaction of business in this State is to engage in any activity which cannot lawfully be engaged in without first obtaining a license under the authority of the laws of this State to engage in such activity and such a license cannot lawfully be granted to a corporation.

(3) If among its purposes for the transaction of business in this State, there is included, however worded, a combination of the two businesses listed in either of the following:

(a) The business of raising cattle and owning land therefor, and the business of operating stockyards and of slaughtering, refrigerating, canning, curing or packing meat. Owning and operating feed lots and feeding cattle shall not be considered as engaging in "the business of raising cattle and owning land therefor" within the purview of this paragraph of this subsection.

(b) The business of engaging in the petroleum oil producing business in this State and the business of engaging directly in the oil pipe line business in this State: provided, however, that a corporation engaged in the oil producing business in this State which owns or operates private pipe lines in and about its refineries, fields or stations or which owns stock of corporations engaged in the oil pipe line business shall not be deemed to be engaging directly in the oil pipe line business in this State; and provided that any corporation, or group of corporations acting in partnership or other combination with other corporations, engaged as a common carrier in the pipe line business for transporting oil, oil products, gas, carbon dioxide, salt brine, fuller's earth, sand, clay, liquefied minerals or other mineral solutions, shall have all of the rights and powers conferred by Sections 111.019 through 111.022, Natural Resources Code.

(4) If any one or more of its purposes is to operate any of the following:

(a) Banks, (b) trust companies, (c) building and loan associations or companies, (d) insurance companies of every type and character that operate under the insurance laws of this State, and corporate attorneys in fact for reciprocal or inter-insurance exchanges, (e) railroad companies, (f) cemetery companies, (g) cooperatives or limited cooperative associations, (h) labor unions, (i) abstract and title insurance companies whose purposes are provided for and whose powers are prescribed by Chapter 9 of the Insurance Code of this State.

C. A company may be incorporated under this Article or under Chapter 1, Title 112, Revised Statutes, if the company:

(1) operates a railroad passenger service by contracting with a railroad corporation or other company; and

(2) does not construct, own, or maintain a railroad track.

Art. 2.02. General Powers

A. Subject to the provisions of Sections B and C of this Article, each corporation shall have power:

(1) To have perpetual succession by its corporate name unless a limited period of duration is stated in its articles of incorporation. Notwithstanding the articles of incorporation, the period of duration for any corporation incorporated before September 6, 1955, is perpetual if all fees and franchise taxes have been paid as provided by law.

(2) To sue and be sued, complain and defend, in its corporate name.

(3) To have a corporate seal which may be altered at pleasure, and to use the same by causing it, or a facsimile thereof, to be impressed on, affixed to, or in any manner reproduced upon, instruments of any nature required to be executed by its proper officers.

(4) To purchase, receive, lease, or otherwise acquire, own, hold, improve, use and otherwise deal in and with, real or personal property, or any interest therein, wherever situated, as the purposes of the corporation shall require.

(5) To sell, convey, mortgage, pledge, lease, exchange, transfer and otherwise dispose of all or any part of its property and assets.

(6) To lend money to, and otherwise assist, its employees, officers, and directors if such a loan or assistance reasonably may be expected to benefit, directly or indirectly, the lending or assisting corporation.

(7) To purchase, receive, subscribe for, or otherwise acquire, own, hold, vote, use, employ, mortgage, lend, pledge, sell or otherwise dispose of, and otherwise use and deal in and with, shares or other interests in, or obligations of, other domestic or foreign corporations, associations, partnerships, or individuals, or direct or indirect obligations of the United States or of any other government, state, territory, government district, or municipality, or of any instrumentality thereof.

(8) To purchase or otherwise acquire its own bonds, debentures, or other evidences of its indebtedness or obligations; to purchase or otherwise acquire its own unredeemable shares and hold those acquired shares as treasury shares or cancel or otherwise dispose of those acquired shares; and to redeem or purchase shares made redeemable by the provisions of its articles of incorporation.

(9) To make contracts and incur liabilities, borrow money at such rates of interest as the corporation may determine, issue its notes, bonds, and other obligations, and secure any of its obligations by mortgage or pledge of all or any of its property, franchises, and income.

(10) To lend money for its corporate purposes, invest and reinvest its funds, and take and hold real and personal property as security for the payment of funds so loaned or invested.

(11) To conduct its business, carry on its operations, and have offices and exercise the powers granted by this Act, within or without this State.

(12) To elect or appoint officers and agents of the corporation for such period of time as the corporation may determine, and define their duties and fix their compensation.

(13) To make and alter bylaws, not inconsistent with its articles of incorporation or with the laws of this State, for the administration and regulation of the affairs of the corporation.

(14) To make donations for the public welfare or for charitable, scientific, or educational purposes.

(15) To transact any lawful business which the board of directors shall find will be in aid of government policy.

(16) To indemnify directors, officers, employees, and agents of the corporation and to purchase and maintain liability insurance for those persons.

(17) To pay pensions and establish pension plans, pension trusts, profit sharing plans, stock bonus plans, and other incentive plans for any or all of, or any class or classes of, its directors, officers, or employees.

(18) To be an organizer, partner, member, associate, or manager of any partnership, joint venture, or other enterprise, and to the extent permitted by any other jurisdiction to be an incorporator of any other corporation of any type or kind.

(19) To cease its corporate activities and terminate its existence by voluntary dissolution.

(20) To renounce, in its articles of incorporation or by action of its board of directors, an interest or expectancy of the corporation in, or an interest or expectancy of the corporation in being offered an opportunity to participate in, specified business opportunities or specified classes or categories of business opportunities that are presented to the corporation or one or more of its officers, directors, or shareholders.

(21) Whether included in the foregoing or not, to have and exercise all powers necessary or appropriate to effect any or all of the purposes for which the corporation is organized.

B. Nothing in this Article grants any authority to officers or directors of a corporation for the exercise of any of the foregoing powers, inconsistent with limitations on any of the same which may be expressly set forth in this Act or in the articles of incorporation or in any other laws of this State. Authority of officers and directors to act beyond the scope of the purpose or purposes of a corporation is not granted by any provision of this Article.

C. Nothing contained in this Article shall be deemed to authorize any action in violation of the Anti-Trust Laws of this State, as now existing or hereafter amended.

Art. 2.02-1. Power to Indemnify and to Purchase Indemnity Insurance; Duty to Indemnify

A. In this article:

(1) "Corporation" includes any domestic or foreign predecessor entity of the corporation in a merger, conversion, or other transaction in which some or all of the liabilities of the predecessor are transferred to the corporation by operation of law and in any other transaction in which the corporation assumes the liabilities of the predecessor but does not specifically exclude liabilities that are the subject matter of this article.

(2) "Director" means any person who is or was a director of the corporation and any person who, while a director of the corporation, is or was serving at the request of the corporation as a director, officer, partner, venturer, proprietor, trustee, employee, agent, or similar functionary of another foreign or domestic corporation, employee benefit plan, other enterprise, or other entity.

(3) "Expenses" include court costs and attorneys' fees.

(4) "Official capacity" means

(a) when used with respect to a director, the office of director in the corporation, and

(b) when used with respect to a person other than a director, the elective or appointive office in the corporation held by the officer or the employment or agency relationship undertaken by the employee or agent in behalf of the corporation, but

(c) in both Paragraphs (a) and (b) does not include service for any other foreign or domestic corporation or any employee benefit plan, other enterprise, or other entity.

(5) "Proceeding" means any threatened, pending, or completed action, suit, or proceeding, whether civil, criminal, administrative, arbitrative, or investigative, any appeal in such an action, suit, or proceeding, and any inquiry or investigation that could lead to such an action, suit, or proceeding.

B. A corporation may indemnify a person who was, is, or is threatened to be made a named defendant or respondent in a proceeding because the person is or was a director only if it is determined in accordance with Section F of this article that the person:

(1) conducted himself in good faith;

(2) reasonably believed:

(a) in the case of conduct in his official capacity as a director of the corporation, that his conduct was in the corporation's best interests; and

(b) in all other cases, that his conduct was at least not opposed to the corporation's best interests; and

(3) in the case of any criminal proceeding, had no reasonable cause to believe his conduct was unlawful.

C. Except to the extent permitted by Section E of this article, a director may not be indemnified under Section B of this article in respect of a proceeding:

(1) in which the person is found liable on the basis that personal benefit was improperly received by him, whether or not the benefit resulted from an action taken in the person's official capacity; or

(2) in which the person is found liable to the corporation.

D. The termination of a proceeding by judgment, order, settlement, or conviction, or on a plea of nolo contendere or its equivalent is not of itself determinative that the person did not meet the requirements set forth in Section B of this article. A person shall be deemed to have been found liable in respect of any claim, issue or matter only after the person shall have been so adjudged by a court of competent jurisdiction after exhaustion of all appeals therefrom.

E. A person may be indemnified under Section B of this article against judgments, penalties (including excise and similar taxes), fines, settlements, and reasonable expenses actually incurred by the person in connection with the proceeding; but if the person is found liable to the corporation or is found liable on the basis that personal benefit was improperly received by the person, the indemnification (1) is limited to reasonable expenses actually incurred by the person in connection with the proceeding and (2) shall not be made in respect of any proceeding in which the person shall have been found liable for willful or intentional misconduct in the performance of his duty to the corporation.

F. A determination of indemnification under Section B of this article must be made:

(1) by a majority vote of the directors who at the time of the vote are not named defendants or respondents in the proceeding, regardless of whether the directors not named defendants or respondents constitute a quorum;

(2) by a majority vote of a committee of the board of directors, if:

(a) the committee is designated by a majority vote of the directors who at the time of the vote are not named defendants or respondents in the proceeding, regardless of whether the directors not named defendants or respondents constitute a quorum; and

(b) the committee consists solely of one or more of the directors not named as defendants or respondents in the proceeding;

(3) by special legal counsel selected by the board of directors or a committee of the board by vote as set forth in Subsection (1) or (2) of this section; or

(4) by the shareholders in a vote that excludes the shares held by directors who are named defendants or respondents in the proceeding.

G. Authorization of indemnification and determination as to reasonableness of expenses must be made in the same manner as the determination that indemnification is permissible, except that if the determination that indemnification is permissible is made by special legal counsel, authorization of indemnification and determination as to reasonableness of expenses must be made in the manner specified by Subsection (3) of Section F of this article for the selection of special legal counsel. A provision contained in the articles of incorporation, the bylaws, a resolution of shareholders or directors, or an agreement that makes mandatory the indemnification permitted under Section B of this article shall be deemed to constitute authorization of indemnification in the manner required by this section even though such provision may not have been adopted or authorized in the same manner as the determination that indemnification is permissible.

H. A corporation shall indemnify a director against reasonable expenses incurred by him in connection with a proceeding in which

he is a named defendant or respondent because he is or was a director if he has been wholly successful, on the merits or otherwise, in the defense of the proceeding.

I. If, in a suit for the indemnification required by Section H of this article, a court of competent jurisdiction determines that the director is entitled to indemnification under that section, the court shall order indemnification and shall award to the director the expenses incurred in securing the indemnification.

J. If, upon application of a director, a court of competent jurisdiction determines, after giving any notice the court considers necessary, that the director is fairly and reasonably entitled to indemnification in view of all the relevant circumstances, whether or not he has met the requirements set forth in Section B of this article or has been found liable in the circumstances described by Section C of this article, the court may order the indemnification that the court determines is proper and equitable; but if the person is found liable to the corporation or is found liable on the basis that personal benefit was improperly received by the person, the indemnification shall be limited to reasonable expenses actually incurred by the person in connection with the proceeding.

K. Reasonable expenses incurred by a present director who was, is, or is threatened to be made a named defendant or respondent in a proceeding may be paid or reimbursed by the corporation, in advance of the final disposition of the proceeding and without the determination specified in Section F of this article or the authorization or determination specified in Section G of this article, after the corporation receives a written affirmation by the director of his good faith belief that he has met the standard of conduct necessary for indemnification under this article and a written undertaking by or on behalf of the director to repay the amount paid or reimbursed if it is ultimately determined that he has not met that standard or if it is ultimately determined that indemnification of the director against expenses incurred by him in connection with that proceeding is prohibited by Section E of this article. Notwithstanding any authorization or determination specified in this article, reasonable expenses incurred by a former director or officer, or a present or former employee or agent of the corporation, who was, is, or is threatened to be made a named defendant or respondent in a proceeding may be paid or reimbursed by the corporation, in advance of the final disposition of the proceeding, on any terms the corporation considers appropriate. A provision contained in the articles of incorporation, the bylaws, a resolution of shareholders or directors, or an agreement that makes mandatory the payment or reimbursement permitted under this section shall be deemed to constitute authorization of that payment or reimbursement.

L. The written undertaking required by Section K of this article must be an unlimited general obligation of the director but need not be secured. It may be accepted without reference to financial ability to make repayment.

M. A provision for a corporation to indemnify or to advance expenses to a director who was, is, or is threatened to be made a named defendant or respondent in a proceeding, whether contained in the articles of incorporation, the bylaws, a resolution of shareholders or directors, an agreement, or otherwise, except in accordance with Section R of this article, is valid only to the extent it is consistent with this article as limited by the articles of incorporation, if such a limitation exists.

N. Notwithstanding any other provision of this article, a corporation may pay or reimburse expenses incurred by a director in connection with his appearance as a witness or other participation in a proceeding at a time when he is not a named defendant or respondent in the proceeding.

O. An officer of the corporation shall be indemnified as, and to the same extent, provided by Sections H, I, and J of this article for a director and is entitled to seek indemnification under those sections to the same extent as a director. A corporation may indemnify and advance expenses to an officer, employee, or agent of the corporation to the same extent that it may indemnify and advance expenses to directors under this article. A determination of indemnification for an employee or agent of the corporation is not required to be made in accordance with Section F of this article.

P. A corporation may indemnify and advance expenses to persons who are not or were not officers, employees, or agents of the corporation but who are or were serving at the request of the corporation as a director, officer, partner, venturer, proprietor, trustee, employee, agent, or similar functionary of another foreign or domestic corporation, employee benefit plan, other enterprise, or other entity to the same extent that it may indemnify and advance expenses to directors under this article.

Q. A corporation may indemnify and advance expenses to an officer, employee, agent, or person identified in Section P of this article and who is not a director to such further extent, consistent with law, as may be provided by its articles of incorporation, bylaws, general or specific action of its board of directors, or contract or as permitted or required by common law.

R. A corporation may purchase and maintain insurance or another arrangement on behalf of any person who is or was a director, officer, employee, or agent of the corporation or who is or was serving at the request of the corporation as a director, officer, partner, venturer, proprietor, trustee, employee, agent, or similar functionary of another foreign or domestic corporation, employee benefit plan, other enterprise, or other entity, against any liability asserted against him and incurred by him in such a capacity or arising out of his status as such a person, whether or not the corporation would have the power to indemnify him against that liability under this article. If the insurance or other arrangement is with a person or entity that is not regularly engaged in the business of providing insurance coverage, the insurance or arrangement may provide for payment of a liability with respect to which the corporation would not have the power to indemnify the person only if including coverage for the additional liability has been approved by the shareholders of the corporation. Without limiting the power of the corporation to procure or maintain any kind of insurance or other arrangement, a corporation may, for the benefit of persons indemnified by the corporation, (1) create a trust fund; (2) establish any form of self-insurance; (3) secure its indemnity obligation by grant of a security interest or other lien on the assets of the corporation; or (4) establish a letter of credit, guaranty, or surety arrangement. The insurance or other arrangement may be procured, maintained, or established within the corporation or with any insurer or other person deemed appropriate by the board of directors regardless of whether all or part of the stock or other securities of the insurer or other person are owned in whole or part by the corporation. In the absence of fraud, the judgment of the board of directors as to the terms and conditions of the insurance or other arrangement and the identity of the insurer or other person participating in an arrangement shall be conclusive and the insurance or arrangement shall not be voidable and shall not subject the directors approving the insurance or

arrangement to liability, on any ground, regardless of whether directors participating in the approval are beneficiaries of the insurance or arrangement.

S. Any indemnification of or advance of expenses to a director in accordance with this article shall be reported in writing to the shareholders with or before the notice or waiver of notice of the next shareholders' meeting or with or before the next submission to shareholders of a consent to action without a meeting pursuant to Section A, Article 9.10, of this Act and, in any case, within the 12-month period immediately following the date of the indemnification or advance.

T. For purposes of this article, the corporation is deemed to have requested a director to serve as a trustee, employee, agent, or similar functionary of an employee benefit plan whenever the performance by him of his duties to the corporation also imposes duties on or otherwise involves services by him to the plan or participants or beneficiaries of the plan. Excise taxes assessed on a director with respect to an employee benefit plan pursuant to applicable law are deemed fines. Action taken or omitted by a director with respect to an employee benefit plan in the performance of his duties for a purpose reasonably believed by him to be in the interest of the participants and beneficiaries of the plan is deemed to be for a purpose which is not opposed to the best interests of the corporation.

U. The articles of incorporation of a corporation may restrict the circumstances under which the corporation is required or permitted to indemnify a person under Section H, I, J, O, P, or Q of this article.

Art. 2.04. Defense of Ultra Vires

A. Lack of capacity of a corporation shall never be made the basis of any claim or defense at law or in equity.

B. No act of a corporation and no conveyance or transfer of real or personal property to or by a corporation shall be invalid by reason of the fact that such act, conveyance or transfer was beyond the scope of the purpose or purposes of the corporation as expressed in its articles of incorporation or by reason of limitations on authority of its officers and directors to exercise any statutory power of the corporation, as such limitations are expressed in the articles of incorporation, but that such act, conveyance or transfer was, or is, beyond the scope of the purpose or purposes of the corporation as expressed in its articles of incorporation or inconsistent with any such expressed limitations of authority, may be asserted:

(1) In a proceeding by a shareholder against the corporation to enjoin the doing of any act or acts or the transfer of real or personal property by or to the corporation. If the unauthorized act or transfer sought to be enjoined is being, or is to be, performed or made pursuant to any contract to which the corporation is a party, the court may, if all of the parties to the contract are parties to the proceeding and if it deems the same to be equitable, set aside and enjoin the performance of such contract, and in so doing may allow to the corporation or to the other parties to the contract, as the case may be, compensation for the loss or damage sustained by either of them which may result from the action of the court in setting aside and enjoining the performance of such contract, but anticipated profits to be derived from the performance of the contract shall not be awarded by the court as a part of loss or damage sustained.

(2) In a proceeding by the corporation, whether acting directly or through a receiver, trustee, or other legal representative, or through shareholders in a representative suit, against the incumbent or former officers or directors of the corporation for exceeding their authority.

(3) In a proceeding by the Attorney General, as provided in this Act, to dissolve the corporation, or in a proceeding by the Attorney General to enjoin the corporation from transacting unauthorized business, or to enforce divestment of real property acquired or held contrary to the laws of this State.

Art. 2.05. Corporate Name; Use of Assumed Names

A. The Corporate name shall conform to the following requirements:

(1) It shall contain the word "corporation," "company," or "incorporated," or shall contain an abbreviation of one of such words, and shall contain such additional words as may be required by law.

(2) It shall not contain any word or phrase which indicates or implies that it is organized for any purpose other than one or more of the purposes contained in its articles of incorporation.

(3) It shall not be the same as, or deceptively similar to, the name of any domestic corporation, limited partnership, or limited liability company existing under the laws of this State, or the name of any foreign corporation, non-profit corporation, limited partnership, or limited liability company authorized to transact business in this State, or a name the exclusive right to which is, at the time, reserved in the manner provided in this Act or any other statute providing for reservation of names by a limited partnership or limited liability company, or the name of a corporation, limited partnership, or limited liability company which has in effect a registration of its company name as provided in this Act or any other applicable law; provided that a name may be similar if written consent is obtained from the existing corporation, limited partnership, or limited liability company having the name deemed to be similar or the person for whom the name deemed to be similar is reserved in the office of the Secretary of State.

(4) It shall not contain the word "lottery."

B. Any domestic or foreign corporation having authority to transact business in this State may do so under an assumed name by filing an assumed name certificate in the manner prescribed by law. The assumed name may, but is not required to, comply with the requirements of Section A(1) of this Article.

C. The filing of articles of incorporation under Part Three of this Act, an application to reserve a specified Corporate name under Article 2.06 of this Act, or an application to register a Corporate name by a foreign corporation under Article 2.07 of this Act does not authorize the use of a Corporate name in this State in violation of the rights of another under the federal Trademark Act of 1946 (15 U.S.C., Section 1051 et seq.), the Texas trademark law (Chapter 16, Business & Commerce Code), the Assumed Business or Professional Name Act (Chapter 36, Business & Commerce Code), or the common law. The Secretary of State shall deliver to each newly organized corporation, applicant for reservation of a Corporate name, and newly registered foreign corporation a notice containing the substance of this section.

Art. 2.06. Reserved Name

A. The exclusive right to the use of a corporate name may be reserved by:

(1) Any person intending to organize a corporation under this Act.

(2) Any domestic corporation intending to change its name.

(3) Any foreign corporation intending to make application for a certificate of authority to transact business in this State.

(4) Any foreign corporation authorized to transact business in this State and intending to change its name.

(5) Any person intending to organize a foreign corporation and intending to have such corporation make application for a certificate of authority to transact business in this State.

B. The reservation shall be made by filing with the Secretary of State an application to reserve a specified corporate name, executed by the applicant or the attorney or agent thereof. If the Secretary of State finds that the name is available for corporate use, he shall reserve the same for the exclusive use of the applicant for a period of one hundred and twenty (120) days.

C. The right to the exclusive use of a specified corporate name so reserved may be transferred to any other person or corporation by filing in the office of the Secretary of State a notice of such transfer, executed by the applicant for whom the name was reserved, and specifying the name and address of the transferee.

D. Any person for whom a specified corporate name has been reserved pursuant to Section B of this article may, during the period for which such name is reserved, terminate such reservation by filing with the Secretary of State an application for cancellation of reservation of corporate name, together with the applicable fee.

Art. 2.07. Registered Name

A. Any corporation organized for the purpose of operating a bank, trust company, building and loan association or company, insurance company currently holding a valid certificate of authority to do business in the State of Texas, and any foreign corporation not authorized to transact business in this State may register its corporate name under this Act, provided its corporate name is not the same as, or deceptively similar to, the name of any domestic corporation existing under the laws of this State or the name of any foreign corporation authorized to transact business in this State or any corporate name reserved or registered under this Act. Provided, however, that any bank, trust company, building and loan association, or insurance company will not be prohibited from registering its corporate name even if the corporate name may be deemed to be the same as or deceptively similar to an otherwise authorized corporate name, if such bank, trust company, building and loan association, or insurance company was duly organized on, and in continual existence from, a date preceding the date the conflicting corporate name was authorized by the Secretary of State under this Act.

B. Such registration shall be made by:

(1) Filing with the Secretary of State:

(a) An application for registration executed by the corporation by an officer thereof, setting forth the name of the corporation, the state or territory under the laws of which it is incorporated, the date of its incorporation, a statement that it is carrying on or doing business, and a brief statement of the business in which it is engaged, and

(b) A certificate setting forth that such corporation is in good standing under the laws of the state or territory wherein it is organized, executed by the Secretary of State of such state or territory or by such other official as may have custody of the records pertaining to corporations, and

(2) Paying to the Secretary of State the required registration fee.

C. Such registration shall be effective for a period of one year from the date on which the application for registration is filed, unless voluntarily withdrawn by the filing of a written notice thereof with the Secretary of State.

Art. 2.08. Renewal of Registered Name

A. A corporation which has in effect a registration of its corporate name may renew such registration from year to year by filing annually an application for renewal in the manner prescribed for the filing of an original application. Such renewal application shall be filed during the ninety (90) days preceding the expiration date of the then current registration.

Art. 2.09. Registered Office and Registered Agent

A. Each corporation shall have and continuously maintain in this State:

(1) A registered office which may be, but need not be, the same as its place of business.

(2) A registered agent, which agent may be either an individual resident in this State or a domestic corporation, or other entity organized under the laws of this state or authorized to transact business in this State that has a business office identical with each such registered office that is generally open during normal business hours to accept service of process and otherwise perform the functions of a registered agent.

Art. 2.10. Change of Registered Office or Registered Agent

A. A corporation may change its registered office or change its registered agent, or both, upon filing in the office of the Secretary of State a statement setting forth:

(1) The name of the corporation.

(2) The post-office address of its then registered office.

(3) If the post-office address of its registered office is to be changed, the post-office address to which the registered office is to be changed.

(4) The name of its then registered agent.

(5) If its registered agent is to be changed, the name of its successor registered agent.

(6) That the post-office address of its registered office and the post-office address of the business office of its registered agent, as changed, will be identical.

(7) That such change was authorized by its Board of Directors or by an officer of the corporation so authorized by the Board of Directors.

B. The statement required by this article shall be executed on behalf of the corporation by an officer. The original and a copy of the statement shall be delivered to the Secretary of State. If the Secretary of State finds that such statement conforms to the provisions of this Act, he shall, when the appropriate filing fee is paid as prescribed by law:

(1) Endorse on the original and the copy the word "Filed," and the month, day, and year of the filing thereof.

(2) File the original in his office.

(3) Return the copy to the corporation or its representative.

C. Upon such filing, the change of address of the registered office, or the appointment of a new registered agent, or both, as the case may be, shall become effective.

D. Any registered agent of a corporation may resign

(1) by giving written notice to the corporation at its last known address

(2) and by giving written notice, in duplicate (the original and one copy of the notice), to the Secretary of State within ten days after mailing or delivery of said notice to the corporation. Such notice shall include the last known address of the corporation and shall include the statement that written notice of resignation has been given to the corporation and the date thereof. Upon compliance with the requirements as to written notice, the appointment of such agent shall terminate upon the expiration of thirty (30) days after receipt of such notice by the Secretary of State.

If the Secretary of State finds that such written notice conforms to the provisions of this Act, he shall:

(1) Endorse on the original and the copy the word "filed" and the month, day, and year of the filing thereof.

(2) File the original in his office.

(3) Return the copy to such resigning registered agent.

(4) Notify the corporation of the resignation of the registered agent. No fee shall be required to be paid for the filing of a resignation under this section.

Art. 2.10-1. Change of Address of Registered Agent

A. The location of the registered office in Texas for a corporation, domestic or foreign, may be changed from one address to another upon filing in the office of the Secretary of State a statement setting forth:

(1) The name of the corporation represented by such registered agent.

(2) The address at which such registered agent has maintained the registered office for said corporation.

(3) The new address at which such registered agent will thereafter maintain the registered office for said corporation.

(4) A statement that notice of the change has been given to said corporation in writing at least ten (10) days prior to such filing.

B. The statement required by this article shall be signed by the registered agent, or, if said agent is a corporation, by an officer of such corporate agent on its behalf. If the registered agent is simultaneously filing statements as to more than one corporation, each such statement may contain facsimile signatures in the execution. The original and one copy of the statement shall be delivered to the Secretary of State. If the Secretary of State finds that such statement conforms to the provisions of this Act, he shall:

(1) Endorse on the original and the copy the word "Filed," and the month, day, and year of the filing thereof.

(2) File the original in his office.

(3) Return the copy to such registered agent.

C. The registered office of the corporation named in such statement shall be changed to the new address of the registered agent upon the filing of such statement by the Secretary of State.

Art. 2.11. Service of Process on Corporation

A. The president and all vice presidents of the corporation and the registered agent of the corporation shall be agents of such corporation upon whom any process, notice, or demand required or permitted by law to be served upon the corporation may be served.

B. Whenever a corporation shall fail to appoint or maintain a registered agent in this State, or whenever its registered agent cannot with reasonable diligence be found at the registered office, then the Secretary of State shall be an agent of such corporation upon whom any such process, notice, or demand may be served. Service on the Secretary of State of any process, notice, or demand shall be made by delivering to and leaving with him, or with the Assistant Secretary of State, or with any clerk having charge of the corporation department of his office, duplicate copies of such process, notice, or demand. In the event any such process, notice, or demand is served on the Secretary of State, he shall immediately cause one of the copies thereof to be forwarded by registered mail, addressed to the corporation at its registered office. Any service so had on the Secretary of State shall be returnable in not less than thirty (30) days.

C. The Secretary of State shall keep a record of all processes, notices and demands served upon him under this Article, and shall record therein the time of such service and his action with reference thereto.

D. Service of process, notice, or demand required or permitted by law to be served by a political subdivision of this state or by a person, including another political subdivision or an attorney, acting on behalf of a political subdivision in connection with the collection of a delinquent ad valorem tax may be served on a corporation whose corporate privileges are forfeited under Section 171.251, Tax Code, or is involuntarily dissolved under Article 7.01 of this Act by delivering the process, notice, or demand to any officer or director of the corporation, as listed in the most recent records of the secretary of state. If the officers or directors of the corporation are unknown or cannot be found, service on the corporation may be made in the same manner as service is made on unknown shareholders under law. Notwithstanding any disability or reinstatement of a corporation, service of process under this section is sufficient for a judgment against the corporation or a judgment in rem against any property to which the corporation holds title.

Art. 2.12. Authorized Shares

A. Each corporation may issue the number of shares stated in its articles of incorporation. Such shares may be divided into one or more classes, any or all of which classes may consist of shares with par value or shares without par value, as shall be stated in the articles of incorporation. Any such class of shares may be divided into one or more series, as shall be stated in the articles of incorporation. All shares of the same class shall be of the same par value or be without par value. Unless the shares of a class have been divided into series, all shares of the same class shall be identical in all respects. If the shares of a class have been divided into series, shares of the same class may vary between series, but all shares of the same series shall be identical in all respects. Any such class or series of shares shall be so designated as to distinguish the shares of that class or series from the shares of all other classes and series. Any such class or series shall have such designations, preferences, limitations, and relative rights, including voting rights, as shall be stated in the articles of incorporation. The articles of incorporation may limit or deny the voting rights of, or provide special voting rights for, the shares of any class or series to the extent that such limitation, denial, or provision is not inconsistent with the provisions of this Act. Any of the designations, preferences, limitations, and relative rights, including voting rights, of any class or series of shares may be made dependent upon facts ascertainable outside the articles of incorporation, which facts may include future acts of the corporation, provided that the manner in which such facts shall operate upon the designations, preferences, limitations, and relative rights, including voting rights, of such class or series of shares is clearly and expressly set forth in the articles of incorporation.

B. Without being limited to the authority herein contained, a corporation, when so provided in its articles of incorporation, may issue shares of one or more classes or series:

(1) Redeemable, subject to compliance by the corporation with Articles 2.38 and 4.08 of this Act, at the option of the corporation, the shareholder or another person or upon the occurrence of a designated event.

(2) Entitling the holders thereof to cumulative, noncumulative, or partially cumulative dividends.

(3) Having preference over any other class, classes or series of shares as to the payment of dividends.

(4) Having preference in the assets of the corporation over any other class, classes or series of shares upon the voluntary or involuntary liquidation of the corporation.

(5) Exchangeable, subject to compliance by the corporation with Article 2.38 of this Act, at the option of the corporation, the shareholder or another person or upon the occurrence of a designated event, for shares, obligations, indebtedness, evidence of ownership, rights to purchase securities or other securities of the corporation or one or more other domestic or foreign corporations or other entities or for other property or for any combination of the foregoing.

(6) Convertible at the option of the corporation, the shareholder or another person or upon the occurrence of a designated event, into shares of any other class or series, but shares without par value shall not be converted into shares with par value unless that part of the stated capital of the corporation represented by such shares without par value is, at the time of conversion, at least equal to the aggregate par value of the shares into which shares without par value are to be converted or the amount of any such deficiency is transferred from surplus to stated capital.

C. (1) The board of directors of a corporation registered as an open-end company under the Investment Company Act may:

(a) establish classes of shares and series of unissued shares of any class by fixing and determining the designations, preferences, limitations, and relative rights, including voting rights, of the shares of any class or series so established to the same extent that the designations, preferences, limitations, and relative rights could be stated if fully set forth in the articles of incorporation; and

(b) increase or decrease the aggregate number of shares or the number of shares of, or eliminate and remove from the articles of incorporation, a class or series of shares that the corporation has authority to issue, unless a provision has been included in the articles of incorporation of the corporation after September 1, 1993, expressly prohibiting those actions by the board of directors. The board of directors may not:

(i) decrease the number of shares within a class or series to less than the number of shares of that class or series that are then outstanding; or

(ii) eliminate or remove from the articles of incorporation any reference to any class or series of which shares are then outstanding.

To establish a class or series, the board of directors shall adopt a resolution setting forth the designation of the class or series and fixing and determining the designations, preferences, limitations, and relative rights, including voting rights, of the class or series. In order to increase or decrease the number of shares of, or eliminate and remove from the articles of incorporation any reference to, a class or series of shares, the board of directors shall adopt a resolution fixing and determining the new number of shares of each class or series in which the number of shares is increased or decreased or eliminating the class or series and removing references to the class or series from the articles of incorporation. The shares of any eliminated series shall resume the status of authorized but unissued shares of the class of shares from which the series was established unless otherwise provided in the resolution or the articles of incorporation.

(2) Before the first issuance of any shares of a class or series established or increased or decreased by resolution adopted by the board of directors under Subsection (1) of this section, and in order to eliminate from the articles of incorporation a class or series of shares and all references to the class or series contained in the articles, the corporation shall file with the Secretary of State a statement setting forth:

(a) the name of the corporation;

(b) if the statement relates to the establishment of a class or series of shares, a copy of the resolution establishing and designating the class or series and fixing and determining the preferences, limitations, and relative rights of the class or series;

(c) if the statement relates to an increase or decrease in the number of shares of any class or series, a copy of the resolution fixing and determining the new number of shares of each class or series in which the number of shares is increased or decreased;

(d) if the statement relates to the elimination of a class or series of shares and to the removal of all references to the class or series from the articles of incorporation, a copy of the resolution eliminating the class or series and removing all references to the class or series from the articles of incorporation;

(e) the date of adoption of the resolution; and

(f) that the resolution was duly adopted by all necessary action on the part of the corporation.

(3) The statement shall be executed on behalf of the corporation by an officer. The original and a copy of the statement shall be delivered to the Secretary of State. If the Secretary of State finds that the statement conforms to law, when the appropriate filing fee is paid as provided by law, the Secretary of State shall:

(a) endorse on the original and the copy the word "Filed," and the month, day, and year of the filing of the statement;

(b) file the original in the Secretary of State's office; and

(c) return the copy to the corporation or its representative.

(4) On the filing of a statement by the Secretary of State, the resolution establishing and designating the class or series and fixing and determining the preferences, limitations, and relative rights of the class or series, the resolution fixing the new number of shares of each class or series in which the number of shares is increased or decreased, or the resolution eliminating a class or series and all references to the class or series from the articles of incorporation, as appropriate, becomes an amendment of the articles of incorporation. An amendment of the articles of incorporation effected as provided by this Article is not subject to the procedure to amend the articles contained in Article 4.02 of this Act.

Art. 2.13. Series of Shares Established by Board of Directors

A. If the articles of incorporation shall expressly vest such authority in the board of directors, then the board of directors shall have authority to establish series of unissued shares of any class by fixing and determining the designations, preferences, limitations, and relative rights, including voting rights, of the shares of any series so established to the same extent that such designations, preferences, limitations, and relative rights could be stated if fully set forth in the articles of incorporation, but subject to and within the limitations set forth in the articles of incorporation. In order to establish a series, where authority so to do is contained in the articles of incorporation, the board of directors shall adopt a resolution setting forth the designation of the series and fixing and determining the designations, preferences, limitations and relative rights, including voting rights, thereof or so much thereof as shall not be fixed and determined by the articles of incorporation.

B. If the articles of incorporation shall expressly vest authority in the board of directors to establish series of unissued shares of a class and do not expressly restrict the board of directors from increasing or decreasing the number of shares of such a series, then the board of directors shall have authority to increase or decrease the number of shares within each such series; provided, however, that the board of directors may not decrease the number of shares within a series to less than the number of shares within such series that are then issued.

In order to so increase or decrease the number of shares of a series, the board of directors shall adopt a resolution fixing and determining the new number of shares of each series in which the number of shares is increased or decreased. In case the number of shares of a series shall be so decreased, the shares by which the series is decreased shall resume the status of authorized but unissued shares of the class of shares from which such series was established, unless otherwise provided in the articles of incorporation or the terms of such class or series.

C. If the articles of incorporation shall expressly vest authority in the board of directors to establish series of unissued shares, then if no shares of a series established by resolution of the board of directors are outstanding, either because none were issued or because no issued shares of such series remain outstanding or held as treasury shares, the board of directors shall have authority to eliminate from the articles of incorporation such series and all references to such series contained therein. In order to eliminate such series and such references from the articles of incorporation, the board of directors shall adopt a resolution eliminating such series and all reference to such series from the articles of incorporation. The shares of any such eliminated series shall resume the status of authorized but unissued shares of the class of shares from which such series was established, unless otherwise provided in the articles of incorporation.

D. Prior to the issuance of any shares of a series established by resolution adopted by the board of directors, and prior to the issuance of any shares of a series in which the number of shares has been increased or decreased by resolution adopted by the board of directors, if such issuance is the first issuance of shares of such series since such resolution was adopted, and in order to eliminate from the articles of incorporation a series of shares and all references to such series contained therein, the corporation shall file with the Secretary of State a statement setting forth:

(1) The name of the corporation.

(2) If the statement relates to the establishment of a series of shares, a copy of the resolution establishing and designating the series and fixing and determining the preferences, limitations, and relative rights thereof.

(3) If the statement relates to an increase or decrease in the number of shares of any series, a copy of the resolution fixing and determining the new number of shares of each series in which the number of shares is increased or decreased.

(4) If the statement relates to the elimination of a series of shares and all references thereto from the articles of incorporation, a copy of the resolution eliminating such series and all references to such series from the articles of incorporation.

(5) The date of adoption of such resolution.

(6) That such resolution was duly adopted by all necessary action on the part of the corporation.

E. If the articles of incorporation expressly authorize the board of directors to establish series of unissued shares of a class and if no shares of a series established by resolution of the board of directors have been issued, the board of directors may amend the designations, preferences, limitations, and relative rights, including voting rights, of the series, unless otherwise provided in the articles of incorporation. To amend the designations, preferences, limitations, and relative rights of a series, the board of directors shall adopt a resolution amending the designations, preferences, limitations, and relative rights of the series. Before the issuance of any shares of the series, the corporation shall file with the secretary of state a statement setting forth:

(1) The name of the corporation.

(2) That no shares of the series have been issued.

(3) If the designation of the series is being changed, a statement of the original designation and the new designation.

(4) A copy of the resolution amending the designations, preferences, limitations, or relative rights of the series.

(5) The date of adoption of the resolution.

(6) That the resolution was adopted by all necessary action on the part of the corporation.

F. A statement filed in accordance with Section D or E of this article shall be executed on behalf of the corporation by an officer. The original and a copy of the statement shall be delivered to the Secretary of State. If the Secretary of State finds that such statement conforms to law, he shall, when the appropriate filing fee is paid as prescribed by law:

(1) Endorse on the original and the copy the word "Filed," and the month, day, and year of the filing thereof.

(2) File the original in his office.

(3) Return the copy to the corporation or its representative.

G. Upon the filing of a statement described in Section D or E of this article by the Secretary of State, the resolution establishing and designating the series and fixing and determining the preferences, limitations, and relative rights thereof, the resolution fixing the new number of shares of each series in which the number of shares is increased or decreased, the resolution eliminating a series and all references to such series from the articles of incorporation, or the resolution amending the preferences, limitations, and relative rights of the series, as appropriate, shall become an amendment of the articles of incorporation. The filing of the statement or the filing of a restated certificate of incorporation under Article 4.07 of this Act does not prohibit the board of directors from subsequently adopting a resolution as authorized by this article. An amendment of the articles of incorporation effected pursuant to this Article 2.13 is not subject to the procedure to amend the articles of incorporation contained in Article 4.02 of this Act.

Art. 2.14. Subscription for Shares

A. Unless otherwise provided therein, a subscription for shares of a corporation to be organized may not be revoked within six (6) months, except with the consent of all other subscribers.

B. Repealed.

C. Acceptance of a subscription shall be effected by a resolution of acceptance by the board of directors or by a written memorandum of acceptance executed by one authorized by the board of directors and delivered to the subscriber or his assignee.

D. Subscriptions for shares, whether made before or after the organization of a corporation, shall be paid in full at such time, or in such installments and at such times, as shall be determined by the board of directors unless the payment terms are specified by the subscription. Unless otherwise specified by the subscription, a call made by the board of directors for payment on subscriptions shall be uniform as to all shares of the same class or as to all shares of the same series, as the case may be, as far as practicable. In case of default in the payment of any installment or call when such payment is due, the corporation may proceed to collect the amount due in the same manner as any debt due the corporation or declare the subscription forfeited if the amount due remains unpaid for a period of twenty (20) days after written demand has been made therefor to the subscriber. If mailed, such written demand shall be deemed to be made when deposited in the United States mail in a sealed envelope addressed to the subscriber at his last post office address known to the corporation, with postage thereon prepaid. The effect of such declaration of forfeiture shall be to terminate all the rights and obligations of the subscriber as such, but the corporation may retain any amount previously paid on the subscription.

E. Before acquiring shares in a corporation, a person may commit to act in a specified manner with respect to the shares after the acquisi-

tion, including with respect to the voting of the shares or the retention or disposition of the shares. To be binding, the commitment must be in writing and be signed by the person acquiring the shares. A written commitment entered into under this section is a contract between the shareholder and the corporation.

Art. 2.14-1. Stock Rights, Options, and Convertible Indebtedness

A. Subject to any limitations in its articles of incorporation, a corporation may create and issue, whether or not in connection with the issuance and sale of any of its shares or other securities, (1) rights or options entitling the holders thereof to purchase or receive from the corporation any of its shares of any class, classes or series or other securities and (2) indebtedness convertible into any of its shares of any class, classes or series or other securities.

B. The terms of rights or options may:

(1) prohibit or limit the exercise, transfer, or receipt of the rights or options by certain persons or classes of persons, including:

(a) a person who beneficially owns or offers to acquire a specified number or percentage of the outstanding common shares, voting power, or other securities of the corporation; or

(b) a transferee of a person described by Paragraph (a) of this subsection; or

(2) invalidate the rights or options held by a person or transferee described by Subsection (1) of this section.

C. Such rights, options or indebtedness shall be evidenced in such manner as the board of directors shall approve and, subject to the provisions of the articles of incorporation, shall set forth:

(1) in the case of rights or options, the terms upon which, the time or times within which, and any consideration, including a formula by which the consideration may be determined, for which such shares may be purchased or received from the corporation upon the exercise of any such right or option; or

(2) in the case of convertible indebtedness, the terms and conditions upon which, the time or times within which, and the conversion ratio or ratios at which, such indebtedness may be converted into such shares.

D. In the absence of fraud in the transaction, the judgment of the board of directors as to the adequacy of the consideration received for such rights, options, or indebtedness shall be conclusive; provided that rights or options may be issued by a corporation to its shareholders, employees, or directors without consideration if, in the judgment of the board of directors, the issuance of those rights or options is in the interests of the corporation. The consideration to be received for any shares having a par value, other than treasury shares, to be issued upon the exercise of such rights or options shall not be less than the par value thereof. No privilege of conversion shall be conferred upon, or altered in respect to, any indebtedness that would result in receipt by the corporation of less than the minimum consideration required to be received upon issuance of the shares. The consideration for shares issued upon the exercise of convertible indebtedness shall be that provided in Section E of Article 2.15 of this Act. The consideration for shares issued upon the exercise of rights or options shall be that provided in Section F of Article 2.15 of this Act.

E. Except as provided by Section F of this article, the authority to grant, amend, redeem, extend, or replace the rights or options on behalf of a corporation is vested exclusively in the board of directors of the corporation. A bylaw may not require the board to grant, amend, redeem, extend, or replace the rights or options.

F. The terms of the rights or options or the agreement or plan under which the rights or options are issued may provide that the board of directors may by resolution authorize one or more officers of the corporation to do one or both of the following:

(1) designate officers and employees of the corporation or of any of its subsidiaries to receive rights or options created by the corporation; or

(2) determine the number of the rights or options to be received by the officers and employees.

G. A resolution adopted under Section F of this article authorizing an officer of the corporation to designate recipients of rights or options shall specify the total number of rights or options the officer may award. The board of directors may not authorize an officer to designate himself or herself as a recipient of any rights or options.

Art. 2.15. Consideration for Shares

A. Shares having a par value may be issued for such consideration, not less than the par value thereof, as shall be fixed from time to time by the board of directors or, in the case of shares issued by a converted entity, in the plan of conversion or, in the case of a corporation created by a merger, in the plan of merger.

B. Shares without par value may be issued for such consideration, as may be fixed:

(1) by the board of directors from time to time, unless the articles of incorporation reserve to the shareholders the right to fix the consideration, in which case, prior to the issuance of such shares, the shareholders shall fix the consideration to be received for such shares, by a vote of the holders of a majority of all shares entitled to vote thereon;

(2) by a plan of conversion, in the case of shares to be issued pursuant to the plan of conversion by a corporation that is a converted entity; or

(3) by a plan of merger, in the case of shares to be issued pursuant to the plan of merger by a corporation created pursuant to the plan of merger.

C. Treasury shares may be disposed of by the corporation for such consideration as may be fixed from time to time by the board of directors.

D. That part of the surplus of a corporation which is transferred to stated capital upon the issuance of shares as a share dividend shall be deemed to be the consideration for the issuance of such shares.

E. In the event of the issuance of shares by a corporation upon the conversion or exchange of its indebtedness or shares, the consideration for the shares so issued shall be:

(1) The principal sum of, and accrued interest on, the indebtedness so exchanged or converted, or the stated capital then represented by the shares so exchanged or converted, and

(2) That part of surplus, if any, transferred to stated capital upon the issuance of shares for the shares so exchanged or converted, and

(3) Any additional consideration paid to the corporation upon the issuance of shares for the indebtedness or shares so exchanged or converted.

F. In the event of the issuance of shares by a corporation upon the exercise of rights or options entitling the holders thereof to purchase or receive from the corporation any of its shares, the consideration for the shares so issued shall be:

(1) The consideration, if any, received by the corporation for such rights or options, and

(2) The consideration, if any, received by the corporation for the issuance of shares upon the exercise of such rights or options.

Art. 2.16. Payment for Shares

A. The board of directors or, in the case of shares to be issued pursuant to a plan of conversion by a corporation that is a converted entity, the plan of conversion, or, in the case of shares to be issued pursuant to a plan of merger by a corporation created pursuant to the plan of merger, the plan of merger may authorize shares to be issued for con-

sideration consisting of any tangible or intangible benefit to the corporation or other property of any kind or nature, including cash, promissory notes, services performed, contracts for services to be performed, other securities of the corporation, or securities of any other corporation, domestic or foreign, or other entity. In addition, shares may be issued pursuant to a plan of conversion or plan of merger in the manner and for such consideration as may be provided for in the plan of conversion or plan of merger. Shares may not be issued until the full amount of the consideration, fixed as provided by law, has been paid or delivered as required in connection with the authorization of the shares. When such consideration shall have been so paid or delivered, the shares shall be deemed to have been issued and the subscriber or shareholder entitled to receive such issue shall be a shareholder with respect to such shares, and the shares shall be considered fully paid and non-assessable.

B. In the absence of fraud in the transaction, the judgment of the board of directors or the shareholders or the party or parties approving the plan of conversion or the plan of merger, as the case may be, as to the value and sufficiency of the consideration received for shares shall be conclusive.

Art. 2.18. Expenses of Organization, Reorganization, and Financing

A. The reasonable charges and expenses of organization or reorganization of a corporation, and the reasonable expenses of and compensation for the sale or underwriting of its shares, may be paid or allowed by such corporation out of the consideration received by it in payment for its shares without thereby rendering such shares not fully paid and non-assessable.

Art. 2.19. Certificates Representing Shares

A. A corporation shall deliver certificates representing shares to which shareholders are entitled, or the shares of a corporation may be uncertificated shares. Unless otherwise provided by the articles of incorporation or bylaws, the board of directors of a corporation may provide by resolution that some or all of any or all classes and series of its shares shall be uncertificated shares, provided that such resolution shall not apply to shares represented by a certificate until such certificate is surrendered to the corporation. Certificates representing shares shall be signed by such officer or officers as the bylaws of the corporation shall prescribe, and may be sealed with the seal of the corporation or a facsimile thereof. The signatures of such officer or officers as the bylaws of the corporation shall prescribe upon a certificate may be facsimiles. In case any officer who has signed or whose facsimile signature has been placed upon such certificate shall have ceased to be such officer before such certificate is issued, it may be issued by the corporation with the same effect as if he were such officer at the date of its issuance.

B. In the event a corporation is authorized to issue shares of more than one class or series, each certificate representing shares issued by such corporation (1) shall conspicuously set forth on the face or back of the certificate a full statement of all the designations, preferences, limitations, and relative rights of the shares of each class or series to the extent they have been fixed and determined and the authority of the board of directors to fix and determine the designations, preferences, limitations, and relative rights of subsequent series; or (2) shall conspicuously state on the face or back of the certificate that (a) such a statement is set forth in the articles of incorporation on file in the office of the Secretary of State and (b) the corporation will furnish a copy of such statement to the record holder of the certificate without charge on written request to the corporation at its principal place of business or registered office. In the event a corporation has by its articles of incorporation limited or denied the preemptive right of shareholders to acquire unissued or treasury shares of the corporation, each certificate representing shares issued by such corporation (1) shall conspicuously set forth on the face or back of the certificate a full statement of the limitation or denial of preemptive rights contained in the articles of incorporation, or (2) shall conspicuously state on the face or back of the certificate that (a) such a statement is set forth in the articles of incorporation on file in the office of the Secretary of State and (b) the corporation will furnish a copy of such statement to the record holder of the certificate without charge on request to the corporation at its principal place of business or registered office.

C. Each certificate representing shares shall state upon the face thereof:

(1) That the corporation is organized under the laws of this State.

(2) The name of the person to whom issued.

(3) The number and class of shares and the designation of the series, if any, which such certificate represents.

(4) The par value of each share represented by such certificate, or a statement that the shares are without par value.

D. In accordance with Chapter 8, Business & Commerce Code, a corporation shall, after the issuance or transfer of uncertificated shares, send to the registered owner of uncertificated shares a written notice containing the information required to be set forth or stated on certificates pursuant to this Act. Except as otherwise expressly provided by law, the rights and obligations of the holders of uncertificated shares and the rights and obligations of the holders of certificates representing shares of the same class and series shall be identical. No share shall be issued until the consideration therefor, fixed as provided by law, has been fully paid.

E. No requirement of this Act with respect to matters to be set forth on certificates representing shares of a corporation shall apply to or affect certificates outstanding, when such requirement first becomes applicable to such certificates; but such requirements shall apply to all certificates thereafter issued whether in connection with an original issue of shares, a transfer of shares or otherwise. No certificate representing shares in which any provision of the articles of incorporation, or by-laws, or resolution, or agreement restricting the transfer of shares, shall have been incorporated by reference pursuant to the provisions of Section F of this Article prior to its amendment shall be invalidated or affected by such amendment; but such incorporation by reference shall not be used on certificates hereafter issued whether in connection with an original issue of shares, a transfer of shares, or otherwise.

F. Repealed.

G. In the event any restriction on the transfer, or registration of the transfer, of shares shall be imposed or agreed to by the corporation, as permitted by this Act, each certificate representing shares so restricted (1) shall conspicuously set forth a full or summary statement of the restriction on the face of the certificate, or (2) shall set forth such statement on the back of the certificate and conspicuously refer to the same on the face of the certificate, or (3) shall conspicuously state on the face or back of the certificate that such a restriction exists pursuant to a specified document and (a) that the corporation will furnish to the record holder of the certificate without charge upon written request to the corporation at its principal place of business or registered office a copy of the specified document, or (b) if such document is one required or permitted to be and has been filed under this Act, that such specified document is on file in the office of the Secretary of State and contains a full statement of such restriction. Unless such

document was on file in the office of the Secretary of State at the time of the request, a corporation which fails within a reasonable time to furnish the record holder of a certificate upon such request and without charge a copy of the specified document shall not be permitted thereafter to enforce its rights under the restriction imposed on the shares represented by such certificate.

H. Repealed.

Art. 2.20. Issuance of Fractional Shares or Scrip

A. A corporation may (1) issue fractions of a share, either represented by a certificate or uncertificated, (2) arrange for the disposition of fractional interests by those entitled thereto, (3) pay in cash the fair value of fractions of a share as of the time when those entitled to receive such fractions are determined, or (4) issue scrip in registered or bearer form which shall entitle the holder to receive a certificate for a full share or an uncertificated full share upon the surrender of such scrip aggregating a full share. A certificate for a fractional share or an uncertificated fractional share shall, but scrip shall not unless otherwise provided therein, entitle the holder to exercise voting rights, to receive dividends thereon, and to participate in any of the assets of the corporation in the event of liquidation. The board of directors may cause scrip to be issued subject to the condition that it shall become void if not exchanged for certificates representing full shares or uncertificated full shares before a specified date, or subject to the condition that the shares for which such scrip is exchangeable may be sold by the corporation and the proceeds thereof distributed to the holders of scrip, or subject to any other conditions which the board of directors may determine advisable.

Art. 2.21. Liability of Subscribers and Shareholders

A. A holder of shares, an owner of any beneficial interest in shares, or a subscriber for shares whose subscription has been accepted, or any affiliate thereof or of the corporation, shall be under no obligation to the corporation or to its obligees with respect to:

(1) such shares other than the obligation, if any, of such person to pay to the corporation the full amount of the consideration, fixed in compliance with Article 2.15 of this Act, for which such shares were or are to be issued;

(2) any contractual obligation of the corporation or any matter relating to or arising from the obligation on the basis that the holder, owner, subscriber, or affiliate is or was the alter ego of the corporation, or on the basis of actual fraud or constructive fraud, a sham to perpetrate a fraud, or other similar theory, unless the obligee demonstrates that the holder, owner, subscriber, or affiliate caused the corporation to be used for the purpose of perpetrating and did perpetrate an actual fraud on the obligee primarily for the direct personal benefit of the holder, owner, subscriber, or affiliate; or

(3) any obligation of the corporation on the basis of the failure of the corporation to observe any corporate formality, including without limitation: (a) the failure to comply with any requirement of this Act or of the articles of incorporation or bylaws of the corporation; or (b) the failure to observe any requirement prescribed by this Act or by the articles of incorporation or bylaws for acts to be taken by the corporation, its board of directors, or its shareholders.

B. The liability of a holder, owner, or subscriber of shares of a corporation or any affiliate thereof or of the corporation for an obligation that is limited by Section A of this article is exclusive and preempts any other liability imposed on a holder, owner, or subscriber of shares of a corporation or any affiliate thereof or of the corporation for that obligation under common law or otherwise, except that nothing contained in this article shall limit the obligation of a holder, owner, subscriber, or affiliate to an obligee of the corporation when:

(1) the holder, owner, subscriber, or affiliate has expressly assumed, guaranteed, or agreed to be personally liable to the obligee for the obligation; or

(2) the holder, owner, subscriber, or affiliate is otherwise liable to the obligee for the obligation under this Act or another applicable statute.

C. Any person becoming an assignee or transferee of certificated shares or of uncertificated shares or of a subscription for shares in good faith and without knowledge or notice that the full consideration therefor has not been paid shall not be personally liable to the corporation or its creditors for any unpaid portion of such consideration.

D. An executor, administrator, conservator, guardian, trustee, assignee for the benefit of creditors, or receiver shall not be personally liable as a holder of or subscriber to shares of a corporation, but the estate and funds in his hands shall be so liable.

E. No pledgee or other holder of shares as collateral security shall be personally liable as a shareholder.

Art. 2.22. Transfer of Shares and Other Securities and Restrictions on Transfer

A. The shares and other securities of a corporation shall be personal property for all purposes and shall be transferable in accordance with the provisions of Chapter 8—Investment Securities—of the Business & Commerce Code, as amended, except as otherwise provided in this Act.

B. A restriction on the transfer or registration of transfer of a security, or on the amount of the corporation's securities that may be owned by any person or group of persons, may be imposed by the articles of incorporation, or by-laws, or a written agreement among any number of the holders of such securities, or a written agreement among any number of the holders and the corporation provided a counterpart of such agreement shall be placed on file by the corporation at its principal place of business or its registered office and shall be subject to the same right of examination by a shareholder of the corporation, in person or by agent, attorney or accountant, as are the books and records of the corporation. No restriction so imposed shall be valid with respect to any security issued prior to the adoption of the restriction unless the holder of the security voted in favor of the restriction or is a party to the agreement imposing it.

C. Any restriction on the transfer or registration of transfer of a security of a corporation, if reasonable and noted conspicuously on the certificate or other instrument representing the security or, in the case of an uncertificated security, if reasonable and if notation of the restriction is contained in the notice sent pursuant to Section D of Article 2.19 of this Act with respect to the security, shall be specifically enforceable against the holder of the restricted security or any successor or transferee of the holder. Unless noted conspicuously on the certificate or other instrument representing the security or, in the case of an uncertificated security, unless notation of the restriction is contained in the notice sent pursuant to Section D of Article 2.19 of this Act with respect to the security, a restriction, even though otherwise enforceable, is ineffective against a transferee for value without actual knowledge of the restriction at the time of the transfer or against any subsequent transferee (whether or not for value), but such a restriction shall be specifically enforceable against any other person who is not a transferee for value from and after the time that the person acquires actual knowledge of the existence of the restriction.

D. In particular and without limiting the general power granted in Sections B and C of this Article to impose reasonable restrictions, a restriction on the transfer or registration of transfer of securities of a corporation shall be valid if it reasonably:

(1) Obligates the holders of the restricted securities to offer to the corporation or to any other holders of securities of the corporation or to any other person or to any combination of the foregoing, a prior opportunity, to be exercised within a reasonable time, to acquire the restricted securities; or

(2) Obligates the corporation to the extent permitted by this Act or any holder of securities of the corporation or any other person, or any combination of the foregoing, to purchase the securities which are the subject of an agreement respecting the purchase and sale of the restricted securities; or

(3) Requires the corporation or the holders of any class of securities of the corporation to consent to any proposed transfer of the restricted securities or to approve the proposed transferee of the restricted securities for the purpose of preventing violations of federal or state laws; or

(4) Prohibits the transfer of the restricted securities to designated persons or classes of persons, and such designation is not manifestly unreasonable; or

(5) Maintains the status of the corporation as an electing small business corporation under Subchapter S of the United States Internal Revenue Code, maintains any other tax advantage to the corporation, or maintains the status of the corporation as a close corporation under Part Twelve of this Act; or

(6) Obligates the holder of the restricted securities to sell or transfer an amount of restricted securities to the corporation, to any other holders of securities of the corporation, or to any other person or combination of persons; or

(7) Causes or results in the automatic sale or transfer of an amount of restricted securities to the corporation, to any other holders of securities of the corporation, or to any other person or combination of persons.

E. A corporation that has adopted a bylaw, or is a party to an agreement, restricting the transfer of its shares or other securities may file such bylaw or agreement as a matter of public record with the Secretary of State, as follows:

(1) The corporation shall file a copy of the bylaw or agreement in the office of the Secretary of State together with an attached statement setting forth:

(a) the name of the corporation;

(b) that the copy of the bylaw or agreement is a true and correct copy of the same; and

(c) that such filing has been duly authorized by the board of directors or, in the case of a close corporation that, in conformance with Part Twelve of this Act, is managed in some other manner pursuant to a shareholders' agreement, by the shareholders or by the persons empowered by the agreement to manage its business and affairs.

(2) Such statement shall be executed on behalf of the corporation by an officer. The original and a copy of the statement shall be delivered to the Secretary of State with copies of such bylaw or agreement restricting the transfer of shares or other securities attached thereto. If the Secretary of State finds that such statement conforms to law and the appropriate filing fee has been paid as prescribed by law, he shall:

(a) endorse on the original and the copy the word "Filed", and the month, day, and year of the filing thereof;

(b) file the original in his office; and

(c) return the copy to the corporation or its representative.

(3) After the filing of such statement by the Secretary of State, the bylaw or agreement restricting the transfer of shares or other securities

shall become a matter of public record and the fact of such filing shall be stated on any certificate representing the shares or other securities so restricted if required by Section G, Article 2.19, of this Act.

F. A corporation that is a party to an agreement restricting the transfer of its shares or other securities may make such agreement part of its articles of incorporation without restating the provisions of such agreement therein by complying with the provisions of Part Four of this Act for amendment of the articles of incorporation. If such agreement shall alter any provision of the original or amended articles of incorporation, the articles of amendment shall identify by reference or description the altered provision. If such agreement is to be an addition to the original or amended articles of incorporation, the articles of amendment shall state that fact. The articles of amendment shall have attached thereto a copy of the agreement restricting the transfer of shares or other securities, and shall state that the attached copy of such agreement is a true and correct copy of the same and that its inclusion as part of the articles of incorporation has been duly authorized in the manner required by this Act to amend the articles of incorporation.

G. When shares are registered on the books of a corporation in the names of two or more persons as joint owners with the right of survivorship, after the death of a joint owner and before the time that the corporation receives actual written notice that parties other than the surviving joint owner or owners claim an interest in the shares or any distributions thereon, the corporation may record on its books and otherwise effect the transfer of those shares to any person, firm, or corporation (including that surviving joint owner individually) and pay any distributions made in respect of those shares, in each case as if the surviving joint owner or owners were the absolute owners of the shares. A corporation permitting such a transfer by and making any distribution to such a surviving joint owner or owners before the receipt of written notice from other parties claiming an interest in those shares or distributions is discharged from all liability for the transfer or payment so made; provided, however, that the discharge of the corporation from liability and the transfer of full legal and equitable title of the shares in no way affects, reduces, or limits any cause of action existing in favor of any owner of an interest in those shares or distributions against the surviving owner or owners.

H. A restriction on the transfer or the registration of a transfer of the securities of a corporation, the amount of securities of a corporation, or the amount of securities of a corporation that may be owned by a person or group of persons for any of the following purposes is conclusively presumed to be for a reasonable purpose:

(1) maintaining a local, state, federal, or foreign tax advantage to the corporation or its shareholders, including:

(a) maintaining the corporation's status as an electing small business corporation under Subchapter S of the Internal Revenue Code of 1986;

(b) maintaining or preserving any tax attribute, including net operating losses; or

(c) qualifying or maintaining the qualification of the corporation as a real estate investment trust under the Internal Revenue Code of 1986 or regulations adopted under the Internal Revenue Code of 1986; or

(2) maintaining a statutory or regulatory advantage or complying with a statutory or regulatory requirement under applicable local, state, federal, or foreign law.

Art. 2.22-1. Shareholders' Preemptive Rights

A. Except as provided by Section F of this article, the shareholders of a corporation shall not have a preemptive right to acquire additional, unissued, or treasury shares of the corporation, or securities of the corporation convertible into or carrying a right to subscribe to or acquire shares, except to the extent provided by the articles of incorporation or by agreement.

B. The articles of incorporation may provide that the shareholders of a corporation shall have a preemptive right by including a statement that the corporation "elects to have a preemptive right" or a similar statement. Section C of this article applies to the shareholders' preemptive right except as otherwise provided by the articles of incorporation.

C. (1) If the shareholders of a corporation have a preemptive right under this article, the shareholders have a preemptive right to acquire proportional amounts of the corporation's additional unissued or treasury shares, or securities of the corporation convertible into or carrying a right to subscribe to or acquire shares on the decision of the corporation's board of directors to issue the shares.

(2) Unless otherwise provided in the articles of incorporation, no preemptive right shall exist with respect to:

(a) shares issued or granted to a director, officer, agent, or employee of the corporation or a subsidiary or affiliate of the corporation;

(b) shares issued or granted to satisfy conversion or option rights created to provide compensation to a director, officer, agent, or employee of the corporation or a subsidiary or affiliate of the corporation;

(c) shares authorized in the corporation's articles of incorporation that are issued not later than the 180th day after the effective date of the corporation's formation; or

(d) shares sold, issued, or granted by the corporation for consideration other than money.

(3) Holders of shares of any class or series without general voting rights but that is preferred as to distributions shall not be entitled to any preemptive right.

(4) Holders of shares of any class or series with general voting rights that is not preferred as to distributions shall not be entitled to any preemptive right to shares of any class or series that is preferred as to distributions or to any obligations, unless the shares with preferential rights or obligations are convertible into or carry a right to subscribe to or acquire shares without preferential rights.

(5) The preemptive right shall be only an opportunity to acquire shares or other securities under such uniform terms and conditions as the board of directors may fix for the purpose of providing a fair and reasonable opportunity for the exercise of such right.

(6) For a one-year period beginning on the date on which the shares are offered to shareholders, shares subject to preemptive rights that are not acquired by a shareholder may be issued to a person for consideration set by the corporation's board of directors that is not lower than the consideration set for the exercise of preemptive rights. An offer at a lower consideration or after the expiration of the period prescribed by this subsection is subject to the shareholders' preemptive rights.

D. An action may not be brought against the corporation, its directors, officers, or agents, any holder of shares or securities of the corporation, or any owner of any beneficial interest in shares or securities of the corporation on account of any violation of any preemptive right of a shareholder to acquire any shares of the corporation, or any securities of the corporation convertible into or carrying a right to subscribe to or acquire shares, unless such action is brought within the earlier of:

(1) One year after the date on which written notice is given to each shareholder whose preemptive right was violated by the issuance, sale, or other distribution of those shares or securities, which notice shall be mailed to the shareholder at the address of the shareholder as it

appears on the share transfer records of the corporation and shall inform the shareholder that the issuance, sale, or other distribution of those shares or securities was in violation of the preemptive right of the shareholder; and

(2) Four years after the date on which the corporation issued, sold, or otherwise distributed those shares or securities or August 28, 1989, whichever is later.

E. In the event of a transfer or other disposition of shares by any shareholder of a corporation whose preemptive right to acquire shares of the corporation, or securities of the corporation convertible into or carrying a right to subscribe to or acquire shares, shall have been violated, the transferee or successor of the shareholder shall not acquire the preemptive right, or any right or claim based on that violation, unless the shareholder shall have assigned the preemptive right to the transferee or successor.

F. Subject to the articles of incorporation, shareholders of a corporation incorporated before September 1, 2003, have a preemptive right to acquire additional unissued or treasury shares of the corporation, or securities of the corporation convertible into or carrying a right to subscribe to or acquire shares, to the extent provided by Sections C, D, and E of this article. After September 1, 2003, a corporation may limit or deny the preemptive right of the shareholders of the corporation by amending the corporation's articles of incorporation.

G. A shareholder may waive a preemptive right granted to the shareholder. A written waiver of a preemptive right is irrevocable regardless of whether the waiver is supported by consideration.

Art. 2.23. Bylaws

A. The initial bylaws of a corporation shall be adopted by its board of directors. The bylaws may contain any provisions for the regulation and management of the affairs of the corporation not inconsistent with law or the articles of incorporation.

B. A corporation's board of directors may amend or repeal the corporation's bylaws, or adopt new bylaws, unless:

(1) the articles of incorporation or this Act reserves the power exclusively to the shareholders in whole or part; or

(2) the shareholders in amending, repealing, or adopting a particular bylaw expressly provide that the board of directors may not amend or repeal that bylaw.

C. Unless the articles of incorporation or a bylaw adopted by the shareholders provides otherwise as to all or some portion of a corporation's bylaws, a corporation's shareholders may amend, repeal, or adopt the corporation's bylaws even though the bylaws may also be amended, repealed, or adopted by its board of directors.

Art. 2.24. Meetings of Shareholders

A. Meetings of shareholders may be held at such place within or without this State as may be stated in or fixed in accordance with the bylaws. If no other place is so stated or fixed, the board of directors of the corporation is not authorized to designate a place, or the board of directors chooses not to designate a place, meetings shall be held at the registered office of the corporation.

(1) If, under the articles of incorporation or the bylaws, the board of directors is authorized to determine the place of a meeting of shareholders, the board of directors may, in its discretion, determine that the meeting may be held solely by means of remote communication as provided by Subsection (2) of this section.

(2) If authorized by the board of directors, and subject to any guidelines and procedures adopted by the board of directors, shareholders not physically present at a meeting of shareholders, by means of remote communication:

(a) may participate in a meeting of shareholders; and

(b) may be considered present in person and may vote at a meeting of shareholders held at a designated place or held solely by means of remote communication if:

(i) the corporation implements reasonable measures to verify that each person considered present and permitted to vote at the meeting by means of remote communication is a shareholder;

(ii) the corporation implements reasonable measures to provide the shareholders at the meeting by means of remote communication a reasonable opportunity to participate in the meeting and to vote on matters submitted to the shareholders, including an opportunity to read or hear the proceedings of a meeting substantially concurrently with the proceedings; and

(iii) the corporation maintains a record of any shareholder vote or other action taken at the meeting by means of remote communication.

B. An annual meeting of the shareholders shall be held at such time as may be stated in or fixed in accordance with the bylaws. If the annual meeting is not held within any 13-month period and a written consent of shareholders has not been executed instead of the meeting, any court of competent jurisdiction in the county in which the principal office of the corporation is located may, on the application of any shareholder, summarily order a meeting to be held unless the meeting is not required to be held under Section D of this article. Failure to hold the annual meeting at the designated time shall not work a dissolution of the corporation.

C. Special meetings of the shareholders may be called (1) by the president, the board of directors, or such other person or persons as may be authorized in the articles of incorporation or the bylaws or (2) by the holders of at least ten (10) percent of all the shares entitled to vote at the proposed special meeting, unless the articles of incorporation provide for a number of shares greater than or less than ten (10) percent, in which event special meetings of the shareholders may be called by the holders of at least the percentage of shares so specified in the articles of incorporation, but in no event shall the articles of incorporation provide for a number of shares greater than fifty (50) percent. If not otherwise stated in or fixed in accordance with the bylaws of the corporation, the record date for determining shareholders entitled to call a special meeting is the date the first shareholder signs the notice of that meeting. Only business within the purpose or purposes described in the notice required by Article 2.25 of this Act may be conducted at a special meeting of the shareholders.

D. If the articles of incorporation or bylaws of a corporation registered under the Investment Company Act so provide, the corporation is not required to hold an annual meeting of shareholders or elect directors in any year that the election of directors is not required to be acted on under the Investment Company Act. If the corporation is required by the Investment Company Act to hold a meeting of shareholders to elect directors, the meeting shall be designated as the annual meeting of shareholders for that year.

Art. 2.25. Notice of Shareholders' Meetings

A. Written or printed notice stating the place, day and hour of the meeting, the means of any remote communications by which shareholders may be considered present and may vote at the meeting, and, in case of a special meeting, the purpose or purposes for which the meeting is called, shall be delivered not less than ten (10) days nor more than sixty (60) days before the date of the meeting, personally, by electronic transmission, or by mail, by or at the direction of the president, the secretary, or the officer or person calling the meeting, to each shareholder entitled to vote at such meeting. If mailed, such notice shall be deemed to be delivered when deposited in the United States mail addressed to the shareholder at his address as it appears on the share transfer records of the corporation, with postage thereon prepaid.

B. Any notice required to be given to any shareholder, under any provision of this Act or the articles of incorporation or bylaws of any corporation, need not be given to the shareholder if (1) notice of two consecutive annual meetings and all notices of meetings held during the period between those annual meetings, if any, or (2) all (but in no event less than two) payments (if sent by first class mail) of distributions or interest on securities during a 12-month period have been mailed to that person, addressed at his address as shown on the share transfer records of the corporation, and have been returned undeliverable. Any action or meeting taken or held without notice to such a person shall have the same force and effect as if the notice had been duly given and, if the action taken by the corporation is reflected in any articles or document filed with the Secretary of State, those articles or that document may state that notice was duly given to all persons to whom notice was required to be given. If such a person delivers to the corporation a written notice setting forth his then current address, the requirement that notice be given to that person shall be reinstated.

Art. 2.25-1. Notice by Electronic Transmission

A. On consent of a shareholder, notice from a corporation under any provision of this Act, the articles of incorporation, or the bylaws may be given to the shareholder by electronic transmission. The shareholder may specify the form of electronic transmission to be used to communicate notice. The shareholder may revoke this consent by written notice to the corporation. The shareholder's consent is deemed to be revoked if the corporation is unable to deliver by electronic transmission two consecutive notices, and the secretary, assistant secretary, or transfer agent of the corporation, or another person responsible for delivering notice on behalf of the corporation knows that delivery of these two electronic transmissions was unsuccessful. The inadvertent failure to treat the unsuccessful transmissions as a revocation of shareholder consent does not invalidate a meeting or other action.

B. Notice under this article is deemed given when the notice is:

(1) transmitted to a facsimile number provided by the shareholder for the purpose of receiving notice;

(2) transmitted to an electronic mail address provided by the shareholder for the purpose of receiving notice;

(3) posted on an electronic network and a message is sent to the shareholder at the address provided by the shareholder for the purpose of alerting the shareholder of a posting; or

(4) communicated to the shareholder by any other form of electronic transmission consented to by the shareholder.

C. An affidavit of the secretary, assistant secretary, transfer agent, or other agent of the corporation that notice has been given by electronic transmission is, in the absence of fraud, prima facie evidence that the notice was given.

Art. 2.26. Registered Holders of Shares, Closing of Share Transfer Records and Record Date

A. Registered Holders as Owners. Unless otherwise provided in this Act, and subject to the provisions of Chapter 8-Investment Securities of the Business & Commerce Code:

(1) A corporation may regard the person in whose name any shares issued by the corporation are registered in the share transfer records of the corporation at any particular time (including, without limitation, as of a record date fixed pursuant to Section B or C of this Article) as the owner of those shares at that time for purposes of voting those shares, receiving distributions thereon or notices in respect thereof, transferring those shares, exercising rights of dissent with respect to those shares, exercising or waiving any preemptive right with respect to those shares, entering into agreements with respect to those shares in accordance with Article 2.22 or 2.30 of this Act, or giving proxies with respect to those shares; and

(2) Neither the corporation nor any of its officers, directors, employees, or agents shall be liable for regarding that person as the owner of those shares at that time for those purposes, regardless of whether that person does not possess a certificate for those shares.

B. Fixing Record Dates for Matters Other Than Consents to Action. For the purpose of determining shareholders entitled to notice of or to vote at any meeting of shareholders or any adjournment thereof, or entitled to receive a distribution by a corporation (other than a distribution involving a purchase or redemption by the corporation of any of its own shares) or a share dividend, or in order to make a determination of shareholders for any other proper purpose (other than determining shareholders entitled to consent to action by shareholders proposed to be taken without a meeting of shareholders), the board of directors of a corporation may provide that the share transfer records shall be closed for a stated period but not to exceed, in any case, sixty (60) days. If the share transfer records shall be closed for the purpose of determining shareholders entitled to notice of or to vote at a meeting of shareholders, such records shall be closed for at least ten (10) days immediately preceding such meeting. In lieu of closing the share transfer records, the bylaws, or in the absence of an applicable bylaw the board of directors, may fix in advance a date as the record date for any such determination of shareholders, such date in any case to be not more than sixty (60) days and, in the case of a meeting of shareholders, not less than ten (10) days, prior to the date on which the particular action requiring such determination of shareholders is to be taken. If the share transfer records are not closed and no record date is fixed for the determination of shareholders entitled to notice of or to vote at a meeting of shareholders, or shareholders entitled to receive a distribution (other than a distribution involving a purchase or redemption by the corporation of any of its own shares) or a share dividend, the date on which notice of the meeting is mailed or the date on which the resolution of the board of directors declaring such distribution or share dividend is adopted, as the case may be, shall be the record date for such determination of shareholders. When a determination of shareholders entitled to vote at any meeting of shareholders has been made as provided in this Article, such determination shall apply to any adjournment thereof except where the determination has been made through the closing of the share transfer records and the stated period of closing has expired.

C. Fixing Record Dates for Consents to Action. Unless a record date shall have previously been fixed or determined pursuant to this section, whenever action by shareholders is proposed to be taken by consent in writing without a meeting of shareholders, the board of directors may fix a record date for the purpose of determining shareholders entitled to consent to that action, which record date shall not precede, and shall not be more than ten (10) days after, the date upon which the resolution fixing the record date is adopted by the board of directors. If no record date has been fixed by the board of directors and the prior action of the board of directors is not required by this Act, the record date for determining shareholders entitled to consent to action in writing without a meeting shall be the first date on which a signed written consent setting forth the action taken or proposed to be taken is delivered to the corporation as provided in Section A of Article 9.10 of this Act. Delivery shall be by hand or by certified or registered mail, return receipt requested. Delivery to the corporation's principal place of business shall be addressed to the president or the principal executive officer of the corporation. If no record date shall have been fixed by the board of directors and prior action of the board of directors is required by this Act, the record date for determining shareholders entitled to consent to action in writing without a meeting shall be at the close of business on the date on which the board of directors adopts a resolution taking such prior action.

D. Distributions Held in Suspense. Distributions made by a corporation, including those that were payable but not paid to a holder of shares, or to his heirs, successors, or assigns, and have been held in suspense by the corporation or were paid or delivered by it into an escrow account or to a trustee or custodian, shall be payable by the corporation, escrow agent, trustee, or custodian to the holder of the shares as of the record date determined for that distribution as provided in Section B of this Article, or to his heirs, successors, or assigns.

Art. 2.27. Voting List

A. The officer or agent having charge of the share transfer records for shares of a corporation shall make, at least ten (10) days before each meeting of shareholders, a complete list of the shareholders entitled to vote at such meeting or any adjournment thereof, arranged in alphabetical order, with the address of and the number of shares held by each, which list, for a period of ten (10) days prior to such meeting, shall be kept on file at the registered office or principal place of business of the corporation and shall be subject to inspection by any shareholder at any time during usual business hours. Alternatively, the list of the shareholders may be kept on a reasonably accessible electronic network, if the information required to gain access to the list is provided with the notice of the meeting. This article does not require the corporation to include any electronic contact information of any shareholder on the list. If the corporation elects to make the list available on an electronic network, the corporation shall take reasonable steps to ensure that the information is available only to shareholders of the corporation. Such list shall also be produced and kept open at the time and place of the meeting and shall be subject to the inspection of any shareholder during the whole time of the meeting. If the meeting is held by means of remote communication, the list must be open to the examination of any shareholder for the duration of the meeting on a reasonably accessible electronic network, and the information required to access the list must be provided to shareholders with the notice of the meeting. The original share transfer records shall be prima-facie evidence as to who are the shareholders entitled to examine such list or transfer records or to vote at any meeting of shareholders.

B. Failure to comply with the requirements of this Article shall not affect the validity of any action taken at such meeting.

C. An officer or agent having charge of the share transfer records who shall fail to prepare the list of shareholders or keep the same accessible to shareholders electronically or physically on file at the principal place of business for a period of ten (10) days, or produce and keep it accessible for inspection during the meeting, as provided in this Article, shall be liable to any shareholder suffering damages on account of such failure, to the extent of such damage. In the event that such officer or agent does not receive notice of the date of the meeting reasonably to enable him to comply with the duties prescribed by this Article, the corporation, not such officer or agent, shall be liable to any shareholder suffering damage on account of such failure, to the extent of such damage.

Art. 2.28. Quorum of and Voting by Shareholders

A. Quorum. With respect to any meeting of shareholders, a quorum shall be present for any matter to be presented at that meeting if the holders of a majority of the shares entitled to vote at the meeting are represented at the meeting in person or by proxy, unless otherwise provided in the articles of incorporation in accordance with this section. The articles of incorporation may provide:

(1) That a quorum shall be present at a meeting of shareholders only if the holders of a specified greater portion of the shares entitled to vote are represented at the meeting in person or by proxy; or

(2) That a quorum shall be present at a meeting of shareholders if the holders of a specified lesser portion, but not less than one-third (1/3), of the shares entitled to vote are represented at the meeting in person or by proxy.

Unless otherwise provided in the articles of incorporation or the bylaws, once a quorum is present at a meeting of shareholders, the shareholders represented in person or by proxy at the meeting may conduct such business as may be properly brought before the meeting until it is adjourned, and the subsequent withdrawal from the meeting of any shareholder or the refusal of any shareholder represented in person or by proxy to vote shall not affect the presence of a quorum at the meeting. Unless otherwise provided in the articles of incorporation or the bylaws, the shareholders represented in person or by proxy at a meeting of shareholders at which a quorum is not present may adjourn the meeting until such time and to such place as may be determined by a vote of the holders of a majority of the shares represented in person or by proxy at that meeting.

B. Voting on Matters Other Than the Election of Directors. With respect to any matter, other than the election of directors or a matter for which the affirmative vote of the holders of a specified portion of the shares entitled to vote is required by this Act, the affirmative vote of the holders of a majority of the shares entitled to vote on, and that voted for or against or expressly abstained with respect to, that matter at a meeting of shareholders at which a quorum is present shall be the act of the shareholders, unless otherwise provided in the articles of incorporation or the bylaws in accordance with this section. With respect to any matter, other than the election of directors or a matter for which the affirmative vote of the holders of a specified portion of the shares entitled to vote is required by this Act, the articles of incorporation or the bylaws may provide:

(1) That the act of the shareholders shall be the affirmative vote of the holders of a specified portion, but not less than a majority, of the shares entitled to vote on that matter;

(2) That the act of the shareholders shall be the affirmative vote of the holders of a specified portion, but not less than a majority, of the

shares entitled to vote on that matter and represented in person or by proxy at a meeting of shareholders at which a quorum is present;

(3) That the act of the shareholders shall be the affirmative vote of the holders of a specified portion, but not less than a majority, of the shares entitled to vote on, and voted for or against, that matter at a meeting of shareholders at which a quorum is present; or

(4) That the act of the shareholders shall be the affirmative vote of the holders of a specified portion, but not less than a majority, of the shares entitled to vote on, and that voted for or against or expressly abstained with respect to, that matter at a meeting of shareholders at which a quorum is present.

C. Voting in the Election of Directors. Unless otherwise provided in the articles of incorporation or the bylaws in accordance with this section, directors shall be elected by a plurality of the votes cast by the holders of shares entitled to vote in the election of directors at a meeting of shareholders at which a quorum is present. The articles of incorporation or the bylaws may provide:

(1) That a director shall be elected only if the director receives the vote of the holders of a specified portion, but not less than a majority, of the shares entitled to vote in the election of directors;

(2) That a director shall be elected only if the director receives the vote of the holders of a specified portion, but not less than a majority, of the shares entitled to vote in the election of directors and represented in person or by proxy at a meeting of shareholders at which a quorum is present; or

(3) That a director shall be elected only if the director receives a specified portion, but not less than a majority, of the votes cast by the holders of shares entitled to vote in the election of directors at a meeting of shareholders at which a quorum is present.

D. Changes in the Vote Required for Certain Matters. With respect to any matter for which the affirmative vote of the holders of a specified portion of the shares entitled to vote is required by this Act, the articles of incorporation may provide that the act of the shareholders on that matter shall be the affirmative vote of the holders of a specified portion, but not less than a majority, of the shares entitled to vote on that matter, rather than the affirmative vote otherwise required by this Act. With respect to any matter for which the affirmative vote of the holders of a specified portion of the shares of any class or series is required by this Act, the articles of incorporation also may provide that the act of the holders of shares of that class or series on that matter shall be the affirmative vote of the holders of a specified portion, but not less than a majority, of the shares of that class or series, rather than the affirmative vote of the holders of shares of that class or series otherwise required by this Act. If any provision of the articles of incorporation provides that the act of the shareholders on any matter shall be the affirmative vote of the holders of a specified portion of the shares entitled to vote on that matter that is greater than a majority of the shares so entitled to vote, that provision of the articles of incorporation may not be amended or modified, directly or indirectly, without the affirmative vote of the holders of that greater portion of the shares entitled to vote on that matter, unless otherwise provided in the articles of incorporation. If any provision of the articles of incorporation provides that the act of the holders of shares of any class or series on any matter shall be the affirmative vote of the holders of a specified portion of the shares of that class or series that is greater than a majority of the shares of that class or series, that provision of the articles of incorporation may not be amended or modified, directly or indirectly, without the affirmative vote of the holders of

that greater portion of the shares of that class or series, unless otherwise provided in the articles of incorporation.

E. A corporation may establish procedures in its bylaws, not inconsistent with this Act, for determining the validity of proxies and whether shares that are held of record by a bank, broker, or other nominee are represented at a meeting of shareholders with respect to any matter. The procedures may incorporate or look to rules and determinations of any stock exchange or self-regulatory organization regulating the corporation or that bank, broker, or other nominee.

Art. 2.29. Voting of Shares

A. (1) Each outstanding share, regardless of class, shall be entitled to one vote on each matter submitted to a vote at a meeting of shareholders, except:

(a) To the extent that the articles of incorporation provide for more or less than one vote per share or (if and to the extent permitted by this Act) limit or deny voting rights to the holders of the shares of any class or series, or

(b) As otherwise provided by this Act.

(2) If the articles of incorporation provide for more or less than one vote per share for all the outstanding shares or for the shares of any class or any series on any matter, every reference in this Act (or in the articles of incorporation or bylaws, unless expressly stated otherwise therein), in connection with such matter, to a specified portion of such shares shall mean such portion of the votes entitled to be cast in respect of such shares by virtue of the provisions of such articles of incorporation.

B. Shares of its own stock owned by a corporation or by another domestic or foreign corporation or other entity, if a majority of the voting stock or voting interest of the other corporation or other entity is owned or controlled by the corporation, shall not be voted, directly or indirectly, at any meeting, and shall not be counted in determining the total number of outstanding shares at any given time. Nothing in this section shall be construed as limiting the right of any domestic or foreign corporation or other entity to vote stock, including but not limited to its own stock, held or controlled by it in a fiduciary capacity, or with respect to which it otherwise exercises voting power in a fiduciary capacity.

C. Any shareholder may vote either in person or by proxy executed in writing by the shareholder. A telegram, telex, cablegram, or other form of electronic transmission, including telephone transmission, by the shareholder, or a photographic, photostatic, facsimile, or similar reproduction of a writing executed by the shareholder, shall be treated as an execution in writing for purposes of this Section. Any electronic transmission must contain or be accompanied by information from which it can be determined that the transmission was authorized by the shareholder. No proxy shall be valid after eleven (11) months from the date of its execution unless otherwise provided in the proxy. A proxy shall be revocable unless the proxy form conspicuously states that the proxy is irrevocable and the proxy is coupled with an interest. Proxies coupled with an interest include the appointment as proxy of:

(1) a pledgee;

(2) a person who purchased or agreed to purchase, or owns or holds an option to purchase, the shares;

(3) a creditor of the corporation who extended it credit under terms requiring the appointment;

(4) an employee of the corporation whose employment contract requires the appointment; or

(5) a party to a voting agreement created under Section B, Article 2.30, of this Act.

An irrevocable proxy, if noted conspicuously on the certificate representing the shares that are subject to the irrevocable proxy or, in the case of uncertificated shares, if notation of the irrevocable proxy is contained in the notice sent pursuant to Section D of Article 2.19 of this Act with respect to the shares that are subject to the irrevocable proxy, shall be specifically enforceable against the holder of those shares or any successor or transferee of the holder. Unless noted conspicuously on the certificate representing the shares that are subject to the irrevocable proxy or, in the case of uncertificated shares, unless notation of the irrevocable proxy is contained in the notice sent pursuant to Section D of Article 2.19 of this Act with respect to the shares that are subject to the irrevocable proxy, an irrevocable proxy, even though otherwise enforceable, is ineffective against a transferee for value without actual knowledge of the existence of the irrevocable proxy at the time of the transfer or against any subsequent transferee (whether or not for value), but such an irrevocable proxy shall be specifically enforceable against any other person who is not a transferee for value from and after the time that the person acquires actual knowledge of the existence of the irrevocable proxy.

D. (1) At each election for directors every shareholder entitled to vote at such election shall have the right (a) to vote the number of shares owned by him for as many persons as there are directors to be elected and for whose election he has a right to vote or (b) only if expressly permitted by the articles of incorporation (in general or with respect to a specified class or series of shares or group of classes or series of shares) and subject to subsection (2) of this Section D, to cumulate his votes by giving one candidate as many votes as the number of such directors multiplied by his shares shall equal, or by distributing such votes on the same principle among any number of such candidates.

(2) Cumulative voting shall not be allowed in an election of directors unless the articles of incorporation expressly grant that right, and a shareholder who intends to cumulate his votes as herein authorized shall have given written notice of such intention to the secretary of the corporation on or before the day preceding the election at which such shareholder intends to cumulate his votes. All shareholders entitled to vote cumulatively may cumulate their votes if any shareholder gives the written notice provided for herein.

(3) Except as provided by the articles of incorporation, a shareholder of a corporation incorporated before September 1, 2003, has the right to cumulatively vote the number of shares the shareholder owns in the election of directors to the extent permitted by this article. A corporation may limit or deny a shareholder's right to cumulatively vote any time after September 1, 2003, by amending its articles of incorporation.

E. Shares standing in the name of another corporation, domestic or foreign, may be voted by such officer, agent, or proxy as the bylaws of such corporation may authorize or, in the absence of such authorization, as the board of directors of such corporation may determine; provided, however, that when any foreign corporation without a permit to do business in this State lawfully owns or may lawfully own or acquire stock in Texas corporation, it shall not be unlawful for such foreign corporation to vote said stock and participate in the management and control of the business and affairs of such Texas corporation, as other stockholders, subject to all laws, rules and regulations governing Texas corporations and especially subject to the provisions of the Anti-Trust laws of the State of Texas.

F. Shares held by an administrator, executor, guardian, or conservator may be voted by him so long as such shares forming a part of an estate are in the possession and forming a part of the estate being served by

him, either in person or by proxy, without a transfer of such shares into his name. Shares standing in the name of a trustee may be voted by him, either in person or by proxy, but no trustee shall be entitled to vote shares held by him without a transfer of such shares into his name as trustee.

G. Shares standing in the name of a receiver may be voted by such a receiver, and shares held by or under the control of a receiver may be voted by such receiver without the transfer thereof into his name if authority so to do be contained in an appropriate order of the court by which such receiver was appointed.

H. A shareholder whose shares are pledged shall be entitled to vote such shares until the shares have been transferred into the name of the pledgee, and thereafter the pledgee shall be entitled to vote the shares so transferred.

Art. 2.30. Voting Trusts and Voting Agreements

A. Any number of shareholders of a corporation may enter into a written voting trust agreement for the purpose of conferring upon a trustee or trustees the right to vote or otherwise represent shares of the corporation. The shares that are to be subject to the agreement shall be transferred to the trustee or trustees for purposes of the agreement, and a counterpart of the agreement shall be deposited with the corporation at its principal place of business or registered office. The counterpart of the voting trust agreement so deposited with the corporation shall be subject to the same right of examination by a shareholder of the corporation, in person or by agent or attorney, as are the books and records of the corporation, and shall be subject to examination by any holder of a beneficial interest in the voting trust, either in person or by agent or attorney, at any reasonable time for any proper purpose.

B. Any number of shareholders of a corporation, or any number of shareholders of a corporation and the corporation itself, may enter into a written voting agreement for the purpose of providing that shares of the corporation shall be voted in the manner prescribed in the agreement. A counterpart of the agreement shall be deposited with the corporation at its principal place of business or registered office and shall be subject to the same right of examination by a shareholder of the corporation, in person or by agent or attorney, as are the books and records of the corporation. The agreement, if noted conspicuously on the certificate representing the shares that are subject to the agreement or, in the case of uncertificated shares, if notation of the agreement is contained in the notice sent pursuant to Section D of Article 2.19 of this Act with respect to the shares that are subject to the agreement, shall be specifically enforceable against the holder of those shares or any successor or transferee of the holder. Unless noted conspicuously on the certificate representing the shares that are subject to the agreement or, in the case of uncertificated shares, unless notation of the agreement is contained in the notice sent pursuant to Section D of Article 2.19 of this Act with respect to the shares that are subject to the agreement, the agreement, even though otherwise enforceable, is ineffective against a transferee for value without actual knowledge of the existence of the agreement at the time of the transfer or against any subsequent transferee (whether or not for value), but the agreement shall be specifically enforceable against any other person who is not a transferee for value from and after the time that the person acquires actual knowledge of the existence of the agreement. A voting agreement entered into pursuant to this Section B is not subject to the provisions of Section A of this Article.

Art. 2.30-1. Shareholder Agreements

A. Scope of Agreement. An agreement among the shareholders of a corporation that complies with this article is effective among the shareholders and the corporation even though it is inconsistent with one or more provisions of this Act in that it:

(1) restricts the discretion or powers of the board of directors;

(2) eliminates the board of directors and permits management of the business and affairs of the corporation by its shareholders, or in whole or in part by one or more of its shareholders, or by one or more persons not shareholders;

(3) establishes the natural persons who shall be the directors or officers of the corporation, their term of office or manner of selection or removal, or terms or conditions of employment of any director, officer, or other employee of the corporation, regardless of the length of employment;

(4) governs the authorization or making of distributions whether in proportion to ownership of shares, subject to the limitations in Article 2.38 of this Act, or determines the manner in which profits and losses shall be apportioned;

(5) governs, in general or in regard to specific matters, the exercise or division of voting power by and between the shareholders, directors (if any), or other persons or by or among any of them, including use of disproportionate voting rights or director proxies;

(6) establishes the terms and conditions of any agreement for the transfer or use of property or the provision of services between the corporation and any shareholder, director, officer, or employee of the corporation, or other person or among any of them;

(7) authorizes arbitration or grants authority to any shareholder or other person as to any issue about which there is a deadlock among the directors, shareholders, or other person or persons empowered to manage the corporation to resolve that issue;

(8) requires dissolution of the corporation at the request of one or more of the shareholders or on the occurrence of a specified event or contingency, in which case the dissolution of the corporation shall proceed as if all the shareholders had consented in writing to dissolution of the corporation as provided in Article 6.02 of this Act; or

(9) otherwise governs the exercise of corporate powers, the management of the business and affairs of the corporation, or the relationship among the shareholders, the directors, and the corporation, or among any of them, as if the corporation were a partnership or in a manner that would otherwise be appropriate only among partners, and is not contrary to public policy.

B. Procedures Required. An agreement authorized by this article shall be:

(1) set forth (a) in the articles of incorporation or bylaws and approved by all persons who are shareholders at the time of the agreement, or (b) in a written agreement that is signed by all the persons who are shareholders at the time of the agreement and is made known to the corporation;

(2) subject to amendment only by all persons who are shareholders at the time of the amendment, unless the agreement provides otherwise; and

(3) valid for 10 years, unless the agreement provides otherwise.

C. Notation of Existence. The existence of an agreement authorized by this article shall be noted conspicuously on the front or back of each certificate for outstanding shares or on the information statement required for uncertificated shares by Article 2.19 of this Act and shall include the following: "These shares are subject to the provisions of a shareholders' agreement that may provide for management of the corporation in a manner different than in other corporations and may

subject a shareholder to certain obligations or liabilities not otherwise imposed on shareholders in other corporations." If at the time of the agreement the corporation has shares outstanding represented by certificates, the corporation shall recall the outstanding certificates and issue substitute certificates that comply with this section. The failure to note the existence of the agreement on the certificate or information statement shall not affect the validity of the agreement or any action taken pursuant to it.

D. Right of Rescission. Any purchaser of shares who, at the time of purchase, did not have knowledge of the existence of an agreement authorized by this article shall be entitled to rescission of the purchase. A purchaser shall be deemed to have knowledge of the existence of the agreement if its existence is noted on the certificate or information statement for the shares in compliance with Section C of this article and, if the shares are not represented by a certificate, the information statement noting existence of the agreement is delivered to the purchaser at or prior to the time of purchase of the shares. An action to enforce the right of rescission authorized by this section must be commenced within the earlier of 90 days after discovery of the existence of the agreement or two years after time of the purchase of the shares.

E. Cessation. An agreement authorized by this article shall cease to be effective when shares of the corporation are listed on a national securities exchange, quoted on an interdealer quotation system of a national securities association, or regularly traded in a market maintained by one or more members of a national or affiliated securities association. If the agreement ceases to be effective for any reason and the corporation does not have a board of directors, governance by a board of directors shall be instituted or reinstated in the manner provided in Section C, Article 12.23, of this Act. If the agreement is contained or referred to in the corporation's articles of incorporation or bylaws, the board of directors may adopt an amendment to the articles of incorporation or bylaws, without shareholder action, to delete the agreement and any references to it.

F. Managerial Liabilities. An agreement authorized by this article that limits the discretion or powers of the board of directors or supplants the board of directors shall relieve the directors of, and impose on the person or persons in whom such discretion or powers or management of the business and affairs of the corporation are vested, liability for action or omissions imposed by this Act or other law on directors to the extent that the discretion or powers of the directors are limited or supplanted by the agreement.

G. Limitation of Liability. The existence or performance of an agreement authorized by this article shall not be grounds for imposing personal liability on any shareholder for the acts or obligations of the corporation by disregarding the separate entity of the corporation or otherwise, even if the agreement or its performance:

(1) treats the corporation as if it were a partnership or in a manner that otherwise is appropriate only among partners;

(2) results in the corporation being considered a partnership for purposes of taxation; or

(3) results in failure to observe the corporate formalities otherwise applicable to the matters governed by the agreement.

H. If No Shares Issued. Incorporators or subscribers for the shares may act as shareholders with respect to an agreement authorized by this article if no shares have been issued when the agreement is signed.

Art. 2.31. Board of Directors

A. Except as provided by Article 2.30-1 and Part Twelve of this Act, the powers of a corporation shall be exercised by or under the authority of, and the business and affairs of a corporation shall be managed under the direction of, the board of directors of the corporation. Directors need not be residents of this State or shareholders of the corporation unless the articles of incorporation or bylaws so require. The articles of incorporation or bylaws may prescribe other qualifications for directors.

Art. 2.32. Number and Election of Directors

A. The board of directors of a corporation shall consist of one or more members. The number of directors shall be fixed by, or in the manner provided in, the articles of incorporation or the bylaws, except as to the number constituting the initial board of directors, which number shall be fixed by the articles of incorporation. The number of directors may be increased or decreased from time to time by amendment to, or in the manner provided in, the articles of incorporation or the bylaws, but no decrease shall have the effect of shortening the term of any incumbent director. In the absence of a bylaw or a provision of the articles of incorporation fixing the number of directors or providing for the manner in which the number of directors shall be fixed, the number of directors shall be the same as the number constituting the initial board of directors as fixed by the articles of incorporation. The names and addresses of the members of the initial board of directors shall be stated in the articles of incorporation. Unless otherwise provided by the articles of incorporation or the bylaws, a director may resign at any time by giving notice in writing or by electronic transmission to the corporation. Absent resignation or removal in accordance with the provisions of the bylaws or the articles of incorporation, such persons shall hold office until the first annual meeting of shareholders, and until their successors shall have been elected and qualified. At the first annual meeting of shareholders and at each annual meeting thereafter, the holders of shares entitled to vote in the election of directors shall elect directors to hold office until the next succeeding annual meeting, except in case of the classification of directors as permitted by this Act.

B. The articles of incorporation may provide that the holders of any class or series of shares or any group of classes or series of shares shall be entitled to elect one or more directors, who shall hold office for such terms as shall be stated in the articles of incorporation. The articles of incorporation may provide that any directors elected by the holders of any such class or series of shares or any such group shall be entitled to more or less than one vote on all or any specified matters, in which case every reference in this Act (or in the articles of incorporation or bylaws, unless expressly stated otherwise therein) to a specified portion of the directors shall mean such portion of the votes entitled to be cast by the directors to which such reference is applicable. Absent resignation or removal in accordance with provisions of the bylaws or the articles of incorporation, each director shall hold office for the term for which he is elected and until his successor shall have been elected and qualified.

C. Except as otherwise provided in this Article, the bylaws, or the articles of incorporation, at any meeting of shareholders called expressly for that purpose, any director or the entire board of directors may be removed, with or without cause, by a vote of the holders of a majority of the shares then entitled to vote at an election of the director or directors. Whenever the holders of any class or series of shares or any such group are entitled to elect one or more directors by the provisions of the articles of incorporation, only the holders of shares of that class or series or group shall be entitled to vote for or against the removal of any director elected by the holders of shares of that class or series or group. In the case of a corporation having cumulative voting, if less than the entire board is to be removed, no one of the directors may be removed if the votes cast against his removal would be sufficient to elect him if then cumulatively voted at an election of the entire board of directors, or if there be classes of directors, at an election of the class of directors of which he is a part. In the case of a corporation whose directors have been classified as permitted by this Act, unless the articles of incorporation otherwise provide, a director may not be removed except for cause.

D. Notwithstanding Section B of this Article, a director of a corporation registered under the Investment Company Act, absent resignation or removal in accordance with the provisions of the articles of incorporation or bylaws, holds office for the term for which the director is elected and until the director's successor has been elected and qualified.

Art. 2.33. Classification of Directors

A. The bylaws of a corporation may provide that the directors, the directors elected by any class or series of shares or any group of classes or series of shares, or any portion of the directors or of the directors elected by any class or series of shares or any such group shall be divided into either two or three classes, each class to be as nearly equal in number as possible, the terms of office of directors of the first class to expire at the first annual meeting of shareholders after their election, that of the second class to expire at the second annual meeting after their election, and that of the third class, if any, to expire at the third annual meeting after their election. If the bylaws provide for the classification of directors, (1) the whole number of directors of the corporation need not be elected annually, and (2) at each annual meeting after such classification, the number of directors equal to the number of the class whose term expires at the time of such meeting shall be elected to hold office until the second succeeding annual meeting, if there be two classes, or until the third succeeding annual meeting, if there be three classes. No classification of directors shall be effective prior to the next annual meeting of shareholders at which directors are elected unless the classification is effected by a bylaw adopted by the shareholders. No classification of directors shall be effective for any corporation if any shareholder has the right to cumulate his votes for the election of directors of the corporation unless the board of directors of the corporation consists of nine or more members.

Art. 2.34. Vacancies

A. Any vacancy occurring in the initial board of directors before the issuance of shares may be filled by the affirmative vote or written consent of a majority of the incorporators or by the affirmative vote of a majority of the remaining directors though less than a quorum of the board of directors. A director elected to fill a vacancy shall be elected for the unexpired term of the director's predecessor in office.

B. Any vacancy occurring in the board of directors after the issuance of shares may be filled in accordance with Section D of this article or may be filled by the affirmative vote of a majority of the remaining directors though less than a quorum of the board of directors. A director elected to fill a vacancy shall be elected for the unexpired term of his predecessor in office.

C. A directorship to be filled by reason of an increase in the number of directors may be filled in accordance with Section D of this article or may be filled by the board of directors for a term of office continuing only until the next election of one or more directors by the shareholders; provided that the board of directors may not fill more than two such directorships during the period between any two successive annual meetings of shareholders.

D. Any vacancy occurring in the board of directors or any directorship to be filled by reason of an increase in the number of directors may be filled by election at an annual or special meeting of shareholders called for that purpose.

E. Notwithstanding Sections B, C, and D of this article, whenever the holders of any class or series of shares or group of classes or series of shares are entitled to elect one or more directors by the provisions of the articles of incorporation, any vacancies in such directorships and any newly created directorships of such class or series to be filled by reason of an increase in the number of such directors may be filled by the affirmative vote of a majority of the directors elected by such class or series, or by such group, then in office, or by a sole remaining director so elected, or by the vote of the holders of the outstanding shares of such class or series or of such group, and such directorships shall not in any case be filled by the vote of the remaining directors or the holders of the outstanding shares as a whole unless otherwise provided in the articles of incorporation.

Art. 2.35. Quorum of and Action by Directors

A. A majority of the number of directors fixed by, or in the manner provided in, the articles of incorporation or the bylaws shall constitute a quorum for the transaction of business unless a different number or portion is required by law or the articles of incorporation or the bylaws. In no case may the articles of incorporation or bylaws provide that less than one-third of the number of directors so fixed constitute a quorum. The act of the majority of the directors present at a meeting at which a quorum is present shall be the act of the board of directors, unless the act of a greater number is required by law or the articles of incorporation or the bylaws.

Art. 2.35-1. Interested Directors

A. An otherwise valid contract or transaction between a corporation and one or more of its directors or officers, or between a corporation and any other domestic or foreign corporation or other entity in which one or more of its directors or officers are directors or officers or have a financial interest, shall be valid notwithstanding whether the director or officer is present at or participates in the meeting of the board or committee thereof which authorizes the contract or transaction, or solely because his or their votes are counted for such purpose, if any one of the following is satisfied:

(1) The material facts as to his relationship or interest and as to the contract or transaction are disclosed or are known to the board of directors or the committee, and the board or committee in good faith authorizes the contract or transaction by the affirmative vote of a majority of the disinterested directors, even though the disinterested directors be less than a quorum; or

(2) The material facts as to his relationship or interest and as to the contract or transaction are disclosed or are known to the shareholders entitled to vote thereon, and the contract or transaction is specifically approved in good faith by vote of the shareholders; or

(3) The contract or transaction is fair as to the corporation as of the time it is authorized, approved, or ratified by the board of directors, a committee thereof, or the shareholders.

B. Common or interested directors may be counted in determining the presence of a quorum at a meeting of the board of directors or of a committee which authorizes the contract or transaction.

Art. 2.36. Committees of the Board of Directors

A. If the articles of incorporation or the bylaws so provide, the board of directors may designate from among its members one or more committees, each of which shall be comprised of one or more of its members, and may designate one or more of its members as alternate members of any committee, who may, subject to any limitations imposed by the board of directors, replace absent or disqualified members at any meeting of that committee. Any such committee, to the extent provided in the resolution of the board of directors or in the articles of incorporation or the bylaws, shall have and may exercise all of the authority of the board of directors, subject to the limitations set forth in Sections B and C of this Article.

B. No committee of the board of directors shall have the authority of the board of directors in reference to:

(1) amending the articles of incorporation, except that a committee may, to the extent provided in the resolution designating that committee or in the articles of incorporation or the bylaws, exercise the authority of the board of directors vested in it in accordance with Article 2.13 of this Act;

(2) proposing a reduction of the stated capital of the corporation in the manner permitted by Article 4.12 of this Act;

(3) approving a plan of merger, share exchange, or conversion of the corporation;

(4) recommending to the shareholders the sale, lease, or exchange of all or substantially all of the property and assets of the corporation otherwise than in the usual and regular course of its business;

(5) recommending to the shareholders a voluntary dissolution of the corporation or a revocation thereof;

(6) amending, altering, or repealing the bylaws of the corporation or adopting new bylaws of the corporation;

(7) filling vacancies in the board of directors;

(8) filling vacancies in or designating alternate members of any such committee;

(9) filling any directorship to be filled by reason of an increase in the number of directors;

(10) electing or removing officers of the corporation or members or alternate members of any such committee;

(11) fixing the compensation of any member or alternate members of such committee; or

(12) altering or repealing any resolution of the board of directors that by its terms provides that it shall not be so amendable or repealable.

C. Unless the resolution designating a particular committee, the articles of incorporation, or the bylaws expressly so provide, no committee of the board of directors shall have the authority to authorize a distribution or to authorize the issuance of shares of the corporation.

D. The designation of a committee of the board of directors and the delegation thereto of authority shall not operate to relieve the board of directors, or any member thereof, of any responsibility imposed by law.

Art. 2.37. Place and Notice of Directors' Meetings

A. Meetings of the board of directors, regular or special, may be held either within or without this State.

B. Regular meetings of the board of directors may be held with or without notice as prescribed in the bylaws. Special meetings of the board of directors shall be held upon such notice as is prescribed in the bylaws. Attendance of a director at a meeting shall constitute a waiver of notice of such meeting, except where a director attends a meeting for the express purpose of objecting to the transaction of any business on the ground that the meeting is not lawfully called or convened. Neither the business to be transacted at, nor the purpose of, any regular or special meeting of the board of directors need be specified in the notice or waiver of notice of such meeting, unless required by the bylaws.

C. On consent of a director, notice of the date, time, place, or purpose of a regular or special meeting of the board of directors may be given to the director by electronic transmission. The director may specify the form of electronic transmission to be used to communicate notice. The director may revoke this consent by written notice to the corporation. The director's consent is deemed to be revoked if the corporation is unable to deliver by electronic transmission two consecutive notices and the secretary of the corporation or other person responsible for delivering the notice on behalf of the corporation knows that the delivery of these two electronic transmissions was unsuccessful. The inadvertent failure to treat the unsuccessful transmissions as a revocation of the director's consent does not invalidate a meeting or other action. An affidavit of the secretary or other agent of the corporation that notice has been given by electronic transmission is, in the absence of fraud, prima facie evidence that the notice was given. Notice under this section is deemed given when the notice is:

(1) transmitted to a facsimile number provided by the director for the purpose of receiving notice;

(2) transmitted to an electronic mail address provided by the director for the purpose of receiving notice;

(3) posted on an electronic network and a message is sent to the director at the address provided by the director for the purpose of alerting the director of a posting; or

(4) communicated to the director by any other form of electronic transmission consented to by the director.

Art. 2.38. Distributions

A. The board of directors of a corporation may authorize and the corporation may make distributions subject to any restrictions in its articles of incorporation and to the limitations set forth in this Article.

B. A distribution may not be made by a corporation if:

(1) after giving effect to the distribution, the corporation would be insolvent; or

(2) the distribution exceeds the surplus of the corporation.

C. Notwithstanding the limitation set forth in Subsection (2) of Section B of this Article, if the net assets of a corporation are not less than the amount of the proposed distribution:

(1) the corporation may make a distribution involving a purchase or redemption of any of its own shares if the corporation is an open-end investment company, registered as such under the Federal Investment Company Act of 1940 (15 U.S.C.A. Sec. 80a-1 (1986)), and its articles of incorporation provide in effect that it may purchase its own shares out of stated capital;

(2) the corporation may make a distribution involving a purchase or redemption of any of its own shares if the purchase or redemption is made by the corporation to:

(a) eliminate fractional shares;

(b) collect or compromise indebtedness owed by or to the corporation;

(c) pay dissenting shareholders entitled to payment for their shares under this Act; or

(d) effect the purchase or redemption of redeemable shares in accordance with this Act; and

(3) the corporation may make a distribution not involving a purchase or redemption of any of its own shares if the corporation is a consuming assets corporation.

D. Notwithstanding the limitations set forth in Section B of this Article, the corporation may make distributions in compliance with Article 6.04, 7.09, or 7.12 of this Act.

E. A corporation's indebtedness to a shareholder incurred by reason of a distribution made in accordance with this Article shall be at parity with the corporation's indebtedness to its general, unsecured creditors, except to the extent the indebtedness is subordinated, or payment of that indebtedness is secured, by agreement.

Art. 2.38-1. Share Dividends

A. The board of directors of a corporation may authorize and the corporation may pay share dividends subject to any restrictions in its articles of incorporation and to the limitations set forth in this Article.

B. A share dividend payable in authorized but unissued shares may not be paid by a corporation if the surplus of the corporation is less than the amount required by this Article to be transferred to stated capital at the time that share dividend is paid.

C. If a share dividend is payable in authorized but unissued shares having a par value, those shares shall be issued at the par value and at the time that share dividend is paid an amount of surplus designated by the board of directors not less than the aggregate par value of the shares to be issued as a share dividend shall be transferred to stated capital.

D. If a share dividend is payable in authorized but unissued shares without par value, those shares shall be issued at the value fixed by resolution of the board of directors adopted at the time the share dividend is authorized, and at the time the share dividend is paid an amount of surplus equal to the aggregate value so fixed in respect of those shares shall be transferred to stated capital.

E. A share dividend payable in shares of any class may not be paid to the holders of shares of any other class unless the articles of incorporation so provide or unless the payment is authorized by the affirmative vote or the written consent of the holders of at least a majority of the outstanding shares of the class in which the payment is to be made.

Art. 2.38-2. Split-Up or Division Without Stated Capital Increase

A split-up or division of the issued shares of any class of a corporation into a greater number of shares of the same class without increasing the stated capital of the corporation does not constitute a share dividend or a distribution.

Art. 2.38-3. Determination of Net Assets, Stated Capital, and Surplus

A. Determinations whether a corporation is insolvent and of the value of the net assets, and determination of stated capital, and surplus of the corporation, and each of their components, may, but is not required to, be based on:

(1) financial statements of the corporation, including without limitation financial statements that include subsidiary corporations or other corporations accounted for on a consolidated basis or on the equity method of accounting, that present the financial condition of the corporation in accordance with generally accepted accounting principles;

(2) financial statements prepared on the basis of accounting used to file the corporation's federal income tax return or any other accounting practices and principles that are reasonable in the circumstances;

(3) financial information, including without limitation condensed or summary financial statements, that is prepared on a basis consistent with the financial statements referred to in Subsections (1) and (2) of this section;

(4) projection, forecast, or other forward looking information relating to the future economic performance, financial condition, or liquidity of the corporation that is reasonable in the circumstances;

(5) a fair valuation or information from any other method that is reasonable in the circumstances; or

(6) any combination of the statements, valuations, or information authorized by this section.

B. Section A of this Article and the determinations made in accordance therewith do not apply to the calculation of the Texas franchise tax or any other tax imposed on corporations under the laws of this state.

Art. 2.38-4. Date of Determination of Surplus

A. In the case of a distribution by a corporation or the payment of a share dividend, the surplus of the corporation shall be determined, and the determination whether the corporation would be insolvent after giving effect to the distribution shall be made:

(1) on the date that action is authorized by the board of directors if the action is taken on or before the 120th day after the date of authorization;

(2) if the action is taken after the 120th day after the date of authorization and the board of directors designates a date, within 120 days before the date the action is taken, on which the determination is to be made, on the date so designated by the board of directors; or

(3) if the action is taken after the 120th day after the date of authorization and the board of directors does not make the designation described by Subsection (2) of this section, on the date the action is taken.

B. For the purposes of this Article, a distribution that involves the incurrence by a corporation of any indebtedness or deferred payment obligation or that involves a requirement in the corporation's articles of incorporation or other contract by the corporation to redeem, exchange, or otherwise acquire any of its own shares is deemed to have been made on the date the indebtedness or obligation is incurred or, in the case of a provision in the articles of incorporation of a corporation or other contract to purchase, redeem, exchange, or otherwise acquire shares, at the option of the corporation, is deemed to have been made on either the date the provision or other contract is made or takes effect or the date on which the shares to be redeemed, exchanged, or acquired are redeemed, exchanged, or acquired.

Art. 2.41. Liability of Directors and Shareholders in Certain Cases

A. In addition to any other liabilities imposed by law upon directors of a corporation:

(1) Directors of a corporation who vote for or assent to a distribution by the corporation that is not permitted by Article 2.38 of this Act shall be jointly and severally liable to the corporation for the amount by which the distributed amount exceeds the amount permitted by Article 2.38 of this Act to be distributed; provided that a director shall have no liability for the excess amount, or any part of that excess, if on any date after the date of the vote or assent authorizing the distribution, a distribution of that excess or that part would have been permitted by Article 2.38.

(2) An action may not be brought against a director for liability imposed by this section after two years after the date on which the act alleged to give rise to the liability occurred.

B. A director of a corporation who is present at a meeting of its board of directors at which action on any corporate matter is taken shall be presumed to have assented to the action taken unless his dissent shall be entered in the minutes of the meeting or unless he shall file his written dissent to such action with the person acting as the secretary of the meeting before the adjournment thereof or shall forward such dissent by registered mail to the secretary of the corporation immedi-

ately after the adjournment of the meeting. Such right to dissent shall not apply to a director who voted in favor of such action.

C. A director shall not be liable under Subsection (1) of Section A of this Article if, in voting for or assenting to the distribution, the director:

(1) relied in good faith and with ordinary care upon the statements, valuations, or information referred to in Article 2.38-3 of this Act, or upon other information, opinions, reports, or statements, including financial statements and other financial data, concerning the corporation or another person, that were prepared or presented by:

(a) one or more officers or employees of the corporation;

(b) legal counsel, public accountants, investment bankers, or other persons as to matters the director reasonably believes are within the person's professional or expert competence; or

(c) a committee of the board of directors of which the director is not a member;

(2) acting in good faith and with ordinary care, considered the assets of the corporation to be at least of their book value; or

(3) in determining whether the corporation made adequate provision for payment, satisfaction or discharge of all of its liabilities and obligations as provided in Articles 6.04 and 7.12 of this Act, relied in good faith and with ordinary care upon financial statements of, or other information concerning, any person who was or became contractually obligated to pay, satisfy, or discharge some or all of those liabilities or obligations.

D. In the discharge of any duty imposed or power conferred upon a director, including as a member of a committee, the director, may in good faith and with ordinary care, rely on information, opinions, reports, or statements, including financial statements and other financial data, concerning the corporation or another person, that were prepared or presented by:

(1) one or more officers or employees of the corporation;

(2) legal counsel, public accountants, investment bankers, or other persons as to matters the director reasonably believes are within the person's professional or expert competence; or

(3) a committee of the board of directors of which the director is not a member.

A director is not relying in good faith within the meaning of this Section if the director has knowledge concerning the matter in question that makes reliance otherwise permitted by this Section unwarranted.

E. A director against whom a claim shall be asserted under this Article for a distribution made by the corporation, and who shall be held liable thereon, shall be entitled to contribution from the shareholders who accepted or received such distribution knowing that such distribution was not permitted by Article 2.38, in proportion to the amounts received by them, respectively.

F. A director found liable with respect to a claim shall be entitled to contribution as appropriate to achieve equity from each of the other directors who are liable with respect to that claim.

G. The liability provided in Subsection (1) of Section A of this Article shall be the only liability of directors to a corporation or its creditors for authorizing a distribution by the corporation that is not permitted by Article 2.38 of this Act. The liability provided in Section E of this Article shall be the only liability of shareholders to a corporation or its creditors for accepting or receiving a distribution by the corporation that is not permitted by Article 2.38 of this Act; provided, however, that this Section does not limit any liability under the Uniform Fraudulent Transfer Act or the United States Bankruptcy Code.

Art. 2.42. Officers

A. The officers of a corporation shall consist of a president and a secretary, each of whom shall be elected by the board of directors at such time and in such manner as may be prescribed by the bylaws. Such other officers, including assistant officers, and agents as may be deemed necessary may be elected or appointed by the board of directors or chosen in such other manner as may be prescribed by the bylaws. Any two (2) or more offices may be held by the same person.

B. All officers and agents of the corporation, as between themselves and the corporation, shall have such authority and perform such duties in the management of the corporation as may be provided in the bylaws, or as may be determined by resolution of the board of directors not inconsistent with the bylaws.

C. In the discharge of any duty imposed or power conferred upon an officer, of a corporation the officer may in good faith and ordinary care rely on information, opinions, reports, or statements, including financial statements and other financial data, concerning the corporation or another person, that were prepared or presented by:

(1) one or more other officers or employees of the corporation including members of the board of directors; or

(2) legal counsel, public accountants, investment bankers, or other persons as to matters the officer reasonably believes are within the person's professional or expert competence.

An officer is not relying in good faith within the meaning of this section if the officer has knowledge concerning the matter in question that makes reliance otherwise permitted by this subsection unwarranted.

Art. 2.43. Removal of Officers

A. Any officer or agent or member of a committee elected or appointed by the board of directors may be removed by the board of directors whenever in its judgment the best interests of the corporation will be served thereby, but such removal shall be without prejudice to the contract rights, if any, of the person so removed. Election or appointment of an officer or agent or member of a committee shall not of itself create contract rights.

Art. 2.44. Books and Records

A. Each corporation shall keep books and records of account and shall keep minutes of the proceedings of its shareholders, its board of directors, and each committee of its board of directors. Each corporation shall keep at its registered office or principal place of business, or at the office of its transfer agent or registrar, a record of the original issuance of shares issued by the corporation and a record of each transfer of those shares that have been presented to the corporation for registration of transfer. Such records shall contain the names and addresses of all past and current shareholders of the corporation and the number and class or series of shares issued by the corporation held by each of them. Any books, records, minutes, and share transfer records may be in written form or in any other form capable of being converted into written paper form within a reasonable time. The principal place of business of a corporation, or the office of its transfer agent or registrar, may be located outside the State of Texas.

B. A director may examine the corporation's books and records of account, share transfer records, corporate minutes and any other corporate books and records for any purpose reasonably related to the director's service as a director. A court of competent jurisdiction may compel a corporation to open its books and records of account, share transfer records, corporate minutes or any other corporate books and records to permit the director to inspect the books or

records and make copies or extracts from the books or records on a showing by a director that:

(1) he is a director;

(2) he demanded to inspect the corporate books and records;

(3) his purpose for inspecting the corporate books and records was reasonably related to his service as a director; and

(4) his right of access to the books and records was refused by the corporation.

The court may also award the director attorneys' fees and any other relief that the court deems just and proper.

C. Any person who shall have been a shareholder for at least six (6) months immediately preceding his demand, or shall be the holder of at least five per cent (5%) of all the outstanding shares of a corporation, upon written demand stating the purpose thereof, shall have the right to examine, in person or by agent, accountant, or attorney, at any reasonable time or times, for any proper purpose, its relevant books and records of account, minutes, and share transfer records, and to make extracts therefrom.

D. Any corporation which shall refuse to allow any such shareholder or his agent, accountant or attorney, so to examine and make extracts from its books and records of account, minutes, and share transfer records, for any proper purpose, shall be liable to such shareholder for all costs and expenses, including attorneys' fees, incurred in enforcing his rights under this Article in addition to any other damages or remedy afforded him by law. It shall be a defense to any action for penalties under this section that the person suing therefor has within two (2) years sold or offered for sale any list of shareholders or of holders of voting trust certificates for shares of such corporation or any other corporation or has aided or abetted any person in procuring any list of shareholders or of holders of voting trust certificates for any such purpose, or has improperly used any information secured through any prior examination of the books and records of account, minutes, or share transfer records of such corporation or any other corporation, or was not acting in good faith or for a proper purpose in making his demand.

E. Nothing herein contained shall impair the power of any court of competent jurisdiction, upon proof of proper purpose by a beneficial or record holder of shares, irrespective of the period of time during which such holder shall have been a beneficial or record holder and irrespective of the number of shares held by him, to compel the production for examination by such holder of the books and records of account, minutes, and share transfer records of a corporation.

F. Upon the written request of any shareholder of a corporation, the corporation shall mail to such shareholder its annual statements for its last fiscal year showing in reasonable detail its assets and liabilities and the results of its operations and the most recent interim statements, if any, which have been filed in a public record or otherwise published. The corporation shall be allowed a reasonable time to prepare such annual statements.

G. A holder of a beneficial interest in a voting trust entered into pursuant to Article 2.30 of this Act shall be regarded as a holder of the shares represented by such beneficial interest for the purposes of this Article.

Business Corporation Act

Part 3.

Art. 3.01. Incorporators

A. Any natural person of the age of eighteen (18) years or more, or any domestic or foreign corporation, estate, or other entity may act as an incorporator of a corporation by signing the articles of incorporation for such corporation and by delivering the original and a copy of the articles of incorporation to the Secretary of State.

Art. 3.02. Articles of Incorporation

A. The articles of incorporation shall set forth:

(1) The name of the corporation;

(2) The period of duration, which may be perpetual;

(3) The purpose or purposes for which the corporation is organized which may be stated to be, or to include, the transaction of any or all lawful business for which corporations may be incorporated under this Act;

(4) The aggregate number of shares which the corporation shall have authority to issue; if such shares are to consist of one class only, the par value of each of such shares, or a statement that all of such shares are without par value; or, if such shares are to be divided into classes, the number of shares of each class, and a statement of the par value of the shares of each class or that such shares are to be without par value;

(5) If the shares are to be divided into classes, the designation of each class and statement of the preferences, limitations, and relative rights in respect of the shares of each class;

(6) If the corporation is to issue the shares of any class in series, then the designation of each series and a statement of the variations in the preferences, limitations and relative rights as between series insofar as the same are to be fixed in the articles of incorporation, and a statement of any authority to be vested in the board of directors to establish series and fix and determine the preferences, limitations and relative rights of each series;

(7) Any provision limiting or denying to shareholders the preemptive right to acquire additional or treasury shares of the corporation;

(8) If a corporation elects to become a close corporation in conformance with Part Twelve of this Act, any provision (a) required or permitted by this Act to be stated in the articles of incorporation of a close corporation, but not in the articles of incorporation of an ordinary corporation, (b) contained or permitted to be contained in a shareholders' agreement in conformance with Part Twelve of this Act which the incorporators elect to set forth in articles of incorporation, or (c) that makes a shareholders' agreement in conformance with Part Twelve of this Act part of the articles of incorporation of a close corporation in the manner prescribed in Section F, Article 2.22 of this Act, but any such provision, other than the statement required by Section A, Article 12.11 of this Act, shall be preceded by a statement that the provision shall be subject to the corporation remaining a close corporation in conformance with Part Twelve of this Act;

(9) Any provision, not inconsistent with law, including any provision which under this Act is required or permitted to be set forth in the bylaws or which is permitted to be included pursuant to Article 2.30-1 of this Act, providing for the regulation of the internal affairs of the corporation;

(10) The street address of its initial registered office and the name of its initial registered agent at such address;

(11) Subject to Article 2.30-1 of this Act, the number of directors constituting the initial board of directors and the names and addresses of the person or persons who are to serve as directors until the first annual meeting of shareholders or until their successors be elected and qualify, or, in the case of a close corporation that, in conformance with Part Twelve of this Act, is to be managed in some other manner pursuant to a shareholders' agreement by the shareholders or by the persons empowered by the agreement to manage its business and affairs, the names and addresses of the person or persons who, pursuant to the shareholders' agreement, will perform the functions of the initial board of directors provided for by this Act;

(12) The name and address of each incorporator, unless the corporation is being incorporated pursuant to a plan of conversion or a plan of merger, in which case the articles need not include such information; and

(13) If the corporation is being incorporated pursuant to a plan of conversion or a plan of merger, a statement to that effect, and in the case of a plan of conversion, the name, address, date of formation, and prior form of organization and jurisdiction of incorporation or organization of the converting entity.

B. It shall not be necessary to set forth in the articles of incorporation any of the corporate powers enumerated in this Act.

Art. 3.03. Filing of Articles of Incorporation

A. Except as provided by Section C of this Article, the original and a copy of the articles of incorporation shall be delivered to the Secretary of State. If the Secretary of State finds that the articles of incorporation conform to law, he shall, when all fees have been paid as required by law:

(1) Endorse on the original and the copy the word "Filed," and the month, day, and year of the filing thereof.

(2) File the original in his office.

(3) Issue a certificate of incorporation to which he shall affix the copy.

B. The certificate of incorporation, together with the copy of the articles of incorporation affixed thereto by the Secretary of State, shall be delivered to the incorporators or their representatives.

C. In the case of a new domestic corporation being incorporated pursuant to a plan of conversion or a plan of merger pursuant to Part Five of this Act, the articles of incorporation of the corporation shall be filed with the Secretary of State with the articles of conversion or merger and need not be filed separately pursuant to Section A of this Article. If the Secretary of State finds that the articles of incorporation conform to the law, he shall file the articles of incorporation in his office and issue a certificate of incorporation, to which he shall affix a copy of the articles of incorporation, and deliver the same to the party or parties filing the articles of conversion or merger, or their representatives, with the certificate of conversion or merger that is issued in connection with the conversion or merger. In the case of a conversion or a merger, the certificate of incorporation of a domestic corporation that is a converted entity or that is to be created pursuant to the plan of merger shall become effective on the effectiveness of the conversion or the merger, as the case may be.

Art. 3.04. Effect of Issuance of Certificate of Incorporation

A. Except as provided by Section B of this Article, on the issuance of the certificate of incorporation, the corporate existence of the corporation being incorporated shall begin.

B. In the case of a new domestic corporation being incorporated pursuant to a plan of conversion or a plan of merger pursuant to Part Five of this Act, the corporate existence of the corporation shall begin upon the effectiveness of the conversion or the merger, as the case may be.

C. The certificate of incorporation on effectiveness shall be conclusive evidence that all conditions precedent required to be performed for the valid incorporation of the corporation have been complied with and that the corporation has been duly incorporated under this Act, except as against the State in a proceeding for involuntary dissolution.

Art. 3.06. Organization Meeting of Directors

A. Except as provided by Section B of this Article, after the issuance of the certificate of incorporation, an organization meeting of the initial board of directors named in the articles of incorporation (or of the person or persons who, in conformance with Section A(12), Article 3.02 of this Act, are named in the articles of incorporation as the person or persons who will perform the functions of the initial board of directors provided for by this Act) shall be held, either within or without this State, at the call of a majority of the directors named in the articles of incorporation, for the purpose of adopting bylaws, electing officers, and transacting such other business as may come before the meeting. The directors calling the meeting shall give at least three (3) days notice thereof by mail to each director so named, stating the time and place of the meeting.

B. The provisions of Section A of this Article shall not apply to a corporation that is a converted entity or a corporation that is created pursuant to a plan of merger if the plan of conversion or the plan of merger, as the case may be, sets forth the bylaws and officers of the corporation.

Business Corporation Act
Part 4.

Art. 4.01. Right to Amend Articles of Incorporation

A. A corporation may amend its articles of incorporation, from time to time, in any and as many respects as may be desired, so long as its articles of incorporation as amended contain only such provisions as might be lawfully contained in original articles of incorporation at the time of making such amendment, and, if a change in shares or the rights of shareholders, or an exchange, reclassification, subdivision, combination, or cancellation of shares or rights of shareholders is to be made, such provisions as may be necessary to effect such change, exchange, reclassification, subdivision, combination, or cancellation.

B. A shareholder of the corporation does not have a vested property right resulting from any provision in the articles of incorporation, including provisions relating to management, control, capital structure, dividend entitlement, or purpose or duration of the corporation.

C. Repealed.

Art. 4.02. Procedure to Amend Articles of Incorporation

A. The articles of incorporation may be amended in the following manner:

(1) The board of directors shall adopt a resolution setting forth the proposed amendment and, unless the amendment is undertaken under authority granted to the board of directors in the articles of incorporation in accordance with Article 2.13 of this Act, if shares have been issued, directing that it be submitted to a vote at a meeting of shareholders, which may be either an annual or a special meeting. If no shares have been issued, the amendment shall be adopted by resolution of the board of directors and the provisions for adoption by shareholders shall not apply. The resolution may incorporate the proposed amendment in restated articles of incorporation which contain a statement that except for the designated amendment the restated articles of incorporation correctly set forth without change the corresponding provisions of the articles of incorporation as heretofore amended, and that the restated articles of incorporation together with the designated amendment supersede the original articles of incorporation and all amendments thereto.

(2) Written or printed notice setting forth the proposed amendment or a summary of the changes to be effected thereby shall be given to each shareholder of record entitled to vote thereon within the time and in the manner provided in this Act for the giving of notice of meetings of shareholders. If the meeting be an annual meeting, the proposed amendment or such summary may be included in the notice of such annual meeting.

(3) At such meeting a vote of the shareholders entitled to vote thereon shall be taken on the proposed amendment. The proposed amendment shall be adopted upon receiving the affirmative vote of the holders of at least two-thirds of the outstanding shares entitled to vote thereon, unless any class or series of shares is entitled to vote thereon as a class, in which event the proposed amendment shall be adopted upon receiving the affirmative vote of the holders of at least two-thirds of the shares within each class or series of outstanding shares entitled to vote thereon as a class and of at least two-thirds of the total outstanding shares entitled to vote thereon.

(4) The resolution authorizing a proposed amendment to the articles of incorporation may provide that at any time before the filing of the amendment with the secretary of state is effective, notwithstanding authorization of the proposed amendment by the shareholders of the corporation, the board of directors may abandon the proposed amendment without further action by the shareholders.

B. Any number of amendments may be submitted to the shareholders, and voted upon by them, at one meeting.

C. Repealed.

Art. 4.03. Class Voting on Amendments

A. The holders of the outstanding shares of a class shall be entitled to vote as a class upon a proposed amendment, and the holders of the outstanding shares of a series shall be entitled to vote as a class upon a proposed amendment, whether or not entitled to vote thereon by the provisions of the articles of incorporation, if the amendment would accomplish any of the following, unless the amendment is undertaken pursuant to authority granted to the board of directors in the articles of incorporation in accordance with Article 2.13 of this Act:

(1) Increase or decrease the aggregate number of authorized shares of such class or series.

(2) Increase or decrease the par value of the shares of such class, including changing shares having a par value into shares without par value, or shares without par value into shares with par value.

(3) Effect an exchange, reclassification, or cancellation of all or part of the shares of such class or series.

(4) Effect an exchange, or create a right of exchange, of all or any part of the shares of another class into the shares of such class or series.

(5) Change the designations, preferences, limitations, or relative rights of the shares of such class or series.

(6) Change the shares of such class or series, whether with or without par value, into the same or a different number of shares, either with or without par value, of the same class or series or another class or series.

(7) Create a new class or series of shares having rights and preferences equal, prior, or superior to the shares of such class or series, or increase the rights and preferences of any class or series having rights and preferences equal, prior, or superior to the shares of such class or series, or increase the rights and preferences of any class or series having rights or preferences later or inferior to the shares of such class or series in such a manner as to become equal, prior, or superior to the shares of such class or series.

(8) Divide the shares of such class into series and fix and determine the designation of such series and the variations in the relative rights and preferences between the shares of such series.

(9) Limit or deny the existing preemptive rights of the shares of such class or series.

(10) Cancel or otherwise affect dividends on the shares of such class or series which had accrued but had not been declared.

(11) Include in or delete from the articles of incorporation any provisions required or permitted to be included in the articles of incorporation of a close corporation in conformance with Part Twelve of this Act.

B. Unless otherwise provided in a corporation's articles of incorporation, if the holders of the outstanding shares of a class that is divided into series are entitled to vote as a class on a proposed amendment and the amendment would affect all series of such class (other than any series of which no shares are outstanding or any series that is not affected by the amendment) equally, than the holders of the separate series shall not be entitled to separate class votes.

C. Unless otherwise provided in a corporation's articles of incorporation, the approval of a proposed amendment to the corporation's articles of incorporation that would solely effect changes in the designations, preferences, limitations, and relative rights, including voting rights, of one or more series of shares of the corporation that have been established pursuant to the authority granted the board of directors in the articles of incorporation in accordance with Article 2.13 of this Act shall not require the approval of the holders of the outstanding shares of any class or series other than such series if the preferences, limitations and relative rights of such series after giving effect to such amendment and of any series that may be established as a result of a reclassification of such series are, in each case, within those permitted to be fixed and determined by the board of directors with respect to the establishment of any new series of shares pursuant to the authority granted the board of directors in the articles of incorporation in accordance with Article 2.13 of this Act.

Art. 4.04. Articles of Amendment

A. The articles of amendment shall be executed on behalf of the corporation by an officer. If no shares have been issued, however, and the articles of amendment are adopted by the board of directors, the articles of amendment may be executed on behalf of the corporation by a majority of the directors.

B. The articles of amendment shall set forth:

(1) The name of the corporation.

(2) If the amendment alters any provision of the original or amended articles of incorporation, an identification by reference or description of the altered provision and a statement of its text as it is amended to read. If the amendment is an addition to the original or amended articles of incorporation, a statement of that fact and the full text of each provision added.

(3) The date of the adoption of the amendment by the shareholders, or by the board of directors where no shares have been issued.

(4) A statement that the amendment has been approved in the manner required by this Act and the constituent documents of the corporation.

Art. 4.05. Filing of Articles of Amendment

A. The original and a copy of the articles of amendment shall be delivered to the Secretary of State. If the Secretary of State finds that the articles of amendment conform to law, he shall, when the appropriate filing fee is paid as required by law:

(1) Endorse on the original and the copy the word "Filed" and the month, day, and year of the filing thereof.

(2) File the original in his office.

(3) Issue a certificate of amendment to which he shall affix the copy.

B. The certificate of amendment, together with the copy of the articles of amendment affixed thereto by the Secretary of State, shall be delivered to the corporation or its representative.

Art. 4.06. Effect of Certificate of Amendment

A. Upon the issuance of the certificate of amendment by the Secretary of State, the amendment shall become effective and the articles of incorporation shall be deemed to be amended accordingly.

B. No amendment shall affect any existing cause of action in favor of or against such corporation, or any pending suit to which such corporation shall be a party, or the existing rights of persons other than shareholders; and, in the event the corporate name shall be changed by amendment, no suit brought by or against such corporation under its former name shall abate for that reason.

Art. 4.07. Restated Articles of Incorporation

A. A corporation may, by following the procedure to amend the articles of incorporation provided by this Act (except that no shareholder approval shall be required where no amendment is made), authorize, execute, and file restated articles of incorporation which may restate either:

(1) The entire text of the articles of incorporation as amended or supplemented by all certificates of amendment previously issued by the Secretary of State; or

(2) The entire text of the articles of incorporation as amended or supplemented by all certificates of amendment previously issued by the Secretary of State, and as further amended by such restated articles of incorporation.

B. If the restated articles of incorporation restate the entire articles of incorporation as amended and supplemented by all certificates of amendments previously issued by the Secretary of State, without making any further amendment thereof, the introductory paragraph shall contain a statement that the instrument accurately copies the articles of incorporation and all amendments thereto that are in effect to date and that the instrument contains no change in any provision thereof; provided that the number of directors then constituting the board of directors and the names and addresses of the persons then serving as directors may be inserted in lieu of similar information concerning the initial board of directors, and the name and address of each incorporator may be omitted.

C. If the restated articles of incorporation restate the entire articles of incorporation as amended and supplemented by all certificates of amendments previously issued by the Secretary of State, and as further amended by such restated articles of incorporation, the instrument containing such articles shall:

(1) Set forth, for any amendment made by such restated articles of incorporation, a statement that each such amendment has been effected in conformity with the provisions of this Act, and shall further set forth the statements required by this Act to be contained in articles of amendment.

(2) Contains a statement that the instrument accurately copies the articles of incorporation and all amendments thereto that are in effect to date and as further amended by such restated articles of incorporation and that the instrument contains no other change in any provision thereof; provided that the number of directors then constituting the board of directors and the names and addresses of the persons then serving as directors may be inserted in lieu of similar

information concerning the initial board of directors, and the names and addresses of each incorporator may be omitted.

(3) Restate the text of the entire articles of incorporation as amended and supplemented by all certificates of amendment previously issued by the Secretary of State and as further amended by the restated articles of incorporation.

D. Such restated articles of incorporation shall be executed on behalf of the corporation by an officer. If no shares have been issued, however, and the restated articles of incorporation are adopted by the board of directors, the restated articles of incorporation may be executed on behalf of the corporation by a majority of the directors. The original and a copy of the restated articles of incorporation shall be delivered to the Secretary of State. If the Secretary of State finds that the restated articles of incorporation conform to law, he shall, when the appropriate filing fee is paid as required by law:

(1) Endorse on the original and the copy the word "Filed," and the month, day, and year of the filing thereof.

(2) File the original in his office.

(3) Issue a restated certificate of incorporation to which he shall affix the copy.

E. The restated certificate of incorporation, together with the copy of the restated articles of incorporation affixed thereto by the Secretary of State, shall be delivered to the corporation or its representative.

F. Upon the issuance of the restated certificate of incorporation by the Secretary of State, the original articles of incorporation and all amendments thereto shall be superseded and the restated articles of incorporation shall be deemed to be the articles of incorporation of the corporation.

Art. 4.08. Procedure for Redemption

A. A corporation may at any time, subject to Article 2.38 of this Act and to the provisions of its articles of incorporation, proceed, by resolution of its board of directors, to redeem any or all outstanding shares subject to redemption. If less than all such shares are to be redeemed, the shares to be redeemed shall be selected for redemption in accordance with the provisions in the articles of incorporation, or, in the absence of such provisions therein, may be selected ratably or by lot in such manner as may be prescribed by resolution of the board of directors. Such redemption shall be effected by call and written or printed notice in the following manner:

(1) The notice of redemption of such shares shall set forth:

(a) The class or series of shares or part of any class or series of shares to be redeemed.

(b) The date fixed for redemption.

(c) The redemptive price.

(d) The place at which the shareholders may obtain payment of the redemptive price and, in the case of holders of certificated shares, upon surrender of their respective share certificates.

(2) The notice shall be given to each holder of redeemable shares being called, either personally or by mail, not less than twenty (20) nor more than sixty (60) days before the date fixed for redemption. If mailed, such notice shall be deemed to be delivered when deposited in the United States mail addressed to the shareholder at his address as it appears on the stock transfer book of the corporation, with postage thereon prepaid.

B. A corporation may, on or prior to the date fixed for redemption of redeemable shares, deposit with any bank or trust company in this State, or any bank or trust company in the United States duly appointed and acting as transfer agent for such corporation, as a trust fund, a sum sufficient to redeem shares called for redemption, with irrevocable instructions and authority to such bank or trust company to give or complete the notice of redemption thereof and to pay, on or after the date fixed for such redemption, to the respective holders of shares, as evidenced by a list of holders of such shares certified by an officer of the corporation, the redemptive price upon the surrender of their respective share certificates. From and after the date fixed for redemption, such shares shall be deemed to be redeemed and dividends thereon shall cease to accrue. Such deposit shall be deemed to constitute full payment of such shares to their holders. From and after the date such deposit is made and such instructions are given, such shares shall no longer be deemed to be outstanding, and the holders thereof shall cease to be shareholders with respect to such shares, and shall have no rights with respect thereto except the right to receive from the bank or trust company payment of the redemptive price of such shares without interest and, in the case of holders of certificated shares, upon the surrender of their respective certificates therefor, and any right to convert such shares which may exist. In case the holders of such shares shall not, within six (6) years after such deposit, claim the amount deposited for redemption thereof, such bank or trust company shall upon demand pay over to the corporation the balance of such amount so deposited to be held in trust and such bank or trust company shall thereupon be relieved of all responsibility to the holders thereof.

Art. 4.10. Reduction of Stated Capital by Redemption or Purchase of Redeemable Shares

A. When redeemable shares of a corporation are redeemed or purchased by the corporation, the redemption or purchase shall effect a cancellation of such shares. Thereupon such shares shall be restored to the status of authorized but unissued shares, unless the articles of incorporation provide that such shares when redeemed or purchased shall not be reissued, in which case the number of shares of the class so cancelled which the corporation is authorized to issue shall be reduced by the number of shares so cancelled. If the shares so redeemed and purchased constitute all the outstanding shares of any particular class of shares and if the articles of incorporation provide that the shares of such class when redeemed and repurchased shall not be reissued, the corporation may not issue any additional shares of the class of shares.

B. Repealed.

C. Repealed.

D. The cancellation of shares under this article shall effect a reduction of the stated capital of the corporation by an amount equal to that part of the stated capital which was, at the time of the cancellation, represented by the shares so cancelled.

E. Nothing contained in this Article shall be construed to forbid a cancellation of shares or a reduction of stated capital in any other manner permitted by law.

Art. 4.11. Cancellation of Treasury Shares

A. A corporation may, at any time, by resolution of its board of directors, cancel all or any part of its treasury shares.

B. Repealed.

C. Repealed.

D. Upon the cancellation of the treasury shares, the stated capital of the corporation shall be deemed to be reduced by that part of the stated capital which was, at the time of such cancellation, represented by the shares so cancelled, and the shares so cancelled shall be restored to the status of authorized but unissued shares.

E. Nothing contained in this Article shall be construed to forbid a cancellation of shares or a reduction of stated capital in any other manner permitted by law.

Art. 4.12. Reduction of Stated Capital Without Amendment of Articles and Without Cancellation of Shares

A. If all or part of the stated capital of a corporation is represented by shares without par value, the stated capital of the corporation may be reduced in the following manner:

(1) The board of directors shall adopt a resolution setting forth the amount of the proposed reduction and the manner in which the reduction shall be effected, and directing that the question of such reduction be submitted to a vote at a meeting of shareholders, which may be either an annual or a special meeting.

(2) Written or printed notice, stating that the purpose or one of the purposes of such meeting is to consider the question of reducing the stated capital of the corporation in the amount and manner proposed by the board of directors, shall be given to each shareholder of record entitled to vote thereon within the time and in the manner provided in this Act for the giving of notice of meetings of shareholders.

(3) At the meeting for which such notice has been given, the affirmative vote of the holders of at least a majority of the shares entitled to vote on the question shall be required for approval of the resolution proposing the reduction of stated capital.

B. Repealed.

C. Repealed.

D. Upon the approval of such resolution by the shareholders, the stated capital of the corporation shall be reduced as therein set forth.

E. No reduction of stated capital shall be made under the provisions of this Article which would reduce the amount of the aggregate stated capital of the corporation to an amount equal to or less than the aggregate preferential amounts payable upon all issued shares having a preferential right in the assets of the corporation in the event of voluntary liquidation, plus the aggregate par value of all issued shares having a par value but no preferential right in the assets of the corporation in the event of voluntary liquidation.

Art. 4.13. Special Provisions Relating to Surplus and Reserves

A corporation may, by resolution of its board of directors, create a reserve or reserves out of its surplus or designate or allocate any part or all of surplus in any manner for any proper purpose or purposes, and may increase, decrease, or abolish any such reserve, designation, or allocation in the same manner.

Art. 4.14. Reorganization Under a Federal Statute; Amendment of Articles, Merger, Share Exchange, Conversion, and Dissolution Pursuant to Federal Reorganization Proceedings

A. Authorization. Notwithstanding any other provision of this Act to the contrary, a trustee appointed for a corporation being reorganized under a federal statute, the designated officers of the corporation, or any other individual or individuals designated by the court to act on behalf of the corporation may do any of the following without action by or notice to its board of directors or shareholders in order to carry out a plan of reorganization ordered or decreed by a court of competent jurisdiction under the federal statute:

(1) amend or restate its articles of incorporation if the articles after amendment or restatement contain only provisions required or permitted in articles;

(2) merge or engage in a share exchange with one or more domestic or foreign corporations or other entities pursuant to a plan of merger or exchange having such terms and provisions as required or permitted by Articles 5.01 and 5.02 of this Act;

(3) change the location of its registered office, change its registered agent, and remove or appoint any agent to receive service of process;

(4) alter, amend, or repeal its bylaws;

(5) constitute or reconstitute and classify or reclassify its board of directors, and name, constitute, or appoint directors and officers in place of or in addition to all or some of the officers or directors then in place;

(6) sell, lease, exchange or otherwise dispose of all, or substantially all, of its property and assets;

(7) authorize and fix the terms, manner, and conditions of the issuance of bonds, debentures, or other obligations, whether or not convertible into shares of any class or bearing warrants or other evidences of optional rights to purchase or subscribe for any shares of any class;

(8) dissolve; or

(9) effect a conversion.

Actions taken under Subsection (4) or (5) of this section are effective on entry of the order or decree approving the plan of reorganization or on another effective date as may be specified, without further action of the corporation, as and to the extent set forth in the plan of reorganization or the order or decree approving the plan of reorganization.

B. Authority to Sign Documents. A trustee appointed for a corporation being reorganized under a federal statute, the designated officers of the corporation, or any other individual or individuals designated by the court may sign on behalf of a corporation that is being reorganized:

(1) articles of amendment or restated articles of incorporation setting forth:

(a) the name of the corporation;

(b) the text of each amendment or the restatement approved by the court;

(c) the date of the court's order or decree approving the articles of amendment or restatement;

(d) the court, file name, and case number of the reorganization case in which the order or decree was entered; and

(e) a statement that the court had jurisdiction of the case under federal statute; or

(2) articles of merger or exchange setting forth:

(a) the name of the corporation;

(b) the text of the part of the plan of reorganization that contains the plan of merger or exchange approved by the court, which shall include the information required by Article 5.04A or 5.16B of this Act, as applicable, but need not include the resolution of the board of directors referred to in Article 5.16B(3) of this Act;

(c) the date of the court's order or decree approving the plan of merger or consolidation;

(d) the court, file name, and case number of the reorganization case in which the order or decree was entered; and

(e) a statement that the court had jurisdiction of the case under federal statute; or

(3) articles of dissolution setting forth:

(a) the name of the corporation;

(b) the information required by Articles 6.06A(1)(2) and (3) of this Act;

(c) the date of the court's order or decree approving the articles of dissolution;

(d) that the debts, obligations and liabilities of the corporation have been paid or discharged as provided in the plan of reorganization and that the remaining property and assets of the corporation have been distributed as provided in the plan of reorganization;

(e) the court, file name, and case number of the reorganization case in which the order or decree was entered; and

(f) a statement that the court had jurisdiction of the case under federal statute; or

(4) a statement of change of registered office or registered agent, or both, setting forth:

(a) the name of the corporation;

(b) the information required by Article 2.10A of this Act, as applicable, but not the information included in the statement referred to in Article 2.10A(7) of this Act;

(c) the date of the court's order or decree approving the statement of change of registered office or registered agent, or both;

(d) the court, file name, and case number of the reorganization case in which the order or decree was entered; and

(e) a statement that the court had jurisdiction of the case under federal statute; or

(5) articles of conversion setting forth:

(a) the name of the corporation;

(b) the text of the part of the plan of reorganization that contains the plan of conversion approved by the court, which shall include the information required by Article 5.18 of this Act;

(c) the date of the court's order or decree approving the plan of conversion;

(d) the court, file name, and case number of the reorganization case in which the order or decree was entered; and

(e) a statement that the court had jurisdiction of the case under federal statute.

C. Procedure for Merger or Share Exchange. When a domestic or foreign corporation or other entity that is not being reorganized merges or engages in a share exchange with a corporation that is being reorganized pursuant to a plan of reorganization:

(1) Articles 5.01, 5.02, 5.03, 5.11, 5.12, and 5.13 of this Act shall apply to the domestic or foreign corporation or other entity that is not being reorganized to the same extent they would apply if it were merging or engaging in a share exchange with a corporation that is not being reorganized;

(2) Article 5.06 of this Act shall apply to the domestic or foreign corporation or other entity that is not being reorganized to the same extent it would apply if that domestic or foreign corporation or other entity were merging or engaging in a share exchange with a corporation that is not being reorganized, except as otherwise provided in the plan of reorganization ordered or decreed by a court of competent jurisdiction under the federal statute;

(3) Article 5.16E of this Act shall apply to a subsidiary corporation that is not being reorganized to the same extent it would apply if that corporation were merging with a parent corporation that is not being reorganized;

(4) Upon the receipt of all required authorization for all action required by this Act for each corporation that is a party to the plan of merger or exchange that is not being reorganized and all action by each corporation, foreign corporation, or other entity that is a party to the plan of merger or exchange required by the laws under which it is incorporated or organized and its constituent documents, articles of merger or exchange shall be signed by each domestic or foreign corporation or other entity that is a party to the merger or exchange other than the corporation that is being reorganized as provided in Article 5.04 of this Act and on behalf of the corporation that is being reorganized by the persons specified in Section B of this Article;

(5) The articles of merger or exchange shall set forth the information required in Section B(2) of this Article;

(6) The articles of merger or exchange shall be filed with the Secretary of State in the manner and with such number of copies as is provided in Article 5.04B of this Act; and

(7) Upon the issuance of the certificate of merger or share exchange by the Secretary of State as provided in Article 5.04 of this Act, the merger or share exchange shall become effective with the same effect as if it had been adopted by unanimous action of the directors and shareholders of the corporation being reorganized. The effectiveness of the merger or share exchange shall be determined as provided in Article 5.05 of this Act.

D. Dissenters' Rights. Shareholders of a corporation being reorganized under a federal statute do not have a right to dissent under Article 5.11, 5.16E, or 5.20 of this Act, except as the plan of reorganization may provide.

E. When Applicable. This Article shall not apply after the entry of a final decree in the reorganization case even though the court may retain jurisdiction of the case for limited purposes unrelated to consummation of the plan of reorganization.

F. Nonexclusivity. This Article shall not preclude other changes in a corporation or its securities by a plan of reorganization ordered or decreed by a court of competent jurisdiction under federal statute.

Business Corporation Act
Part 5.
Art. 5.01. Merger

A. A domestic corporation may adopt a plan of merger and one or more domestic corporations may merge with one or more domestic or foreign corporations or other entities if:

(1) the board of directors of each domestic corporation that is a party to the plan of merger acts upon and its shareholders (if required by Article 5.03 of this Act) approve the plan of merger in the manner prescribed in Article 5.03 of this Act;

(2) if one or more foreign corporations or other entities is a party to the merger or is to be created by the terms of the plan of merger, (a) the merger is permitted by the laws of the state or country under whose law each foreign corporation, if any, that is a party to the merger is incorporated, (b) the merger is either permitted by the laws under which each other entity that is a party to the merger is incorporated or organized or by the constituent documents of the other entity that are not inconsistent with such laws, and (c) each foreign corporation or other entity that is a party to the merger complies with such laws or documents in effecting the merger; and

(3) no shareholder of a domestic corporation that is a party to the merger will, as a result of such merger, become personally liable, without his consent, for the liabilities or obligations of any other person or entity.

B. A plan of merger shall set forth:

(1) the name of each domestic or foreign corporation or other entity that is a party to the merger and the name of each domestic or foreign corporation or other entity, if any, that shall survive the merger, which may be one or more of the domestic or foreign corporations or other entities party to the merger, and the name of each new domestic or

foreign corporation or other entity, if any, that may be created by the terms of the plan of merger;

(2) the terms and conditions of the merger including, if more than one domestic or foreign corporation or other entity is to survive or to be created by the terms of the plan of merger, (a) the manner and basis of allocating and vesting the real estate and other property of each domestic or foreign corporation and of each other entity that is a party to the merger among one or more of the surviving or new domestic or foreign corporations and other entities, (b) the name of the surviving or new domestic or foreign corporation or other entity that is to be obligated for the payment of the fair value of any shares held by a shareholder of any domestic corporation that is a party to the merger who has complied with the requirements of Article 5.12 of this Act for the recovery of the fair value of his shares, and (c) the manner and basis of allocating all other liabilities and obligations of each domestic or foreign corporation and other entity that is a party to the merger (or making adequate provision for the payment and discharge thereof) among one or more of the surviving or new domestic or foreign corporations and other entities;

(3) the manner and basis of converting any of the shares or other evidences of ownership of each domestic or foreign corporation and other entity that is a party to the merger into shares, obligations, evidences of ownership, rights to purchase securities or other securities of one or more of the surviving or new domestic or foreign corporations or other entities, into cash or other property, including shares, obligations, evidences of ownership, rights to purchase securities or other securities of any other person or entity, or into any combination of the foregoing, and if any shares or other evidences of ownership of any holder of a class or series of shares or other evidence of ownership is to be converted in a manner or basis different than any other holder of shares of such class or series or other evidence of ownership, the manner and basis applicable to such holder;

(4) as an exhibit or attachment, the articles of incorporation of any new domestic corporation to be created by the terms of the plan of merger; and

(5) the articles of incorporation or other organizational documents of each other entity that is a party to the merger and that is to survive the merger or is to be created by the terms of the plan of merger.

C. The plan of merger may set forth:

(1) any amendments to the articles of incorporation of any surviving corporation;

(2) provisions relating to a share exchange; and

(3) any other provisions relating to the merger, including a provision requiring that the plan of merger be submitted to shareholders regardless of whether the board of directors determines after adopting the resolution or making the determination required by Section B, Article 5.03 of this Act, that the plan of merger is not advisable and recommends that the shareholders reject it.

D. Upon the merger's taking effect, the surviving or new foreign corporation or other entity, if any, that is the sole surviving or new foreign corporation or other entity in the merger, or if more than one domestic or foreign corporation or other entity is to survive or to be created by the terms of the plan of merger, the surviving or new foreign corporation or other entity that is designated in the plan of merger to be the entity obligated for the payment of the fair value of any shares held by a shareholder who has complied with the requirements of Article 5.12 of this Act for the recovery of the fair value of his shares, is deemed:

(1) to appoint the Secretary of State in this State as its agent for service of process in a proceeding to enforce any obligation or the rights of dissenting shareholders of each domestic corporation that is a party to the merger; and

(2) to agree that it will promptly pay to the dissenting shareholders of each domestic corporation that is a party to the merger the amount, if any, to which they are entitled under Article 5.11 of this Act.

E. This Article does not limit the power of a domestic or foreign corporation or other entity to acquire all or part of the shares of one or more classes or series of a domestic corporation through a voluntary exchange or otherwise.

F. This Article does not limit the power of domestic or foreign corporations to merge pursuant to Article 5.16 of this Act.

Art. 5.02. Share Exchange or Acquisition

A. One or more domestic or foreign corporations or other entities may acquire all of the outstanding shares of one or more classes or series of one or more domestic corporations if:

(1) the board of directors of each domestic corporation that is a party to the plan of exchange acts on a plan of exchange in the manner prescribed by Article 5.03 of this Act and its shareholders (if required by Article 5.03 of this Act) approve the plan of exchange;

(2) one or more foreign corporations or other entities is to issue shares or other interests as part of the plan of exchange, the issuance of such shares or interests is either permitted by the laws under which such foreign corporation or other entity is incorporated, organized, or not inconsistent with such laws; and

(3) each acquiring domestic or foreign corporation or other entity takes all action that may be required by the laws of the state or country under which it was incorporated or organized and by its constituent documents to effect the exchange.

B. A plan of exchange must set forth:

(1) the name of the corporation or corporations whose shares will be acquired and the name of each acquiring domestic or foreign corporation and other entity;

(2) the terms and conditions of the exchange including, if there is more than one acquiring domestic or foreign corporation or other entity, the shares to be acquired by each such corporation or other entity; and

(3) the manner and basis of exchanging the shares to be acquired for shares, obligations, evidences of ownership, rights to purchase securities or other securities of one or more of the acquiring domestic or foreign corporations or other entities that is a party to the plan of exchange, or for cash or other property, including shares, obligations, evidences of ownership, rights to purchase securities or other securities of any other person or entity, or for any combination of the foregoing, and if any shares or other evidences of ownership of any holder of a class or series of shares or other evidence of ownership is to be exchanged in a manner or basis different than any other holder of shares of such class or series or other evidence of ownership, the manner and basis applicable to such holder.

C. The plan of exchange may set forth any other provisions relating to the exchange and may be contained in and be a part of a plan of merger, including a provision requiring that the plan of exchange be submitted to shareholders regardless of whether the board of directors determines after adopting the resolution or making the determination required by Section B, Article 5.03 of this Act, that the plan of exchange is not advisable and recommends that the shareholders reject it.

D. A plan of exchange may not be effected if any shareholder of a domestic corporation that is a party to the share exchange will, as a result of the share exchange, become personally liable, without his consent, for the liabilities or obligations of any other person or entity.

E. This Article does not limit the power of a domestic or foreign corporation or other entity to acquire all or part of the shares of one or more classes or series of a domestic corporation through a voluntary exchange or otherwise.

Art. 5.03. Action on Plan of Merger or Exchange

A. Except as provided by Sections G and H of this Article, after acting on a plan of merger or exchange in the manner prescribed by Subsection (1) of Section B of this Article, the board of directors of each domestic corporation that is a party to the merger, and the board of directors of each domestic corporation whose shares are to be acquired in the share exchange, shall submit the plan of merger or exchange for approval by its shareholders. Unless the articles of incorporation otherwise require, no approval by shareholders of a plan of merger is required under this Article for any corporation that is a party to the plan of merger unless that corporation is also a party to the merger.

B. Except as provided by Sections G and H of this Article, for a plan of merger or exchange to be approved:

(1) the board of directors of the corporation shall adopt a resolution recommending that the plan of merger or exchange be approved by the shareholders of the corporation, unless the board of directors determines that for any reason it should not make that recommendation, in which case the board of directors shall adopt a resolution directing that the plan of merger or exchange be submitted to shareholders for approval without recommendation and, in connection with the submission, communicate the basis for its determination that the plan be submitted to shareholders without any recommendation; and

(2) the shareholders entitled to vote on the plan of merger or exchange must approve the plan.

C. The board of directors may condition its submission to shareholders of a plan of merger or exchange on any basis. If, after the adoption of a resolution recommending that the plan of merger or exchange be approved or after a determination by the board of directors that a recommendation should not be made, the board of directors determines that the plan of merger or exchange is not advisable, the plan of merger or exchange may be submitted to the shareholders with a recommendation that the shareholders not approve the plan of merger or exchange.

D. The corporation shall notify each shareholder, whether or not entitled to vote, of the meeting of shareholders at which the plan of merger or exchange is to be submitted for approval in accordance with Article 2.25 of this Act. The notice shall be given at least 20 days before the meeting and shall state that the purpose, or one of the purposes, of the meeting is to consider the plan of merger or exchange and shall contain or be accompanied by a copy or summary of the plan.

E. Unless the board of directors (acting pursuant to Section C of this Article) requires a greater vote or a vote by class or series, the vote of shareholders required for approval of a plan of merger or exchange shall be the affirmative vote of the holders of at least two-thirds of the outstanding shares of each corporation entitled to vote thereon, unless any class or series of shares of any such corporation is entitled to vote as a class thereon, in which event the vote required for approval by the holders of such corporation shall be the affirmative vote of the holders of at least two-thirds of the outstanding shares within each class or series of shares entitled to vote thereon as a class and at least

two-thirds of the outstanding shares otherwise entitled to vote thereon. Shares entitled to vote as a class shall be entitled to vote only as a class unless otherwise entitled to vote on each matter submitted to the shareholders generally or provided in the articles of incorporation.

F. Separate voting by a class or series of shares of a corporation shall be required:

(1) for approval of a plan of merger if (a) the plan contains a provision that if contained in a proposed amendment to the articles of incorporation would require approval by that class or series of shares under Article 4.03 of this Act, or (b) that class or series of shares is entitled under the articles of incorporation to vote as a class thereon; and

(2) on a plan of exchange if (a) shares of that class or series are to be exchanged pursuant to the terms of the plan, or (b) that class or series is entitled under the articles of incorporation to vote as a class thereon.

G. Unless the articles of incorporation otherwise require, approval by the shareholders of a corporation on a plan of merger shall not be required and the provisions of Sections A, B, C, D, E, and F of this Article do not apply if:

(1) the corporation is the sole surviving corporation in the merger;

(2) the articles of incorporation of the corporation will not differ from its articles of incorporation before the merger;

(3) each shareholder of the corporation whose shares were outstanding immediately before the effective date of the merger will hold the same number of shares, with identical designations, preferences, limitations, and relative rights, immediately after the effective date of the merger;

(4) the voting power of the number of voting shares outstanding immediately after the merger, plus the voting power of the number of voting shares issuable as a result of the merger (either by the conversion of securities issued pursuant to the merger or the exercise of rights to purchase securities issued pursuant to the merger), will not exceed by more than 20 percent the voting power of the total number of voting shares of the corporation outstanding immediately before the merger;

(5) the number of participating shares outstanding immediately after the merger, plus the number of participating shares issuable as a result of the merger (either by the conversion of securities issued pursuant to the merger or the exercise of rights to purchase securities issued pursuant to the merger), will not exceed by more than 20 percent the total number of participating shares of the corporation outstanding immediately before the merger; and

(6) the board of directors of the corporation adopts a resolution approving the plan of merger.

H. Unless the articles of incorporation otherwise require, approval by the shareholders of a corporation of a plan of merger shall not be required and Sections A, B, C, D, E, and F of this Article do not apply if:

(1) the merger is a merger of the corporation with or into a direct or indirect wholly owned subsidiary of the corporation and after the merger the corporation or its successor is a direct or indirect wholly owned subsidiary of a holding company;

(2) the corporation and the direct or indirect wholly owned subsidiary of the corporation are the only parties to the merger;

(3) each share or a fraction of a share of stock of the corporation outstanding immediately prior to the effectiveness of the merger is converted in the merger into a share or fraction of share of capital stock of the holding company having the same designations, preferences, limitations, and relative rights as a share of stock of the corporation being converted in the merger;

(4) the holding company and the corporation are domestic corporations and the direct or indirect wholly owned subsidiary that is the other party to the merger is a domestic corporation or domestic limited liability company;

(5) the articles of incorporation and bylaws of the holding company immediately following the effective time of the merger contain provisions identical to the articles of incorporation and bylaws of the corporation immediately prior to the effective time of the merger (other than provisions, if any, regarding the incorporator or incorporators, the corporate name, the registered office and agent, the initial board of directors, and the initial subscribers of shares and such provisions contained in any amendment to the certificate as were necessary to effect a change, exchange, reclassification, or cancellation of shares, if such change, exchange, reclassification, or cancellation has become effective);

(6) the organizational documents or corresponding documents of the surviving entity immediately following the effective time of the merger contain provisions identical to the organizational documents or corresponding documents of the corporation immediately prior to the effective time of the merger (other than provisions, if any, regarding the incorporator or incorporators, the corporate or entity name, the registered office and agent, the initial board of directors, and the initial subscribers of shares, references to members rather than shareholders, references to interests, units, or similar property rather than stock or shares, references to managers, managing members, or other members of the governing body rather than directors, and such provisions contained in any amendment to the certificate as were necessary to effect a change, exchange, reclassification, or cancellation of shares, if such change, exchange, reclassification, or cancellation has become effective); provided, however, that:

(a) if the organizational documents of the surviving entity do not contain the following provisions, they shall be amended in the merger to contain provisions requiring that:

(i) any act or transaction by or involving a surviving entity, other than the election or removal of directors or managers, managing members, or other members of the governing body of the surviving entity, that requires for its approval under this Act or its organizational documents the approval of shareholders or members of the surviving entity shall, by specific reference to this section, require the approval of the shareholders of the holding company (or any successor by merger) by the same vote as is required by this Act or by the organizational documents of the surviving entity;

(ii) a surviving entity that is not a corporation obtain the approval of the shareholders of the holding company for any act or transaction by or involving the surviving entity, other than the election or removal of directors or managers, managing members, or other members of the governing body of the surviving entity, that would require the approval of the shareholders of the surviving entity if the surviving entity were a corporation subject to this Act;

(iii) any amendment of the organizational documents of a surviving entity that is not a corporation, that would, if adopted by a corporation subject to this Act, be required to be included in the articles of incorporation of the corporation, shall also require, by specific reference to this section, the approval of the shareholders of the holding company, or any successor by merger, by the same vote as is required by this Act or by the organizational documents of the surviving entity; and

(iv) the business affairs of a surviving entity that is not a corporation shall be managed by or under the direction of a board of directors, board of managers, or other governing body consisting of individuals who are subject to the same fiduciary duties applicable to directors of a corporation subject to this Act, and who are liable for breach of the duties to the same extent as directors of a corporation subject to this Act;

(b) the organizational documents of the surviving entity may be amended in the merger to change the classes and series of shares and the number of shares that the surviving entity is authorized to issue; and

(c) Subsection (6)(a) of this section or a provision of a surviving entity's organizational documents required by Subdivision (a) may not be construed as requiring approval of the shareholders of the holding company to elect or remove directors, managers, managing members, or other members of the governing body of the surviving entity;

(7) the directors of the corporation become or remain directors of the holding company on the effective time of the merger;

(8) the shareholders of the corporation will not recognize gain or loss for United States federal income tax purposes as determined by the board of directors of the corporation; and

(9) the board of directors of the corporation adopts a resolution approving the plan of merger.

H-1. The term "organizational documents," as used in Section H(6) of this article, means:

(1) in reference to a corporation, the articles of incorporation of the corporation; or

(2) in reference to a limited liability company, the limited liability company agreement of the limited liability company.

I. As used in this Article:

(1) "Direct or indirect wholly owned subsidiary" means, with respect to any corporation, another corporation, all of the outstanding voting stock of which is owned by the corporation or by one or more other domestic or foreign corporations or other entities, all of the outstanding voting stock or interests of which is owned by the corporation or one or more of such other wholly owned domestic or foreign corporations or other entities.

(2) "Holding company" means a corporation which, from its incorporation until the effectiveness of a merger pursuant to Section H of this Article, was at all times a direct or indirect wholly owned subsidiary of the corporation and whose stock is issued in the merger permitted by Section H of this Article.

(3) "Participating shares" means shares that entitle the holders thereof to participate without limitation in distributions.

(4) "Party to the merger" means:

(a) a domestic corporation that is to be divided into two or more new domestic corporations or into a surviving corporation and one or more new domestic or foreign corporations or other entities pursuant to a plan of merger; or

(b) a domestic or foreign corporation or other entity that is to be combined with one or more domestic or foreign corporations or other entities pursuant to a plan of merger resulting in (i) one or more surviving domestic or foreign corporations or other entities, (ii) the creation of one or more new domestic or foreign corporations or other entities, or (iii) one or more surviving domestic or foreign corporations or other entities and the creation of one or more new domestic or foreign corporations or other entities. A domestic or foreign corporation or other entity that is a party to a plan of merger that is not to be divided or combined into or with one or more domestic or foreign corporations or other entities is not considered to be a party to the merger even if shares, securities, or other property of such party is to be issued pursuant to the plan of merger.

(5) "Voting shares" means shares that entitle the holders thereof to vote unconditionally in elections of directors.

(6) "Shares" means, without limitation, a receipt or other instrument issued by a depositary representing an interest in one or more shares of stock, or fractions thereof, solely of a domestic or foreign corporation, which stock is deposited with a depositary.

J. To the extent the provisions contained in Part Thirteen of this Act apply to the corporation and its shareholders at the effective time of a merger pursuant to Section H of this Article, those provisions shall continue to apply to the holding company and its shareholders immediately after the effective time of the merger as though it were the corporation, and all shares of the holding company acquired in the merger shall, for purposes of Part Thirteen, be deemed to have been acquired at the time that the shares of stock of the corporation converted in the merger were acquired, and any shareholder who, immediately prior to the effective time of the merger, was not an affiliated shareholder within the meaning of Article 13.02 of this Act shall not solely by reason of the merger become an affiliated shareholder of the holding company.

K. If the corporate name of a holding company immediately following the effective time of a merger pursuant to Section H of this Article is the same as the corporate name of the corporation immediately prior to the effective time of the merger, the shares of the holding company into which the shares of the corporation are converted in the merger shall be represented by the stock certificates that previously represented the shares of the corporation.

L. After a merger or share exchange is approved, and at any time before the merger or share exchange has become effective, the plan of merger or share exchange may be abandoned (subject to any contractual rights) by any of the corporations that are a party to the merger, without shareholder action, in accordance with the procedures set forth in the plan of merger or exchange or, if no such procedures are set forth in the plan, in the manner determined by the board of directors. If articles of merger or exchange have been filed with the Secretary of State but the merger or share exchange has not yet become effective, the merger or share exchange may be abandoned if a statement, executed on behalf of each domestic corporation and foreign corporation or other entity that is a party to the merger or share exchange by an officer or other duly authorized representative, stating that the plan of merger or exchange has been abandoned in accordance with applicable law is filed with the Secretary of State prior to the effectiveness of the merger or share exchange. If the Secretary of State finds that such statement conforms to law, he shall, when all fees have been paid as required by law:

(1) Endorse on the original and each copy the word "Filed" and the month, day, and year the filing thereof.

(2) File the original in his office.

(3) Issue a certificate of abandonment to each domestic or foreign corporation or other entity that is a party to the merger or exchange.

Upon the filing of such statement by the Secretary of State, the merger or share exchange shall be deemed abandoned and shall not become effective.

M. To the extent a shareholder of a corporation has standing to institute or maintain derivative litigation on behalf of the corporation immediately before a merger, nothing in this article may be construed to limit or extinguish the shareholder's standing.

Art. 5.04. Articles of Merger or Exchange

A. If a plan of merger or exchange has been approved in accordance with Article 5.03 of this Act and has not been abandoned, or approved by the board of directors if shareholder approval is not required under that Article, articles of merger or exchange shall be executed on behalf of each domestic or foreign corporation or other entity that is a party to the merger or exchange by an officer or other duly authorized representative thereof and shall set forth:

(1) The plan of merger or exchange or statement certifying the following:

(a) the name and state of incorporation or organization of each domestic or foreign corporation or other entity that is a party to the plan of merger or exchange or that is to be created thereby;

(b) that a plan of merger or exchange has been approved;

(c) in the case of a merger, such amendments or changes in the articles of incorporation of each domestic surviving corporation, or if no such amendments are desired to be effected by the merger, a statement to that effect;

(d) that the articles of incorporation of each new domestic corporation to be created pursuant to the terms of the plan of merger are being filed with the Secretary of State with the articles of merger or exchange;

(e) that an executed plan of merger or exchange is on file at the principal place of business of each surviving, acquiring, or new domestic or foreign corporation or other entity, stating the address thereof; and

(f) that a copy of the plan of merger or exchange will be furnished by each surviving, acquiring, or new domestic or foreign corporation or other entity, on written request and without cost, to any shareholder of each domestic corporation that is a party to or created by the plan of merger or exchange and, in the case of a merger with multiple surviving domestic or foreign corporations or other entities, to any creditor or obligee of the parties to the merger at the time of the merger if such obligation is then outstanding.

(2) If shareholder approval is not required by Article 5.03 of this Act, a statement to that effect.

(3) As to each corporation the approval of whose shareholders is required, the number of shares outstanding, and, if the shares of any class or series are entitled to vote as a class, the designation and number of outstanding shares of each such class or series.

(4) As to each corporation the approval of whose shareholders is required, the number of shares, not entitled to vote only as a class, voted for and against the plan, respectively, and, if the shares of any class or series are entitled to vote as a class, the number of shares of each such class or series voted for and against the plan, respectively.

(5) As to each acquiring domestic or foreign corporation or other entity in a plan of exchange, a statement that the plan and performance of its terms were duly authorized by all action required by the laws under which it was incorporated or organized and by its constituent documents.

(6) As to each foreign corporation or other entity that is a party to the merger, a statement that the approval of the plan of merger was duly authorized by all action required by the laws under which it was incorporated or organized and by its constituent documents.

B. The original of the articles of merger or exchange, and such number of copies of the articles equal to the number of surviving, new, and acquiring domestic or foreign corporations and other entities that are a party to the merger or exchange or that will be created by the terms thereof, shall be delivered to the Secretary of State. An equal number of copies of the articles of incorporation of each domestic corporation that is to be incorporated pursuant to the plan of merger shall also be delivered to the Secretary of State with the articles of merger.

C. If the Secretary of State finds that the articles of merger or exchange conform to law, he shall, when all fees and franchise taxes have been paid as required by law, or if the plan of merger or exchange (or statement provided in lieu thereof) provides that one or more of the surviving, new, or acquiring domestic or foreign corporations or other entities will be responsible for the payment of all such fees and franchise taxes and that all of such surviving, new, or acquiring domestic or foreign corporations and other entities will be obligated to pay such fees and franchise taxes if the same are not timely paid:

(1) Endorse on the original and each copy the word "Filed," and the month, day, and year of the filing thereof.

(2) File the original in his office.

(3) Issue a certificate of merger or exchange, together with a copy of the articles affixed thereto, to each surviving, new, and acquiring domestic or foreign corporation or other entity that is a party to the merger or exchange or that is created thereby, or its or their respective representatives.

Art. 5.05. Effective Date of Merger or Share Exchange

A. Except as otherwise provided by Article 10.03 of this Act, upon the issuance of the certificate of merger or exchange by the Secretary of State, the merger or share exchange shall be effective.

Art. 5.06. Effect of Merger or Share Exchange

A. When a merger takes effect:

(1) the separate existence of every domestic corporation that is a party to the merger, except any surviving or new domestic corporation, shall cease;

(2) all rights, title and interests to all real estate and other property owned by each domestic or foreign corporation and by each other entity that is a party to the merger shall be allocated to and vested in one or more of the surviving or new domestic or foreign corporations and other entities as provided in the plan of merger without reversion or impairment, without further act or deed, and without any transfer or assignment having occurred, but subject to any existing liens or other encumbrances thereon;

(3) all liabilities and obligations of each domestic or foreign corporation and other entity that is a party to the merger shall be allocated to one or more of the surviving or new domestic or foreign corporations and other entities in the manner set forth in the plan of merger, and each surviving or new domestic or foreign corporation, and each surviving or new other entity to which a liability or obligation shall have been allocated pursuant to the plan of merger, shall be the primary obligor therefor and, except as otherwise set forth in the plan of merger or as otherwise provided by law or contract, no other party to the merger, other than a surviving domestic or foreign corporation or other entity liable thereon at the time of the merger and no other new domestic or foreign corporation or other entity created thereby, shall be liable therefor;

(4) a proceeding pending by or against any domestic or foreign corporation or by or against any other entity that is a party to the merger may be continued as if the merger did not occur, or the surviving or new domestic or foreign corporation or corporations or the surviving or new other entity or other entities to which the liability, obligation, asset or right associated with such proceeding is allocated to and vested in pursuant to the plan of merger may be substituted in the proceeding;

(5) the articles of incorporation of each surviving corporation shall be amended to the extent provided in the plan of merger;

(6) each new domestic corporation, the articles of incorporation of which are set forth in the plan of merger pursuant to Article 5.01 of this Act, shall be incorporated as a corporation under this Act; and each other entity to be incorporated or organized under the laws of this State, the organizational documents of which are set forth in the plan of merger shall, upon an executed copy of the articles of merger being delivered to or filed with any required governmental entity with which organizational documents of such other entity are required to be delivered or filed, and upon meeting such additional requirements, if any, of law for its incorporation or organization, shall be incorporated or organized as provided in the plan of merger; and

(7) the shares of each domestic or foreign corporation and the shares or evidences of ownership in each other entity that is a party to the merger that are to be converted or exchanged, in whole or part, into shares, obligations, evidences of ownership, rights to purchase securities or other securities of one or more of the surviving or new domestic or foreign corporations or other entities, into cash or other property, including shares, obligations, evidences of ownership, rights to purchase securities or other securities of any other person or entity, or into any combination of the foregoing, shall be so converted and exchanged and the former holders of the shares of each domestic corporation that is a party to the merger shall be entitled only to the rights provided in the plan of merger or to their rights under Article 5.11 of this Act.

B. When a share exchange takes effect, the shares of each acquired corporation shall be deemed to have been exchanged as provided in the plan of exchange, and the former holders of the shares exchanged pursuant to the plan of exchange shall be entitled only to the exchange rights provided in the articles of exchange or to their rights under Article 5.11 of this Act and the acquiring domestic or foreign corporation or corporations and the acquiring other entity or other entities of the shares to be acquired and exchanged in the share exchange shall be entitled to all rights, title, and interests with respect to the shares so acquired and exchanged subject to the provisions in the articles of exchange.

C. If the plan of merger shall fail to provide for the allocation and vesting of the right, title, and interest in any particular item of real estate or other property or for the allocation of any liability or obligation of any party to the merger, such item of real estate or other property shall be owned in undivided interest by, or such liability or obligation shall be the joint and several liability and obligation of, each of the surviving and new domestic and foreign corporations and other entities, pro rata to the total number of surviving and new domestic and foreign corporations and other entities resulting from the merger.

Art. 5.08. Conveyance by Corporation

A. Any corporation may convey land by deed, with or without the seal of the corporation, signed by an officer or attorney in fact of the corporation when authorized by appropriate resolution of the board of directors. Such deed, when acknowledged by such officer or attorney in fact to be the act of the corporation, or proved in the manner prescribed for other conveyances of lands, may be recorded in like manner and with the same effect as other deeds. Any such deed when recorded, if signed by an officer of the corporation, shall constitute prima facie evidence that such resolution of the board of directors was duly adopted.

Art. 5.09. Disposition of Assets Authorized by Board of Directors

A. Except as otherwise provided in the articles of incorporation and except as provided in the next sentence of this section, the sale, lease, exchange or other disposition of all, or substantially all, the property and assets of a corporation, when made in the usual and regular course of the business of the corporation, may be made upon such terms and conditions and for such considerations, which may consist in whole or in part of money or property, real or personal, including shares of any other corporation, domestic or foreign, as shall be authorized by its board of directors, without authorization or consent of the shareholders. Except as otherwise provided in the articles of incorporation, the board of directors may authorize any pledge, mortgage, deed of trust or trust indenture and no authorization or consent of the shareholders shall be required for the validity thereof or for any sale pursuant to the terms thereof.

B. A transaction referred to in this Article and in Article 5.10 of this Act shall be in the usual and regular course of business if the corporation shall, directly or indirectly, either continue to engage in one or more businesses or apply a portion of the consideration received in connection with the transaction to the conduct of a business in which it engages following the transaction.

Art. 5.10. Disposition of Assets Requiring Special Authorization of Shareholders; Effect of Disposition Requiring or Not Requiring Authorization; Liability of Acquiring Corporation

A. A sale, lease, exchange, or other disposition (not including any pledge, mortgage, deed of trust or trust indenture unless otherwise provided in the articles of incorporation) of all, or substantially all, the property and assets, with or without the good will of a corporation, if not made in the usual and regular course of its business, may be made upon such terms and conditions and for such consideration, which may consist in whole or in part of money or property, real or personal, including shares of any corporation, domestic or foreign, as may be authorized in the following manner:

(1) The board of directors may adopt a resolution recommending that such sale, lease, exchange, or other disposition be approved by shareholders of the corporation, unless the board of directors determines that for any reason it should not make the recommendation in which case the board of directors may adopt a resolution directing that such sale, lease, exchange, or other disposition be submitted to shareholders without recommendation and, in connection with the submission, communicate the basis for its determination that the sale, lease, exchange or other disposition be submitted without recommendation.

(2) The board of directors may submit the proposed sale, lease, exchange or other disposition for authorization by the corporation's shareholders at a meeting of shareholders, which may be either an annual or a special meeting.

(3) Written or printed notice shall be given to each shareholder of record entitled to vote at such meeting within the time and in the manner provided for in this Act for the giving of notice of meetings of shareholders, and, whether the meeting be an annual or a special meeting shall state that the purpose, or one of the purposes, of such meeting is to consider the proposed sale, lease, exchange, or other disposition.

(4) At such meeting, the shareholders may authorize such sale, lease, exchange or other disposition and may fix, or may authorize the board of directors to fix, any or all of the terms and conditions thereof and the consideration to be received by the corporation therefor. Such authorization shall require the affirmative vote of the holders of at least two-thirds of the outstanding shares of the corporation entitled

to vote thereon, unless any class or series of shares of the corporation is entitled to vote as a class thereon, in which event the vote required for authorization by the shareholders shall be the affirmative vote of the holders of at least two-thirds of the outstanding shares within each such class or series entitled to vote thereon as a class and at least two-thirds of the outstanding shares otherwise entitled to vote thereon. Shares entitled to vote as a class shall be entitled to vote only as a class unless otherwise entitled to vote on each matter submitted to the shareholders generally or provided in the articles of incorporation.

(5) After such authorization by vote of shareholders, the board of directors, nevertheless, in its discretion, may abandon such sale, lease, exchange or other disposition of assets, subject to the rights of third parties under any contracts relating thereto, without further action or approval by shareholders.

B. A disposition of any, all, or substantially all, of the property and assets of a corporation, whether or not it requires the special authorization of the shareholders of the corporation, effected under Section A of this article or under Article 5.09 of this Act or otherwise:

(1) is not considered to be a merger or conversion pursuant to this Act or otherwise; and

(2) except as otherwise expressly provided by another statute, does not make the acquiring corporation, foreign corporation, or other entity responsible or liable for any liability or obligation of the selling corporation that the acquiring corporation, foreign corporation, or other entity did not expressly assume.

Art. 5.11. Rights of Dissenting Shareholders in the Event of Certain Corporate Actions

A. Any shareholder of a domestic corporation shall have the right to dissent from any of the following corporate actions:

(1) Any plan of merger to which the corporation is a party if shareholder approval is required by Article 5.03 or 5.16 of this Act and the shareholder holds shares of a class or series that was entitled to vote thereon as a class or otherwise;

(2) Any sale, lease, exchange or other disposition (not including any pledge, mortgage, deed of trust or trust indenture unless otherwise provided in the articles of incorporation) of all, or substantially all, the property and assets, with or without good will, of a corporation if special authorization of the shareholders is required by this Act and the shareholders hold shares of a class or series that was entitled to vote thereon as a class or otherwise;

(3) Any plan of exchange pursuant to Article 5.02 of this Act in which the shares of the corporation of the class or series held by the shareholder are to be acquired.

B. Notwithstanding the provisions of Section A of this Article, a shareholder shall not have the right to dissent from any plan of merger in which there is a single surviving or new domestic or foreign corporation, or from any plan of exchange, if:

(1) the shares, or depository receipts in respect of the shares, held by the shareholder are part of a class or series, shares, or depository receipts in respect of the shares, of which are on the record date fixed to determine the shareholders entitled to vote on the plan of merger or plan of exchange:

(a) listed on a national securities exchange;

(b) listed on the Nasdaq Stock Market (or successor quotation system) or designated as a national market security on an interdealer quotation system by the National Association of Securities Dealers, Inc., or successor entity; or

(c) held of record by not less than 2,000 holders;

(2) the shareholder is not required by the terms of the plan of merger or plan of exchange to accept for the shareholder's shares any consideration that is different than the consideration (other than cash in lieu of fractional shares that the shareholder would otherwise be entitled to receive) to be provided to any other holder of shares of the same class or series of shares held by such shareholder; and

(3) the shareholder is not required by the terms of the plan of merger or the plan of exchange to accept for the shareholder's shares any consideration other than:

(a) shares, or depository receipts in respect of the shares, of a domestic or foreign corporation that, immediately after the effective time of the merger or exchange, will be part of a class or series, shares, or depository receipts in respect of the shares, of which are:

(i) listed, or authorized for listing upon official notice of issuance, on a national securities exchange;

(ii) approved for quotation as a national market security on an inter-dealer quotation system by the National Association of Securities Dealers, Inc., or successor entity; or

(iii) held of record by not less than 2,000 holders;

(b) cash in lieu of fractional shares otherwise entitled to be received; or

(c) any combination of the securities and cash described in Subdivisions (a) and (b) of this subsection.

Art. 5.12. Procedure for Dissent by Shareholders as to Said Corporate Actions

A. Any shareholder of any domestic corporation who has the right to dissent from any of the corporate actions referred to in Article 5.11 of this Act may exercise that right to dissent only by complying with the following procedures:

(1)(a) With respect to proposed corporate action that is submitted to a vote of shareholders at a meeting, the shareholder shall file with the corporation, prior to the meeting, a written objection to the action, setting out that the shareholder's right to dissent will be exercised if the action is effective and giving the shareholder's address, to which notice thereof shall be delivered or mailed in that event. If the action is effected and the shareholder shall not have voted in favor of the action, the corporation, in the case of action other than a merger, or the surviving or new corporation (foreign or domestic) or other entity that is liable to discharge the shareholder's right of dissent, in the case of a merger, shall, within ten (10) days after the action is effected, deliver or mail to the shareholder written notice that the action has been effected, and the shareholder may, within ten (10) days from the delivery or mailing of the notice, make written demand on the existing, surviving, or new corporation (foreign or domestic) or other entity, as the case may be, for payment of the fair value of the shareholder's shares. The fair value of the shares shall be the value thereof as of the day immediately preceding the meeting, excluding any appreciation or depreciation in anticipation of the proposed action. The demand shall state the number and class of the shares owned by the shareholder and the fair value of the shares as estimated by the shareholder. Any shareholder failing to make demand within the ten (10) day period shall be bound by the action.

(b) With respect to proposed corporate action that is approved pursuant to Section A of Article 9.10 of this Act, the corporation, in the case of action other than a merger, and the surviving or new corporation (foreign or domestic) or other entity that is liable to discharge the shareholder's right of dissent, in the case of a merger, shall, within ten (10) days after the date the action is effected, mail to each shareholder of record as of the effective date of the action notice of the fact and

date of the action and that the shareholder may exercise the shareholder's right to dissent from the action. The notice shall be accompanied by a copy of this Article and any articles or documents filed by the corporation with the Secretary of State to effect the action. If the shareholder shall not have consented to the taking of the action, the shareholder may, within twenty (20) days after the mailing of the notice, make written demand on the existing, surviving, or new corporation (foreign or domestic) or other entity, as the case may be, for payment of the fair value of the shareholder's shares. The fair value of the shares shall be the value thereof as of the date the written consent authorizing the action was delivered to the corporation pursuant to Section A of Article 9.10 of this Act, excluding any appreciation or depreciation in anticipation of the action. The demand shall state the number and class of shares owned by the dissenting shareholder and the fair value of the shares as estimated by the shareholder. Any shareholder failing to make demand within the twenty (20) day period shall be bound by the action.

(2) Within twenty (20) days after receipt by the existing, surviving, or new corporation (foreign or domestic) or other entity, as the case may be, of a demand for payment made by a dissenting shareholder in accordance with Subsection (1) of this Section, the corporation (foreign or domestic) or other entity shall deliver or mail to the shareholder a written notice that shall either set out that the corporation (foreign or domestic) or other entity accepts the amount claimed in the demand and agrees to pay that amount within ninety (90) days after the date on which the action was effected, and, in the case of shares represented by certificates, upon the surrender of the certificates duly endorsed, or shall contain an estimate by the corporation (foreign or domestic) or other entity of the fair value of the shares, together with an offer to pay the amount of that estimate within ninety (90) days after the date on which the action was effected, upon receipt of notice within sixty (60) days after that date from the shareholder that the shareholder agrees to accept that amount and, in the case of shares represented by certificates, upon the surrender of the certificates duly endorsed.

(3) If, within sixty (60) days after the date on which the corporate action was effected, the value of the shares is agreed upon between the shareholder and the existing, surviving, or new corporation (foreign or domestic) or other entity, as the case may be, payment for the shares shall be made within ninety (90) days after the date on which the action was effected and, in the case of shares represented by certificates, upon surrender of the certificates duly endorsed. Upon payment of the agreed value, the shareholder shall cease to have any interest in the shares or in the corporation.

B. If, within the period of sixty (60) days after the date on which the corporate action was effected, the shareholder and the existing, surviving, or new corporation (foreign or domestic) or other entity, as the case may be, do not so agree, then the shareholder or the corporation (foreign or domestic) or other entity may, within sixty (60) days after the expiration of the sixty (60) day period, file a petition in any court of competent jurisdiction in the county in which the principal office of the domestic corporation is located, asking for a finding and determination of the fair value of the shareholder's shares. Upon the filing of any such petition by the shareholder, service of a copy thereof shall be made upon the corporation (foreign or domestic) or other entity, which shall, within ten (10) days after service, file in the office of the clerk of the court in which the petition was filed a list containing the names and addresses of all shareholders of the domestic corporation who have demanded payment for their shares and with whom agreements as to the value of their shares have not been reached by the corporation (foreign or domestic) or other entity. If the petition shall be filed by the corporation (foreign or domestic) or other entity, the petition shall be accompanied by such a list. The clerk of the court shall give notice of the time and place fixed for the hearing of the petition by registered mail to the corporation (foreign or domestic) or other entity and to the shareholders named on the list at the addresses therein stated. The forms of the notices by mail shall be approved by the court. All shareholders thus notified and the corporation (foreign or domestic) or other entity shall thereafter be bound by the final judgment of the court.

C. After the hearing of the petition, the court shall determine the shareholders who have complied with the provisions of this Article and have become entitled to the valuation of and payment for their shares, and shall appoint one or more qualified appraisers to determine that value. The appraisers shall have power to examine any of the books and records of the corporation the shares of which they are charged with the duty of valuing, and they shall make a determination of the fair value of the shares upon such investigation as to them may seem proper. The appraisers shall also afford a reasonable opportunity to the parties interested to submit to them pertinent evidence as to the value of the shares. The appraisers shall also have such power and authority as may be conferred on Masters in Chancery by the Rules of Civil Procedure or by the order of their appointment.

D. The appraisers shall determine the fair value of the shares of the shareholders adjudged by the court to be entitled to payment for their shares and shall file their report of that value in the office of the clerk of the court. Notice of the filing of the report shall be given by the clerk to the parties in interest. The report shall be subject to exceptions to be heard before the court both upon the law and the facts. The court shall by its judgment determine the fair value of the shares of the shareholders entitled to payment for their shares and shall direct the payment of that value by the existing, surviving, or new corporation (foreign or domestic) or other entity, together with interest thereon, beginning 91 days after the date on which the applicable corporate action from which the shareholder elected to dissent was effected to the date of such judgment, to the shareholders entitled to payment. The judgment shall be payable to the holders of uncertificated shares immediately but to the holders of shares represented by certificates only upon, and simultaneously with, the surrender to the existing, surviving, or new corporation (foreign or domestic) or other entity, as the case may be, of duly endorsed certificates for those shares. Upon payment of the judgment, the dissenting shareholders shall cease to have any interest in those shares or in the corporation. The court shall allow the appraisers a reasonable fee as court costs, and all court costs shall be allotted between the parties in the manner that the court determines to be fair and equitable.

E. Shares acquired by the existing, surviving, or new corporation (foreign or domestic) or other entity, as the case may be, pursuant to the payment of the agreed value of the shares or pursuant to payment of the judgment entered for the value of the shares, as in this Article provided, shall, in the case of a merger, be treated as provided in the plan of merger and, in all other cases, may be held and disposed of by the corporation as in the case of other treasury shares.

F. The provisions of this Article shall not apply to a merger if, on the date of the filing of the articles of merger, the surviving corporation is the owner of all the outstanding shares of the other corporations, domestic or foreign, that are parties to the merger.

G. In the absence of fraud in the transaction, the remedy provided by this Article to a shareholder objecting to any corporate action referred to in Article 5.11 of this Act is the exclusive remedy for the recovery of the value of his shares or money damages to the shareholder with respect to the action. If the existing, surviving, or new corporation (foreign or domestic) or other entity, as the case may be, complies with the requirements of this Article, any shareholder who fails to comply with the requirements of this Article shall not be entitled to bring suit for the recovery of the value of his shares or money damages to the shareholder with respect to the action.

Art. 5.13. Provisions Affecting Remedies of Dissenting Shareholders

A. Any shareholder who has demanded payment for his shares in accordance with either Article 5.12 or 5.16 of this Act shall not thereafter be entitled to vote or exercise any other rights of a shareholder except the right to receive payment for his shares pursuant to the provisions of those articles and the right to maintain an appropriate action to obtain relief on the ground that the corporate action would be or was fraudulent, and the respective shares for which payment has been demanded shall not thereafter be considered outstanding for the purposes of any subsequent vote of shareholders.

B. Upon receiving a demand for payment from any dissenting shareholder, the corporation shall make an appropriate notation thereof in its shareholder records. Within twenty (20) days after demanding payment for his shares in accordance with either Article 5.12 or 5.16 of this Act, each holder of certificates representing shares so demanding payment shall submit such certificates to the corporation for notation thereon that such demand has been made. The failure of holders of certificated shares to do so shall, at the option of the corporation, terminate such shareholder's rights under Articles 5.12 and 5.16 of this Act unless a court of competent jurisdiction for good and sufficient cause shown shall otherwise direct. If uncertificated shares for which payment has been demanded or shares represented by a certificate on which notation has been so made shall be transferred, any new certificate issued therefor shall bear similar notation together with the name of the original dissenting holder of such shares and a transferee of such shares shall acquire by such transfer no rights in the corporation other than those which the original dissenting shareholder had after making demand for payment of the fair value thereof.

C. Any shareholder who has demanded payment for his shares in accordance with either Article 5.12 or 5.16 of this Act may withdraw such demand at any time before payment for his shares or before any petition has been filed pursuant to Article 5.12 or 5.16 of this Act asking for a finding and determination of the fair value of such shares, but no such demand may be withdrawn after such payment has been made or, unless the corporation shall consent thereto, after any such petition has been filed. If, however, such demand shall be withdrawn as hereinbefore provided, or if pursuant to Section B of this Article the corporation shall terminate the shareholder's rights under Article 5.12 or 5.16 of this Act, as the case may be, or if no petition asking for a finding and determination of fair value of such shares by a court shall have been filed within the time provided in Article 5.12 or 5.16 of this Act, as the case may be, or if after the hearing of a petition filed pursuant to Article 5.12 or 5.16, the court shall determine that such shareholder is not entitled to the relief provided by those articles, then, in any such case, such shareholder and all persons claiming under him shall be conclusively presumed to have approved and ratified the corporate action from which he dissented and shall be bound thereby, the right of such shareholder to be paid the fair value of his shares shall cease, and his status as a shareholder shall be restored without prejudice to any corporate proceedings which may have been taken during the interim, and such shareholder shall be entitled to receive any dividends or other distributions made to shareholders in the interim.

Art. 5.14. Derivative Proceedings

A. Certain Definitions. For purposes of this Article:

(1) "Derivative proceeding" means a civil suit in the right of a domestic corporation or, to the extent provided in Section K of this Article, in the right of a foreign corporation.

(2) "Shareholder" includes a beneficial owner whose shares are held in a voting trust or by a nominee on the beneficial owner's behalf.

B. Standing. A shareholder may not commence or maintain a derivative proceeding unless the shareholder:

(1) was a shareholder of the corporation at the time of the act or omission complained of or became a shareholder by operation of law from a person that was a shareholder at that time; and

(2) fairly and adequately represents the interests of the corporation in enforcing the right of the corporation.

C. Demand. No shareholder may commence a derivative proceeding until:

(1) a written demand is filed with the corporation setting forth with particularity the act, omission, or other matter that is the subject of the claim or challenge and requesting that the corporation take suitable action; and

(2) 90 days have expired from the date the demand was made, unless the shareholder has earlier been notified that the demand has been rejected by the corporation or unless irreparable injury to the corporation is being suffered or would result by waiting for the expiration of the 90-day period.

D. Stay; Discovery. (1) If the domestic or foreign corporation commences an inquiry into the allegations made in a demand or petition and the person or group described in Section H of this Article is conducting an active review of the allegations in good faith, the court shall stay a derivative proceeding until the review is completed and a determination is made by the person or group as to what further action, if any, should be taken. To obtain a stay, the domestic or foreign corporation must provide the court with a written statement containing an undertaking to advise the court and the shareholder making the demand of the determination promptly on the completion of the review of the matter. A stay shall, on motion, be reviewed as to its continued necessity every 60 days thereafter. If the review and determination by the person or group described in Section H of this Article is not completed within 60 days, the stay may be renewed for one or more additional 60-day periods on the domestic or foreign corporation providing the court and the shareholder making the demand with a written statement of the status of the review and the reasons a continued extension of the stay is necessary.

(2) If a domestic or foreign corporation proposes to dismiss a derivative proceeding pursuant to Section F of this Article, discovery by a shareholder following the filing of the derivative proceeding in accordance with the provisions of this Article shall be limited to facts relating to whether the person or group described in Section H of this Article is independent and disinterested, the good faith of the inquiry and review by such person or group, and the reasonableness of the procedures followed by such person or group in conducting its review

and will not extend to any facts or substantive matters with respect to the act, omission, or other matter that is the subject matter of the action in the derivative proceeding. The scope of discovery may be expanded if the court determines after notice and hearing that a good faith review of the allegations for purposes of Section F of this Article has not been made by an independent and disinterested person or group in accordance with Section F of this Article.

E. Tolling of the Statute of Limitations. A written demand filed with the corporation under Section C of this Article tolls the statute of limitations on the claim on which demand is made until the earlier of (1) 90 days or (2) 30 days after the corporation advises the shareholder that the demand has been rejected or the review has been completed.

F. Dismissal of Derivative Proceeding. A court shall dismiss a derivative proceeding on a motion by the corporation if the person or group described in Section H of this Article determines in good faith, after conducting a reasonable inquiry and based on the factors as the person or group deems appropriate under the circumstances, that the continuation of the derivative proceeding is not in the best interests of the corporation. In determining whether the requirements of the previous sentence have been met, the burden of proof shall be on:

(1) the plaintiff shareholder, if a majority of the board of directors consists of independent and disinterested directors at the time the determination is made or if the determination is made by a panel of one or more independent and disinterested persons appointed under Section H(3) of this Article; or

(2) the corporation, in all other circumstances; provided that if the corporation presents prima facie evidence that demonstrates that the directors appointed pursuant to Section H(2) of this Article are independent and disinterested, the burden of proof is on the plaintiff shareholder.

G. Commencement of Proceeding After Rejection of Demand. If a derivative proceeding is commenced after a demand is rejected, the petition must allege with particularity facts that establish that the rejection was not made in accordance with the requirements of Sections F and H of this Article.

H. Determination by Directors or Independent Persons. The determination described in Section F of this Article must be made by:

(1) a majority vote of independent and disinterested directors present at a meeting of the board of directors at which interested directors are not present (at the time of the vote) if the independent and disinterested directors constitute a quorum of the board of directors;

(2) a majority vote of a committee consisting of two or more independent and disinterested directors appointed by a majority vote of one or more independent and disinterested directors present at a meeting of the board of directors, whether or not the independent and disinterested directors so acting constitute a quorum of the board of directors; or

(3) a panel of one or more independent and disinterested persons appointed by the court on a motion by the corporation setting forth the names of the persons to be so appointed together with a statement that to the best of its knowledge the persons so proposed are disinterested persons and qualified to make the determinations contemplated by Section F of this Article. Such panel shall be appointed if the court finds that such persons are independent and disinterested persons and are otherwise qualified in regard to expertise, experience, independent judgment, and other factors deemed appropriate by the court under the circumstances to make such determinations. Persons appointed by the court shall have no liability to the corporation or its shareholders

for any action or omission taken by them in that capacity, absent fraud or wilful misconduct.

I. Discontinuance or Settlement. A derivative proceeding may not be discontinued or settled without the approval of the court. If the court determines that a proposed discontinuance or settlement may substantially affect the interest of other shareholders, it shall direct that notice be given to the affected shareholders.

J. Payment of Expenses. (1) On termination of a derivative proceeding, the court may order:

(a) the domestic or foreign corporation to pay the expenses of the plaintiff incurred in the proceeding if it finds that the proceeding has resulted in a substantial benefit to the domestic or foreign corporation;

(b) the plaintiff to pay the expenses of the domestic or foreign corporation or any defendant incurred in investigating and defending the proceeding if it finds that the proceeding was commenced or maintained without reasonable cause or for an improper purpose; or

(c) a party to pay the expenses incurred by another party (including the domestic or foreign corporation) because of the filing of a pleading, motion, or other paper, if it finds that the pleading, motion, or other paper (i) was not well grounded in fact after reasonable inquiry, (ii) was not warranted by existing law or a good faith argument for the extension, modification, or reversal of existing law, or (iii) was interposed for an improper purpose, such as to harass or to cause unnecessary delay or needless increase in the cost of litigation.

(2) For purposes of this section, "expenses" mean reasonable expenses incurred in the defense of a derivative proceeding, including without limitation:

(a) attorney's fees;

(b) costs in pursuing an investigation of the matter that was the subject of the derivative proceeding; and

(c) expenses for which the domestic or foreign corporation or a corporate defendant may be required to indemnify another person.

K. Application to Foreign Corporations. In any derivative proceeding brought in the right of a foreign corporation, the matters covered by this Article are governed by the laws of the jurisdiction of incorporation of the foreign corporation, except for Sections D, I, and J of this Article, which are procedural and not matters relating to the internal affairs of the foreign corporation. In the case of matters relating to a foreign corporation under Section D of this Article, references to a person or group described in Section H of this Article are to be deemed to refer to a person or group entitled under the laws of the jurisdiction of incorporation of the foreign corporation to review and dispose of a derivative proceeding, and the standard of review of a decision by the person or group to dismiss the derivative proceeding is to be governed by the laws of the jurisdiction of incorporation of the foreign corporation.

L. Closely Held Corporations. (1) The provisions of Sections B through H of this Article are not applicable to a closely held corporation. If justice requires:

(a) a derivative proceeding brought by a shareholder of a closely held corporation may be treated by a court as a direct action brought by the shareholder for his own benefit; and

(b) a recovery in a direct or derivative proceeding by a shareholder may be paid either directly to the plaintiff or to the corporation if necessary to protect the interests of creditors or other shareholders of the corporation.

(2) For purposes of this section, a "closely held corporation" means a corporation:

(a) with less than 35 shareholders; and

(b) that has no shares listed on a national securities exchange or regularly quoted in an over-the-counter market by one or more members of a national securities association.

Art. 5.15. Antitrust Laws; Creditors

Nothing contained in Part 5 of this Act shall ever be construed as affecting, nullifying or repealing the Anti-trust laws or as abridging any right or rights of any creditor under existing laws.

Art. 5.16. Merger with Subsidiary Entities

A. In any case in which at least ninety (90%) per cent of the outstanding shares of each class and series of shares, membership interests, or other ownership interests of one or more domestic or foreign corporations or other entities, other than a corporation that has in its articles of incorporation the provision required by Article 5.03(H)(6)(a) of this Act, of which there are outstanding shares that would be entitled to vote on the merger absent this section, is owned by another domestic or foreign corporation or other entity, and at least one of the parent or subsidiary entities is a domestic corporation and the other or others are domestic corporations, foreign corporations, or other entities organized under the laws of a jurisdiction that permit such a merger or whose organizational documents or other constituent documents not inconsistent with those laws permit such a merger, the corporation or other entity may enter into a merger:

(a) in the event that the corporation or other entity having at least 90 percent ownership will be a surviving entity in the merger, by executing and filing articles of merger in accordance with Section B of this Article; or

(b) in the event that the corporation or other entity having at least 90 percent ownership will not be a surviving entity in the merger, by the entity having such ownership adopting a plan of merger in the manner required by the laws of its jurisdiction of organization or formation and its organizational or other constituent documents, except that no action under Section 5.03 shall be required to be taken by the corporation or corporations whose shares are so owned, and executing and filing articles of merger in accordance with Section B of this Article.

B. The articles of merger shall be signed on behalf of the parent entity by an officer or other duly authorized representative of the parent entity and shall set forth:

(1) The name of the parent entity and the name of each subsidiary entity and the type of entity and respective jurisdiction under which each subsidiary entity is organized.

(2) The total number or percentage of outstanding shares, membership interests, or other ownership interests, identified by class, series, or group, and the number or percentage of shares, membership interests, or other ownership interests in each class, series, or group owned by the parent entity.

(3) A copy of the resolution or merger adopted by the parent entity in accordance with the laws of its jurisdiction of organization or formation and its organizational or other constituent documents together with a statement that the resolution was so adopted and the date of the adoption thereof. If the parent entity does not own all the outstanding shares, membership interests, or other ownership interests of each class of each subsidiary entity that is a party to the merger, the resolution shall state the terms and conditions of the merger, including the cash or other property, including shares, obligations, evidences of ownership, rights to purchase securities, or other securities of any person or entity or any combination of the shares, obligations, evi-

dences of ownership, rights, or other securities, to be used, paid or delivered by the surviving entity upon surrender of each share, membership interest, or other ownership interest of the subsidiary entity or entities not owned by the parent entity.

(4) If the surviving entity is a foreign corporation or other entity, the address, including street number if any, of its registered or principal office in the jurisdiction under whose laws it is governed. If the surviving entity is a foreign corporation or other entity, on the merger taking effect the surviving entity is deemed to (a) appoint the Secretary of State of this state as its agent for service of process to enforce an obligation or the rights of dissenting shareholders of each domestic corporation that is a party to the merger, and (b) agree that it will promptly pay to the dissenting shareholders of each domestic corporation that is a party to the merger the amount, if any, to which they are entitled under this Article.

(5) If a plan of merger is required by Section A of this Article to be adopted in the manner required by Article 5.03 of this Act, the information required by Section A of Article 5.04 of this Act.

C. The articles of merger shall be delivered to the Secretary of State and filed as provided by Sections B and C of Article 5.04 of this Act.

D. The effective date and the effect of such merger shall be the same as provided in Articles 5.05 and 5.06 of this Act if the surviving entity is a domestic corporation. If the surviving entity is a foreign corporation or other entity, the effective date and the effect of such merger shall be the same as in the case of the merger of domestic corporations except in so far as the laws of such other jurisdiction provide otherwise.

E. In the event all of the shares of a subsidiary domestic corporation that is a party to a merger effected under this Article are not owned by the parent entity immediately prior to the merger, the surviving parent entity shall, within ten (10) days after the effective date of the merger, mail to each shareholder of record of each subsidiary domestic corporation a copy of the articles of merger and notify the shareholder that the merger has become effective. Any such shareholder who holds shares of a class or series that would have been entitled to vote on the merger if it had been effected pursuant to Article 5.03 of this Act shall have the right to dissent from the merger and demand payment of the fair value for the shareholder's shares in lieu of the cash or other property to be used, paid or delivered to such shareholder upon the surrender of such shareholder's shares pursuant to the terms and conditions of the merger, with the following procedure:

(1) Such shareholder shall within twenty (20) days after the mailing of the notice and copy of the articles of merger make written demand on the surviving parent entity for payment of the fair value of the shareholder's shares. The fair value of the shares shall be the value thereof as of the day before the effective date of the merger, excluding any appreciation or depreciation in anticipation of such act. The demand shall state the number and class of the shares owned by the dissenting shareholder and the fair value of such shares as estimated by the shareholder. Any shareholder failing to make demand within the twenty (20) day period shall be bound by the corporate action.

(2) Within ten (10) days after receipt by the surviving entity of a demand for payment by the dissenting shareholder of the fair value of the shareholder's shares in accordance with Subsection (1) of this section, the surviving entity shall deliver or mail to the dissenting shareholder a written notice which shall either set out that the surviving entity accepts the amount claimed in the demand and agrees to pay such amount within ninety (90) days after the date on which the corporate action was effected and, in the case of shares represented by

certificates, upon the surrender of the shares certificates duly endorsed, or shall contain an estimate by the surviving parent entity of the fair value of such shares, together with an offer to pay the amount of that estimate within ninety (90) days after the date on which such corporate action was effected, upon receipt of notice within sixty (60) days after that date from the shareholder that the shareholder agrees to accept that amount and, in the case of shares represented by certificates, upon the surrender of the shares certificates duly endorsed.

(3) If, within sixty (60) days after the date on which the corporate action was effected, the value of the shares is agreed upon between the dissenting shareholder and the surviving entity, payment for the shares shall be made within ninety (90) days after the date on which the corporate action was effected and, in the case of shares represented by certificates, upon surrender of the certificate or certificates representing such shares. Upon payment of the agreed value, the dissenting shareholder shall cease to have any interest in such shares or in the corporation.

(4) If, within sixty (60) days after the date on which such corporate action was effected, the shareholder and the surviving entity do not so agree, then the dissenting shareholder or the surviving entity may, within sixty (60) days after the expiration of the sixty (60) day period, file a petition in any court of competent jurisdiction in the county in which the principal office of the corporation is located, asking for a finding and determination of the fair value of the shareholder's shares as provided in Section B of Article 5.12 of this Act and thereupon the parties shall have the rights and duties and follow the procedure set forth in Sections B to D inclusive of Article 5.12.

(5) In the absence of fraud in the transaction, the remedy provided by this Article to a shareholder objecting to the corporate action is the exclusive remedy for the recovery of the value of the shareholder's shares or money damages to the shareholder with respect to the corporate action. If the surviving entity complies with the requirements of this Article, any such shareholder who fails to comply with the requirements of this Article shall not be entitled to bring suit for the recovery of the value of the shareholder's shares or money damages to such shareholder with respect to such corporate action.

F. If a plan of merger is required by Section A of this Article to be adopted in the manner required by Article 5.03 of this Act, the provisions of Articles 5.11 and 5.12 of this Act shall apply to the rights of the shareholders of a parent corporation to dissent from such merger. Except as otherwise provided in this Article, the provisions of Articles 5.11 and 5.12 of this Act shall not be applicable to a merger effected under the provisions of this Article. The provisions of Article 5.13 of this Act shall be applicable to any merger effected under the provisions of this Article to the extent provided in Article 5.13 of this Act.

Art. 5.17. Conversion

A. A domestic corporation may adopt a plan of conversion and convert to a foreign corporation or any other entity if:

(1) the converting entity acts on and its shareholders approve a plan of conversion in the manner prescribed by Article 5.03 of this Act as if the conversion were a merger to which the converting entity were a party and not the survivor;

(2) the conversion (a) is permitted by, or not inconsistent with, the laws of the state or country in which the converted entity is to be incorporated, formed, or organized, and (b) the incorporation, formation, or organization of the converted entity is effected in compliance with such laws;

(3) at the time the conversion becomes effective, each shareholder of the converting entity (other than those who receive payment of their shares under Article 5.12 of this Act) will, unless otherwise agreed to by that shareholder, own an equity interest or other ownership or security interest in, and be a shareholder, partner, member, owner, or other security holder of, the converted entity;

(4) no shareholder of the domestic corporation will, as a result of the conversion, become personally liable, without the shareholder's consent, for the liabilities or obligations of the converted entity; and

(5) the converted entity shall be incorporated, formed, or organized as part of or pursuant to the plan of conversion.

B. Any foreign corporation or other entity may adopt a plan of conversion and convert to a domestic corporation if:

(1) the conversion is permitted by the laws of the state or country in which the foreign corporation is incorporated, if a foreign corporation is converting;

(2) the conversion is either permitted by the laws under which the other entity is formed or organized or by the constituent documents of the other entity that are not inconsistent with the laws of the state or country in which the other entity is formed or organized, if another entity is converting; and

(3) the converting entity takes all action that may be required by the laws of the state or country under which it is incorporated, formed, or organized and by its constituent documents to effect the conversion.

C. A plan of conversion shall set forth:

(1) the name of the converting entity and the converted entity;

(2) a statement that the converting entity is continuing its existence in the organizational form of the converted entity;

(3) a statement as to the type of entity that the converted entity is to be and the state or country under the laws of which the converted entity is to be incorporated, formed, or organized;

(4) the manner and basis of converting the shares or other evidences of ownership of the converting entity into shares or other evidences of ownership or securities of the converted entity, or any combination thereof;

(5) in an attachment or exhibit, the articles of incorporation of the domestic corporation, if the converted entity is a domestic corporation; and

(6) in an attachment or exhibit, the articles of incorporation or other organizational documents of the converted entity, if the converted entity is not a domestic corporation.

D. A plan of conversion may set forth such other provisions relating to the conversion not inconsistent with law, including the initial bylaws and officers of the converted entity.

E. After a conversion of a corporation is approved, and at any time before the conversion has become effective, the plan of conversion may be abandoned (subject to any contractual rights) by the converting entity, without shareholder action, in accordance with the procedures set forth in the plan of conversion or, if any such procedures are not set forth in the plan, in the manner determined by the board of directors. If articles of conversion have been filed with the Secretary of State but the conversion has not become effective, the conversion may be abandoned if a statement, executed on behalf of the converting entity by an officer or other duly authorized representative and stating that the plan of conversion has been abandoned in accordance with applicable law, is filed with the Secretary of State prior to the effectiveness of the conversion. If the Secretary of State finds that such statement conforms to law, the Secretary of State shall, when all fees have been paid as required by law:

(1) endorse on the original and each copy the word "Filed" and the month, day, and year of the filing;

(2) file the original in his office; and

(3) issue a certificate of abandonment to the converting entity or its representatives.

F. On the filing of the statement described by Section E of this Article by the Secretary of State, the conversion shall be deemed abandoned and shall not become effective.

Art. 5.18. Articles of Conversion

A. If a plan of conversion has been approved in accordance with Article 5.17 of this Act and has not been abandoned, articles of conversion shall be executed by the converting entity by an officer or other duly authorized representative and shall set forth:

(1) the plan of conversion or a statement certifying the following:

(a) the name, state or country of incorporation, formation, and organization of the converting entity, and organizational form of the converting entity;

(b) that a plan of conversion has been approved;

(c) that an executed plan of conversion is on file at the principal place of business of the converting entity, stating the address thereof, and that an executed plan of conversion will be on file, from and after the conversion, at the principal place of business of the converted entity, stating the address thereof; and

(d) that a copy of the plan of conversion will be furnished by the converting entity (prior to the conversion) or the converted entity (after the conversion), on written request and without cost, to any shareholder of the converting entity or the converted entity;

(2) if the converting entity is a domestic corporation, the number of shares outstanding and, if the shares of any class or series are entitled to vote as a class, the designation and number of outstanding shares of each such class or series;

(3) if the converting entity is a domestic corporation, the number of outstanding shares, not entitled to vote only as a class, voted for and against the plan, respectively, and, if the shares of any class or series are entitled to vote as a class, the number of shares of each such class or series voted for and against the plan, respectively; and

(4) if the converting entity is a foreign corporation or other entity, a statement that the approval of the plan of conversion was duly authorized by all action required by the laws under which it was incorporated, formed, or organized and by its constituent documents.

B. The original and one copy of the articles of conversion shall be delivered to the Secretary of State. Two copies of the articles of incorporation of the domestic corporation, if the converted entity is a domestic corporation, shall also be delivered to the Secretary of State with the articles of conversion.

C. If the Secretary of State finds that the articles of conversion conform to law, has received all filings required to be received, and has issued all certificates required to be issued in connection with the incorporation, formation, or organization of the converted entity, if any, the Secretary of State shall, when all fees and franchise taxes have been paid as required by law or if the articles of conversion provide that the converted entity will be liable for the payment of all such fees and franchise taxes:

(1) endorse on the original and each copy the word "Filed" and the month, day, and year of the filing;

(2) file the original in his office; and

(3) issue a certificate of conversion, together with a copy of the articles affixed thereto, to the converted entity or its representatives.

Art. 5.19. Effective Date of Conversion

A. Except as otherwise provided by Article 10.03 of this Act, on the issuance of the certificate of conversion by the Secretary of State, the conversion of a converting entity shall be effective.

Art. 5.20. Effect of Conversion

A. When a conversion of a converting entity takes effect:

(1) the converting entity shall continue to exist, without interruption, but in the organizational form of the converted entity rather than in its prior organizational form;

(2) all rights, title, and interests to all real estate and other property owned by the converting entity shall continue to be owned by the converted entity in its new organizational form without reversion or impairment, without further act or deed, and without any transfer or assignment having occurred, but subject to any existing liens or other encumbrances thereon;

(3) all liabilities and obligations of the converting entity shall continue to be liabilities and obligations of the converted entity in its new organizational form without impairment or diminution by reason of the conversion;

(4) all rights of creditors or other parties with respect to or against the prior interest holders or other owners of the converting entity in their capacities as such in existence as of the effective time of the conversion will continue in existence as to those liabilities and obligations and may be pursued by such creditors and obligees as if the conversion had not occurred;

(5) a proceeding pending by or against the converting entity or by or against any of the converting entity's interest holders or owners in their capacities as such may be continued by or against the converted entity in its new organizational form and by or against the prior interest holders or owners, as the case may be, without any need for substitution of parties;

(6) the shares and other evidences of ownership in the converting entity that are to be converted into shares, evidences of ownership, or other securities in the converted entity as provided in the plan of conversion shall be so converted, and if the converting entity is a domestic corporation, the former holders of shares in the domestic corporation shall be entitled only to the rights provided in the plan of conversion or to their rights under Article 5.11 of this Act;

(7) if, after the effectiveness of the conversion, a shareholder, partner, member, or other owner of the converted entity would be liable under applicable law, in such capacity, for the debts or obligations of the converted entity, such shareholder, partner, member, or other owner of the converted entity shall be liable for the debts and obligations of the converting entity that existed before the conversion takes effect only to the extent that such shareholder, partner, member, or other owner: (a) agreed in writing to be liable for such debts or obligations, (b) was liable under applicable law, prior to the effectiveness of the conversion, for such debts or obligations, or (c) by becoming a shareholder, partner, member, or other owner of the converted entity, becomes liable under applicable law for existing debts and obligations of the converted entity;

(8) if the converted entity is a foreign corporation or other entity, such converted entity shall be deemed to: (a) appoint the Secretary of State in this state as its agent for service of process in a proceeding to enforce any obligation or the rights of dissenting shareholders of the converting domestic corporation, and (b) agree that it will promptly pay the dissenting shareholders of the converting domestic corporation the amount, if any, to which they are entitled under Article 5.11 of this Act; and

(9) if the converting corporation is a domestic corporation, the provisions of Articles 5.11, 5.12, and 5.13 of this Act shall apply as if the converted entity were the survivor of a merger with the converting entity.

Business Corporation Act
Part 6.

Art. 6.01. Voluntary Dissolution by Incorporators or Directors

A. A corporation which has not commenced business and which has not issued any shares, may be voluntarily dissolved by its incorporators or its directors at any time in the following manner:

(1) Articles of dissolution shall be signed by a majority of the incorporators or directors and shall set forth:

(a) The name of the corporation.

(b) The date of issuance of its certificate of incorporation.

(c) That none of its shares has been issued.

(d) That the corporation has not commenced business.

(e) That the amount, if any, actually paid on subscriptions for its shares, less any part thereof disbursed for necessary expenses, has been returned to those entitled thereto.

(f) That no debts of the corporation remain unpaid.

(g) That a majority of the incorporators or directors elect that the corporation be dissolved.

(2) The original and a copy of the articles of dissolution shall be delivered to the Secretary of State, along with a certificate from the Comptroller of Public Accounts that all franchise taxes have been paid. If the Secretary of State finds that the articles of dissolution conform to law, he shall, when the appropriate filing fee is paid as required by law:

(a) Endorse on the original and the copy the word "Filed," and the month, day, and year of the filing thereof.

(b) File the original in his office.

(c) Issue a certificate of dissolution, to which he shall affix the copy.

(3) The certificate of dissolution, together with the copy of the articles of dissolution affixed thereto by the Secretary of State, shall be delivered to the incorporators, the directors, or their representatives. Upon the issuance of such certificate of dissolution by the Secretary of State, the existence of the corporation shall cease.

Art. 6.02. Voluntary Dissolution by Consent of Shareholders

A. A corporation may be voluntarily dissolved by the written consent of all of its shareholders.

B. Upon the execution of such written consent and after compliance with other provisions of this Act, the corporation shall file articles of dissolution as provided in this Act.

Art. 6.03. Voluntary Dissolution by Act of Corporation

A. A corporation may be dissolved by the act of the corporation when authorized in the following manner:

(1) The board of directors shall adopt a resolution recommending that the corporation be dissolved, and directing that the question of such dissolution be submitted to a vote at a meeting of shareholders, which may be either an annual or a special meeting.

(2) Written or printed notice shall be given to each shareholder of record entitled to vote at such meeting within the time and in the manner provided in this Act for the giving of notice of meetings of shareholders, and, whether the meeting be an annual or special meet-

ing, shall state that the purpose, or one of the purposes, of such meeting is to consider the advisability of dissolving the corporation.

(3) At such meeting a vote of shareholders entitled to vote thereat shall be taken on a resolution to dissolve the corporation. Such resolution shall be adopted on receiving the affirmative vote of the holders of at least two-thirds of the outstanding shares of the corporation entitled to vote thereon unless any class or series of shares is entitled to vote as a class thereon, in which event the resolution shall require for its adoption the affirmative vote of the holders of at least two-thirds of the outstanding shares within each class or series of shares entitled to vote as a class thereon and at least two-thirds of the outstanding shares otherwise entitled to vote thereon. Shares entitled to vote as a class shall be entitled to vote only as a class unless otherwise entitled to vote on each matter generally as provided in the articles of incorporation.

B. Upon the adoption of such resolution and after compliance with other provisions of this Act, the corporation shall file articles of dissolution as provided in this Act.

Art. 6.04. Procedure Before Filing Articles of Dissolution

A. Before filing articles of dissolution:

(1) The corporation shall cease to carry on its business, except insofar as may be necessary for the winding up thereof.

(2) The corporation shall cause written notice by registered or certified mail of its intention to dissolve to be mailed to each known claimant against the corporation.

(3) The directors of the corporation shall manage the process of winding up the business or affairs of the corporation. The corporation shall proceed to collect its assets, dispose of such of its properties as are not to be distributed in kind to its shareholders, pay, satisfy, or discharge all its debts, liabilities, and obligations, or make adequate provision for payment, satisfaction, or discharge thereof, and do all other acts required to liquidate its business and affairs, except that if the properties and assets of the corporation are not sufficient to pay, satisfy, or discharge all the corporation's debts, liabilities, and obligations, the corporation shall apply its properties and assets so far as they will go to the just and equitable payment, satisfaction, or discharge of its debts, liabilities, and obligations or shall make adequate provision for such application. After paying, satisfying, or discharging all its debts, liabilities, and obligations, or making adequate provision for payment, satisfaction, or discharge thereof, the corporation shall then distribute the remainder of its properties and assets, either in cash or in kind, to its shareholders according to their respective rights and interests.

(4) The corporation, at any time during the liquidation of its business and affairs, may make application to any district court of this State in the county in which the registered office of the corporation is situated to have the liquidation continued under the supervision of such court as provided in this Act.

Art. 6.05. Revocation of Voluntary Dissolution Proceedings

A. At any time prior to the issuance of a certificate of dissolution by the Secretary of State, or within 120 days thereafter, a corporation may revoke voluntary dissolution proceedings:

(1) By the written consent of all of its shareholders.

(2) By the act of the corporation in the following manner:

(a) The board of directors shall adopt a resolution recommending that the question of such revocation be submitted to a vote at a special meeting of shareholders.

(b) Written or printed notice, stating that the purpose or one of the purposes of such meeting is to consider the advisability of revoking the voluntary dissolution proceedings, shall be given to each share-

holder of record entitled to vote at such meeting within the time and in the manner provided in this Act for the giving of notice of special meetings of shareholders.

(c) At such meeting a vote of the shareholders entitled to vote thereat shall be taken on a resolution to revoke the voluntary dissolution proceedings. Such resolution shall be adopted upon receiving the affirmative vote of the holders of at least two-thirds of the outstanding shares of the corporation entitled to vote thereon unless any class or series of shares is entitled to vote as a class thereon, in which event the resolution shall require for its adoption the affirmative vote of the holders of at least two-thirds of the outstanding shares within each class or series of shares entitled to vote as a class thereon and at least two-thirds of the outstanding shares otherwise entitled to vote thereon. Shares entitled to vote as a class shall be entitled to vote only as a class unless otherwise entitled to vote on each matter generally as provided in the articles of incorporation.

B. After revocation of voluntary dissolution is authorized as provided in Section A of this Article, the corporation shall, if a certificate of dissolution of the corporation has been issued by the Secretary of State, deliver to the Secretary of State for filing within 120 days after such issuance the original and a copy of articles of revocation of dissolution executed on behalf of the corporation by an officer, that set forth:

(1) the name of the corporation;

(2) the date that the revocation of dissolution was authorized and, if the dissolution has become effective, the effective date of the dissolution that was revoked; and

(3) if the corporation elected to revoke voluntary dissolution proceedings by the written consent of all of its shareholders, a copy of the consent, together with a statement that the consent was signed by all shareholders of the corporation or was signed in their names by their attorneys thereunto duly authorized; or

(4) if the corporation elected to revoke voluntary dissolution proceedings by act of the corporation:

(a) a statement that a resolution revoking the voluntary dissolution was adopted by the shareholders of the corporation and of the date of the adoption thereof;

(b) the number of shares outstanding and entitled to vote on the resolution, and, if the shares of any class or series were entitled to vote as a class, the designation and number of outstanding shares of each such class or series; and

(c) the number of shares entitled to vote on the resolution generally that voted for and against such resolution, respectively, and if the shares of any class or series were entitled to vote as a class, the number of shares of each such class or series voted for and against such resolution, respectively.

C. If the Secretary of State finds that the articles of revocation of dissolution conform to law, the Secretary shall, when the appropriate filing fee is paid as required by law:

(1) Endorse on the original and the copy the word "Filed" and the month, day, and year of the filing thereof;

(2) File the original in his office;

(3) Issue a certificate of revocation of dissolution to which he shall affix the copy; and

(4) Deliver to the corporation or its representative the certificate of revocation of dissolution, together with the affixed copy.

Notwithstanding the foregoing provisions of this Section C, if the corporation's name is the same as or deceptively similar to a corporate name already on file or reserved or registered pursuant to this Act, the

Secretary of State shall not issue to the corporation a certificate of revocation of dissolution unless the corporation contemporaneously amends its articles of incorporation to change its name.

D. If a corporation revokes voluntary dissolution proceedings prior to the issuance by the Secretary of State of a certificate of dissolution of the corporation, the corporation may again carry on its business as though voluntary dissolution proceedings had not occurred. If a corporation revokes voluntary dissolution proceedings after the issuance by the Secretary of State of a certificate of dissolution of the corporation, then upon the issuance by the Secretary of State of a certificate of revocation of dissolution, the revocation shall be effective, the existence of the corporation shall be deemed to have continued without interruption after the issuance by the Secretary of State of the certificate of dissolution, the corporation may carry on its business as though voluntary dissolution proceedings had not occurred, and the existence of the corporation shall continue until the corporation is subsequently dissolved or otherwise ceases to exist pursuant to the provisions of this Act.

Art. 6.06. Articles of Dissolution

A. If voluntary dissolution proceedings have been taken and have not been revoked, then when all debts, liabilities, and obligations of the corporation have been paid, satisfied, or discharged or adequate provision has been made for payment, satisfaction, or discharge thereof or, if the properties and assets of the corporation are not sufficient to pay, satisfy, or discharge all the corporation's debts, liabilities, and obligations, then when all properties and assets of the corporation have been applied so far as they will go to the just and equitable payment of the corporation's debts, liabilities, and obligations or when adequate provision has been made for such application, and the remainder of its properties and assets have been distributed to its shareholders according to their respective rights and interests, articles of dissolution shall be executed on behalf of the corporation by an officer, which shall set forth:

(1) The name of the corporation.

(2) The names and respective addresses of its officers.

(3) The names and respective addresses of its directors.

(4) That all debts, liabilities, and obligations of the corporation have been paid, satisfied, or discharged or that adequate provision has been made for payment, satisfaction, or discharge thereof or, if the properties and assets of the corporation were not sufficient to pay, satisfy, or discharge all the corporation's debts, liabilities, and obligations, that all properties and assets of the corporation have been applied so far as they would go to the just and equitable payment of those debts, liabilities, and obligations or that adequate provision has been made for such application.

(5) That the remainder of the properties and assets of the corporation have been distributed to its shareholders according to their respective rights and interests or that no properties or assets of the corporation remained for distribution to shareholders after applying the properties and assets of the corporation so far as they would go to the just and equitable payment of the debts, liabilities, and obligations of the corporation or making adequate provision for such application.

(6) If the corporation elected to dissolve by the written consent of all of its shareholders, a statement that a consent approving a dissolution of the corporation was signed by all shareholders of the corporation or was signed in their names by their attorneys thereunto duly authorized.

(7) If the corporation elected to dissolve by act of the corporation:

(a) A statement that a resolution approving a dissolution of the corporation was adopted by the shareholders of the corporation and of the date of adoption.

(b) The number of shares outstanding and entitled to vote on the resolution, and, if the shares of any class or series were entitled to vote as a class, the designation and number of outstanding shares of each such class or series.

(c) The number of shares entitled to vote on the resolution generally that voted for and against such resolution, respectively, and if the shares of any class or series were entitled to vote as a class, the number of shares of each such class or series voted for and against such resolution, respectively.

Art. 6.07. Filing Articles of Dissolution

A. The original and a copy of such articles of dissolution shall be delivered to the Secretary of State, along with a certificate from the Comptroller of Public Accounts that all taxes administered by the Comptroller under Title 2, Tax Code, have been paid. If the Secretary of State finds that such articles of dissolution conform to law, he shall, when the appropriate filing fee is paid as required by law:

(1) Endorse on the original and the copy the word "Filed," and the month, day, and year of the filing thereof.

(2) File the original in his office.

(3) Issue a certificate of dissolution to which he shall affix the copy.

B. The certificate of dissolution, together with the copy of the articles of dissolution affixed thereto by the Secretary of State, shall be delivered to the representative of the dissolved corporation. Upon the issuance of such certificate of dissolution, the existence of the corporation shall cease, except as otherwise provided in Article 6.05 or Article 7.12 of this Act.

Art. 6.08. Fraudulent Termination

A. Notwithstanding any other provision of this Act, a court may order the revocation of dissolution of a corporation that was dissolved as a result of actual or constructive fraud. In an action under this Article, any limitation period provided by law is tolled in accordance with the discovery rule.

B. The Secretary of State shall take any action necessary to implement an order under this Article.

Business Corporation Act
Part 7.
Art. 7.01. Involuntary Dissolution

A. A corporation may be dissolved involuntarily by a decree of the district court of the county in which the registered office of the corporation is situated or of any district court in Travis County in an action filed by the Attorney General when it is established that it is in default in any of the following particulars:

(1) The corporation or its incorporators have failed to comply with a condition precedent to incorporation; or

(2) The original articles of incorporation or any amendments thereof were procured through fraud; or

(3) The corporation has continued to transact business beyond the scope of the purpose or purposes of the corporation as expressed in its articles of incorporation; or

(4) A misrepresentation has been made of any material matter in any application, report, affidavit, or other document submitted by such corporation pursuant to this Act.

B. A corporation may be dissolved involuntarily by order of the Secretary of State when it is established that it is in default in any of the following particulars:

(1) The corporation has failed to file any report within the time required by law, or has failed to pay any fees, franchise taxes or penalties prescribed by law when the same have become due and payable;

(2) The corporation has failed to maintain a registered agent in this state as required by law; or

(3) The corporation has failed to pay the filing fee for the corporation's articles of incorporation or the initial franchise tax deposit, or the fee or tax was paid by an instrument that was dishonored when presented by the state for payment.

C. (1) No corporation shall be involuntarily dissolved under Subsection (1) or (2) of Section B hereof unless the Secretary of State, or other state agency with which such report, fees, taxes, or penalties is required to be made, gives the corporation not less than 90 days notice of its neglect, delinquency, or omission by certified mail addressed to its registered office or to its principal place of business, or to the last known address of one of its officers or directors, or to any other known place of business of said corporation, and the corporation has failed prior to such involuntary dissolution to correct the neglect, omission or delinquency.

(2) When a corporation is involuntarily dissolved under Subsection (3) of Section B of this article, the Secretary of State shall give the corporation notice of the dissolution by regular mail addressed to its registered office, its principal place of business, the last known address of one of its officers or directors, or any other known place of business of the corporation.

D. Whenever a corporation has given cause for involuntary dissolution and has failed to correct the neglect, omission or delinquency as provided in Sections B and C, the Secretary of State shall thereupon dissolve the corporation by issuing a certificate of involuntary dissolution, which shall include the fact of such involuntary dissolution and the date and cause thereof. The original of such certificate shall be placed in his office and a copy thereof mailed to the corporation at its registered office, or to its principal place of business, or the last known address of one of its officers or directors, or to any other known place of business of said corporation. Upon the issuance of such certificate of involuntary dissolution, the existence of the corporation shall cease, except for purposes otherwise provided by law.

E. Any corporation dissolved by the Secretary of State under the provisions of Section B of this article may be reinstated by the Secretary of State at any time within a period of 36 months from the date of such dissolution, upon approval of an application for reinstatement signed by an officer or director of the dissolved corporation. Such application shall be filed by the Secretary of State whenever it is established to the Secretary's satisfaction that in fact there was no cause for the dissolution, or whenever the neglect, omission or delinquency resulting in dissolution has been corrected and payment of all fees, taxes, penalties and interest due thereon which accrued before the dissolution plus an amount equal to the total taxes from the date of dissolution to the date of reinstatement which would have been payable had the corporation not been dissolved. A reinstatement filing fee of $50 shall accompany the application for reinstatement. Reinstatement shall not be authorized if the corporate name is the same as or deceptively similar to a corporate, limited partnership, or limited liability company name already on file or reserved or registered, unless the corporation being reinstated contemporaneously amends the articles of incorporation to change its name.

When the application for reinstatement is approved and filed by the Secretary of State, the corporate existence shall be deemed to have continued without interruption from the date of dissolution except the reinstatement shall have no effect upon any issue of personal liability of the directors, officers, or agents of the corporation during the period between dissolution and reinstatement.

F. When a corporation is convicted of a felony or when a high managerial agent is convicted of a felony in the conduct of the affairs of the corporation, the Attorney General may file an action to involuntarily dissolve the corporation in a district court of the county in which the registered office of the corporation is situated or in a district court of Travis County. The court may dissolve the corporation involuntarily if it is established that:

(1) The corporation, or a high managerial agent acting in behalf of the corporation, has engaged in a persistent course of felonious conduct; and

(2) To prevent future felonious conduct of the same character, the public interest requires such dissolution.

G. Article 7.02 of this Act does not apply to Section F of this article.

Art. 7.02. Notification to Attorney General, Notice to Corporation and Opportunity of Corporation to Cure Default

A. The Secretary of State shall certify to the Attorney General, from time to time, the names of all corporations which have given cause for judicial dissolution of their charters or revocation of their certificates of authority as provided in this Act, together with the facts pertinent thereto. Every such certificate from the Secretary of State to the Attorney General shall be taken and received in all courts as prima facie evidence of the facts therein stated.

B. Whenever the Secretary of State shall certify the name of any such corporation to the Attorney General as having given any cause for dissolution or revocation of its certificate of authority, the Secretary of State shall concurrently mail to such corporation at its registered office in this State a notice that such certification has been made and the grounds therefor. A record of the date of mailing such notice shall be kept in the office of the Secretary of State, and a certificate by the Secretary of State that such notice was mailed as indicated by such record shall be taken and received in all courts as prima facie evidence of the facts therein stated.

C. If at the expiration of thirty (30) days after the date of such mailing the corporation has not cured the defaults so certified by the Secretary of State, the Attorney General shall then file an action in the name of the State against such corporation for its dissolution or revocation of its certificate of authority, as the case may be.

D. If, after any such action is filed but before judgment is pronounced in the district court, the corporation against whom such action has been filed shall cure its default and pay the costs of such action, the action shall abate.

E. If, after the issues made in any such action have been heard by the court trying same and it is found that the corporate defendant has been guilty of any default of such nature as to justify its dissolution or revocation of its certificate of authority as provided in this Act, the court shall, without rendering or entering any judgment for a period of five (5) days pending the filing of an action upon a sworn application for stay of judgment as hereinafter provided, promptly pronounce its findings to such effect. If the corporation has proved by a preponderance of the evidence that the defaults of which the corporation has been found guilty were neither willful nor the result of failure to take reasonable precautions and has procured a finding to such effect it may promptly make sworn application to the court for a stay of entry of judgment in order to allow the corporation reasonable opportunity to cure the defaults of which it has been found guilty. If the court is reasonably satisfied on the basis of the corporation's sworn application and any evidence heard in support of or opposed to the application that the corporation is able and intends in good faith to cure the defaults of which it has been found guilty and that such stay is not applied for without just cause, the court shall grant such application and stay entry of judgment for such time as in the discretion of the court is reasonably necessary to afford the corporation opportunity to cure such defaults if it acts with reasonable diligence, but in no event shall such stay be for more than sixty (60) days after the date of the pronouncement of the court's findings. If during such period of time as shall be allowed by the court the corporation shall cure its defaults and pay the costs of such action, the court shall then enter judgment dismissing the action. If the corporation does not satisfy the court that it has cured its default within said period of time, the court shall enter final judgment at the expiration thereof.

F. If the corporation does not make application for stay of such judgment but does appeal therefrom and the trial court's judgment is affirmed and if the appellate court is satisfied that the appeal was taken in good faith and not for purpose of delay or with no sufficient cause and further finds that the defaults of which the corporation has been adjudged guilty are capable of being cured, it shall, if the appealing corporation has so prayed, remand the case to the trial court with instructions to grant the corporation opportunity to cure such defaults, such cure to be accomplished within such time after issuance of the mandate as the appellate court shall determine but in no event more than sixty (60) days thereafter. If during such period of time as shall have been so allowed the corporation shall cure such defaults and pay all costs accrued in such action, the trial court shall then enter judgment dismissing such action. If the corporation does not satisfy the trial court that it has cured its defaults within such period of time, the judgment shall thereupon become final.

Art. 7.03. Venue and Process

A. Every action for the involuntary dissolution of a domestic corporation or revocation of the certificate of authority of a foreign corporation shall be commenced by the Attorney General either in the district court of the county in which the registered office of the corporation in this State is situated, or in any district court of Travis County. Citation shall issue and be served as provided by law. If process is returned not found, the Attorney General shall cause publication to be made as in other civil cases in some newspaper published in the county where the registered office of the corporation in this State is situated, containing a notice of the pendency of such action, the title of the court, the title of the action, and the date on or after which default judgment may be entered. The Attorney General may include in one notice the name of any number of such corporations against which such actions are then pending in the same court. The Attorney General shall cause a copy of such notice to be mailed to the corporation at its registered office in this State within ten days after the first publication thereof. The certificate of the Attorney General of the mailing of such notice shall be prima facie evidence thereof. Such notice shall be published at least once a week for two successive weeks, and the first publication thereof may begin at any time after the citation has been returned. Unless a corporation shall have been served with citation, no default judgment shall be taken against it earlier than thirty days after the first publication of such notice.

Art. 7.04. Appointment of Receiver for Specific Corporate Assets

A. A receiver may be appointed by any court having jurisdiction of the subject matter for specific corporate assets located within the State, whether owned by a domestic or a foreign corporation, which are involved in litigation, whenever circumstances exist deemed by the court to require the appointment of a receiver to conserve such assets and to avoid damage to parties at interest, but only if all other requirements of law are complied with and if other remedies available either at law or in equity are determined by the court to be inadequate and only in the following instances:

(1) In an action by a vendor to vacate a fraudulent purchase of property; or by a creditor to subject any property or fund to his claim; or between partners or others jointly owning or interested in any property or fund, on the application of the plaintiff or any party whose right to or interest in the property or fund or the proceeds thereof is probable, and where it is shown that the property or fund is in danger of being lost, removed, or materially injured.

(2) In an action by a mortgagee for the foreclosure of his mortgage and sale of the mortgaged property, when it appears that the mortgaged property is in danger of being lost, removed, or materially injured, or that the condition of the mortgage has not been performed and that the property is probably insufficient to discharge the mortgage debt.

(3) In any other actions where receivers for specific assets have heretofore been appointed by the usages of the court of equity.

B. The court appointing such receiver shall have and retain exclusive jurisdiction over the specific assets placed in receivership and shall determine the rights of the parties in these assets or their proceeds.

Art. 7.05. Appointment of Receiver to Rehabilitate Corporation

A. A receiver may be appointed for the assets and business of a corporation by the district court for the county in which the registered office of the corporation is located, whenever circumstances exist deemed by the court to require the appointment of a receiver to conserve the assets and business of the corporation and to avoid damage to parties at interest, but only if all other requirements of law are complied with and if all other remedies available either at law or in equity, including the appointment of a receiver for specific assets of the corporation, are determined by the court to be inadequate, and only in the following instances:

(1) In an action by a shareholder when it is established:

(a) That the corporation is insolvent or in imminent danger of insolvency; or

(b) That the directors are deadlocked in the management of the corporate affairs and the shareholders are unable to break the deadlock, and that irreparable injury to the corporation is being suffered or is threatened by reason thereof; or

(c) That the acts of the directors or those in control of the corporation are illegal, oppressive or fraudulent; or

(d) That the corporate assets are being misapplied or wasted.

(e) That the shareholders are deadlocked in voting power, and have failed, for a period which includes at least two consecutive annual meeting dates, to elect successors to directors whose terms have expired or would have expired upon the election and qualification of their successors.

(2) In an action by a creditor when it is established:

(a) That the corporation is insolvent and the claim of the creditor has been reduced to judgment and an execution thereon returned unsatisfied; or

(b) That the corporation is insolvent and the corporation has admitted in writing that the claim of the creditor is due and owing.

(3) In any other actions where receivers have heretofore been appointed by the usages of the court of equity.

B. In the event that the condition of the corporation necessitating such an appointment of a receiver is remedied, the receivership shall be terminated forthwith and the management of the corporation shall be restored to the directors and officers, the receiver being directed to redeliver to the corporation all its remaining properties and assets.

Art. 7.06. Jurisdiction of Court to Liquidate Assets and Business of Corporation and Receiverships Therefor

A. The district court for the county in which the registered office of a corporation is located may order the liquidation of the assets and business of the corporation and may appoint a receiver to effect such liquidation, whenever circumstances demand liquidation in order to avoid damage to parties at interest, but only if all other requirements of law are complied with and if all other remedies available either at law or in equity, including the appointment of a receiver of specific assets of the corporation and appointment of a receiver to rehabilitate the corporation, are determined by the court to be inadequate and only in the following instances:

(1) When an action has been filed by the Attorney General, as provided in this Act, to dissolve a corporation and it is established that liquidation of its business and affairs should precede the entry of a decree of dissolution.

(2) Upon application by a corporation to have its liquidation continued under the supervision of the court.

(3) If the corporation is in receivership and no plan for remedying the condition of the corporation requiring appointment of the receiver, which the court finds to be feasible, has been presented within twelve (12) months after the appointment of the receiver.

(4) Upon application of any creditor if it is established that irreparable damage will ensue to the unsecured creditors of the corporation, generally, as a class, unless there be an immediate liquidation of the assets of the corporation.

B. In the event the condition of the corporation necessitating the appointment of a receiver is remedied, the receivership shall be terminated forthwith and the management of the corporation shall be restored to the directors and officers, the receiver being directed to redeliver to the corporation all its remaining properties and assets.

Art. 7.07. Qualifications, Powers, and Duties of Receivers; Other Provisions Relating to Receiverships

A. No receiver shall be appointed for any corporation to which this Act applies or for any of its assets or for its business except as provided for and on the conditions set forth in this Act. A receiver shall in all cases be a citizen of the United States or a corporation authorized to act as receiver, which corporation may be a domestic corporation or a foreign corporation authorized to transact business in this State, and shall in all cases give such bond as the court may direct with such sureties as the court may require.

B. A receiver appointed by authority of this Act shall have authority to sue and be sued in all courts in his own name and shall have those powers and duties provided by laws of general applicability relating to receivers and in addition thereto may be accorded such other powers and duties as the court shall deem appropriate to accomplish the objec-

tives for which the receiver was appointed. Such additional and unusual powers and duties shall be stated in the order appointing the receiver and may be increased or diminished at any time during the proceedings.

C. In proceedings involving any receivership of the assets or business of a corporation, the court may require all creditors of the corporation to file with the clerk of the court or with the receiver, in such form as the court may prescribe, proofs of their respective claims under oath. If the court requires the filing of claims, it shall fix a date as the last day for the filing thereof, which shall be not less than four months from the date of the order, and shall prescribe the notice that shall be given to creditors and claimants of the date so fixed. Prior to the date so fixed, the court may extend the time for the filing of claims. Creditors and claimants failing to file proofs of claim on or before the date fixed therefor may be barred, by order of court (unless presenting to the court a justifiable excuse for delay in the filing), from participating in the distribution of the assets of the corporation; but no discharge shall be decreed or effected.

D. The court shall have power from time to time to make allowances to the receiver or receivers and to attorneys in the proceeding, and to direct the payment thereof out of the assets of the corporation within the scope of the receivership or the proceeds of any sale or disposition of such assets.

E. A court authorized to appoint a receiver for a corporation to which this Act applies, and no other court in this State, shall be authorized to appoint a receiver for the corporation or its assets and business; when such a court does appoint a receiver, as authorized by this Act, for the corporation or its assets and business, that court shall have exclusive jurisdiction of the corporation and all its properties, wherever situated.

F. Notwithstanding any provision of this Article or in this Act to the contrary, the district court for the county in which the registered office of any foreign corporation doing business in this State is located shall have jurisdiction to appoint an ancillary receiver for the assets and business of such corporation, to serve ancillary to the receiver for the assets and business of the corporation acting under orders of a court having jurisdiction to appoint such a receiver for the corporation, located in any other state, whenever circumstances exist deemed by the court to require the appointment of such ancillary receiver. Moreover, such district court, whenever circumstances exist deemed by it to require the appointment of a receiver for all the assets in and out of this State, and the business, of a foreign corporation doing business in this State, in accordance with the ordinary usages of equity, may appoint such a receiver for all its assets in and out of this State, and its business, even though no receiver has been appointed elsewhere; such receivership shall be converted into an ancillary receivership when deemed appropriate by such district court in the light of orders entered by a court of competent jurisdiction in some other State, providing for a receivership of all assets and business of such corporation.

Art. 7.08. Shareholders Not Necessary Parties Defendant to Receivership or Liquidation Proceedings

A. It shall not be necessary to make shareholders parties to any action or proceeding for a receivership or liquidation of the assets and business of a corporation unless relief is sought against them personally.

Art. 7.09. Decree of Involuntary Dissolution

A. In proceedings to liquidate the assets and business of a corporation, when the costs and expenses of such proceedings and all debts, obligations, and liabilities of the corporation shall have been paid and discharged, or adequate provision shall have been made therefor, and all of its remaining property and assets distributed to its shareholders, or, in case its property and assets are not sufficient to satisfy and discharge such costs, expenses, debts, and obligations, when all the property and assets have been applied so far as they will go to their payment, the court shall enter a decree dissolving the corporation, whereupon the existence of the corporation shall cease.

Art. 7.10. Filing of Decree of Dissolution

A. In any case in which the court shall enter a decree dissolving a corporation, it shall be the duty of the clerk of such court to cause a certified copy of the decree to be filed with the Secretary of State. No fee shall be charged by the Secretary of State for the filing thereof.

Art. 7.11. Deposit With Comptroller of Amount Due Certain Shareholders and Creditors

A. Upon the voluntary or involuntary dissolution of a corporation, the portion of the assets distributable to a creditor or shareholder who is unknown or cannot be found after the exercise of reasonable diligence by the person or persons responsible for the distribution in liquidation of the corporation's assets shall be reduced to cash and deposited with the Comptroller, together with a statement giving the name of the person, if known, entitled to such fund, his last known address, the amount of his distributive portion, and such other information about such person as the Comptroller may reasonably require, whereupon the person or persons responsible for the distribution in liquidation of the corporation's assets shall be released and discharged from any further liability with respect to the funds so deposited. The Comptroller shall issue his receipt for such fund and shall deposit same in a special account to be maintained by him.

B. On receipt of satisfactory written proof of ownership or of right to such fund within seven (7) years from the date such fund was so deposited, the Comptroller shall issue proper warrant therefor in favor of the person or persons then entitled thereto. If no claimant has made satisfactory proof of right to such fund within seven (7) years from the time of such deposit the Comptroller shall then cause to be published in one issue of a newspaper of general circulation in Travis County, Texas, a notice of the proposed escheat of such fund, giving the name of the creditor or shareholder apparently entitled thereto, his last known address, if any, the amount of the fund so deposited, and the name of the dissolved corporation from whose assets such fund was derived. If no claimant makes satisfactory proof of right to such fund within two months from the time of such publication, the fund so unclaimed shall thereupon automatically escheat to and become the property of the General Revenue Fund of the State of Texas.

Art. 7.12. Limited Survival After Dissolution

A. A dissolved corporation shall continue its corporate existence for a period of three years from the date of dissolution, for the following purposes:

(1) prosecuting or defending in its corporate name any action or proceeding by or against the dissolved corporation;

(2) permitting the survival of any existing claim by or against the dissolved corporation;

(3) holding title to and liquidating any properties or assets that remained in the dissolved corporation at the time of, or are collected by the dissolved corporation after, dissolution, and applying or distributing those properties or assets, or the proceeds thereof, as provided in Subsections (3) and (4) of Section A of Article 6.04 of this Act; and

(4) settling any other affairs not completed before dissolution.

However, a dissolved corporation may not continue its corporate existence for the purpose of continuing the business or affairs for which the dissolved corporation was organized.

B. During the three-year period, the members of the board of directors of a dissolved corporation serving at the time of dissolution or the majority of them then living, however reduced in number, or their successors selected by them, shall continue to manage the affairs of the dissolved corporation for the limited purposes specified in this Article and shall have the powers necessary to accomplish those purposes. In the exercise of those powers, the directors shall have the same duties to the dissolved corporation that they had immediately prior to the dissolution and shall be liable to the dissolved corporation for actions taken by them after the dissolution to the same extent that they would have been liable had those actions been taken by them prior to the dissolution.

C. A corporation shall not be liable for any claim other than an existing claim. An existing claim by or against a dissolved corporation shall be extinguished unless an action or proceeding on such existing claim is brought before the expiration of the three-year period following the date of dissolution. If an action or proceeding on an existing claim by or against a dissolved corporation is brought before the expiration of the three-year period following the date of dissolution and such existing claim was not extinguished pursuant to Section D of this Article, the dissolved corporation shall continue to survive (1) for purposes of that action or proceeding until all judgments, orders, and decrees therein have been fully executed, and (2) for purposes of applying or distributing any properties or assets of the dissolved corporation as provided in Subsections (3) and (4) of Section A of Article 6.04 of this Act until such properties or assets are so applied or distributed.

D. A dissolved corporation may give written notice to a person having or asserting an existing claim against the dissolved corporation to present such existing claim to the dissolved corporation in accordance with the notice. The notice shall be sent by registered or certified mail, return receipt requested, to the person having or asserting the existing claim at such person's last known address, and the notice shall:

(1) state that such person's claim against the dissolved corporation must be presented in writing to the dissolved corporation on or before the date stated in the notice, which shall be not earlier than 120 days after the date the notice is sent to such person;

(2) state that the written presentation of the claim must describe such claim in sufficient detail to reasonably inform the dissolved corporation of the identity of such person and of the nature and amount of the claim;

(3) state a mailing address where the written presentation of the person's claim against the dissolved corporation is to be sent;

(4) state that if the written presentation of the claim is not received at such address on or before the date stated in the notice, the claim will be extinguished; and

(5) be accompanied by a copy of this Section D.

If a written presentation of such person's claim against the dissolved corporation that meets the requirements of this section is received at the address of the dissolved corporation stated in the notice on or before the date stated in the notice, the dissolved corporation may thereafter give written notice to such person that such claim is rejected by the dissolved corporation. The notice shall be sent by registered or certified mail, return receipt requested, addressed to such person at such person's last known address, and the notice shall state:

(1) that such claim is rejected by the dissolved corporation;

(2) that such claim will be extinguished unless an action or proceeding on such claim is brought within 180 days after the date such notice of rejection was sent to such person and before the expiration of the three-year period following the date of dissolution; and

(3) the date such notice of rejection was sent and the date of dissolution. Such person's claim against the dissolved corporation shall be extinguished if (a) a written presentation of that claim meeting the requirements of this section is not received at the address of the dissolved corporation stated in the notice to such person on or before the date stated in the notice or (b) an action or proceeding on such claim is not brought within 180 days after the date a notice of rejection was sent to such person and before the expiration of the three-year period following the date of dissolution.

E. A dissolved corporation that was dissolved by the expiration of the period of its duration may, during the three-year period following the date of dissolution, amend its articles of incorporation by following the procedure prescribed in this Act to extend or perpetuate its period of existence. That expiration shall not of itself create any vested right on the part of any shareholder or creditor to prevent such an action. No act or contract of such a dissolved corporation during a period within which it could have extended its existence as permitted by this Article, whether or not it has taken action so to extend its existence, shall be in any degree invalidated by the expiration of its period of duration.

F. In this Article:

(1) The term "dissolved corporation" means a corporation (a) that was voluntarily dissolved by the issuance of a certificate of dissolution by the Secretary of State and was not issued a certificate of revocation of dissolution pursuant to Section C of Article 6.05 of this Act, (b) that was involuntarily dissolved by the Secretary of State and was not reinstated pursuant to Section E of Article 7.01 of this Act, (c) that was dissolved by decree of a court when the court has not liquidated all the assets and business of the corporation as provided in this Act, (d) that was dissolved by the expiration of its period of duration and has not revived its existence as provided in this Act, or (e) whose charter was forfeited pursuant to the Tax Code, unless the forfeiture has been set aside.

(2) The term "claim" means a right to payment, damages, or property, whether liquidated or unliquidated, accrued or contingent, matured or unmatured.

(3) The term "existing claim" means a claim that existed before dissolution and is not otherwise barred by limitations or a contractual obligation incurred after dissolution.

Business Corporation Act
Part 8.
Art. 8.01. Admission of Foreign Corporation

A. No foreign corporation shall have the right to transact business in this State until it shall have procured a certificate of authority so to do from the Secretary of State. No foreign corporation shall be entitled to procure a certificate of authority under this Act to transact in this State any business which a corporation organized under this Act is not permitted to transact. A foreign corporation shall not be denied a certificate of authority by reason of the fact that the laws of the State or country under which such corporation is organized governing its organization and internal affairs differ from the laws of this State, and nothing in this Act contained shall be construed to authorize this State to regulate the organization of such corporation or its internal affairs.

B. Without excluding other activities which may not constitute transacting business in this state, a foreign corporation shall not be considered to be transacting business in this state, for the purposes of this Act, by reason of carrying on in this state any one (1) or more of the following activities:

(1) Maintaining or defending any action or suit or any administrative or arbitration proceedings, or effecting the settlement thereof or the settlement of claims or disputes to which it is a party;

(2) Holding meetings of its directors or shareholders or carrying on other activities concerning its internal affairs;

(3) Maintaining bank accounts;

(4) Maintaining offices or agencies for the transfer, exchange, and registration of securities issued by it, or appointing and maintaining trustees or depositaries with relation to its securities;

(5) Voting the stock of any corporation which it has lawfully acquired;

(6) Effecting sales through independent contractors;

(7) Creating as borrower or lender, or acquiring, indebtedness or mortgages or other security interests in real or personal property.

(8) Securing or collecting debts due to it or enforcing any rights in property securing the same;

(9) Transacting any business in interstate commerce;

(10) Conducting an isolated transaction completed within a period of thirty (30) days and not in the course of a number of repeated transactions of like nature;

(11) Exercising the powers of executor or administrator of the estate of a non-resident decedent under ancillary letters issued by a court of this state, or exercising the powers of a trustee under the will of a non-resident decedent, or under a trust created by one or more non-residents of this state, or by one or more foreign corporations, if the exercise of such powers, in any such case, will not involve activities which would be deemed to constitute the transacting of business in this state in the case of a foreign corporation acting in its own right;

(12) Acquiring, in transactions outside Texas, or in interstate commerce, of debts secured by mortgages or liens on real or personal property in Texas, collecting or adjusting of principal and interest payments thereon, enforcing or adjusting any rights and property securing said debts, taking any actions necessary to preserve and protect the interest of the mortgagee in said security, or any combination of such transactions;

(13) Investing in or acquiring, in transactions outside of Texas, royalties and other non-operating mineral interests, and the execution of division orders, contracts of sale and other instruments incidental to the ownership of such non-operating mineral interests.

Art. 8.02. Powers of Foreign Corporation

A. A foreign corporation which shall have received a certificate of authority under this Act shall, until its certificate of authority shall have been revoked in accordance with the provisions of this Act or until a certificate of withdrawal shall have been issued by the Secretary of State as provided in this Act, enjoy the same, but no greater, rights and privileges as a domestic corporation organized for the purposes set forth in the application pursuant to which such certificate of authority is issued; and, as to all matters affecting the transaction of intrastate business in this State, it and its officers and directors shall be subject to the same duties, restrictions, penalties, and liabilities now or hereafter imposed upon a domestic corporation of like character and its officers and directors; provided, however, that only the laws of the jurisdiction of incorporation of a foreign corporation shall govern (1) the internal affairs of the foreign corporation, including but not limited to the rights, powers, and duties of its board of directors and shareholders and matters relating to its shares, and (2) the liability, if any, of shareholders of the foreign corporation for the debts, liabilities, and obligations of the foreign corporation for which they are not otherwise liable by statute or agreement.

Art. 8.03. Corporate Name of Foreign Corporation

A. No certificate of authority shall be issued to a foreign corporation unless the corporate name of such corporation:

(1) Shall contain the word "corporation," "company," "incorporated," or "limited," or shall contain an abbreviation of one (1) of such words, or such corporation shall, for use in this state, add at the end of its name one (1) of such words or an abbreviation thereof.

(2) Shall not be the same as, or deceptively similar to, the name of any domestic corporation, limited partnership, or limited liability company existing under the laws of this state or of any foreign corporation, limited partnership, or limited liability company authorized to transact business in this state, or a name the exclusive right to which is, at the time, reserved or registered in the manner provided in this Act or any other statute providing for the reservation or registration of names by a limited partnership or limited liability company; provided that a name may be similar if written consent is obtained from the existing corporation, limited partnership, or limited liability company having the name deemed to be similar or the person for whom the name deemed to be similar is reserved or registered in the office of the Secretary of State. A certificate of authority shall be issued as provided in this Act to any foreign corporation having a name the same as, deceptively similar to, or, if no consent is given, similar to the name of any domestic corporation, limited partnership, or limited liability company existing under the laws of this state or of any foreign corporation, limited partnership, or limited liability company authorized to transact business in this state, or a name the exclusive right to which is, at the time, reserved or registered in accordance with this Act or any other applicable law, provided such foreign corporation qualifies and does business under a name that meets the requirements of this article. The foreign corporation shall set forth in the application for a certificate of authority the name under which it is qualifying and shall file an assumed name certificate in accordance with Chapter 36, Business & Commerce Code, as amended.

Art. 8.04. Change of Name by Foreign Corporation

A. Whenever a foreign corporation which is authorized to transact business in this State shall change its name to one under which a certificate of authority would not be granted to it on application therefor, the certificate of authority of such corporation shall be suspended and it shall not thereafter transact any business in this State until it has changed its name to a name which is available to it under the laws of this State or has otherwise complied with the provisions of this Act.

Art. 8.05. Application for Certificate of Authority

A. In order to procure a certificate of authority to transact business in this State, a foreign corporation shall make application therefor to the Secretary of State, which application shall set forth:

(1) The name of the corporation and the State or country under the laws of which it is incorporated.

(2) If the name of the corporation does not contain the word "corporation," "company," "incorporated," or "limited," and does not contain an abbreviation of one (1) of such words, then the name of the corporation with the word or abbreviation which it elects to add thereto for use in this State; if the corporation is required to qualify under a name other than its corporate name, then the name under which the corporation is to be qualified.

(3) The date of incorporation and the period of duration of the corporation.

(4) The address of the principal office of the corporation in the state or country under the laws of which it is incorporated.

(5) The address of the registered office of the corporation in this State, and the name of its registered agent in this State at such address.

(6) The purpose or purposes of the corporation which it proposes to pursue in the transaction of business in this State and a statement that it is authorized to pursue such purpose or purposes in the state or country under the laws of which it is incorporated.

(7) The names and respective addresses of the directors and officers of the corporation.

(8) A statement that the corporation exists as a valid corporation under the laws of the corporation's jurisdiction of formation.

B. Such application shall be made on forms promulgated by the Secretary of State and shall be executed on behalf of the corporation by an officer.

Art. 8.06. Filing of Application for Certificate of Authority

A. The original and a copy of the application of the corporation for a certificate of authority shall be delivered to the Secretary of State. If the Secretary of State finds that the application conforms to law, he shall, when the appropriate filing fee is paid as required by law:

(1) Endorse on the original and the copy the word "Filed," and the month, day, and year of the filing thereof.

(2) File in his office the original.

(3) Issue a certificate of authority to transact business in this State to which he shall affix the copy.

B. The certificate of authority, together with the copy of the application affixed thereto by the Secretary of State, shall be delivered to the corporation or its representative.

Art. 8.07. Effect of Certificate of Authority

A. Upon the issuance of a certificate of authority by the Secretary of State, the corporation shall be authorized to transact business in this State for those purposes set forth in its application, and such certificate shall be conclusive evidence of such right of the corporation to transact business in this State for such purposes, except as against this State in a proceeding to revoke such certificate.

Art. 8.08. Registered Office and Registered Agent of Foreign Corporation

A. Each foreign corporation authorized to transact business in this State shall have and continuously maintain in this State:

(1) A registered office which may be, but need not be, the same as its place of business in this State.

(2) A registered agent, which agent may be either an individual resident in this State whose business office is identical with such registered office, or a domestic corporation, or a foreign corporation authorized to transact business in this State, having a business office identical with such registered office.

Art. 8.09. Change of Registered Office or Registered Agent of Foreign Corporation

A. A foreign corporation authorized to transact business in this state may change its registered office or its registered agent, or both, upon filing in the office of the Secretary of State a statement setting forth:

(1) The name of the corporation.

(2) The post-office address of its then registered office.

(3) If the post-office address of its registered office is to be changed, the post-office address to which the registered office is to be changed.

(4) The name of its then registered agent.

(5) If its registered agent is to be changed, the name of its successor registered agent.

(6) That the post-office address of its registered office and the post-office address of the business office of its registered agent, as changed, will be identical.

(7) That such change was authorized by its Board of Directors or by an officer of the corporation so authorized by the Board of Directors.

B. Such statement shall be executed on behalf of the corporation by an officer. The original and a copy of such statement shall be delivered to the Secretary of State. If the Secretary of State finds that such statement conforms to the provisions of this Act, he shall, when all fees have been paid as required by law:

(1) Endorse on the original and the copy the word "Filed," and the month, day, and year of the filing thereof.

(2) File the original in his office.

(3) Return the copy to the corporation or its representative.

C. Upon the filing of such statement by the Secretary of State, the change of address of the registered office, or the appointment of a new registered agent, or both, as the case may be, shall become effective.

D. Any registered agent of a corporation may resign

(1) by giving written notice to the corporation at its last known address

(2) and by giving written notice, in duplicate (the original and one copy of the notice), to the Secretary of State within ten days after mailing or delivery of said notice to the corporation. Such notice shall include the last known address of the corporation and shall include the statement that written notice of resignation has been given to the corporation and the date thereof.

Upon compliance with the requirements as to written notice, the appointment of such agent shall terminate upon the expiration of thirty (30) days after receipt of such notice by the Secretary of State.

If the Secretary of State finds that such written notice conforms to the provisions of this Act, he shall:

(1) Endorse on the original and the copy the word "filed" and the month, day, and year of the filing thereof.

(2) File the original in his office.

(3) Return the copy to such resigning registered agent.

(4) Notify the corporation of the resignation of the registered agent.

No fee shall be required to be paid for the filing of a resignation under this section.

Art. 8.10. Service of Process on Foreign Corporation

A. The president and all vice presidents of a foreign corporation authorized to transact business in this State and the registered agent so appointed by a foreign corporation shall be agents of such corporation upon whom any process, notice, or demand required or permitted by law to be served upon the corporation may be served.

B. Whenever a foreign corporation authorized to transact business in this State shall fail to appoint or maintain a registered agent in this State, or whenever any such registered agent cannot with reasonable diligence be found at the registered office, or whenever the certificate of authority of a foreign corporation shall be revoked, then the Secretary of State shall be an agent of such corporation upon whom any such process, notice, or demand may be served. Service on the Secretary of State of any such process, notice, or demand shall be made by delivering to and leaving with him, or with the Assistant Secretary of State, or with any clerk having charge of the corporation department of his office, duplicate copies of such process, notice, or demand. In the event any such process, notice or demand is served on the Secretary of State, he shall immediately cause one of such copies thereof to be forwarded by registered mail, addressed to the corporation at its principal office in the state or country under the laws of which it is incorporated. Any service so had on the Secretary of State shall be returnable in not less than thirty days.

C. The Secretary of State shall keep a record of all processes, notices and demands served upon him under this Article, and shall record therein the time of such service and his action with reference thereto.

D. Nothing herein contained shall limit or affect the right to serve any process, notice, or demand required or permitted by law to be served upon a foreign corporation in any other manner now or hereafter permitted by law.

E. Service of process, notice, or demand required or permitted by law to be served by a political subdivision of this state or by a person, including another political subdivision or an attorney, acting on behalf of a political subdivision in connection with the collection of a delinquent ad valorem tax may be served on a foreign corporation whose privileges to transact business in this state are forfeited under Section 171.251, Tax Code, or whose certificate of authority is revoked under Article 8.16 of this Act by delivering the process, notice, or demand to any officer or director of the foreign corporation, as listed in the most recent records of the secretary of state. If the officers or directors of the foreign corporation are unknown or cannot be found, service on the foreign corporation may be made in the same manner as service is made on unknown shareholders under law. Notwithstanding any disability or reinstatement of a foreign corporation, service of process under this section is sufficient for a judgment against the foreign corporation or a judgment in rem against any property to which the foreign corporation holds title.

Art. 8.13. Amended Certificate of Authority

A. If a foreign corporation authorized to transact business in this State shall change its corporate name, or if such corporation desires to pursue in this State purposes other than, or in addition to, those authorized by its existing certificate of authority, it shall procure an amended certificate of authority by making application therefor to the Secretary of State.

B. To change any statement on an original application for a certificate of authority a foreign corporation shall file with the Secretary of State an application for an amended certificate of authority setting forth the change.

C. An application for an amended certificate of authority submitted because of a name change must be accompanied by a certificate from the proper filing officer in the jurisdiction of incorporation evidencing the name change.

D. The requirements in respect to the form and contents of such application, the manner of its execution, the filing of the application and a copy of it with the Secretary of State, the issuance of an amended certificate of authority and the effect thereof, shall be the same as in the case of an original application for a certificate of authority.

Art. 8.14. Withdrawal or Termination of Foreign Corporation

A. A foreign corporation authorized to transact business in this state may withdraw from this state upon procuring from the Secretary of State a certificate of withdrawal. In order to procure such certificate of withdrawal, such foreign corporation shall deliver to the Secretary of State an application for withdrawal, which shall set forth:

(1) The name of the corporation and the state or country under the laws of which it is incorporated;

(2) That the corporation is not transacting business in this state;

(3) That the corporation surrenders its authority to transact business in this state;

(4) That the corporation revokes the authority of its registered agent in this state to accept service of process and consents that service of process in any action, suit, or proceeding based upon any cause of action arising in this state during the time the corporation was authorized to transact business in this state may thereafter be made on such corporation by service thereof on the Secretary of State;

(5) A post office address to which the Secretary of State may mail a copy of any process against the corporation that may be served on him; and

(6) A statement that all sums due, or accrued, to this state have been paid, or that adequate provision has been made for the payment thereof.

B. The application for withdrawal may be made on forms promulgated by the Secretary of State and shall be executed on behalf of the corporation by an officer.

C. When the existence of a foreign corporation terminates because of dissolution, merger, conversion, or otherwise, a certificate from the proper officer in the jurisdiction of the corporation's incorporation evidencing the termination shall be filed with the Secretary of State.

Art. 8.15. Filing of Application for Withdrawal

A. The original and a copy of such application for withdrawal, along with a certificate from the comptroller that all taxes, including all applicable penalties and interest, administered by the comptroller under Title 2, Tax Code, have been paid, shall be delivered to the secretary of state. If the secretary of state finds that such application conforms to the provisions of this Act, the secretary of state shall, when the appropriate filing fee is paid as required by law:

(1) Endorse on the original and the copy the word "Filed," and the month, day, and year of the filing thereof.

(2) File the original in the office of the secretary of state.

(3) Issue a certificate of withdrawal to which shall be affixed the copy.

B. The certificate of withdrawal, together with the copy of the application for withdrawal affixed thereto by the Secretary of State, shall be delivered to the corporation or its representative. Upon the issuance of such certificate of withdrawal, the authority of the corporation to transact business in this State shall cease.

Art. 8.16. Revocation of Certificate of Authority

A. The certificate of authority of a foreign corporation to transact business in this state may be revoked by a decree of the district court for the county in which the registered office of the corporation in this state is situated or of any district court in Travis County in an action filed by the Attorney General when it is established that:

(1) The corporation has failed to comply with a condition precedent to the issuance of its certificate of authority or a renewal or amendment thereof; or

(2) The certificate of authority to transact business in this state or any amendment thereof was procured through fraud; or

(3) The corporation has continued to transact business beyond the scope of the purpose or purposes expressed in its certificate of authority to transact business in this state; or

(4) A misrepresentation has been made of any material matter in any application, report, affidavit, or other document submitted by such corporation as required by law.

B. The certificate of authority of a foreign corporation to transact business in this state may be revoked by order of the Secretary of State when it is established that it is in default in any of the following particulars:

(1) The corporation has failed to file any report within the time required by law, or has failed to pay any fees, franchise taxes, or penalties prescribed by law when the same have become due and payable; or

(2) The corporation has failed to maintain a registered agent in this state as required by law; or

(3) The corporation has changed its corporate name and has failed to file with the Secretary of State within thirty days after such change of name became effective, an application for an amended certificate of authority, or that the corporation has changed its corporate name and that the newly adopted name is not available for use in this state; or

(4) The corporation has failed to pay the filing fee for the corporation's certificate of authority or the initial franchise tax deposit, or the fee or tax was paid by an instrument that was dishonored when presented by the state for payment.

C. (1) No foreign corporation shall have its certificate of authority to transact business in this state revoked under Subsection (1), (2), or (3) of Section B hereof unless the Secretary of State, or other state agency to which such report, taxes, fees, penalties is required to be made, gives the corporation not less than 90 days notice of its neglect, delinquency, or omission by certified mail addressed to its registered office or to its principal place of business, or to the last known address of one of its officers or directors, or to any other known place of business of said corporation, and the corporation has failed prior to such revocation to correct the neglect, omission or delinquency.

(2) When the certificate of authority of a foreign corporation to transact business in this state is revoked under Subsection (4) of Section B of this article, the Secretary of State shall give the corporation notice of the revocation by regular mail addressed to its registered office, its principal place of business, the last known address of one of its officers or directors, or any other known place of business of the corporation.

D. Whenever a corporation has given cause for revocation of its certificate of authority and has failed to correct the neglect, omission or delinquency as provided in Sections B and C, the Secretary of State shall thereupon revoke the certificate of authority of the corporation by issuing a certificate of revocation which shall include the fact of such revocation and the date and cause thereof. The original of such certificate shall be placed in his office and a copy thereof mailed to the corporation at its registered office or to its principal place of business, or to the last known address of one of its officers or directors, or to any other known place of business of said corporation. Upon the issuance of such certificate of revocation, the authority to transact business in this state shall cease.

E. Any corporation whose certificate of authority has been revoked by the Secretary of State under the provisions of Section B of this article may be reinstated by the Secretary of State at any time within a period of 36 months from the date of such revocation , upon approval of an application for reinstatement signed by an officer or director of the corporation. Such application shall be filed by the Secretary of State whenever it is established to the Secretary's satisfaction that in fact there was no cause for the revocation, or whenever the neglect, omission or delinquency resulting in revocation has been corrected and payment made of all fees, taxes, penalties and interest due thereon which accrued before the revocation plus an amount equal to the total taxes from the date of revocation to the date of reinstatement which would have been payable had the corporation's certificate not been revoked. A reinstatement filing fee of $50 shall accompany the application for reinstatement.

Reinstatement shall not be authorized if the corporate name is the same as or deceptively similar to a corporate, limited partnership, or limited liability company name already on file or reserved or registered, unless the corporation being reinstated contemporaneously amends its certificate of authority to change its name.

When the application for reinstatement is approved and filed by the Secretary of State, the corporate authority to do business in Texas shall be deemed to have continued without interruption from the date of revocation, except that reinstatement shall have no effect upon any issue of personal liability of the directors, officers, or agents of the corporation during the period between revocation and reinstatement.

F. When a foreign corporation is convicted of a felony, or when a high managerial agent is convicted of a felony committed in the conduct of the affairs of the foreign corporation, the Attorney General may file an action to revoke the certificate of authority of the foreign corporation to transact business in this State in a district court of the county in which the registered office of the foreign corporation in this State is situated or in a district court of Travis County. The court may revoke the foreign corporation's certificate of authority if it is established that:

(1) The foreign corporation, or a high managerial agent acting in behalf of the foreign corporation, has engaged in a persistent course of felonious conduct; and

(2) To prevent future felonious conduct of the same character, the public interest requires such revocation.

G. Article 7.02 of this Act does not apply to Section F of this article.

Art. 8.17. Filing of Decree of Revocation

In case the court shall enter a decree revoking the certificate of authority of a foreign corporation to transact business in this State, it shall be the duty of the clerk of such court to cause a certified copy of the decree to be filed with the Secretary of State. No fee shall be charged by the Secretary of State for the filing thereof.

Art. 8.18. Transacting Business without Certificate of Authority

A. No foreign corporation which is transacting, or has transacted, business in this State without a certificate of authority shall be permitted to maintain any action, suit, or proceeding in any court of this State (whether brought directly by the corporation or in the form of a derivative action by a shareholder) on any cause of action arising out of the transaction of business in this State, until such corporation shall have obtained a certificate of authority. Nor shall any action, suit, or proceeding on any such cause of action be maintained in any court of this State by any successor, assignee, or legal representative of such foreign corporation, until a certificate of authority shall have been obtained by such corporation or by a foreign corporation which has acquired all or substantially all of its assets. It is expressly provided, however, that the provisions of this article shall not affect the rights of any assignee of the foreign corporation as the holder in due course of a negotiable promissory note, check, or bill of exchange, or as the bona fide purchaser for value of a warehouse receipt, stock certificate, or other instrument made negotiable by law.

B. The failure of a foreign corporation to obtain a certificate of authority to transact business in this State shall not impair the validity of any contract or act of such corporation, and shall not prevent such corporation from defending any action, suit or proceeding in any court of this State.

C. A foreign corporation which transacts business in this State without a certificate of authority shall be liable to this State, for the years or parts thereof during which it transacted business in this State without a certificate of authority, in an amount equal to all fees and franchise taxes which would have been imposed by law upon such corporation had it duly applied for and received a certificate of authority to transact business in this State as required by law and thereafter filed all reports required by law, plus all penalties imposed by law for failure to pay such fees and franchise taxes. In addition to the penalties and payments thus prescribed, such corporation shall forfeit to this State an amount not less than One Hundred Dollars ($100) nor more than Five Thousand Dollars ($5,000) for each month or fraction thereof it shall have transacted business in this State without a certificate. The Attorney General shall bring suit to recover all amounts due this State under the provisions of this section.

Business Corporation Act
Part 9.

Art. 9.01. Interrogatories by Secretary of State

A. The Secretary of State may propound to any corporation, domestic or foreign, subject to the provisions of this Act, and to any officer or director thereof, such interrogatories as may be reasonably necessary and proper to enable him to ascertain whether such corporation has complied with all the provisions of this Act. Such interrogatories shall be answered within thirty days after the mailing thereof, or within such additional time as shall be fixed by the Secretary of State, and the answers thereto shall be full and complete and shall be made in writing and under oath. If such interrogatories be directed to an individual, they shall be answered by him, and if directed to a corporation, they shall be answered by an officer of the corporation. The Secretary of State need not file any document to which such interrogatories relate until such interrogatories be answered as herein provided, and not then if the answers thereto disclose that such document is not in conformity with the provisions of this Act. The Secretary of State shall certify to the Attorney General, for such action as the Attorney General may deem appropriate, all interrogatories and answers thereto which disclose a violation of the provisions of this Act.

Art. 9.02. Information Disclosed by Interrogatories

A. Interrogatories propounded by the Secretary of State and the answers thereto shall not be open to public inspection nor shall the Secretary of State disclose any facts or information obtained therefrom except insofar as his official duty may require the same to be made public or in the event such interrogatories or the answers thereto are required for evidence in any criminal proceedings or in any other action by this State.

Art. 9.03. Powers of Secretary of State

A. The Secretary of State shall have the power and authority reasonably necessary to enable him to administer this Act efficiently and to perform the duties therein imposed upon him.

Art. 9.04. Appeals from Secretary of State

A. If the Secretary of State shall fail to approve any articles of incorporation, application for certificate of authority to transact business in this State, amendment, merger, share exchange, conversion , or dissolution, or any other document required by this Act to be approved by the Secretary of State before the same shall be filed in his office, he shall, within ten days after the delivery thereof to him, give written notice of his disapproval to the person, corporation, or other entity, domestic or foreign, delivering the same, specifying in such notice the reasons therefor. From such disapproval such person, corporation, or other entity may appeal to any district court of Travis County by filing with the clerk of such court a petition setting forth a copy of the articles or other document sought to be filed and a copy of the written disapproval thereof by the Secretary of State; whereupon the matter shall be tried de novo by the court, and the court shall either sustain the action of the Secretary of State or direct him to take such action as the court may deem proper.

B. Appeals from all final orders and judgments entered by the district court under this Article in review of any ruling or decision of the Secretary of State may be taken as in other civil actions.

Art. 9.05. Certificates and Certified Copies to be Received in Evidence

A. All certificates issued by the Secretary of State in accordance with the provisions of this Act, and all copies of documents filed in his office in accordance with the provisions of this Act, when certified by him, shall be taken and received in all courts, public offices, and official bodies as prima facie evidence of the facts therein stated, and shall be subject to recordation. A certificate by the Secretary of State, under the state seal, as to the existence or non-existence of the facts relating to corporations which would not appear from a certified copy of any of the foregoing documents or certificates shall be taken and received in all courts, public offices, and official bodies as prima facie evidence of the existence or non-existence of the facts therein stated.

Art. 9.06. Forms to be Promulgated by Secretary of State

A. Forms may be promulgated by the Secretary of State for all reports and all other documents required to be filed in the office of the Secretary of State. The use of such forms, however, shall not be mandatory, except in instances in which the law may specifically so provide.

Art. 9.07. Time for Filing Documents in the Office of the Secretary of State

A. Except as provided by Section B of this article, if a document is required to be filed in the office of the Secretary of State by any provision of this Act, that requirement shall be construed to include the requirement that the document be filed with reasonable promptness.

B. A person required under this Act to file with the Secretary of State a change of registered office or agent, an application or certificate of withdrawal or termination, or articles of dissolution commits an offense if the person does not file the required filing with the Secretary of State before the earlier of:

(1) the 30th day after the date of the change, withdrawal, or termination; or

(2) the date the filing is otherwise required by law.

C. A person who violates Section B of this article is liable to the state for a civil penalty in an amount not to exceed $2,500 for each violation. In determining the amount of a penalty under this section, the court shall consider all the circumstances giving rise to the offense. The attorney general or the prosecuting attorney in the county in which the violation occurs may bring suit to recover the civil penalty imposed under this article.

D. The attorney general may bring an action in the name of the state to restrain or enjoin a person from violating Section B of this article.

E. In an action or proceeding brought against a person who has not complied with Section B of this article, the plaintiff or other party bringing the suit or proceeding may recover, at the court's discretion, reasonable costs and attorney's fees incurred by locating and effecting service of process on the person. Any damages recovered must be in conjunction with a pending action or proceeding and shall be awarded as costs under the Texas Rules of Civil Procedure. This sec-

tion does not create a private independent cause of action for failure to comply with Section B of this article.

F. A person who is entitled to recover damages under Section E of this article may request from the attorney general nonconfidential information on the other person for the purpose of effecting service of process. The attorney general shall comply with a request made under this section to the extent practicable.

Art. 9.09. Waiver of Notice

Whenever any notice is required to be given to any shareholder or director of a corporation under the provisions of this Act or under the provisions of the articles of incorporation or bylaws of the corporation, a waiver thereof in writing signed by the person or persons entitled to such notice, or a waiver by electronic transmission by the person entitled to notice, whether before or after the time stated therein, shall be equivalent to the giving of such notice. The business to be transacted at a regular or special meeting of the shareholders, directors, or members of a committee of directors or the purpose of a meeting is not required to be specified in a written waiver of notice or a waiver by electronic transmission unless required by the articles of incorporation or the bylaws.

Art. 9.10. Actions Without a Meeting; Telephone Meetings

A. (1) Any action required by this Act to be taken at any annual or special meeting of shareholders, or any action which may be taken at any annual or special meeting of shareholders, may be taken without a meeting, without prior notice, and without a vote, if a consent or consents in writing, setting forth the action so taken, shall have been signed by the holder or holders of all the shares entitled to vote with respect to the action that is the subject of the consent. The articles of incorporation may provide that any action required by this Act to be taken at any annual or special meeting of shareholders, or any action which may be taken at any annual or special meeting of shareholders, may be taken without a meeting, without prior notice, and without a vote, if a consent or consents in writing, setting forth the action so taken, shall be signed by the holder or holders of shares having not less than the minimum number of votes that would be necessary to take such action at a meeting at which holders of all shares entitled to vote on the action were present and voted.

(2) Every written consent signed by the holders of less than all the shares entitled to vote with respect to the action that is the subject of the consent shall bear the date of signature of each shareholder who signs the consent. No written consent signed by the holder of less than all the shares entitled to vote with respect to the action that is the subject of the consent shall be effective to take the action that is the subject of the consent unless, within 60 days after the date of the earliest dated consent delivered to the corporation in a manner required by this Article, a consent or consents signed by the holder or holders of shares having not less than the minimum number of votes that would be necessary to take the action that is the subject of the consent are delivered to the corporation by delivery to its registered office, registered agent, principal place of business, transfer agent, registrar, exchange agent or an officer or agent of the corporation having custody of the books in which proceedings of meetings of shareholders are recorded. Delivery shall be by hand or certified or registered mail, return receipt requested. Delivery to the corporation's principal place of business shall be addressed to the president or principal executive officer of the corporation.

(3) A telegram, telex, cablegram, or other electronic transmission by a shareholder consenting to an action to be taken is considered to be

written, signed, and dated for the purposes of this article if the transmission sets forth or is delivered with information from which the corporation can determine that the transmission was transmitted by the shareholder and the date on which the shareholder transmitted the transmission. The date of transmission is the date on which the consent was signed. Consent given by telegram, telex, cablegram, or other electronic transmission may not be considered delivered until the consent is reproduced in paper form and the paper form is delivered to the corporation at its registered office in this state or its principal place of business, or to an officer or agent of the corporation having custody of the book in which proceedings of shareholder meetings are recorded. Notwithstanding Subsection (2) of this section, consent given by telegram, telex, cablegram, or other electronic transmission may be delivered to the principal place of business of the corporation or to an officer or agent of the corporation having custody of the book in which proceedings of shareholder meetings are recorded to the extent and in the manner provided by resolution of the board of directors of the corporation.

(4) Any photographic, photostatic, facsimile, or similarly reliable reproduction of a consent in writing signed by a shareholder may be substituted or used instead of the original writing for any purpose for which the original writing could be used, if the reproduction is a complete reproduction of the entire original writing.

(5) Prompt notice of the taking of any action by shareholders without a meeting by less than unanimous written consent shall be given to those shareholders who did not consent in writing to the action.

(6) If any action by shareholders is taken by written consent, any articles or documents filed with the Secretary of State as a result of the taking of the action shall state, in lieu of any statement required by the Act concerning the number of shares outstanding and entitled to vote on the action or concerning any vote of shareholders, that written consent has been given in accordance with the provisions of this Article and that any written notice required by this Article has been given.

B. Unless otherwise restricted by the articles of incorporation or bylaws, any action required or permitted to be taken at a meeting of the board of directors or any committee may be taken without a meeting if a consent in writing, setting forth the action so taken, is signed by all the members of the board of directors or committee, as the case may be. A telegram, telex, cablegram, or other electronic transmission by a director consenting to an action to be taken and transmitted by a director is considered written, signed, and dated for the purposes of this article if the transmission sets forth or is delivered with information from which the corporation can determine that the transmission was transmitted by the director and the date on which the director transmitted the transmission. Such consent shall have the same force and effect as a unanimous vote at a meeting, and may be stated as such in any document or instrument filed with the Secretary of State.

C. Subject to the provisions required or permitted by this Act for notice of meetings, unless otherwise restricted by the articles of incorporation or by-laws, shareholders, members of the board of directors, or members of any committee designated by such board, may participate in and hold a meeting of such shareholders, board, or committee by means of conference telephone or similar communications equipment by means of which all persons participating in the meeting can hear each other, and participation in a meeting pursuant to this Section shall constitute presence in person at such meeting, except where a person participates in the meeting for the express purpose of objecting to the transaction of any business on the ground that the meeting is not lawfully called or convened.

D. If action is taken with respect to a particular matter by the holders of shares of a class or series by means of a written consent in compliance with Section A of this Article, any provision of this Act that requires advance notice of a meeting or of the proposed action will not apply as to that class or series for such action.

Art. 9.11. Application to Foreign and Interstate Commerce

A. The provisions of this Act shall apply to commerce with foreign nations and among the several states only in so far as the same may be permitted under the provisions of the Constitution of the United States.

Art. 9.12. Reservation of Power

A. The Legislature shall at all times have power to prescribe such regulations, provisions, and limitations as it may deem advisable, which regulations, provisions, and limitations shall be binding upon any and all corporations subject to the provisions of this Act, and the Legislature shall have power to amend, repeal, or modify this Act.

Art. 9.13. Effect of Invalidity of Part of This Act

A. If a court of competent jurisdiction shall adjudge to be invalid or unconstitutional any clause, sentence, subsection, section, or Article of this Act, such judgment or decree shall not affect, impair, invalidate, or nullify the remainder of this Act, but the effect thereof shall be confined to the clause, sentence, subsection, section, or Article of this Act so adjudged to be invalid or unconstitutional.

Art. 9.14. To what Corporations This Act Applies; Procedure for Adoption of Act by Existing Corporations

A. This Act applies to each domestic corporation and to each foreign corporation that is transacting business in this state, regardless of whether the foreign corporation is registered to transact business in this state. This Act does not apply to domestic corporations organized under any statute other than this Act or to any foreign corporations granted authority to transact business within this State under any statute other than this Act; provided, however, that if any domestic corporation was heretofore or is hereafter organized under or is governed by a statute other than this Act or the Texas Non-Profit Corporation Act (Article 1396-1.01 et seq., Vernon's Texas Civil Statutes) that contains no provisions in regard to some of the matters provided for in this Act, or any foreign corporation was heretofore or is hereafter granted authority to transact business within this State under a statute other than this Act or the Texas Non-Profit Corporation Act that contains no provisions in regard to some of the matters provided for in this Act in respect of foreign corporations, or if such a statute specifically provides that the general laws for incorporation or for the granting of a certificate of authority to transact business in this State, as the case may be, shall supplement the provisions of such statute, then the provisions of this Act shall apply to the extent that they are not inconsistent with the provisions of such other statute; provided further, however, that this Act shall not apply to any domestic corporation organized under or governed by the Texas Non-Profit Corporation Act or any foreign corporation granted authority to transact business within this State under the Texas Non-Profit Corporation Act.

B. For a period of five (5) years from and after the effective date of this Act, it shall not apply to any domestic corporation duly chartered or existing on said effective date or to any foreign corporation holding, on that date, a valid permit to do business in this State, unless such domestic or foreign corporation shall, during such period of five (5) years, voluntarily elect to adopt the provisions of this Act and shall comply with the procedure prescribed by Section C of this Article.

C. During the period of five (5) years from and after the effective date of this Act, any domestic corporation duly chartered or existing prior to said effective date and any foreign corporation holding a valid permit to do business in this State, prior to the effective date of this Act, may voluntarily elect to adopt the provisions of this Act and may become subject to its provisions by taking the following steps:

(1) As to domestic corporations, a resolution reciting that the corporation voluntarily adopts this Act shall be adopted by the board of directors and shareholders by the procedure prescribed by this Act for the amendment of articles of incorporation. As to foreign corporations, a resolution shall be adopted by the board of directors, reciting that the corporation voluntarily adopts this Act.

(2) Upon adoption of the required resolution or resolutions, an instrument shall be executed in duplicate by the corporation by its president or a vice president and by its secretary or an assistant secretary, and verified by one of the officers signing such statement, which shall set forth:

(a) The name of the corporation.

(b) Each resolution adopted by the corporation.

(c) The date of the adoption of each resolution.

(d) The post office address of its initial registered office, and the name of its initial registered agent at such address.

(3) Duplicate originals of such document shall be delivered to the Secretary of State. If the Secretary of State finds that such document conforms to law, he shall, when all fees and franchise taxes have been paid as prescribed by law:

(a) Endorse on each of such duplicate originals the word "Filed," and the month, day, and year of the filing thereof.

(b) File one of such duplicate originals in his office.

(c) Deliver the other duplicate original to the corporation or its representative.

(4) Upon the filing of such document, all provisions of this Act shall thereafter apply to the corporation.

D. Except for the exceptions and limitations of Section A of this Article, this Act shall apply to all domestic corporations organized after the date on which this Act becomes effective and to all foreign corporations transacting, or seeking to transact, business within this State and not holding, on the effective date of this Act, a valid permit so to do, and to all domestic and foreign corporations electing within five (5) years to adopt this Act and manifesting their election in the manner provided in Section C of this Article.

E. Effective September 6, 1960, this Act shall apply to all domestic corporations and to all foreign corporations transacting or seeking to transact business in this State, except for the exceptions and limitations of Section A of this Article and with the further exception that no domestic corporation existing at the time that this Act becomes effective and no foreign corporation holding a valid permit to do business in this State at the time this Act becomes effective, which has not adopted this Act prior to September 6, 1960 by complying with Section C of this Article and which has not amended its articles of incorporation or its certificate of authority, as the case may be, after this Act becomes applicable thereto, shall be deemed to have failed to comply with the provisions of this Act by reason of the fact that:

(1) The name of such corporation does not conform with the provisions of Articles 2.05A(1) and 8.03A(1) of this Act provided such name does conform with the other provisions of this Act and all other laws of this State.

(2) Such corporation has never received for the issuance of shares consideration of the value of at least One Thousand Dollars ($1,000) in conformity with the minimum requirements of this Act.

If any such corporation should amend its articles of incorporation or its certificate of authority, as the case may be, after this Act becomes applicable thereto, such corporation must, simultaneously with or prior to filing such amendment with the Secretary of State, take such action as may be necessary to bring such corporation into conformity with the provisions of this Act.

F. Except for domestic and foreign corporations organized for the purposes set forth in Section A above, each domestic corporation existing on September 6, 1955, which meanwhile has not been dissolved nor adopted this Act by complying with Section C of this Article and each foreign corporation holding a valid permit to do business in this State on September 6, 1955, which meanwhile has not surrendered its permit nor adopted this Act by complying with Section C of this Article, shall execute and file, as a part of its annual report required to be filed for franchise tax purposes under Article 7089 of the Revised Civil Statutes of Texas between January 1 and March 15, 1960, the following described statement:

(1) Such statement shall be executed in duplicate by the president or a vice-president and by the secretary or an assistant secretary of the corporation, and verified by one of the officers signing such statement, and shall set forth:

(a) The name of the corporation;

(b) The post office address of its initial registered office, and the name of its initial registered agent at such address;

(c) That such designation and appointment was authorized by resolution duly adopted by its board of directors.

(2) Duplicate originals of such statement shall be delivered to the Secretary of State. If the Secretary of State finds that such statement conforms to law, he shall when all fees and franchise taxes have been paid as prescribed by law:

(a) Endorse on each of such duplicate originals the word "Filed", and the month, day and year of the filing thereof;

(b) File one of such duplicate originals in his office;

(c) Deliver the other duplicate original to the corporation or its representative.

(3) No fee shall be charged for the filing of such statement.

(4) Such statement shall not become effective until September 6, 1960, and the registered office and registered agent designated therein may be changed at any time in accordance with the provisions of this Act.

(5) Such statement shall be deemed to be a part of the annual report for franchise tax purposes, and failure to file such statement shall subject the corporation to the penalties set forth in Articles 7089 et seq. of the Revised Civil Statutes of Texas for failure to file an annual report.

Art. 9.15. Extent to Which Existing Laws Shall Remain Applicable to Corporations

A. Except as provided in the last preceding Article, existing corporations shall continue to be governed by the laws heretofore applicable thereto.

B. Except as provided in Section B of Article 9.16 of this Act, any special limitations, obligations, liabilities, and powers, applicable to a particular kind of corporation for which special provision is made by the laws of this State, including, (but not excluding other corporations) those corporations subject to supervision under Article 1524a of the Revised Civil Statutes of Texas, shall continue to be applicable to any such corporation, and this Act is not intended to repeal and does not repeal the statutory provisions providing for these special limitations, obligations, liabilities, and powers.

C. Provided that nothing in this Act shall in anywise affect or nullify the Antitrust Laws of this State.

Art. 9.16. Repeal of Existing Laws; Extent and Effect Thereof

A. Subject to the provisions of the two last preceding Articles of this Act and of Section C of Article 2.02 of this Act and Section B of this Article, and excluding any existing general act not inconsistent with any provision of this Act, no law of this State pertaining to private corporations, domestic or foreign, shall hereafter apply to corporations organized under this Act, or which obtain authority to transact business in this State under this Act, or to existing corporations which adopt this Act.

B. Chapter 15 of Title 32, Revised Civil Statutes of Texas, 1925, as amended, is hereby repealed effective five (5) years after the date on which this Act becomes effective; provided that such Chapter 15, Title 32, shall not hereafter apply to corporations organized under this Act, or which obtain authority to transact business in this State under this Act, or to existing corporations which adopt this Act.

C. The repeal of a prior act by this Act shall not affect any right accrued or established, or any liability or penalty incurred, under the provisions of such Act, prior to the repeal thereof.

Business Corporation Act
Part 10.

Art. 10.01. Filing and Filing Fees

A. The Secretary of State is authorized and required to collect for the use of the State the following fees:

(1) Filing articles of incorporation of a domestic corporation and issuing a certificate of incorporation, Three Hundred Dollars ($300.00).

(2) Filing articles of amendment of a domestic corporation and issuing a certificate of amendment, One Hundred Fifty Dollars ($150.00).

(3) Filing articles of merger, whether the surviving or new corporation be a domestic or foreign corporation, or articles of exchange Three Hundred Dollars ($300.00).

(4) Filing an application of a foreign corporation for a certificate of authority to transact business in this State and issuing such a certificate of authority, Seven Hundred Fifty Dollars ($750.00).

(5) Filing an application of a foreign corporation for an amended certificate of authority to transact business in this State and issuing such an amended certificate of authority, One Hundred Fifty Dollars ($150.00).

(6) Filing restated articles of incorporation of a domestic corporation, Three Hundred Dollars ($300.00).

(7) Filing application for reservation of corporate name and issuing a certificate therefor, Forty Dollars ($40.00).

(8) Filing notice of transfer of reserved corporate name and issuing a certificate therefor, Fifteen Dollars ($15.00).

(9) Filing application for registration of corporate name and issuing a certificate therefor, Seventy-Five Dollars ($75.00).

(10) Filing application for renewal of registration of corporate name and issuing a certificate therefor, Seventy-Five Dollars ($75.00).

(11) Filing statement of change of registered office or registered agent, or both, Fifteen Dollars ($15.00).

(12) Filing statement of change of address of registered agent, Fifteen Dollars ($15.00); provided, however, that the maximum fee for simultaneous filings by a registered agent for more than one corporation shall not exceed Seven Hundred Fifty Dollars ($750.00).

(13) Filing statement of resolution establishing series of shares, Fifteen Dollars ($15.00).

(14) Filing statement of cancellation of redeemable shares, Fifteen Dollars ($15.00).

(15) Filing statement of cancellation of re-acquired shares, Fifteen Dollars ($15.00).

(16) Filing statement of reduction of stated capital, Fifteen Dollars ($15.00).

(17) Filing articles of dissolution and issuing certificate therefor, Forty Dollars ($40.00).

(18) Filing application for withdrawal and issuing certificate therefor, Fifteen Dollars ($15.00).

(19) Filing certificate from home state that foreign corporation is no longer in existence in said state, Fifteen Dollars ($15.00).

(20) Filing a bylaw or agreement restricting transfer of shares or securities other than as an amendment to the articles of incorporation, Fifteen Dollars ($15.00).

(21) Filing any instrument pursuant to this Act not expressly provided for above, Fifteen Dollars ($15.00).

(22) Filing application for reinstatement of corporate charter or certificate of authority following forfeiture under the Tax Code, Seventy-Five Dollars ($75.00).

(23) Blank

(24) Filing articles of conversion and issuing a certificate of conversion, Three Hundred Dollars ($300.00).

B. Except as otherwise expressly provided in this Act, any instrument to be filed pursuant to this Act shall be signed on behalf of the filing corporation by an officer, and the original and a copy of the instrument shall be delivered to the Secretary of State with copies attached thereto of any document incorporated by reference in or otherwise made a part of such instrument, or to be filed by means of such instrument. If the Secretary of State finds that such instrument conforms to law, he shall, when all franchise taxes and fees have been paid as prescribed by law:

(a) endorse on the original and the copy the word "Filed", and the month, day, and year of the filing thereof;

(b) file the original in his office;

(c) issue any certificate required by this Act relating to the subject matter of the filed instrument; and

(d) return the copy, affixed to any certificate required to be issued by the Secretary of State, to the corporation or its representative.

Art. 10.02. Penalty for Signing False Document

A. A person commits an offense if he signs a document he knows is false in any material respect with intent that the document be delivered on behalf of a corporation to the Secretary of State for filing.

B. An offense under this article is a Class A misdemeanor.

Art. 10.03. Delayed Effectiveness of Certain Filings

A. The effectiveness of (i) the incorporation of a corporation under this Act, (ii) an amendment to a corporation's articles of incorporation, including an amendment effected pursuant to a statement of resolution establishing a series of shares, (iii) the restatement of articles of incorporation of a corporation, (iv) a merger or share exchange, (v) a cancellation of redeemable or reacquired shares or a reduction in stated capital, (vi) a voluntary dissolution, (vii) the authorization or withdrawal of a foreign corporation to transact business in this State, (viii) an amendment to the certificate of authority of a foreign corporation, (ix) a bylaw or agreement restricting the transfer of shares or securities of a corporation pursuant to this Act, (x) a change in registered office or registered agent, (xi) a change of address of a registered agent (each such act or document being a "Permitted Act"), or (xii) a conversion may be made effective as of a time and date after the time and date otherwise provided in this Act or may be made effective upon the occurrence of events or facts that may occur in the future, which events or facts may include future acts of any person or entity, if:

(1) the articles, statement, application, or other filing that is required by this Act to be filed with the Secretary of State to make effective such Permitted Act clearly and expressly set forth, in addition to any other statement or information required to be set forth therein, (i) the time and date on which such Permitted Act is to become effective or (ii) if such Permitted Act is to become effective upon the occurrence of events or facts that may occur in the future, (a) the manner in which such events or facts shall operate to cause such Permitted Act to become effective and (b) the date of the 90th day after the date of the filing of such articles, statement, application or other filing;

(2) in the case of a Permitted Act that is to become effective as of a time or date after the time and date otherwise provided in this Act, (i) such subsequent time and date is not more than 90 days after the date of the filing of the articles, statement, application, or other filing that is otherwise required by this Act to be filed with the Secretary of State to make effective such Permitted Act and (ii) the time on which the Permitted Act is to become effective is not midnight or 12:00 p.m.; and

(3) in the case of a Permitted Act that is to be made effective upon the occurrence of events or facts that may occur in the future, other than the mere passage of time, a statement that all such events or facts upon which the effectiveness of such Permitted Act is conditioned have been satisfied or waived, and of the date on which such condition was satisfied or waived, is filed with the Secretary of State within 90 days of the date of the filing of the articles, statement, application or other filing that is otherwise required by this Act for such Permitted Act to become effective.

B. The statement required by Subsection 3 of Section A of this Article shall be executed on behalf of each domestic or foreign corporation or other entity that was required to execute the articles, statement, application, or other filing that is otherwise required by this Act to be filed with the Secretary of State to make effective such Permitted Act by an officer or other duly authorized representative, including an officer or duly authorized representative of any successor domestic or foreign corporation or other entity, and an original and a copy thereof shall be filed with the Secretary of State. If the Secretary of State finds that such statement conforms to the provisions of this Act, he shall:

(1) Endorse on the original and the copy the word "Filed" and the month, day, and year of the filing thereof.

(2) File the original in his office.

(3) Return the copy to the filing party or its representative.

C. If any Permitted Act is to become effective as of a time or date after the time and date otherwise provided in this Act for such Permitted Act to become effective, notwithstanding any other provision of this Act to the contrary, such Permitted Act shall become, to the extent permitted by Section A of this Article, effective as of such subsequent time and date, and any certificate issued by the Secretary of State upon the filing of the articles, statement, application or other filing that is otherwise required by this Act for such Permitted Act to

become effective shall expressly set forth the time and date upon which such Permitted Act is to become effective.

D. If any Permitted Act is to be made effective upon the occurrence of events or facts that may occur in the future, other than the mere passage of time, and the statement required by Subsection 3 of Section A of this Article is filed with the Secretary of State within the time prescribed therein, such Permitted Act shall become effective as of the time and date on which the latest specified event or fact shall have occurred or the time and date on which such condition is otherwise satisfied or waived. Any certificate issued or notation, acknowledgement or other statement made by the Secretary of State upon the filing of the articles, statement, application or other filing that is otherwise required by this Act for such Permitted Act to become effective shall state that "The effectiveness of the action to which this instrument relates is conditioned upon the occurrence of certain facts or events described in the filing to which this instrument relates" or shall make reference in such manner as the Secretary of State shall approve to the fact that the effectiveness of the action is so conditioned. The time and date on which a condition to the effectiveness of a Permitted Act is satisfied or waived as set forth in a statement filed with the Secretary of State pursuant to Subsection 3 of Section A of this Article shall be conclusively regarded as the time and date on which such condition was satisfied or waived for purposes of this Article.

E. If the effectiveness of any Permitted Act is conditioned upon the occurrence of events or facts that may occur in the future, other than the mere passage of time, and the statement required by Subsection 3 of Section A of this Article is not filed with the Secretary of State within the time prescribed therein, such Permitted Act shall not become effective unless there is subsequently filed with the Secretary of State the articles, statement, application, or other filing required by this Act to be filed with the Secretary of State to make effective such Permitted Act.

Business Corporation Act
Part 11.

Art. 11.01. Emergency Clause

A. The fact that existing laws of the State of Texas have been amended from time to time over a period of some seventy (70) years and more without any adoption meanwhile of a complete Act relating to business corporations generally, the provisions of which are consistent with one another; the fact that with so many amendments of the corporation laws applicable to business corporations generally over so many years there have developed many uncertainties in the corporation laws of this State and with the result that there is now an imperative need for clarification of certain provisions of the existing laws; the fact that all of the other states than Texas in which large and important business is transacted have adopted in recent years modern corporation laws and with the result that Texas citizens are increasingly prone to organize their corporate ventures under the laws of other states than the laws of Texas because Texas does not have such a modern act; and the fact that Texas in such connection is losing a substantial volume of corporate enterprise which it should otherwise gain from and after the time that a modern business corporation Act becomes effective in Texas and is losing tax income from ad valorem taxes, filing fees and otherwise meanwhile; all such facts create an emergency and public necessity that the Constitutional Rule requiring bills to be read on three separate days in each House be suspended and said Rule is hereby suspended; and require that this Act take effect and be in force from and after the date of its enactment, and it is so enacted.

Art. 11.02. Applicability; Expiration

A. Except as provided by Title 8, Business Organizations Code, this Act does not apply to a corporation to which the Business Organizations Code applies.

B. This Act expires January 1, 2010.

Business Corporation Act
Part 12.

Art. 12.01. Short Title

A. Citation. This part may be cited as the "Texas Close Corporation Law."

Art. 12.02. Definitions

A. In General. In this part, unless the context otherwise requires:

(1) "Close corporation" means a domestic corporation formed in conformance with the requirements of this part.

(2) "Ordinary corporation" means a domestic corporation that is not a close corporation.

(3) "Shareholders' agreement" means a written agreement regulating any aspect of the business and affairs of a close corporation or the relations among its shareholders that has been executed in conformance with Article 12.33 of this Act.

(4) "Close corporation provision" means a provision in the articles of incorporation of a close corporation or in a shareholders' agreement.

B. Cross-Reference. Article 12.51 of this Act provides definitions of terms that pertain to judicial proceedings concerning a close corporation.

Art. 12.03. Applicability

A. Part Twelve. This part applies only to a close corporation.

B. Other Parts. To the extent not inconsistent with this part, all other parts of this Act apply to a close corporation.

Art. 12.11. Articles of Incorporation

A. In General. In addition to any provision required or permitted to be set forth in the articles by Article 3.02 of this Act the articles of incorporation of a close corporation, whether original, amended, or restated, must include the following statement: "This corporation is a close corporation."

Art. 12.12. Formation of a Close Corporation

A. In General. A close corporation shall be formed in conformance with Part Three and Article 12.11 of this Act.

Art. 12.13. Adoption of Close Corporation Status

A. By Amendment of Articles of Incorporation. An ordinary corporation may become a close corporation by amending its articles of incorporation in conformance with Part Four and Article 12.11 of this Act. An amendment adopting close corporation status must be approved by the affirmative vote of the holders of all the outstanding shares of each class, whether or not entitled to vote on the amendment by the articles of incorporation of the ordinary corporation.

B. Through Merger, Conversion, or Share Exchange. A surviving or new corporation resulting from a merger, a corporation incorporated as part of a conversion, or a corporation that acquires a corporation pursuant to a share exchange in conformance with Part Five of this Act may become a close corporation if as part of the plan of merger, conversion, or exchange its articles of incorporation conform with Article 12.11 of this Act. Any plan of merger, conversion, or exchange adopting close corporation status must be approved by the affirmative vote of the holders of all the outstanding shares, and of each class or series of shares, of each corporation that is party to the merger, conversion, or share exchange, whether or not entitled to vote on the plan by the articles of incorporation of the corporation.

Art. 12.14. Existing Close Corporation

A. In General. If an existing corporation that elected to become a close corporation in conformance with former Article 2.30-1 of this Act has not terminated that status before the effective date of this part:

(1) the corporation is considered to be a close corporation under this part;

(2) a provision in its articles of incorporation authorized by Section G or H of former Article 2.30-1 of this Act or by former Article 2.30-5 of this Act continues to be valid and enforceable so long as its status as a close corporation has not been terminated;

(3) an agreement among its shareholders in conformance with former Article 2.30-2 of this Act is considered to be a shareholders' agreement, if the agreement conforms with Articles 12.32 through 12.37 of this Act; and

(4) any certificate representing its shares issued or delivered after the effective date of this part, whether in connection with an original issue of shares, a transfer of shares, or otherwise, must conform with Article 12.39 of this Act.

Art. 12.15. Bylaws of Close Corporation

A. A close corporation need not adopt bylaws if provisions required by law to be contained in the bylaws are contained in either the articles of incorporation or a shareholders' agreement.

B. If a close corporation does not have bylaws when it terminates its status as a close corporation under Article 12.21 of this Act, the corporation shall immediately adopt bylaws in conformance with Article 2.23 of this Act.

Art. 12.21. Termination of Close Corporation Status

A. In General. A close corporation terminates its status as a close corporation:

(1) on filing a statement of termination in conformance with Article 12.22 of this Act;

(2) by amending its articles of incorporation in conformance with Part Four of this Act to delete from its articles the statement that it is a close corporation;

(3) through a merger, conversion, or share exchange in conformance with Part Five of this Act unless the plan of merger, conversion, or exchange provides that the surviving or new corporation will continue as or become a close corporation and the plan has been approved by the affirmative vote or consent of the holders of all the outstanding shares, and of each class and series of shares, of the close corporation, whether or not entitled to vote on the plan by the articles of incorporation; or

(4) when termination is decreed in a judicial proceeding to enforce a close corporation provision providing for the termination.

Art. 12.22. Statement of Termination; Filing; Notice

A. In General. If a close corporation provision specifies a time or event, whether or not identifiable by persons dealing with the close corporation, that will terminate close corporation status, the termination becomes effective on the occurrence of the specified time or event and the filing of a statement of termination of close corporation status in conformance with this article.

B. Execution, Delivery and Form. Promptly after the time or event specified in a close corporation provision for termination of close corporation status has occurred, a statement of termination of close corporation status shall be signed on behalf of the close corporation by an officer. A copy of the applicable close corporation provision must be included in or attached to the statement. The original and a copy of the statement and the inclusion or attachment shall be delivered to the Secretary of State. The statement must set forth:

(1) the name of the corporation;

(2) a statement that the corporation has terminated its status as a close corporation in accordance with the included or attached close corporation provision; and

(3) the time or event that caused the termination and, in the case of an event, the approximate date of the event.

C. Filing. If the Secretary of State finds that the statement of termination of close corporation status conforms to law, the Secretary of State shall, when all fees and franchise taxes have been paid as required by law:

(1) endorse on the original and the copy the word "Filed" and the month, day, and year of the filing of the statement;

(2) file the original in the office of the Secretary of State; and

(3) return the copy to the corporation or its representative.

D. Effect of Filing. On the filing of the statement of termination of close corporation status, the articles of incorporation of the close corporation are considered to be amended to delete from the articles the statement that it is a close corporation and the corporation's status as a close corporation terminates.

E. Notice to Shareholders. On receipt of the filed copy of the statement of termination from the Secretary of State as provided by Section C of this article, the corporation shall deliver a copy of the statement to each shareholder of the corporation, either personally or by mail. If mailed, the copy is considered to be delivered when deposited in the United States mail, postage prepaid, addressed to the shareholder at his address as it appears on the stock transfer books of the corporation. Failure to deliver the notice does not affect the validity of termination of close corporation status.

Art. 12.23. Effect of Termination of Close Corporation Status

A. In General. A close corporation that terminates its status as a close corporation and becomes an ordinary corporation is subject to the provisions of this Act as if it had not elected close corporation status under this part.

B. Effect on Shareholders' Agreement. The effect of termination of close corporation status on a shareholders' agreement is governed by Section E, Article 12.36 of this Act.

C. Reinstatement of Governance by Board of Directors. If, at the time termination of close corporation status has become effective, the close corporation's business and affairs have been managed other than by a board of directors, as permitted by Article 12.31 of this Act, governance by a board of directors is instituted or reinstated:

(1) if a shareholders' agreement so provides, in the manner stated therein or by the persons named in the agreement to serve as the interim board of directors; or

(2) regardless of whether or not a shareholders' agreement contains a governing provision if all the parties to the agreement so agree, by a shareholders' meeting, to elect a board of directors.

D. Shareholders' Meeting. A shareholders' meeting required by Section C of this article shall be promptly called after termination of close corporation status has become effective. If a meeting is not called before the 31st day after the day on which termination becomes effective, any shareholder, whether or not entitled to call a shareholders' meeting or vote at such a meeting, has the power to call the meeting on the notice required by Article 2.25 of this Act. At the meeting

there shall be elected the number of directors specified in the articles of incorporation or bylaws, or in the absence of such a specification, three directors.

E. Term of Service. The directors succeeding to the management of the corporation as provided in Section C of this article shall serve until the next annual meeting of shareholders and until their successors shall have been elected and qualified. Until directors are elected, the shareholders of the corporation shall act as the board of directors and the business and affairs of the corporation shall be conducted in conformance with Article 12.37 of this Act.

Art. 12.31. Governance of Close Corporation Affairs

A. Management. A close corporation shall be managed:

(1) by a board of directors in the same manner an ordinary corporation is managed by its board of directors under this Act; or

(2) in the manner provided for in its articles of incorporation or in a shareholders' agreement.

Art. 12.32. Shareholders' Agreement—In General

A. Close Corporation Provisions. All shareholders of a close corporation may make one or more shareholders' agreements. The business and affairs of a close corporation or the relations among the shareholders that may be regulated by a shareholders' agreement include without limitation:

(1) management of the business and affairs of the close corporation with or without a board of directors, by its shareholders, or in whole or part by one or more of its shareholders or by one or more persons not shareholders;

(2) buy-sell, first option, first refusal, or similar arrangements with respect to the close corporation's shares or other securities, and restrictions on their transfer, including restrictions beyond those permitted to be imposed by Article 2.22 of this Act;

(3) declaration and payment of dividends and other distributions, whether or not in proportion to ownership of shares, in amounts permitted by this Act or the manner in which profits or losses shall be apportioned;

(4) restrictions on the rights of a transferee of shares or assignee to participate in the management or administration of the close corporation's business and affairs during the term of the shareholders' agreement;

(5) rights of one or more shareholders to dissolve the close corporation at will or on the occurrence of a specified event or contingency in which case the dissolution of the close corporation shall proceed as if all of its shareholders had consented in writing to dissolution of the close corporation as provided by Article 6.02 of this Act;

(6) exercise or division of voting power either in general or in regard to specified matters by or among the shareholders of the close corporation or other persons, including without limitation:

(a) voting agreements and voting trusts that need not conform with Article 2.30 of this Act;

(b) requiring the vote or consent of the holders of a greater or lesser number of shares than is otherwise required by this Act or other law, including any action for termination of close corporation status;

(c) granting one or some other specified number of votes for each shareholder; and

(d) permitting any action for which this Act requires approval by the vote of the board of directors or by a vote of the shareholders of an ordinary corporation or by both, to be taken without such a vote, in the manner provided in the shareholders' agreement;

(7) terms and conditions of employment of any shareholder, director, officer, or other employee of the close corporation, regardless of the length of the period of employment;

(8) the natural persons who shall be directors, if any, and officers of the close corporation;

(9) arbitration of issues about which the shareholders may become deadlocked in voting or about which the directors or those empowered to manage the close corporation may become deadlocked and the shareholders are unable to break the deadlock;

(10) termination of close corporation status, including any right of dissent or other rights that shareholders who object to the termination may be granted;

(11) qualifications of persons who are or are not entitled to be shareholders of the close corporation;

(12) amendments to or termination of the shareholders' agreement; and

(13) any provision required or permitted by this Act to be set forth in the bylaws.

Art. 12.33. Shareholders' Agreements—Procedures Required

A. Execution. A shareholders' agreement shall be executed:

(1) in the case of an existing close corporation, by each person who is then a shareholder, whether or not the shareholder has voting power;

(2) in the case of an existing ordinary corporation that pursuant to the agreement will adopt close corporation status in conformance with Article 12.13 of this Act, by each person who is then a shareholder, whether or not the shareholder has voting power; or

(3) in the case of a close corporation that is being formed in conformance with Article 12.12 of this Act, by each person who either is a subscriber to its shares or by the shareholders' agreement agrees to become a holder of its shares.

B. Amendment of Agreement. Unless otherwise provided in a shareholders' agreement, an amendment to the shareholders' agreement may be adopted only by the written consent of each person who would be required to execute the shareholders' agreement if it were being executed originally at the time of adoption of the amendment, whether or not the person has voting power in the close corporation.

C. Delivery of Shareholders' Agreement. The close corporation shall deliver a complete copy of any shareholders' agreement to each person who is bound by the shareholders' agreement and who is or will become a shareholder in the close corporation as provided in Section A of this article when a certificate or certificates representing shares in the close corporation are delivered to the person. The close corporation shall also deliver a complete copy of any shareholders' agreement to each person to whom a certificate representing shares is issued and who has not received a complete copy of the agreement. Failure to deliver a complete copy of a shareholders' agreement as required by this section does not affect the validity or enforceability of the shareholders' agreement.

Art. 12.34. Statement of Operation as a Close Corporation

A. In General. If on or after the formation of a close corporation or adoption of close corporation status, a close corporation begins to conduct its business and affairs pursuant to a shareholders' agreement that has become effective, the close corporation shall promptly execute and file a statement of operation as a close corporation with the Secretary of State.

B. Execution and Delivery. A statement of operation as a close corporation shall be signed on behalf of the close corporation by an officer. The close corporation shall deliver the original and a copy of the statement to the Secretary of State. The statement must set forth:

(1) the name of the close corporation;

(2) a statement that the close corporation is being operated and its business and affairs are being conducted under the terms of a shareholders' agreement made pursuant to the Texas Close Corporation Law; and

(3) the date when the operation of the corporation began.

C. Filing. If the Secretary of State finds that the statement of operation as a close corporation conforms to law, the Secretary of State shall, when all fees and franchise taxes have been paid as required by law:

(1) endorse on the original and the copy the word "Filed" and the month, day, and year of the filing of the statement;

(2) file the original in the office of the Secretary of State; and

(3) return the copy to the close corporation or its representative.

D. Effect of Filing. On the filing of the statement of operation as a close corporation, the fact that the close corporation is being operated and its business and affairs are being conducted under the terms of a shareholders' agreement becomes a matter of public record.

Art. 12.35. Validity and Enforceability of Shareholders' Agreement

A. In General. A shareholders' agreement, if executed in conformance with Article 12.33 of this Act, is valid and enforceable in accordance with its terms notwithstanding the elimination of a board of directors, notwithstanding any restriction imposed on the discretion or powers of the board of directors or those empowered to manage the close corporation, and notwithstanding that the effect of the shareholders' agreement is to treat the business and affairs of the close corporation as if it were a partnership or in a manner that would otherwise be appropriate only among partners.

B. Enforcement. The close corporation, any of its shareholders, or any person who is a party to a shareholders' agreement may initiate a proceeding to enforce the shareholders' agreement in conformance with Article 12.52 of this Act.

Art. 12.36. Binding Effect of Shareholders' Agreement

A. Persons Bound. A shareholders' agreement, if executed in conformance with Article 12.33 of this Act, is considered to be an agreement among all the shareholders of the close corporation and is binding and enforceable in accordance with its terms on all shareholders of the close corporation regardless of whether a particular shareholder acquired shares in the close corporation by purchase, gift, bequest, or otherwise, or whether the shareholder had actual knowledge of the existence of the shareholders' agreement at the time of acquiring shares. A transferee or assignee of shares of a close corporation with respect to which there is a shareholders' agreement is bound by the shareholders' agreement for all purposes whether or not the transferee or assignee executed or was aware of the agreement.

B. Delivery of Copy to Transferee. Before the transfer of any shares of a close corporation as to which there is a shareholders' agreement, the transferor shall deliver a complete copy of the shareholders' agreement to the transferee. If the transferor fails to do so:

(1) the validity and enforceability of the shareholders' agreement against all shareholders of the corporation, including the transferee, is not affected;

(2) the right, title, or interest of the transferee in the shares transferred is not adversely affected; and

(3) the transferee is entitled to obtain on demand a complete copy of the shareholders' agreement from the transferor or from the close corporation at the expense of the transferor.

C. Effect of Statement on Share Certificate and Delivery of Shareholders' Agreement. If the certificates representing shares of a close corporation contain the statements required by Section A, Article 12.39 of this Act, and a complete copy of each shareholders' agreement has been delivered as required by Section C, Article 12.33 of this Act, each holder, transferee, or other person claiming an interest in the shares of the close corporation is conclusively presumed to have knowledge of any close corporation provision in effect at the time of the transfer.

D. When Party No Longer Bound. A person ceases to be a party to, and bound by, a shareholders' agreement, notwithstanding the person's signature to the agreement, when the person ceases to be a shareholder of the close corporation unless the person's attempted cessation as a shareholder was in violation of Section B of this article or the shareholders' agreement or unless the shareholders' agreement provides to the contrary. Cessation as a party to a shareholders' agreement or as a shareholder does not relieve a person of any liability the person may have incurred for breach of the shareholders' agreement.

E. Termination of Agreement. A shareholders' agreement terminates when the close corporation terminates its status as a close corporation except that if the shareholders' agreement so provides, the agreement or any provision of the agreement continues to be valid and enforceable to the extent permitted for an ordinary corporation by this Act or other law.

Art. 12.37. Responsibility of Shareholders for Managerial Acts

A. In General. This article applies only to a close corporation whose business and affairs, pursuant to a shareholders' agreement, are managed in whole or in part by its shareholders or any other person or persons rather than solely by a board of directors.

B. Shareholders Deemed Directors. Whenever the context of this Act requires, the shareholders of the close corporation are considered to be directors of the close corporation for purposes of applying any provision of this Act other than with respect to the election and removal of directors. Any requirement that an instrument filed with any governmental agency contain a statement that a specified action has been taken by the board of directors is satisfied by a statement that the corporation is a close corporation having no board of directors and that the action was approved by the shareholders of the close corporation, or by the persons empowered to manage the business and affairs of the close corporation, pursuant to a shareholders' agreement.

C. Liabilities. The shareholders of the close corporation are subject to the liabilities imposed on directors by this Act or other law for any managerial acts or omissions, relating to any aspect of the business and affairs of the close corporation, taken by the shareholders or by any other persons empowered to manage the business and affairs of the close corporation pursuant to a shareholders' agreement if the action is required by this Act or other law to be taken by the board of directors.

D. Mode of Taking Action. Any action that this Act requires or permits to be taken by the board of directors of an ordinary corporation shall be taken, if required, or may be taken, if permitted, by action of the shareholders of the close corporation at a meeting of the shareholders or in the manner permitted by a shareholders' agreement, this article, or this Act, without a meeting. Unless otherwise provided in the articles of incorporation of the close corporation or a shareholders' agreement, such an action is binding on the close corporation if taken on the basis of:

(1) the affirmative vote of the holders of a majority of all outstanding shares entitled to vote on the action; or

(2) consent by all the shareholders of the close corporation, which may be proven by:

(a) the full knowledge of the action by all the shareholders and their failure to object to the action in a timely manner;

(b) a consent in writing to the action in conformance with Article 9.10 of this Act or any other writing executed by or on behalf of all the shareholders reasonably evidencing the consent; or

(c) any other means reasonably evidencing the consent.

E. Limitation of Liability. A shareholder of a close corporation is not liable by virtue of a shareholders' vote or shareholder action without a vote unless the shareholder had the right to vote or consent to the action. A shareholder of a close corporation, whether with or without right to vote or consent, is not liable for any action taken by the shareholders, or by the persons empowered to manage the business and affairs of the close corporation pursuant to a shareholders' agreement if the shareholder dissents from, and has not voted for or consented to, the action. The dissent may be proven by:

(1) an entry in the minutes of the meeting of shareholders;

(2) a written dissent filed with the person acting as secretary of the meeting before the adjournment of the meeting;

(3) a written dissent sent by registered mail to the secretary of the close corporation promptly after the meeting or after a consent in writing was obtained from the other shareholders; or

(4) any other means reasonably evidencing the dissent.

F. Lack of Formalities; Treatment as Partnership. Neither the failure of a close corporation to observe usual formalities or requirements prescribed for an ordinary corporation by this Act relating to the exercise of corporate powers or the management of a corporation's business and affairs nor the performance of a shareholders' agreement that treats the close corporation as if it were a partnership or in a manner that otherwise is appropriate only among partners:

(1) shall be a factor in determining whether to impose personal liability on the shareholders for the close corporation's obligations by disregarding the separate entity of the close corporation or otherwise;

(2) is grounds for invalidating an otherwise valid shareholders' agreement; or

(3) shall affect the status of the close corporation as a corporation under this Act or in law.

Art. 12.38. Other Agreements Among Shareholders Permitted

A. In General. Articles 12.31 through 12.37 of this Act do not prohibit or impair any other agreement among two or more shareholders of an ordinary corporation permitted by this Act or by other law.

Art. 12.39. Close Corporation Share Certificates

A. Required Statements. In addition to any matter required or permitted to be stated on a certificate representing shares by this Act or other law, each certificate representing shares issued by a close corporation must state conspicuously on its face or the back: "These shares are issued by a close corporation as defined by the Texas Business Corporation Act. Under that Act, a shareholders' agreement may provide for management of a close corporation by the shareholders or in other ways different from an ordinary corporation. This may subject the holder of this certificate to certain obligations and liabilities not otherwise imposed on shareholders of an ordinary corporation. On any sale or transfer of these shares, the transferor is obligated to deliver to the transferee a complete copy of any shareholders' agreement."

B. Failure to Contain Statements. Notwithstanding any provision of this Act, including Article 2.19, to the contrary, the status of a corporation as a close corporation is not affected by the failure of any share certificate to contain the statements required by Section A of this article.

Art. 12.51. Judicial Proceedings Relating to a Close Corporation
A. Definitions. As used in this article and the succeeding articles of this part, unless the context otherwise requires:
(1) "Court of competent jurisdiction" means a district court in the county in which the close corporation has its principal office.
(2) "Provisional director" means a person appointed by a court of competent jurisdiction in conformance with Article 12.53 of this Act.
(3) "Custodian" means a person appointed by a court of competent jurisdiction in conformance with Article 12.54 of this Act.
(4) "Shareholder" means any person who is a record or beneficial owner of shares in a close corporation, including any person holding a beneficial interest in the shares under an inter vivos, testamentary, or voting trust, or any person who is the personal representative, as that term is defined in the Texas Probate Code, of a record or beneficial owner.
B. Proceedings Authorized. In addition to any other judicial proceeding pertaining to an ordinary corporation provided for in this Act or by law, a proceeding may be brought in a court of competent jurisdiction by a close corporation or a shareholder to:
(1) enforce a close corporation provision;
(2) appoint a provisional director; or
(3) appoint a custodian.
C. Notice; Intervention. Notice of the commencement of a proceeding must be given in the manner prescribed by this Act or other law and otherwise in a manner consistent with due process of law as directed by the court, to the close corporation, if not a plaintiff, and to each shareholder that is not a plaintiff. The close corporation or any shareholder may intervene in the proceeding.
D. Proceeding Nonexclusive. Except as otherwise provided in Section E of this article, the right of the close corporation or a shareholder to commence a proceeding permitted by Section B of this article is in addition to any other right or remedy the plaintiff may have under this Act or other law.
E. Unavailability of Proceeding. A shareholder may not commence a proceeding before any nonjudicial remedy in a close corporation provision, such as arbitration, for resolution of the issues that are in dispute has been exhausted unless the shareholder proves that the close corporation, the shareholders as a whole, or the shareholder will suffer irreparable harm before the nonjudicial remedy is exhausted. A shareholder may not commence a proceeding to seek damages or other monetary relief if the shareholder has the right to dissent from any proposed action and to receive the fair value of his shares under this Act or a shareholders' agreement.
Art. 12.52. Judicial Proceedings to Enforce Close Corporation Provision
A. In General. A court of competent jurisdiction, in a judicial proceeding brought under this article, shall enforce a close corporation provision without regard to whether or not there is an adequate remedy at law. The enforcement may be by injunction, specific performance, or other relief that the court determines is fair and equitable under the circumstances, including without limitation:
(1) damages instead of or in addition to specific enforcement;
(2) appointment of a provisional director or custodian;
(3) appointment of a receiver for specific assets of the close corporation in conformance with Article 7.04 of this Act;
(4) appointment of a receiver to rehabilitate the close corporation in conformance with Article 7.05 of this Act;
(5) subject to Section B of this article, liquidation of the assets and business and involuntary dissolution of the close corporation and appointment of a receiver to effect the liquidation in conformance with Article 7.06 of this Act; and
(6) termination of close corporation status, but termination may not be decreed unless the court determines that all other remedies in law or in equity, including appointment of a provisional director, custodian, or other type of receiver, are inadequate and that the size of the close corporation, the nature of its business, the number of its shareholders, or their relationship to one another or other similar factors make it wholly impractical to continue close corporation status.
B. Liquidation; Involuntary Dissolution; Receivership. Except where a shareholder seeking relief had the right to dissolve the close corporation under a shareholders' agreement, liquidation, involuntary dissolution, and receivership may not be decreed unless the court determines that all other remedies in law or in equity, including appointment of a provisional director, custodian, or other type of receiver, are inadequate.
Art. 12.53. Judicial Proceeding to Appoint Provisional Director for Close Corporation
A. In General. A court of competent jurisdiction, in a proceeding brought under this article, shall appoint a provisional director for a close corporation on proof that the directors or the persons empowered to manage the business and affairs of the close corporation pursuant to a shareholders' agreement are so divided respecting the management of its affairs that the votes or consents required to take action on behalf of the close corporation cannot be obtained with the consequence that its business and affairs can no longer be conducted to the general advantage of the shareholders.
B. Status of Provisional Director. The appointment of a provisional director is subject to the following provisions:
(1) a provisional director must be an impartial person who is not a shareholder, a party to a shareholders' agreement, a person empowered to manage the close corporation pursuant to a shareholders' agreement, or a creditor of the close corporation or of any of its subsidiaries or affiliates and whose further qualifications, if any, are determined by the court;
(2) a provisional director has all the rights and powers of an elected director of the close corporation, or the rights and powers of vote or consent of a shareholder or other persons who have been empowered to manage the business and affairs of the close corporation pursuant to a shareholders' agreement (with the voting power provided by order of the court), including the right to notice of, and to vote at, meetings of directors or shareholders, as the case may be;
(3) a provisional director shall serve until removed by order of the court or by a vote of a majority of the directors or the holders of a majority of the shares having voting power, as the case may be, or if a close corporation provision requires the concurrence of a greater or different majority for action by the directors or the shareholders, as the case may be, then by that majority; and
(4) the compensation of a provisional director shall be determined by an agreement between the provisional director and the close corporation subject to the approval of the court, which may fix the compensation in the absence of an agreement or in the event of a disagreement between the provisional director and the close corporation.
Art. 12.54. Judicial Proceeding to Appoint Custodian for Close Corporation
A. In General. A court of competent jurisdiction in a judicial proceeding brought under this article shall appoint a custodian for a close corporation on proof that:

(1) at any meeting held for the election of directors, the shareholders are so divided that they have failed to elect successors to directors whose terms have expired or would have expired on qualification of their successors;

(2) the business of the close corporation is suffering or is threatened with irreparable injury because the directors, or the shareholders or the persons empowered to manage the business and affairs of the close corporation pursuant to a shareholders' agreement or otherwise, are so divided respecting the management of the affairs of the close corporation that the required vote or consent to take action on behalf of the close corporation cannot be obtained and any remedy with respect to the deadlock in a close corporation provision has failed; or

(3) the plaintiff or intervenor has the right to dissolve the close corporation under a shareholders' agreement as permitted by Article 12.32 of this Act.

B. Status of Custodian. To be eligible to serve as a custodian, a person must comply with all the qualifications required of a receiver under Article 7.07 of this Act. A person who qualifies as a custodian has all of the powers and duties and the title of a receiver appointed under Articles 7.05 through 7.07 of this Act but the authority of the custodian is to continue the business of the close corporation and not to liquidate its affairs and distribute its assets, except when the court otherwise orders or as provided by Subsection A(3) of this article. If the condition necessitating the appointment of a custodian is remedied, other than by liquidation or dissolution, the custodianship is to be terminated immediately and the management of the close corporation shall be restored to the directors or to the shareholders of the close corporation or to the persons empowered to manage the business and affairs of the close corporation pursuant to a shareholders' agreement, as the case may be.

Business Corporation Act
Part 13.

Art. 13.01. Short Title

A. This part may be cited as the Business Combination Law.

Art. 13.02. Definitions

A. In this part:

(1) "Affiliate" means a person who directly or indirectly through one or more intermediaries controls, is controlled by, or is under common control with a specified person.

(2) "Affiliated shareholder" means a person, other than the issuing public corporation or a wholly owned subsidiary of the issuing public corporation, that is the beneficial owner of 20 percent or more of the outstanding voting shares of the issuing public corporation or that, within the preceding three-year period, was the beneficial owner of 20 percent or more of the then outstanding voting shares of the issuing public corporation. For the purpose of determining whether a person is an affiliated shareholder, the number of voting shares of the issuing public corporation considered outstanding includes shares considered beneficially owned by that person under Subdivision (3) of this Article, but does not include other unissued voting shares of the issuing public corporation that may be issuable pursuant to an agreement, arrangement, or understanding, or on exercise of conversion rights, warrants, or options, or otherwise.

(3) "Beneficial owner" means a person who:

(a) individually, or with or through an affiliate or associate, beneficially owns shares or similar securities, directly or indirectly;

(b) individually, or with or through an affiliate or associate, has the right to:

(i) acquire shares or similar securities, whether the right may be exercised immediately or only after the passage of time, pursuant to an agreement, arrangement, or understanding, whether or not in writing, or on the exercise of conversion rights, exchange rights, warrants, or options, or otherwise, except that a person is not considered the beneficial owner of shares or similar securities (A) tendered pursuant to a tender or exchange offer made by the person or an affiliate or associate until the tendered shares or similar securities are accepted for purchase or exchange, or (B) that may be subject to an agreement, arrangement, or understanding that expressly conditions the acquisition or purchase on the approval of the acquisition or purchase pursuant to Article 13.03 of this Act as long as such person has no direct or indirect rights of ownership or voting with respect to such shares until such time that such approval is obtained, at which time such person shall be considered the beneficial owner of such shares; or

(ii) vote the shares or similar securities pursuant to an agreement, arrangement, or understanding, whether or not in writing, except that a person is not considered the beneficial owner of shares or similar securities for purposes of this subparagraph if the agreement, arrangement, or understanding to vote the shares: (A) arises solely from an immediately revocable proxy that authorizes the person named in the proxy to vote at a meeting of shareholders that has been called when the proxy is delivered or at any adjournment of the meeting, and (B) is not then reportable on a Schedule 13D under the Securities Exchange Act of 1934 (15 U.S.C. Section 78a et seq.) or a comparable or successor report; or

(c) has an agreement, arrangement, or understanding, whether or not in writing, to acquire, hold, or dispose (except pursuant to an agreement, arrangement, or understanding permitted by Paragraph (b)(i) of this subdivision) or to vote (except under an immediately revocable proxy under Paragraph (b)(ii) of this subdivision) shares or similar securities with another person who beneficially owns, or whose affiliate or associate beneficially owns, directly or indirectly, the shares or similar securities.

(4) "Business combination" means:

(a) any merger, share exchange, or conversion of an issuing public corporation or a subsidiary with:

(i) an affiliated shareholder;

(ii) a foreign or domestic corporation or other entity that is, or after the merger, share exchange, or conversion would be, an affiliate or associate of the affiliated shareholder; or

(iii) another domestic or foreign corporation or other entity, if the merger, share exchange, or conversion is caused by an affiliated shareholder, or an affiliate or associate of an affiliated shareholder, and as a result of the merger, share exchange, or conversion this part does not apply to the surviving corporation or other entity;

(b) a sale, lease, exchange, mortgage, pledge, transfer, or other disposition, in one transaction or a series of transactions, including an allocation of assets pursuant to a merger, to or with the affiliated shareholder, or an affiliate or associate of the affiliated shareholder, of assets of the issuing public corporation or any subsidiary that:

(i) have an aggregate market value equal to 10 percent or more of the aggregate market value of all the assets, determined on a consolidated basis, of the issuing public corporation;

(ii) have an aggregate market value equal to 10 percent or more of the aggregate market value of all the outstanding voting shares of the issuing public corporation; or

(iii) represent 10 percent or more of the earning power or net income, determined on a consolidated basis, of the issuing public corporation;

(c) the issuance or transfer by an issuing public corporation or a subsidiary to an affiliated shareholder or an affiliate or associate of the affiliated shareholder, in one transaction or a series of transactions, of shares of the issuing public corporation or a subsidiary, except by the exercise of warrants or rights to purchase shares of the issuing public corporation offered, or a share dividend paid, pro rata to all shareholders of the issuing public corporation after the affiliated shareholder's share acquisition date;

(d) the adoption of a plan or proposal for the liquidation or dissolution of an issuing public corporation proposed by, or pursuant to any agreement, arrangement, or understanding, whether or not in writing, with an affiliated shareholder or an affiliate or associate of the affiliated shareholder;

(e) a reclassification of securities, including a reverse share split or a share split-up, share dividend, or other distribution of shares, a recapitalization of the issuing public corporation, a merger of the issuing public corporation with a subsidiary or pursuant to which the assets and liabilities of the issuing public corporation are allocated among two or more surviving or new domestic or foreign corporations or other entities, or any other transaction, whether or not with, into, or otherwise involving the affiliated shareholder, proposed by, or pursuant to an agreement, arrangement, or understanding, whether or not in writing, with an affiliated shareholder or an affiliate or associate of the affiliated shareholder that has the effect, directly or indirectly, of increasing the proportionate ownership percentage of the outstanding shares of a class or series of voting shares or securities convertible into voting shares of the issuing public corporation that is beneficially owned by the affiliated shareholder or an affiliate or associate of the affiliated shareholder, except as a result of immaterial changes due to fractional share adjustments; or

(f) the direct or indirect receipt by an affiliated shareholder or an affiliate or associate of the affiliated shareholder of the benefit of a loan, advance, guarantee, pledge, or other financial assistance or a tax credit or other tax advantage provided by or through the issuing public corporation, except proportionately as a shareholder of the issuing public corporation.

(5) "Control" means the possession, directly or indirectly, of the power to direct or cause the direction of the management and policies of a person, whether through the ownership of equity securities, by contract, or otherwise. A person's beneficial ownership of 10 percent or more of a person's outstanding voting shares or similar interests creates a presumption that the person has control of such other person, but a person is not considered to have control of another person if the person holds such voting shares or similar interests in good faith and not for the purpose of circumventing this part, as an agent, bank, broker, nominee, custodian, or trustee for one or more beneficial owners who do not individually or as a group have control of the person.

(6) "Issuing public corporation" means a domestic corporation that has: (a) 100 or more shareholders, (b) any class or series of its voting shares registered under the Securities Exchange Act of 1934, as amended, or similar or successor statute, or (c) any class or series of its voting shares qualified for trading in a national market system. For the purposes of this definition of issuing public corporation, a shareholder is a shareholder of record as shown by the share transfer records of the corporation.

(7) "Person" means an individual, trust, domestic or foreign corporation or other entity, or a government, or a political subdivision, agency, or instrumentality of a government. If two or more persons act as a partnership, limited partnership, syndicate, or other group under an agreement, arrangement, or other understanding, whether or not in writing, to acquire, hold, vote, or dispose of shares of a corporation, all members of the partnership, limited partnership, syndicate, or other group are considered to be a person.

(8) "Share acquisition date" means the date that a person first becomes an affiliated shareholder of an issuing public corporation.

(9) "Subsidiary" means a domestic or foreign corporation or other entity of which a majority of the outstanding voting shares are owned, directly or indirectly, by an issuing public corporation.

(10) "Voting share" means a share of capital stock of a corporation entitled to vote generally in the election of directors.

Art. 13.03. Three-Year Moratorium on Certain Business Combinations

A. An issuing public corporation shall not, directly or indirectly, enter into or engage in a business combination with an affiliated shareholder, or any affiliate or associate of the affiliated shareholder, during the three-year period immediately following the affiliated shareholder's share acquisition date unless:

(1) the business combination or the purchase or acquisition of shares made by the affiliated shareholder on the affiliated shareholder's share acquisition date is approved by the board of directors of the issuing public corporation before the affiliated shareholder's share acquisition date; or

(2) the business combination is approved, by the affirmative vote of the holders of at least two-thirds of the outstanding voting shares of the issuing public corporation not beneficially owned by the affiliated shareholder or an affiliate or associate of the affiliated shareholder, at a meeting of shareholders and not by written consent, duly called for that purpose not less than six months after the affiliated shareholder's share acquisition date.

Art. 13.04. Application

A. Article 13.03 of this Act does not apply to:

(1) a business combination of an issuing public corporation:

(a) the original articles of incorporation or original bylaws of which contain a provision expressly electing not to be governed by this part;

(b) that adopts an amendment to its articles of incorporation or bylaws before December 31, 1997, expressly electing not to be governed by this part; or

(c) that after December 31, 1997, adopts an amendment to its articles of incorporation or bylaws, approved by the affirmative vote of the shareholders, other than affiliated shareholders and their affiliates and associates, of at least two-thirds of the outstanding voting shares of the issuing public corporation, expressly electing not to be governed by this part, except that the amendment to the articles of incorporation or bylaws takes effect 18 months after the date of the vote and does not apply to a business combination of the issuing public corporation with an affiliated shareholder whose share acquisition date is on or before the effective date of the amendment;

(2) a business combination of an issuing public corporation with an affiliated shareholder that became an affiliated shareholder inadvertently, if the affiliated shareholder:

(a) as soon as practicable divests itself of a sufficient number of the voting shares of the issuing public corporation so that it no longer is the beneficial owner, directly or indirectly, of 20 percent or more of the outstanding voting shares of the issuing public corporation; and

(b) would not at any time within the three-year period preceding the announcement date of the business combination have been an affiliated shareholder but for the inadvertent acquisition;

(3) a business combination with an affiliated shareholder that was the beneficial owner of 20 percent or more of the outstanding voting shares of the issuing public corporation on December 31, 1996, and continuously until the announcement date of the business combination;

(4) a business combination with an affiliated shareholder who became an affiliated shareholder through a transfer of shares of the issuing public corporation by will or intestate succession and continuously was such an affiliated shareholder until the announcement date of the business combination; or

(5) a business combination of an issuing public corporation with a domestic wholly owned subsidiary if the domestic subsidiary is not an affiliate or associate of the affiliated shareholder other than by reason of the affiliated shareholder's beneficial ownership of voting shares in the issuing public corporation.

Art. 13.05. No Effect on Other Actions

A. This part does not affect, directly or indirectly, the validity of another action by the board of directors of an issuing public corporation, nor does it preclude the board of directors from taking other action in accordance with law, nor does the board of directors incur liability for elections made or not made under this part.

Art. 13.06. Duties of Director

A. In discharging the duties of director under this Act or otherwise, a director, in considering the best interests of the corporation, may consider the long-term as well as the short-term interests of the corporation and its shareholders, including the possibility that those interests may be best served by the continued independence of the corporation.

Art. 13.07. Relationship With Other Parts of Act

A. If a provision of this part conflicts with another provision of this Act, the provision of this part controls.

B. The affirmative vote or concurrence of shareholders required for approval of an action required or permitted to be submitted for shareholder vote under Part 13 of this Act may be increased, but not decreased, under Article 2.28 of this Act.

Art. 13.08. Severability

A. If any provision or clause of this part or application thereof to any person or circumstance is held invalid, such invalidity shall not affect other provisions or applications of this part that can be given effect without the invalid provision or application and without being inconsistent with the intent of this part, and to this end the provisions of this part are declared to be severable.

Art. 1528n. Texas Limited Liability Company Act

Text of article effective until January 1, 2010

PART ONE

Short Title, Captions, Parts, Articles, Sections, Subsections, and Paragraphs

Art. 1.01. A. This act shall be known and may be cited as the "Texas Limited Liability Company Act."

B. The divisions of this act into Parts, Articles, Sections, Subsections and Paragraphs and the use of captions in connection therewith are solely for the convenience and shall have no legal effect in construing the provisions of this Act.

C. This act has been organized and subdivided in the following manner:

(1) The act is divided into Parts, containing groups of related Articles. Parts are numbered consecutively with cardinal numbers.

(2) The act is also divided into Articles, numbered consecutively with Arabic numerals.

(3) Articles are divided into Sections. The Sections within each Article are numbered consecutively with capital letters.

(4) Sections are divided into subsections. The subsections within each Section are numbered consecutively with Arabic numerals enclosed in parentheses.

(5) Subsections are divided into paragraphs. The paragraphs within each subsection are numbered consecutively with lower case letters enclosed in parentheses.

Definitions

Art. 1.02. A. As used in this Act, unless the context otherwise requires, the term:

(1) "Bankrupt" means bankrupt under the federal Bankruptcy Act or insolvent under any state insolvency act.

(2) "Court" includes every court and judge having jurisdiction in the action.

(3) "Limited Liability Company" or "Company" means a limited liability company organized and existing under this chapter.

(4) "Person" includes an individual, corporation, business trust, estate, trust, custodian, trustee, executor, administrator, nominee, partnership, registered limited liability partnership, limited partnership, association, limited liability company, government, governmental subdivision, governmental agency, governmental instrumentality, and any other legal or commercial entity, in its own or representative capacity. Any of the foregoing entities may be formed under the laws of this state or any other jurisdiction.

(5) "Real Property" means land and any interest or estate in land.

(6) "Business" means every trade and occupation or profession.

(7) "Conveyance" means every assignment, lease, mortgage, or incumbrance.

(8) "TBCA" means the Texas Business Corporation Act as amended and as it may hereafter be amended.

(9) "Foreign Limited Liability Company" means an entity formed under the laws of a jurisdiction other than this state (a) that is characterized as a limited liability company by such laws or

(b) although not so characterized by such laws, that elects to procure a certificate of authority pursuant to Article 7.01 of this act, that is formed under laws which provide that some or all of the persons entitled to receive a distribution of the assets thereof upon the entity's dissolution or otherwise or to exercise voting rights with respect to an interest in the entity shall not be liable for the debts, obligations or liabilities of the entity and which is not eligible to become authorized to do business in this state under any other statute.

(10) "Merger" means (a) the division of a domestic limited liability company into two or more new domestic limited liability companies or into a surviving limited liability company and one or more new domestic or foreign limited liability companies or other entities, or

(b) the combination of one or more domestic limited liability companies with one or more domestic or foreign limited liability companies or other entities resulting in

(i) one or more surviving domestic or foreign limited liability companies or other entities,

(ii) the creation of one or more new domestic or foreign limited liability companies or other entities, or

(iii) one or more surviving domestic or foreign limited liability companies or other entities and the creation of one or more new domestic or foreign limited liability companies or other entities.

(11) "Conversion" means:

(a) the continuance of a domestic limited liability company as, and in the organizational form of, a foreign limited liability company or other entity; or

(b) the continuance of a foreign limited liability company or other entity as, and in the organizational form of, a domestic limited liability company.

(12) "Converted entity" means any domestic or foreign limited liability company or other entity to which a converting entity has converted or intends to convert as permitted by Article 10.08 of this Act.

(13) "Converting entity" means any domestic or foreign limited liability company or other entity that has converted or intends to convert as permitted by Article 10.08 of this Act.

(14) "Other entity" means any entity, whether organized for profit or not, that is a corporation, limited or general partnership, limited liability company (other than a domestic or foreign limited liability company), real estate investment trust, joint venture, joint stock company, cooperative, association, bank, trust, insurance company, or other legal entity organized pursuant to the laws of this state or any other state or country.

PART TWO

Purposes

Art. 2.01. A. A limited liability company formed under this Act may engage in any lawful business unless a more limited purpose is stated in its articles of organization or regulations.

B. A limited liability company engaging in a business that is subject to regulation by another Texas statute may be formed under this Act only if it is not prohibited by the other statute. The limited liability company is subject to all limitations of the other statute.

Powers

Art. 2.02. A. Each limited liability company shall have the power provided for a corporation under the TBCA and a limited partnership under the Texas Revised Limited Partnership Act.

B. Nothing in this Article grants any authority to managers or members of a limited liability company for the exercise of the powers of a limited liability company, inconsistent with limitations on any of the same which may be expressly set forth in this Act or any articles of organization or regulations or in any laws of this State. Authority of managers and members to act beyond the scope of the purpose or purposes of a limited liability company is not granted by any provision of this Act.

C. Nothing contained in this Act shall be deemed to authorize any action in violation of the Anti-Trust laws of this State, as now existing or hereafter amended.

D. A limited liability company engaged as a common carrier in the pipeline business for transporting oil, oil products, gas, carbon dioxide, salt brine, fuller's earth, sand, clay, liquefied minerals, or other mineral solutions has all of the rights and powers conferred by Sections 111.019-111.022, Natural Resources Code.

Limited liability company names; use of assumed names

Art. 2.03. A. The limited liability company name shall conform to the following requirements:

(1) It shall either contain the words "Limited Liability Company" or "Limited Company" or the abbreviations "L.L.C.," "LLC," "LC," or "L.C." and shall contain such additional words as may be required by law. The word "Limited" may be abbreviated as "Ltd." or "LTD" and the word "Company" may be abbreviated as "Co." However, a limited liability company formed before September 1, 1993, that complied with this Section on the date of formation, but does not comply with this Section as revised, is not required to change its name.

(2) It shall not contain any word or phrase which indicates or implies that it is organized for any purpose other than one or more of the purposes contained in its articles of organization.

(3) It shall not be the same as, or deceptively similar to, the name of any domestic limited liability company, corporation or limited partnership existing under the laws of this state, or the name of any foreign limited liability company, corporation or limited partnership authorized to transact business in this state, or a name the exclusive right to which is, at the time, reserved in the manner provided in this Act or any other statute providing for reservation of names by a corporation or limited partnership, or the name of a limited liability company, corporation or limited partnership which has in effect a registration of its company name as provided in this act or any other applicable law provided that a
name may be similar if written consent is obtained from the existing limited liability company, corporation or limited partnership having the name deemed to be similar or the person for whom the name deemed to be similar is reserved in the office of the Secretary of State.

B. Any domestic or foreign limited liability company having authority to transact business in this State, may do so under an assumed name, by filing an assumed name certificate in the manner prescribed by law.

C. The filing of articles of organization under Part Three of this Act or an application to reserve a specified company name under Article 2.04 of this Act, does not authorize the use of limited liability company name in this State in violation of the rights of another under the Federal Trademark Act of 1946 (15 U.S.C., Section 1051 et seq.), the Texas trademark law (Chapter 16, Business & Commerce Code), the Assumed Business or Professional Name Act (Chapter 36, Business & Commerce Code), or the common law.

Reserved Name

Art. 2.04. A. The exclusive right to the use of a limited liability company name may be reserved by any person.

B. The reservation shall be made by filing with the Secretary of State an application to reserve a specified company name, executed by the applicant or the attorney or agent thereof. If the Secretary of State finds that the name is available for limited liability company use, the Secretary of State shall reserve the same for the exclusive use of the applicant for a period of one hundred and twenty (120) days.

C. The right to the exclusive use of a specified company name so reserved may be transferred to any other person or limited liability company by filing in the office of the Secretary of State a notice of such transfer, executed by the applicant for whom the name was reserved, and specifying the name and address of the transferee.

D. Any person for whom a specified company name has been reserved pursuant to Section B of this article may, during the period for which such name is reserved, terminate such reservation by filing with the Secretary of State an application for cancellation of reservation of company name, together with the applicable fee.

Registered Office and Registered Agent

Art. 2.05. A. Each limited liability company or foreign limited liability company subject to this Act shall have and continuously maintain in this State:

(1) A registered office which may be, but need not be, the same as its place of business.

(2) A registered agent, which agent may be either an individual resident in this State whose business office is identical with such registered office, or a person organized under or authorized to transact business in this State which has a business office identical with such registered office.

Change of Registered Office or Registered Agent

Art. 2.06. A. A limited liability company or foreign limited liability company subject to this Act may change its registered office or change its registered agent, or both, upon filing in the office of the Secretary of State a statement setting forth:

(1) The name of the limited liability company.

(2) The post office address of its then registered office.

(3) If the post office address of its registered office is to be changed, the post office address to which the registered office is to be changed.

(4) The name of its then registered agent.

(5) If its registered agent is to be changed, the name of its successor registered agent.

(6) That the post office address of its registered office and the post office address of the business office of its registered agent, as changed, will be identical.

(7) That such change was authorized by its members or managers.

B. The statement required by this article shall be executed on behalf of the limited liability company or foreign limited liability company by an authorized member or manager. The original and a copy of the statement shall be delivered to the Secretary of State. If the Secretary of State finds that such statement conforms to the provisions of this Act, the Secretary of State shall, when the appropriate filing fee is paid as prescribed by law:

(1) Endorse on the original and the copy the word "filed," and the month, day, and year of the filing thereof.

(2) File the original in the office of the Secretary of State.

(3) Return the copy to the limited liability company or its representative.

C. Upon such filing, the change of address of the registered office, or the appointment of a new registered agent, or both, as the case may be, shall become effective.

D. Any registered agent of a limited liability company or foreign limited liability company may resign:

(1) by giving written notice to the limited liability company at its last known address; and

(2) by giving written notice, in duplicate (the original and one copy of the notice), to the Secretary of State within ten days after mailing or delivery of said notice to the limited liability company. Such notice shall include the last known address of the limited liability company and shall include the statement that written notice of resignation has been given to the limited liability company and the date thereof. Upon compliance with the requirements as to written notice, the appointment of such agent shall terminate upon the expiration of thirty (30) days after receipt of such notice by the Secretary of State.

If the Secretary of State finds that such written notice conforms to the provisions of this Act, the Secretary of State shall:

(1) Endorse on the original and the copy of the word "filed" and the month, day, and year of the filing thereof.

(2) File the original in the office of the Secretary of State.

(3) Return the copy to such resigning registered agent.

(4) Notify the limited liability company of the resignation of the registered agent.

No fee shall be required to be paid for the filing of a resignation under this section.

Change of Address of Registered Agent

Art. 2.07. A. The location of the registered office in Texas for a limited liability company or foreign limited liability company

subject to this Act may be changed from one address to another upon filing in the office of the Secretary of State a statement setting forth:

(1) The name of the limited liability company or foreign limited liability company represented by such registered agent.

(2) The address at which such registered agent has maintained the registered office for the limited liability company or foreign limited liability company.

(3) The new address at which such registered agent will thereafter maintain the registered office for the limited liability company or foreign limited liability company.

(4) A statement that notice of the change has been given to said limited liability company or foreign limited liability company in writing at least ten (10) days prior to such filing.

B. The statement required by this article shall be signed by the registered agent, or, an authorized officer, manager or member on its behalf. If the registered agent is simultaneously filing statements as to more than one limited liability company, each such

statement may contain facsimile signatures in the execution. The original and one copy of the statement shall be delivered to the Secretary of State. If the Secretary of State finds that such statement conforms to the provisions of this Act, the Secretary of State shall:

(1) Endorse on the original and the copy the word "filed," and the month, day, and year of the filing thereof.

(2) File the original in the office of the Secretary of State.

(3) Return the copy to such registered agent.

C. The registered office of the limited liability company or foreign limited liability company named in such statement shall be changed to the new address of the registered agent upon the filing of such statement by the Secretary of State.

Service of Process on a Limited Liability Company

Art. 2.08. A. The managers, if any, and the registered agent shall be agents of a limited liability company or foreign limited liability company upon whom any process, notice, or demand required or permitted by law to be served upon the limited liability company or foreign limited liability company may be served.

B. Whenever a limited liability company or foreign limited liability company shall fail to appoint or maintain a registered agent in this State, or whenever its registered agent cannot with reasonable diligence be found at the registered office, then the Secretary of State shall be an agent of such limited liability company or foreign limited liability company upon whom any such process, notice, or demand may be served. Service on the Secretary of State of any process, notice, or demand shall be made by delivering to and leaving with the Secretary of State, or with the Assistant Secretary of State, or with any clerk having charge of the limited liability company department of the Secretary of State's office, duplicate copies of such process, notice, or demand. In the event any such process, notice, or demand is served on the Secretary of State, the Secretary of State shall immediately cause one of the copies thereof to be forwarded by registered mail, addressed to the limited liability company or foreign limited liability company at its registered office. Any service so had on the Secretary of State shall be returnable in not less than thirty (30) days.

C. The Secretary of State shall keep a record of all processes, notices and demands served under this Article, and shall record therein the time of such service and the action with reference thereto.

D. Nothing herein contained shall limit or affect the right to serve any process, notice, or demand required or permitted by law to be served upon a limited liability company or foreign limited liability company in any manner now or hereafter permitted by law.

Regulations of Limited Liability Company

Art. 2.09. A. The members of a limited liability company have the power to adopt, alter, amend, or repeal the regulations of a limited liability company. The articles of organization or regulations may provide that the manager or managers also have the power to adopt, alter, amend, or repeal the regulations, in whole or in part. Regulations may provide that they may not, in whole or specified part, be altered, amended, or repealed by the managers. The regulations may contain any provisions for the regulation and management of the affairs of the limited liability company not inconsistent with law or the articles of organization. Any provision of this Act subject to variation or modification by the regulations of a limited liability company is also subject to variation or modification by the articles of organization of the limited liability company.

B. Unless otherwise provided in the articles of organization or regulations, adoption, alteration, amendment, or repeal of the regulations of a limited liability company requires the affirmative vote, approval, or consent of all the members or, if the manager or managers have the power to adopt, alter, amend, or repeal the regulations of a limited liability company, the affirmative vote, approval, or consent of all the managers.

C. Unless otherwise provided in the articles of organization or regulations adopted with the affirmative vote, approval, or consent needed to approve an action listed in Section D, G, or H, Article 2.23, of this Act, no regulation that effects an action listed in Section D, G, or H, Article 2.23, of this Act may be indirectly effected through the adoption, alteration, amendment, or repeal of regulations of a limited liability company without the affirmative vote, approval, or consent required by Section D, G, or H, Article 2.23, of this Act.

Limited Liability Company Property

Art. 2.11. A. Real or personal property owned or purchased by a limited liability company may be held and owned, and conveyance may be made, in the name of the limited liability company. Instruments and documents providing for the acquisition, mortgage, or disposition of the property of the limited liability company shall be valid and binding upon the company, if they are executed by one or more persons as provided in Article 2.21 of this Act.

Managers

Art. 2.12. A. Except and to the extent the articles of organization or the regulations shall reserve management of the limited liability company to the members in whole or in part, and subject to provisions in the articles of organization, the regulations, or this Act restricting or enlarging the powers, rights, and duties of any manager or group or class of managers, the powers of a limited liability company shall be exercised by or under the authority of, and the business and affairs of a limited liability company shall be managed under the direction of, the manager or managers of the limited liability company. If management of the limited liability company is fully reserved to the members, the limited liability company need not have managers. Managers need not be residents of this State or members of the limited liability company unless the regulations so require. The regulations may prescribe other qualifications for managers. If the management of the limited liability company is reserved in whole or in part to the members, Articles 2.17, 2.18, 2.19, and 2.20 of this Act apply to the members who manage the limited liability company to the same extent as those articles would otherwise apply to managers of a limited liability company.

Number and Election of Managers

Art. 2.13. A. The managers of a limited liability company, if any, shall consist of one or more persons. The number of managers shall be fixed by, or in the manner provided in, the regulations, except as to the number constituting the initial managers, which number shall be fixed by the articles of organization. The number of managers may be increased or decreased from time to time by amendment to, or in the manner provided in, the regulations, but, unless provided otherwise in the articles of organization or the regulations, no decrease shall have the effect of shortening the term of any incumbent manager. In the absence of a regulation fixing the number of managers or providing for the manner in which the number of managers shall be fixed, the number of managers shall be the same as the number constituting the initial managers. The names and addresses of the initial managers, if any, shall be stated in the articles of organization. Unless otherwise provided in the regulations or in any resolution of the managers or members appointing that manager in accordance with the regulations or articles of organization, each manager shall hold office for the term for which elected, if any term is specified, and until that manager's successor has been elected, or until that manager's earlier death, resignation, or removal. The regulations may provide for the time or times at which the members entitled to vote in the election of managers shall elect managers and the term for which the managers shall hold office. The regulations may provide that any class or group of members shall be entitled to elect one or more managers, who shall hold office for such terms as shall be stated in the regulations. The regulations may provide that at any meeting of members called expressly for that purpose any managers may be removed, with or without cause, as provided therein; however, if any class or group of members is entitled to elect one or more managers by the provisions of the regulations, only the members of that class or group shall be entitled to vote for or against the removal of any managers elected by the members of that class or group.

Classification of Managers

Art. 2.14. A. The regulations may provide that the managers shall be divided into more than one class, each class to be the number specified in the regulations, the terms of managers of each class to expire in the order provided in the regulations and at the meetings of the members at which the regulations provide that managers are to be elected. If the regulations provide for the classification of managers,

(1) the whole number of managers of the limited liability company need not be elected annually or at any regularly scheduled meeting of the members, and

(2) after such classification, at each meeting at which the regulations provide that managers are to be elected, the number of managers equal to the number of the class whose term expires at the time of such meeting shall be elected to hold office until the next succeeding meeting at which the regulations provide that the successors to the managers are to be elected. A classification of managers adopted after the last meeting of members at which managers were elected may not be effective before the next meeting of members at which managers are elected unless the classification is effected by an amendment to the regulations adopted by the members.

Vacancies

Art. 2.15. A. Unless otherwise provided in the articles of organization or the regulations, any vacancy occurring in the managers may be filled in accordance with Section B of this Article or may be filled by the affirmative vote of a majority of the remaining managers though less than a quorum of the managers. Unless otherwise provided in the articles of organization or the regulations, a manager elected to fill a vacancy shall be elected for the unexpired term of the predecessor in office.

B. Unless otherwise provided in the articles of organization or the regulations, any vacancy occurring in the managers to be filled by reason of an increase in the number of managers may be filled by election at an annual or special meeting of members called for that purpose.

C. Notwithstanding Sections A and B of this Article, whenever the holders of any class or series of membership interests are entitled to elect one or more managers by the provisions of the regulations, any vacancies, and any newly created managers of such class or series to be filled by reason of an increase in the number of such managers may be filled by the affirmative vote of a majority of the managers, elected by such class or series then in office or by a sole remaining manager so elected, or by the vote of the holders of the outstanding membership interests of such class or series, and such vacancy shall not in any case be filled by the vote of the remaining managers or the holders of the outstanding membership interests as a whole unless otherwise provided in the regulations.

Interested Managers

Art. 2.17. A. Unless otherwise provided in the articles of organization or the regulations, an otherwise valid contract or transaction between a limited liability company and one or more of its managers or officers, or between a limited liability company and any other domestic or foreign limited liability company or other entity in which one or more of its managers or officers are managers, directors or officers or have a financial interest, shall be valid notwithstanding the manager or officer is present at or participates in the meeting of managers or of a committee of managers which authorizes the contract or transaction, or solely because such manager's or managers' votes are counted for such purpose, if any of the following is satisfied:

(1) The material facts as to the relationship or interest and as to the contract or transaction are disclosed or are known to the managers or the committee, and the managers or committee in good faith authorizes the contract or transaction by the affirmative vote of a majority of the disinterested managers, even though the disinterested managers be less than a quorum; or

(2) The material facts as to the relationship or interest and as to the contract or transaction are disclosed or are known to the members entitled to vote thereon, and the contract or transaction is specifically approved in good faith by vote of the members; or

(3) The contract or transaction is fair as to the limited liability company as of the time it is authorized, approved, or ratified by the managers, a committee thereof, or the members.

B. Unless otherwise provided in the articles of organization or the regulations, common or interested managers may be counted in determining the presence of a quorum at a meeting of the managers or of a committee which authorizes the contract or transaction.

Committees of the Managers

Art. 2.18. A. If the regulations so provide, the managers, by resolution, may designate from among the managers one or more committees, each of which shall be comprised of one or more of the managers, and may designate one or more of the managers as alternate members of any committee, who may, subject to any limitations imposed by the managers, replace absent or disqualified managers at any meeting of that committee. Any such committee, to the extent provided in such resolution or in the regulations, shall have and may exercise all of the authority of the managers, subject to the limitations set forth in Sections B and C of this Article. Unless the resolution designating a particular committee, the articles of organization, or the regulations expressly so provides, a committee of the managers does not have the authority to authorize or make a distribution of limited liability company cash or property to the members or to authorize the issuance of interests in the limited liability company.

B. No committee of the managers shall have the authority of the managers in reference to:

(1) amending the regulations, except that a committee may, to the extent provided in the resolution designating that committee or in the articles of organization or the regulations, exercise the authority of the managers provided in the regulations to establish the relative rights and preferences of the membership interests of any class or series;

(2) approving a plan of merger or share exchange of the limited liability company;

(3) recommending to the members a voluntary dissolution of the limited liability company or a revocation thereof;

(4) filling vacancies in the managers;

(5) fixing the compensation of any member or alternate members of such committee; or

(6) altering or repealing any resolution of the managers that by its terms provides that it shall not be so amendable or repealable.

C. The designation of a committee of the managers and the delegation thereto of authority shall not operate to relieve the managers of any responsibility imposed by law.

Place and Notice of Managers' Meetings

Art. 2.19. A. Except as otherwise provided in the articles of organization or the regulations, regular or special meetings of the members, managers, or any committee may be held either within or without this State.

B. Regular meetings of the managers or committees may be held with or without notice as prescribed in the regulations. Special meetings of the managers or committees shall be held upon such notice as is prescribed in the regulations.

C. Except as otherwise provided in the articles of organization or the regulations, if the limited liability company is without managers, regular meetings of members may be held with or without notice as prescribed in the regulations and special meetings of members may be held with or without notice as prescribed in the regulations, unless any such meeting is to consider any of those matters set forth in Section D, Article 2.23, of this Act. Except as otherwise provided in the articles of organization or the regulations, for any meeting of the members at which any of the matters set forth in Section D, Article 2.23, of this Act are to be considered, written or printed notice stating the place, day, and hour of the meeting and describing the purpose or purposes of such meeting shall be delivered to the members not less than 10 or more than 60 days before the meeting, either personally or by mail.

D. Except as otherwise provided in the articles of organization or the regulations, if the limited liability company has managers, meetings of members shall be held on written or printed notice, stating the place, day, and hour of the meeting and, in the case of a special meeting, the purpose or purposes for which the meeting is called, which notice shall be delivered to the members not less than 10 or more than 60 days before the meeting, either personally or by mail.

E. If mailed, such notice to a member shall be deemed to be delivered when deposited in the United States mail addressed to the member at the member's address that appears on the records of the limited liability company, with postage prepaid.

F. Attendance of a member, manager, or committee member at a meeting shall constitute a waiver of notice of such meeting, except where that member, manager, or committee member attends a meeting for the express purpose of objecting to the transaction of any business on the ground that the meeting is not lawfully called or convened.

G. The articles of organization and regulations may contain provisions relating to giving notice of the time, place, or purpose of a meeting at which a matter is to be voted on by any members or managers, waiver of notice, action by consent without a meeting, the establishment of a record date, quorum requirements, voting in person or by proxy, or any other matter relating to the exercise of the right to vote.

Indemnification

Art. 2.20. A. Subject to such standards and restrictions, if any, as are set forth in its articles of organization or in its regulations, a limited liability company shall have power to indemnify members and managers, officers, and other persons and purchase and maintain liability insurance for such persons.

B. To the extent that at law or in equity, a member, manager, officer, or other person has duties (including fiduciary duties) and liabilities relating thereto to a limited liability company or to another member or manager, such duties and liabilities may be expanded or restricted by provisions in the regulations.

Designation of Officers; Authority and Apparent Authority of Officers, Agents, Managers, and Members

Art. 2.21. A. One or more persons, who may or may not be managers or members, may be designated as officers of the limited liability company by the manager or managers, if management is vested in one or more managers, or by the member or members, if management of the limited liability company is reserved to the members.

B. All officers, agents, managers, and members of the limited liability company, as among themselves and the limited liability company, have authority and perform duties in the management of the limited liability company as may be provided in the regulations or as may be determined by resolution of the manager or managers, if management is vested in one or more managers, or of the member or members, if management is reserved to the members, in each case not inconsistent with the regulations or the articles of organization.

C. Except as otherwise provided in this Article, the following are agents of a limited liability company for the purpose of its business:

(1) any one or more officers or other agents of a limited liability company who are vested with actual or apparent authority;

(2) each manager, to the extent that management of the limited liability company is vested in that manager; and

(3) each member, to the extent that management of the limited liability company has been reserved to that member.

D. An act, including the execution in the name of the limited liability company of any instrument, for the purpose of apparently carrying on in the usual way the business of the limited liability company by any of the persons described in Section C of this Article binds the limited liability company unless:

(1) the officer, agent, manager, or member so acting otherwise lacks the authority to act for the limited liability company; and

(2) the person with whom the officer, agent, manager, or member is dealing has knowledge of the fact that the officer, agent, manager, or member does not have that authority.

Records to be Kept; Access to Information

Art. 2.22. A. A domestic limited liability company shall keep and maintain the following records in its principal office in the United States or make them available in that office within five days after the date of receipt of a written request under Section E of this Article:

(1) a current list that states:

(a) the name and mailing address of each member;

(b) the percentage or other interest in the limited liability company owned by each member; and

(c) if one or more classes or groups are established in or under the articles of organization or regulations, the names of the members who are members of each specified class or group;

(2) copies of the federal, state, and local information or income tax returns for each of the limited liability company's six most recent tax years;

(3) a copy of the articles of organization and, if the regulations of the limited liability company are in writing, a copy of the regulations, copies of all amendments or restatements of the articles of organization or regulations, executed copies of any powers of attorney, and copies of any document that creates, in the manner provided by the articles of organization or regulations, classes or groups of members;

(4) unless contained in the articles of organization or regulations, a written statement of:

(a) the amount of the cash contribution and a description and statement of the agreed value of any other contribution made by each member, and the amount of the cash contribution and a description and statement of the agreed value of any other contribution that the member has agreed to make in the future as an additional contribution;

(b) the times at which additional contributions are to be made or events requiring additional contributions to be made;

(c) events requiring the limited liability company to be dissolved and its affairs wound up; and

(d) the date on which each member in the limited liability company became a member; and

(5) correct and complete books and records of account of the limited liability company.

B. A limited liability company shall maintain such records in written form or in another form capable of conversion into written form within a reasonable time.

C. A limited liability company shall keep in its registered office in Texas and make available to members on reasonable request the street address of its principal United States office in which the records required by this section are maintained or will be available.

D. A member or an assignee of a membership interest, on written request stating the purpose, may examine and copy, in person or by the member's or assignee's representative, at any reasonable time, for any proper purpose, and at the member's expense, records required to be kept under this section and other information regarding the business, affairs, and financial condition of the limited liability company as is just and reasonable for the person to examine and copy.

E. On the written request by any member or an assignee of a membership interest made to the person and address designated in the regulations, the limited liability company shall provide to the requesting member or assignee without charge true copies of:

(1) the articles of organization and regulations and all amendments or restatements; and

(2) any of the tax returns described in Subdivision (2) of Section A of this Article.

Voting, Quorum, and Action

Art. 2.23. A. Except as otherwise provided in this Act, in the articles of organization, or in the regulations, a majority of the members, managers, or members of any committee constitutes a quorum for the transaction of business at any meeting of the members, the managers, or the committee. Except as otherwise provided in the articles of organization or the regulations, an act of a majority of the members entitled to vote, the managers, or the members of a committee, who are present at a meeting of the members, the managers, or the committee at which a quorum is present is the act of the members, the managers, or the committee. Except as otherwise provided in the articles of organization or the regulations, any member may vote either in person or by proxy executed in writing by the member.

B. (1) Unless otherwise provided by the articles of organization or the regulations, any act required or permitted to be taken at any meeting of the members, the managers, or any committee may be taken without a meeting, without prior notice, and without a vote if a consent or consents in writing, setting forth the action so taken, is signed by the members, managers, or committee members, as the case may be, having not fewer than the minimum number of votes that would be necessary to take the action at a meeting at which all members, managers, or committee members, as the case may be, entitled to vote on the action were present and voted.

(2) Unless otherwise provided in the regulations, a telegram, telex, cablegram, or similar transmission by a person, or a photographic, photostatic, facsimile, or similar reproduction of a writing signed by a person, shall be regarded as signed by that person for the purposes of this Article.

C. Subject to the provisions required or permitted by this Act, unless otherwise provided in the articles of organization or the regulations, members, managers, or members of any committee may participate in and hold a meeting of the members, managers, or committee by means of conference telephone or similar communications equipment by means of which all persons participating in the meeting may hear each other. Participation in a meeting pursuant to this Section constitutes presence in person at the meeting except where a person participates in the meeting for the express purpose of objecting to the transaction of any business on the ground that the meeting is not lawfully called or convened.

C-1. Members or managers may take action at a meeting of the members or managers or without a meeting in any manner permitted by the articles of organization, regulations, or this Act. Unless otherwise provided by the articles of organization or the regulations, an action is effective if it is taken by:

(1) an affirmative vote of those persons having not fewer than the minimum number of votes that would be necessary to take the action at a meeting at which all members or managers, as the case may be, entitled to vote on the action were present and voted; or

(2) consent of each member of the limited liability company, which may be established by:

(a) the member's failure to object to the action in a timely manner, if the member has full knowledge of the action;

(b) consent to the action in writing signed by the member; or

(c) any other means reasonably evidencing consent.

D. Except as provided in the articles of organization or the regulations, the affirmative vote, approval, or consent of a majority of all the members is required to:

(1) approve any merger, consolidation, share or interest exchange, or other transaction authorized by or subject to the provisions of Part Ten of this Act;

(2) voluntarily cause the dissolution of the limited liability company; or

(3) authorize any act that would make it impossible to carry on the ordinary business of the limited liability company.

E. Except as provided in the regulations, the affirmative vote, approval, or consent of a majority of all of the managers, if management of the limited liability company is vested in one or more managers, or of the members, if management of the limited liability company is reserved to the members, is required to take any action, other than an action listed in Section D of this Article, that is not apparently for the carrying on of the business of the limited liability company in the usual way.

F. Except as otherwise provided in the articles of organization or the regulations, for purposes of this Act, a "majority" of the members, managers, or any committee of the managers means more than one-half, by number, of all the members, managers, or members of the committee, as the case may be.

G. Except as provided in the articles of organization or the regulations, if the limited liability company has no members, has not received any capital, and has not otherwise commenced business, a majority of the managers named in the articles of organization may amend the articles of organization or dissolve the limited liability company. Except as provided by the articles of organization or the regulations, if the limited liability company has not received any capital, the limited liability company has not otherwise commenced business, and the management has been reserved to the members, a majority of the members named in the articles of organization may amend the articles of organization or dissolve the limited liability company. In

such event, the persons adopting such amendments to the articles of organization or authorizing such dissolution shall sign and file with the Secretary of State the articles of amendment provided for in Articles 3.06 and 3.07 of this Act and the articles of dissolution provided for in Articles 6.05, 6.07, and 6.08 of this Act, as appropriate.

H. Except as provided in the articles of organization or the regulations, if any capital has been paid into the limited liability company or the limited liability company has otherwise commenced business, the affirmative vote, approval, or consent of all members is required to amend the articles of organization.

PART THREE

Formation

Art. 3.01. A. Any natural person of the age of eighteen years or more, or any other person (without regard to place of residence, domicile, or organization) may act as an organizer of a limited liability company by signing the articles of organization for such limited liability company and by delivering the original and a copy of the articles of organization to the Secretary of State.

Articles of Organization

Art. 3.02. A. The initial Articles of Organization shall set forth:

(1) The name of the limited liability company;

(2) The period of duration, which may be perpetual;

(3) The purpose for which the limited liability company is organized which may be stated to be, or to include, the transaction of any or all lawful business for which limited liability companies may be organized under this Act;

(4) The address of its initial registered office and the name of its initial registered agent at that address;

(5) If the limited liability company is to have a manager or managers, a statement to that effect and the names and the addresses of the initial manager or managers, or if the limited liability company will not have managers, a statement to that effect and the names and the addresses of the initial members;

(6) The name and the address of each organizer, unless the limited liability company is being organized pursuant to a plan of conversion or a plan of merger, in which case the articles need not include such information;

(7) Any provision required by Part Eleven of this Act, if the limited liability company is a professional limited liability company;

(8) If the limited liability company is being organized pursuant to a plan of conversion or a plan of merger, a statement to that effect, and in the case of a plan of conversion, the name, address, prior form of organization, date of incorporation, formation, or organization, and jurisdiction of incorporation, formation, or organization of the converting entity; and

(9) Any other provisions, not inconsistent with law, that the members elect to set out in the articles of organization for the regulation of the internal affairs of the limited liability company, including any provisions that under this Act are permitted to be set out in the regulations of the limited liability company.

B. It shall not be necessary to set forth in the articles of organization any of the company powers enumerated in this Act.

Filing of Articles of Organization

Art. 3.03. A. Except as provided by Section C of this Article, the original and a copy of the articles of organization shall be delivered to the Secretary of State. If the Secretary of State finds that the articles of organization conform to law, the Secretary of State shall, when all fees have been paid as required by law:

(1) Endorse on the original and the copy the word "filed," and the month, day, and year of the filing thereof.

(2) File the original in the office of the Secretary of State.

(3) Issue a certificate of organization to which shall be affixed the copy.

B. The certificate of organization, together with the copy of the articles of organization affixed thereto by the Secretary of State, shall be delivered to the organizers or their representatives.

C. In the case of a new domestic limited liability company being organized pursuant to a plan of conversion or a plan of merger pursuant to Part Ten of this Act, the articles of organization of the limited liability company shall be filed with the Secretary of State with the articles of conversion or merger and need not be filed separately pursuant to Section A of this Article. If the Secretary of State finds that the articles of organization conform to the law, the Secretary of State shall file the articles of organization in the office of the Secretary of State and issue a certificate of organization, to which the Secretary of State shall affix a copy of the articles of organization, and deliver the same to the party or parties filing the articles of conversion or merger or their representatives with the certificate of conversion or merger that is issued in connection with the conversion or merger. In the case of a conversion or a merger, the certificate of organization of a domestic limited liability company that is a converted entity or that is to be created pursuant to the plan of merger shall become effective on the effectiveness of the conversion or the merger, as the case may be.

Effect of the Issuance of Certificate of Organization

Art. 3.04. A. Except as provided by Section B of this Article, on the issuance of the certificate of organization, the limited liability company's existence shall begin.

B. In the case of a new domestic limited liability company being organized pursuant to a plan of conversion or a plan of merger pursuant to Part Ten of this Act, the existence of the limited liability company as such shall begin on the effectiveness of the conversion or the merger, as the case may be.

C. On the issuance of the certificate of organization or the effectiveness of the merger or conversion, the certificate of organization shall be conclusive evidence that all conditions precedent required to be performed for the valid organization of the limited liability company have been complied with and that the limited liability company has been duly organized under this Act, except as against the state in a proceeding for involuntary dissolution.

Right to Amend Articles of Organization

Art. 3.05. A. A limited liability company may amend its articles of organization from time to time, in any and as many respects as may be desired, so long as its articles of organization as amended contain only such provisions as might be lawfully contained in original articles of organization at the time of making such amendment.

B. In particular, and without limitation upon such general power of amendment, a limited liability company may amend its articles of organization from time to time so as:

(1) To change its limited liability company name.

(2) To change the time stated in the articles of organization for the dissolution of the limited liability company.

(3) To change, enlarge, or diminish its limited liability company purposes.

(4) To include or modify any provision which could be included in the original articles of organization.

Articles of Amendment

Art. 3.06. A. The articles of amendment shall be executed on behalf of the limited liability company by an authorized manager or member, or in the case of an amendment of the articles of organization by action of a majority of the initial managers or of a majority of the initial members as provided in Section 2.23 of this Act, by a majority of the initial managers or a majority of the initial members as provided in Section 2.23 of this Act.

B. The articles of amendment shall set forth:

(1) The name of the limited liability company.

(2) If the amendment alters any provision of the original or amended articles of organization an identification by reference or description of the altered provision and a statement of its text as it is amended to read. If the amendment is an addition to the original or amended articles of organization a statement of that fact and the text of each provision added.

(3) A statement that the amendment was approved in accordance with Section G or H of Article 2.23 of this Act or as otherwise provided in the articles of organization or regulations and the date of the approval.

Filing of Articles of Amendment

Art. 3.07. A. The original and a copy of the articles of amendment shall be delivered to the Secretary of State. If the Secretary of State finds that the articles of amendment conform to law, the Secretary of State shall, when the appropriate filing fee is paid as required by law:

(1) Endorse on the original and the copy the word "filed," and the month, day, and year of the filing thereof.

(2) File the original in the office of the Secretary of State.

(3) Issue a certificate of amendment to which shall be affixed the copy.

B. The certificate of amendment, together with the copy of the articles of amendment affixed thereto by the Secretary of State shall be delivered to the limited liability company or its representative.

Effect of Certificate of Amendment

Art. 3.08. A. Upon the issuance of the certificate of amendment by the Secretary of State, the amendment shall become effective and the articles of organization shall be amended accordingly.

B. No amendment shall affect any existing cause of action in favor of or against such limited liability company or any pending suit to which such limited liability company shall be a party, or the existing rights of persons other than members, and, in the event the limited liability company name shall be changed by amendment, no suit brought by or against such limited liability company under its former name shall abate for that reason.

Restated Articles of Organization

Art. 3.09. A. By following the procedure to amend the articles of organization provided by this Act, a limited liability company may authorize, execute, and file restated articles of organization that restate the entire text of the articles of organization, as amended or supplemented by:

(1) all certificates of amendment previously issued by the Secretary of State; or

(2) all certificates of amendment previously issued by the Secretary of State and by further amendments included in the restated articles of organization.

Unless otherwise provided by the articles of organization or the regulations, member approval is not required if further amendment is not made by the restated articles of organization.

B. Restated articles of organization that restate the entire articles of organization as amended and supplemented by all certificates of amendment previously issued by the Secretary of State, without making a further amendment, must contain an introductory paragraph stating that the instrument accurately copies the articles of organization and all amendments to the articles of organization that are in effect to date and that the instrument does not contain any other change in a provision of the articles of organization or a previous amendment, other than:

(1) the insertion of the current number of managers, if any, and the names and addresses of the persons then serving as managers, if any, in lieu of similar information concerning the initial managers; and

(2) the omission of the name and address of each organizer.

C. An instrument containing restated articles of organization that restate the entire articles of organization as amended and supplemented by all certificates of amendment previously issued by the Secretary of State and as further amended by the restated articles of organization must:

(1) state that each amendment made by the restated articles of organization has been effected in conformity with this Act;

(2) include the statements required by this Act to be contained in articles of amendment; and

(3) state that the instrument accurately copies the articles of organization and all amendments that are in effect to date and as further amended by the restated articles of organization and that the instrument does not contain any other change in a provision of the articles of organization or the previous amendments, other than:

(a) the insertion of the current number of managers, if any, and the names and addresses of the persons then serving as managers, if any, in lieu of similar information concerning the initial managers; and

(b) the omission of the name and address of each organizer.

D. Restated articles of organization must be executed on behalf of the limited liability company by an authorized manager or member unless capital has not been paid into the limited liability company and the restated articles of organization have been adopted by action of a majority of the initial managers or a majority of the initial members named in the articles of organization as provided by Article 2.23 of this Act, in which case the restated articles of organization may be executed on behalf of the limited liability company by a majority of the persons adopting such restated articles. The original and a copy of the restated articles of organization shall be delivered to the Secretary of State. If the Secretary of State finds that the restated articles of organization conform to law, and the appropriate filing fee is paid as required by law, the Secretary of State shall:

(1) endorse on the original and the copy the word "Filed" and the month, day, and year of filing;

(2) file the original in the Secretary of State's office; and

(3) issue a restated certificate of organization and affix the copy to the restated certificate of organization.

E. The restated certificate of organization, together with the copy of the restated articles of organization affixed to the restated certificate of organization by the Secretary of State, shall be delivered to the limited liability company or its representative.

F. On issuance of a restated certificate of organization by the Secretary of State, the original articles of organization and all amendments to the original articles are superseded, and the restated articles of organization are the articles of organization of the limited liability company.

PART FOUR

Admission of Members and Issuance of Membership Interests

Art. 4.01. A. A limited liability company may have one or more members. In connection with the formation of a limited liability company, a person becomes a member on the latter of:

(1) the date of formation of the limited liability company; or

(2) the date stated in the records of the limited liability company as the date that the person becomes a member or, if no date is stated in those records, on the date that the person's admission is first reflected in the records of the limited liability company.

B. After the formation of a limited liability company, a person becomes a new member:

(1) in the case of a person who is not an assignee of a membership interest, including a person acquiring a membership interest directly from the limited liability company and a person to be admitted as a member of the limited liability company without acquiring a membership interest, on compliance with the provisions of the regulations governing admission of new members or, if the regulations contain no relevant admission provisions, on the written consent of all members; and

(2) in the case of an assignee of a membership interest, as provided by Section A of Article 4.07 of this Act.

B-1. After the formation of a limited liability company, the limited liability company may issue a membership interest in the limited liability company to a person on compliance with the provisions of the regulations governing issuance of membership interests or, if the regulations contain no relevant issuance provisions, upon the consent of all members.

B-2. (1) The regulations may provide that a person may be admitted as a member of a limited liability company and acquire a membership interest in the limited liability company, including a person who will be the sole member, without:

(a) making a contribution to the limited liability company; or

(b) assuming an obligation to make a contribution to the limited liability company.

(2) If one or more persons own a membership interest in a limited liability company, the regulations may provide that a person may be admitted to the limited liability company as a member without acquiring a membership interest in the limited liability company.

C. Any person may be a member unless the person lacks capacity apart from this Act.

Classes and Voting

Art. 4.02. A. The regulations may establish classes or groups of one or more members having certain expressed relative rights, powers, and duties, including voting rights, and may provide for the future creation, in the manner provided in the regulations, of additional classes or groups of members having certain relative rights, powers, or duties, including voting rights, expressed either in the regulations or at the time of creation. The rights, powers, or duties of a class or group may be senior to those of one or more

existing classes or groups of members.

Liability to Third Parties

Art. 4.03. A. Except as and to the extent the regulations specifically provide otherwise, a member or manager is not liable for the debts, obligations or liabilities of a limited liability company including under a judgment decree, or order of a court.

B. Transaction of business outside state. It is the intention of the legislature by the enactment of this Act that the legal existence of limited liability companies formed under this Act be recognized beyond the limits of this state and that, subject to any reasonable registration requirements, any such limited liability company transacting business outside this state be granted the protection of full faith and credit under Section 1 of Article IV of the Constitution of the United States.

C. Parties to actions. A member of a limited liability company is not a proper party to proceedings by or against a limited liability company, except where the object is to enforce a member's right against or liability to the limited liability company.

Nature of Membership Interest

Art. 4.04. A. A membership interest is personal property. A member has no interest in specific limited liability company property.

Assignment of Membership Interest

Art. 4.05. A. Unless otherwise provided by the regulations:

(1) a membership interest is assignable in whole or in part;

(2) an assignment of a membership interest does not of itself dissolve the limited liability company or entitle the assignee to participate in the management and affairs of the limited liability company or to become or exercise any rights of a member;

(3) an assignment entitles the assignee to be allocated income, gain, loss, deduction, credit, or similar items, and to receive distributions, to which the assignor was entitled, to the extent those items are assigned, and, for any proper purpose, to require reasonable information or account of transactions of the limited liability company and to make reasonable inspection of the books and records of the limited liability company; and

(4) until the assignee becomes a member, the assignor member continues to be a member and to have the power to exercise any rights or powers of a member, except to the extent those rights or powers are assigned.

B. The regulations may provide that a member's membership interest may be evidenced by a certificate of membership interest issued by the limited liability company, may provide for the assignment or transfer of membership interests represented by a certificate, and

may make other provisions with respect to the certificate.

C. Until an assignee of the interest of a member in a limited liability company is admitted as a member, the assignee does not have liability as a member solely as a result of the assignment.

Rights of Judgment Creditor

Art. 4.06. A. On application to a court of competent jurisdiction by a judgment creditor of a member or any other owner of a membership interest, the court may charge the membership interest of the member or other owner with payment of the unsatisfied amount of the judgment. Except as otherwise provided in the regulations to the extent that the membership interest is charged in this manner, the judgment creditor has only the rights of an assignee of the interest. This Section does not deprive any member of the benefit of any exemption laws applicable to that member's membership interest.

Right of Assignee to Become Member

Art. 4.07. A. An assignee of a membership interest may become a member if and to the extent that:

(1) the regulations provide; or

(2) all members consent.

B. An assignee who becomes a member has, to the extent assigned, the rights and powers and is subject to the restrictions and liabilities of a member under the regulations and this Act. Unless otherwise provided by regulations, an assignee who becomes a member also is liable for the obligations of the assignor to make contributions but is not obligated for liabilities unknown to the assignee at the time the assignee became a member and which could not be ascertained from the regulations.

C. Whether or not an assignee of a membership interest becomes a member, the assignor is not released from the assignor's liability to the limited liability company.

PART FIVE

Form of Contribution

Art. 5.01. A. The contribution of a member may consist of any tangible or intangible benefit to the limited liability company or other property of any kind or nature, including cash, a promissory note, services performed, a contract for services to be performed, or other interests in or securities or other obligations of any other limited liability company, domestic or foreign, or other entity.

Liability for Contribution Obligations

Art. 5.02. A. A promise by a member to make a contribution to, or otherwise pay cash or transfer property to, a limited liability company is not enforceable unless set out in writing and signed by the member.

B. Except as otherwise provided by the articles of organization or regulations, a member or the member's legal representative or successor is obligated to the limited liability company to perform an enforceable promise to make a contribution to or otherwise pay cash or transfer property to a limited liability company, notwithstanding the member's death, disability, or other change in circumstances. If a member or a member's legal representative or successor does not make a contribution or other payment of cash or transfer of property required by the enforceable promise, whether as a contribution or with respect to a contribution previously made, that member or the member's legal representative or successor is obligated, at the option of the limited liability company, to pay to the limited liability company an amount of cash equal to that portion of the agreed value, as stated in the regulations or in the limited liability company records required to be kept under Article 2.22 of this Act, of the contribution represented by the amount of cash that has not been paid or the value of the property that has not been transferred.

C. The regulations may provide that the interest of a member who fails to make a payment of cash or transfer of property to the limited liability company, whether as a contribution or with respect to a contribution previously made, required by an enforceable promise is subject to specified consequences. A consequence may take the form of a reduction of the defaulting member's percentage or other interest in the limited liability company, subordination of the member's interest to that of nondefaulting members, a forced sale of the member's interest, forfeiture of the member's interest, the lending of money to the defaulting member by other members of the amount necessary to meet the defaulting member's commitment, a determination of the value of the defaulting member's interest by appraisal or by formula and redemption or sale of the interest at that value, or other penalty or consequence.

D. Unless otherwise provided by the regulations, the obligation of a member or a member's legal representative or successor to make a contribution or otherwise pay cash or transfer property or to return cash or property paid or distributed to the member in violation of this Act or the regulations may be compromised or released only by consent of all of the members. Notwithstanding the compromise or release, a creditor of a limited liability company who extends credit or otherwise acts in reasonable reliance on that obligation, after the member signs a writing that reflects the obligation and before the writing is amended or canceled to reflect the compromise or release, may enforce the original obligation. A conditional obligation may not be enforced unless the conditions of the obligation have been satisfied or waived as to or by the applicable member. Conditional obligations include contributions payable on a discretionary call of a limited liability company, prior to the time the call occurs.

Allocation of Profits and Losses

Art. 5.02-1. A. The profits and losses of a limited liability company shall be allocated among the members and among classes of members in the manner provided in the regulations. If the regulations do not otherwise provide, the profits and losses shall be allocated on the basis of the agreed value of the contributions made by each member, as stated in limited liability company records of the kind described in Section A of Article 2.22 of this Act.

Sharing of Distributions

Art. 5.03. A. Distributions of cash or other assets of a limited liability company shall be made to the members in the manner provided by the regulations. If the regulations do not otherwise provide, distributions shall be made on the basis of the agreed value, as stated in the records required to be kept under Article 2.22 of this Act, of the contributions made by each member.

Interim Distributions

Art. 5.04. A. Except as otherwise provided by this Article, a member is entitled to receive distributions from a limited liability company before the member's withdrawal from the limited liability company and before the winding up of the limited liability company to the extent and at the times or on the occurrence of the events specified in the regulations.

Withdrawal or Expulsion of Member

Art. 5.05. A. A member may withdraw or be expelled from a limited liability company only at the time or on the occurrence of events specified in the regulations.

Distribution on Withdrawal

Art. 5.06. A. Except as otherwise provided by this Act, the articles of organization or the regulations, on withdrawal, any withdrawing member is entitled to receive, within a reasonable time after withdrawal, the fair value of that member's interest in the limited liability company as of the date of withdrawal.

Distribution in Kind

Art. 5.07. A. Except as provided by the articles of organization or regulations, a member, regardless of the nature of the member's contribution, may not demand or receive a distribution from a limited liability company in any form other than cash.

Right to Distribution

Art. 5.08. A. Subject to Articles 5.09 and 6.04 of this act, at the time that a member becomes entitled to receive a distribution, with respect to the distribution, that member has the status of and is entitled to all remedies available to a creditor of the limited liability company.

Limitation on Distribution

Art. 5.09. A. A limited liability company may not make a distribution to its members to the extent that, immediately after giving effect to the distribution, all liabilities of the limited liability company, other than liabilities to members with respect to their interests and liabilities for which the recourse of creditors is limited to specified property of the limited liability company, exceed the fair value of the limited liability company assets, except that the fair value of property that is

subject to a liability for which recourse of creditors is limited shall be included in the limited liability company assets only to the extent that the fair value of that property exceeds that liability.

B. A member who receives a distribution that is not permitted under Section A of this Article has no liability under this Act to return the distribution unless the member knew that the distribution violated the prohibition of Section A. This Section does not affect any obligation of the members under the regulations or other applicable law to return the distribution.

PART SIX

Dissolution

Art. 6.01. A. Except as provided by Section B or C of this Article, a limited liability company shall be dissolved on the first of the following to occur:

(1) the period, if any, fixed for the duration of the limited liability company expires;

(2) the occurrence of events specified in the articles of organization or regulations to cause dissolution;

(3) the action of the members to dissolve the limited liability company;

(4) if no capital has been paid into the limited liability company and the limited liability company has not otherwise commenced business, the act of a majority of the managers or members named in the articles of organization to dissolve the limited liability company as provided by Section G of Article 2.23 of this Act;

(5) except as otherwise provided in the regulations, the occurrence of any event that terminates the continued membership of the last remaining member of the limited liability company; or

(6) entry of a decree of judicial dissolution under Section 6.02 of this Act.

B. A limited liability company is not dissolved if an event of dissolution described by Subsection (1) or (2) of Section A of this Article occurs, there is at least one remaining member, and the business of the limited liability company is continued by the vote of the members or class as stated in the articles of organization or regulations of the limited liability company, or if not so stated, by all remaining members. Unless otherwise provided in the articles of organization or in the regulations, an election to continue the business of the limited liability company must be made within 90 days after the date of the occurrence of the event of dissolution. If an election to continue the business of the limited liability company is made following the termination of the period fixed for the duration of the limited liability company or the occurrence of events specified in the articles of organization to cause dissolution, the election is not effective unless an appropriate amendment is made by the limited liability company to its articles of organization during the three-year period following the date of event of dissolution, extending the period fixed for the duration of the limited liability company or deleting the event specified in the articles of organization that caused the dissolution, as applicable.

C. A limited liability company is not dissolved on the occurrence of an event of dissolution described by Subsection (5) of Section A of this Article if the legal representative or successor of the last remaining member agrees to continue the limited liability company and to become a member as of the date of the termination of the last remaining member's membership in the limited liability company or designates another person who agrees to become a member of the limited liability company as of the date of the termination. Unless otherwise provided in the articles of organization or in the regulations, the agreement of the legal representative or successor to continue the limited liability company and to become a member or the designation of another person who agrees to become a member must be made not later than 90 days after the date of termination of the last remaining member's membership in the limited liability company.

Judicial Dissolution

Art. 6.02. A. On application by or for a member, a court of competent jurisdiction may decree dissolution of a limited liability company if it is not reasonably practicable to carry on the business of the limited liability company in conformity with its articles of organization and regulations.

Winding up

Art. 6.03. A. On the dissolution of a limited liability company, the limited liability company's affairs shall be wound up as soon as reasonably practicable. The winding up shall be accomplished by the managers or members or by any other person or persons designated by the articles of organization, by the regulations, or by resolution of the managers or members. In addition, a court of competent jurisdiction, on cause shown, may wind up the limited liability company's affairs on application of any member or the member's legal representative or assignee and, in connection with the winding up, may appoint a person to carry out the liquidation and may make all other orders, directions, and inquiries that the circumstances require.

Transfer of Assets

Art. 6.04. A. On the winding up of a limited liability company, its assets shall be paid or transferred as follows:

(1) To the extent otherwise permitted by law, to creditors, including members who are creditors in satisfaction of liabilities (other than for distributions) of the limited liability company, whether by payment or by establishment of reserves;

(2) Unless otherwise provided by the articles of organization or regulations, to members and former members in satisfaction of the company's liability for distributions; and

(3) Unless otherwise provided by the articles of organization or regulations, to members in the manner provided in Article 6.05.

Procedure Before Filing Articles of Dissolution

Art. 6.05. A. Before filing articles of dissolution:

(1) The limited liability company shall cease to carry on its business, except insofar as may be necessary for the winding up thereof.

(2) The limited liability company shall cause written notice by registered or certified mail of its intention to dissolve to be mailed to each known creditor of and claimant against the limited liability company.

(3) The limited liability company shall proceed to collect its assets, convey and dispose of such of its properties as are not to be distributed in kind to its members, pay, satisfy or discharge its liabilities and obligations, or make adequate provisions for payment and discharge thereof, and do all other acts required to liquidate its business and affairs; in case its property and assets are not sufficient to satisfy or discharge all the limited liability company's liabilities and obligations, the limited liability company shall apply them so far as they will go to the just and equitable payment of the liabilities and obligations. After paying or discharging all of its obligations, or making adequate provisions for payment and discharge thereof, the limited liability company shall then distribute the remainder of its assets, either in cash or in kind, among its members according to their respective rights and interest.

(4) The limited liability company, at any time during the liquidation of its business and affairs, may make application to any district court of this state in the county in which the registered office of the limited liability company is situated to have the liquidation continued under the supervision of such court as provided in this Act.

Revocation of Voluntary Dissolution Proceedings

Art. 6.06. A. At any time before the issuance of a certificate of dissolution by the Secretary of State, or not later than 120 days after the date of the issuance of the certificate of dissolution, a limited liability company may revoke voluntary dissolution proceedings by the written consent of all its members.

A-1. After revocation of voluntary dissolution is authorized as provided in Section A of this Article, the limited liability company shall, if a certificate of dissolution of the limited liability company has been issued by the Secretary of State, deliver to the Secretary of State for filing not later than 120 days after the date the certificate was issued, the original and a copy of the articles of revocation of dissolution executed on behalf of the limited liability company by a manager or authorized member, that set forth:

(1) the name of the limited liability company;

(2) the date that the revocation of dissolution was authorized and, if the dissolution has become effective, the effective date of the dissolution that was revoked; and

(3) a statement that the limited liability company elected to revoke voluntary dissolution proceedings by written consent of all of its members.

A-2. Except as provided by Section A-3 of this Article, if the Secretary of State finds that the articles of revocation of dissolution conform to law, the Secretary of State shall, when the appropriate filing fee is paid as required by law:

(1) endorse the original and the copy with the word "Filed" and the month, day, and year of the filing;

(2) file the original in the Secretary of State's office;

(3) issue a certificate of revocation of dissolution to which the Secretary of State shall affix the copy; and

(4) deliver to the limited liability company or its representative the certificate of revocation of dissolution, together with the affixed copy.

A-3. If the limited liability company's name is the same as or deceptively similar to a name already on file or reserved or registered as specified in Article 2.03 of this Act, the Secretary of State shall issue to the limited liability company a certificate of revocation of dissolution as provided by Section A-2 of this Article only if the limited liability company contemporaneously amends its articles of organization to change its name.

B. Upon the revocation of voluntary dissolution proceedings the limited liability company may again carry on its business. If a limited liability company revokes voluntary dissolution proceedings prior to the issuance by the Secretary of State of a certificate of dissolution of the limited liability company, the limited liability company may again carry on its business as though voluntary dissolution proceedings had not occurred. If a limited liability company revokes voluntary dissolution proceedings after the issuance by the Secretary of State of a certificate of dissolution of the limited liability company, then on the issuance by the Secretary of State of a certificate of revocation of dissolution:

(1) the revocation shall be effective;

(2) the existence of the limited liability company shall be deemed to have continued without interruption after the issuance by the Secretary of State of the certificate of dissolution;

(3) the limited liability company may carry on its business as though voluntary dissolution proceedings had not occurred; and

(4) the existence of the limited liability company shall continue until the limited liability company is subsequently dissolved or otherwise ceases to exist under the provisions of this Act.

Articles of Dissolution

Art. 6.07. A. If voluntary dissolution proceedings have not been revoked, then, when all liabilities and obligations of the limited liability company have been paid or discharged, or adequate provision has been made therefor, or in case its property and assets are not sufficient to satisfy and discharge all the limited liability company's liabilities and obligations, then when all the property and assets have been applied so far as they will go to the just and equitable payment of the limited liability company's liabilities and obligations, and all of the remaining property and assets of the limited liability have been distributed to its members according to their respective rights and interest, articles of dissolution shall be executed on behalf of the limited liability company by a manager or authorized member, or in accordance with Section G, Article 2.23, of this Act, which shall set forth:

(1) The name of the limited liability company.

(2) The names and respective addresses of its managers, if any.

(3) That all debts, obligations, and liabilities of the limited liability company have been paid or discharged or that adequate provision has been made therefor, or, in case the limited liability company's property and assets were not sufficient to satisfy and discharge all its debts, liabilities, and obligations, that all property and assets have been applied so far as they will go to the payment thereof in a just and equitable manner and that no property or assets remain available for distribution among its members, or, that the limited liability company has not acquired any debts, obligations, or liabilities.

(4) That all remaining property and assets of the limited liability company have been distributed among its members in accordance with their respective rights and interest or that no property remained for distribution to members after applying it as far as it would go to the just and equitable payment of the debts, liabilities, and obligations of the limited liability company, or that the limited liability company has not acquired any property or assets and therefore distributions to members were not required.

(5) If capital has not been paid into the limited liability company, a statement that the resolution was adopted by the act of a majority of the initial managers or a majority of the initial members named in the articles of organization in accordance with Section G, Article 2.23, of this Act and of the date of adoption.

(6) If the limited liability company elected to dissolve by action of its members, a statement that the resolution was adopted in accordance with Section D, Article 2.23, of this Act or as otherwise provided in the articles of incorporation or the regulations and the date of adoption.

Filing Articles of Dissolution

Art. 6.08. A. The original and a copy of such articles of dissolution, along with a certificate from the comptroller that all taxes, including all applicable penalties and interest, administered by the comptroller under Title 2, Tax Code, have been paid, shall be delivered to the secretary of state. If the secretary of state finds that such articles of dissolution conform to law, the secretary of state shall, when the appropriate filing fee is paid as required by law:

(1) Endorse on the original and copy the word "Filed," and the month, day, and year of the filing thereof.

(2) File the original in the secretary of state's office.

(3) Issue a certificate of dissolution to which there shall be affixed the copy.

B. The certificate of dissolution, together with the copy of the articles of dissolution affixed thereto by the Secretary of State, shall be delivered to the representative of the dissolved limited liability company. Upon the issuance of such certificate of dissolution the existence of the limited liability company shall cease, except for the purpose of suits, other proceedings in appropriate limited liability company action by members, managers and representatives as provided by the laws of this state.

PART SEVEN

Admission of Foreign Limited Liability Company

Art. 7.01. A. No foreign limited liability company shall have the right to transact business in this State until it shall have procured a certificate of authority so to do from the Secretary of State. No foreign limited liability company shall be entitled to procure a certificate of authority under this Act to transact in this State any business which a limited liability company organized under this Act is not permitted to transact. A foreign limited liability company shall not be denied a certificate of authority by reason of the fact that the laws of the State or country under which such limited liability company is organized governing its organization and internal affairs differ from the laws of this State, and nothing in this Act contained shall be construed to authorize this State to regulate the organization of such limited liability company or its internal affairs.

B. Without excluding other activities which may not constitute transaction of business in this state, a foreign limited liability company shall not be considered to be transacting business in this state, for the purposes of this Act, by reason of carrying on in this state any one (1) or more of the following activities:

(1) Maintaining or defending any action or suit or any administrative or arbitration proceedings, or effecting the settlement thereof or the settlement of claims or disputes to which it is a party;

(2) Holding meetings of its members or managers or carrying on other activities concerning its internal affairs;

(3) Maintaining bank accounts;

(4) Maintaining offices or agencies for the transfer, exchange, and registration of securities issued by it, or appointing and maintaining trustees or depositaries with relation to its securities;

(5) Voting the stock or other equity interest of any person;

(6) Effecting sales through independent contractors;

(7) Creating as borrower or lender, or acquiring, indebtedness or mortgages or other security interests in real or personal property;

(8) Securing or collecting debts due to it or enforcing any rights in property securing the same;

(9) Transacting any business in interstate commerce;

(10) Conducting an isolated transaction completed within a period of thirty (30) days and not in the course of a number of repeated transactions of like nature;

(11) Exercising the powers of executor or administrator of the estate of a non-resident decedent under ancillary letters issued by a court of this state, or exercising the powers of a trustee under the will of a non-resident decedent, or under a trust created by one or more non-residents of this state, or by one or more foreign limited liability companies if the exercise of such powers, in any such case, will not involve activities which would be deemed to constitute the transacting of business in this state in the case of a foreign limited liability company acting in its own right;

(12) Acquiring, in transactions outside Texas, or in interstate commerce, of debts secured by mortgages or liens on real or personal property in Texas, collecting or adjusting of principal and interest payments thereon, enforcing or adjusting any rights and property securing said debts, taking any actions necessary to preserve and protect the interest of the mortgagee in said security, or any combination of such transactions;

(13) Investing in or acquiring, in transactions outside of Texas, royalties and other non-operating mineral interests, and the execution of division orders, contracts of sale and other instruments incidental to the ownership of such non-operating mineral interests.

Powers of Foreign Limited Liability Company

Art. 7.02. A. A foreign limited liability company which shall have received a certificate of authority under this Act shall, until its certificate of authority shall have been revoked in accordance with the provisions of this Act or until a certificate of withdrawal shall have been issued by the Secretary of State as provided in this Act, enjoy the same, but no greater, rights and privileges as a domestic limited liability company organized for the purposes set forth in the application pursuant to which such certificate of authority is issued; and, as to all matters affecting the transaction of intrastate business in this State, it and its managers and members shall be subject to the same duties, restrictions, penalties, and liabilities now or hereafter imposed upon a domestic limited liability company of like character and its managers and members; provided, however, that only the laws of the jurisdiction of organization of a foreign limited liability company shall govern (1) the internal affairs of the foreign limited liability company, including but not limited to the rights, powers, and duties of its manager and members and matters relating to its ownership, and

(2) the liability, if any, of members of the foreign limited liability company for the debts, liabilities and obligations of the foreign limited liability company for which they are not otherwise liable by statute or agreement.

Limited Liability Company Name of Foreign Limited Liability Company

Art. 7.03. A. No certificate of authority shall be issued to a foreign limited liability company unless the limited liability company name of the limited liability company:

(1) Shall contain the word "Limited Liability Company" or "Limited Company" or the abbreviations "L.L.C.," "LLC," "LC," or "L.C." and shall contain any additional words required by law. The word "Limited" may be abbreviated as "Ltd." or "LTD" and the word "Company" may be abbreviated as "Co." However, a foreign limited liability company that procured a certificate of authority to transact business in this state before September 1, 1993, and that complied with this Section on the date of procuring the certificate, but does not comply with this Section as revised, is not required to change its name. This subsection does not apply to a foreign limited liability company that is not characterized as a limited liability company under the laws of the jurisdiction of its formation but elects to procure a certificate of authority pursuant to Article 7.01 of this Act as described by Subsection (9) of Section A of Article 1.02 of this Act.

(2) Shall not contain any word or phrase which indicates or implies that it is organized for any purpose other than one or more of the purposes contained in its articles of organization.

(3) Shall not be the same as, or deceptively similar to, the name of any domestic limited liability company, corporation or limited partnership existing under the laws of this state or of any foreign limited

liability company, corporation or limited partnership authorized to transact business in this state, or a name the exclusive right to which is, at the time, reserved or registered in the manner provided in this Act or any other statute relating to corporations, partnerships, or other business entities; provided that a name may be similar if written consent is obtained from the existing limited liability company, corporation or limited partnership having the name deemed to be similar or the person, or limited liability company, for whom the name deemed to be similar is reserved or registered in the office of the Secretary of State. A certificate of authority shall be issued as provided in this Act to any foreign limited liability company having a name the same as, deceptively similar to, or, if no consent is given, similar to the name of any limited liability company existing under the laws of this state or of any foreign limited liability company authorized to transact business in this state, or a name the exclusive right to which is, at the time, reserved or registered, provided such foreign limited liability company qualifies and does business under a name that meets the requirements of this article. The foreign limited liability company shall set forth in the application for a certificate of authority the name under which it is qualifying and shall file an assumed name certificate as required by law.

Change of Name by Foreign Limited Liability Company

Art. 7.04. A. Whenever a foreign limited liability company which is authorized to transact business in this state shall change its name to one under which a Certificate of Authority would not be granted to it on application therefor, the Certificate of Authority of such foreign limited liability company shall be suspended and it shall not thereafter transact any business in this state until it has changed its name to a name which is available to it under the laws of this State or has otherwise complied with the provisions of this act.

Application for Certificate of Authority

Art. 7.05. A. To procure a Certificate of Authority to transact business in this State, a foreign limited liability company shall make application therefor to the Secretary of State, which application shall set forth:

(1) The name of the foreign limited liability company as stated in the company's formation documents or in any amendments to the company's formation documents in the state or country under the laws of which it is organized.

(2) If the name of the limited liability company does not contain the word "Limited," "Ltd.," or "L.C." or other word or abbreviation the company is required to include in its name under Article 7.03 of this Act, then the name of the foreign limited liability company with the word or abbreviation which it elects to add thereto for use in this state; if the foreign limited liability company is required to qualify under a name other than its foreign limited liability company name, then the name under which the foreign limited liability company is to be qualified.

(3) The date of organization and the period of duration of the foreign limited liability company.

(4) The address of the principal office of the foreign limited liability company in the state or country under the laws of which it is organized.

(5) The address of the registered office of the foreign limited liability company in this state, and the name of its registered agent in this state at such address.

(6) The purpose or purposes of the foreign limited liability company which it proposes to pursue in the transaction of business in this state and a statement that it is authorized to pursue such purpose or purposes in the state or country under the laws of which it is organized.

(7) The names and respective addresses of the managers of the foreign limited liability company.

(8) A statement that the limited liability company exists as a valid entity under the laws of its jurisdiction of formation.

B. Such application shall be made on forms promulgated by the Secretary of State and shall be executed on behalf of the foreign limited liability company by an authorized manager or member.

Filing of Application for Certificate of Authority

Art. 7.06. A. The original and a copy of the application of the foreign limited liability company for a Certificate of Authority shall be delivered to the Secretary of State. If the Secretary of State finds that the application conforms to law, the Secretary of State shall, when the appropriate filing fee is paid as required by law:

(1) Endorse on the original and a copy the word "filed," and the month, day, and year of filing thereof.

(2) File in the office of the Secretary of State the original.

(3) Issue a Certificate of Authority to transact business in this state to which there shall be affixed the copy.

B. The Certificate of Authority, together with a copy of the application affixed thereto by the Secretary of State, shall be delivered to the foreign limited liability company or its representative.

Effect of Certificate of Authority

Art. 7.07. A. Upon the issuance of a Certificate of Authority by the Secretary of State, the foreign limited liability company shall be authorized to transact business in this State for those purposes set forth in its application, and such certificate shall be conclusive evidence of such right of the foreign limited liability company to transact business in the State for such purposes, except as against this State, in preceding to revoke such certificate.

Amended Certificate of Authority

Art. 7.08. A. If a foreign limited liability company authorized to transact business in this State shall change its foreign limited liability company name, or if such foreign limited liability company desires to pursue in this State purposes other than, or in addition to, those authorized by its existing certificate of authority, it shall procure an amended certificate of authority by making application therefor to the Secretary of State.

B. To change any statement on an original application for a certificate of authority a foreign limited liability company shall file with the Secretary of State an application for an amended certificate of authority setting forth the change.

C. An application for an amended certificate of authority submitted because of a name change must be accompanied by a certificate from the proper filing officer in the jurisdiction of organization evidencing the name change.

D. The requirements in respect to the form and contents of such application, the manner of its execution, the filing of the application and a copy of it with the Secretary of State, the issuance of an amended certificate of authority and the effect thereof, shall be the same as in the case of an original application for a certificate of authority.

Withdrawal or Termination of Foreign Limited Liability Company

Art. 7.09. A. A foreign limited liability company authorized to transact business in this state may withdraw from this state upon procuring from the Secretary of State a certificate of withdrawal. In order to procure such certificate of withdrawal, such foreign limited liability company shall deliver to the Secretary of State an application for withdrawal, which shall set forth:

(1) The name of the foreign limited liability company and the state or country under the laws of which it is organized;

(2) That the foreign limited liability company is not transacting business in this state;

(3) That the foreign limited liability company surrenders its authority to transact business in this state;

(4) That the foreign limited liability company revokes the authority of its registered agent in this state to accept service of process and consents that service of process in any action, suit, or proceeding based upon any cause of action arising in this state during the time the foreign limited liability company was authorized to transact business in this state may thereafter be made on such foreign limited liability company by service thereof on the Secretary of State;

(5) A post office address to which the Secretary of State may mail a copy of any process against the foreign limited liability company that may be served on him;

(6) A statement that all sums due, or accrued, to this state have been paid, or that adequate provision has been made for the payment thereof;

(7) A statement that all known creditors or claimants have been paid or provided for and that the foreign limited liability company is not involved in or threatened with litigation in any court in this state.

B. The application for withdrawal may be made on forms promulgated by the Secretary of State and shall be executed on behalf of the foreign limited liability company by an authorized manager or member.

C. When the existence of a foreign limited liability company terminates because of dissolution, merger, or otherwise, a certificate from the proper officer in the jurisdiction of the foreign limited liability company's organization evidencing the termination shall be filed with the Secretary of State.

Filing of Application for Withdrawal

Art. 7.10. A. The original and a copy of such application for withdrawal, along with a certificate from the comptroller that all taxes, including penalties and interest, administered by the comptroller under Title 2, Tax Code, have been paid, shall be delivered to the secretary of state. If the secretary of state finds that such application conforms to the provisions of this Act, the secretary of state shall, when the appropriate filing fee is paid as required by law:

(1) Endorse on the original and the copy the word "Filed," and the month, day, and year of the filing thereof.

(2) File the original in the secretary of state's office.

(3) Issue a certificate of withdrawal to which there shall be affixed the copy.

B. The certificate of withdrawal, together with the copy of the application for withdrawal affixed thereto by the Secretary of State, shall be delivered to the foreign limited liability company or its representative. Upon the issuance of such certificate of withdrawal, the authority of the foreign limited liability company to transact business in this State shall cease.

Revocation of Certificate of Authority

Art. 7.11. A. The certificate of authority of a foreign limited liability company to transact business in this state may be revoked by a decree of the district court for the county in which the registered office of the foreign limited liability company in this state is situated or of any district court in Travis County in an action filed by the Attorney General when it is established that:

(1) The foreign limited liability company has failed to comply with a condition precedent to the issuance of its certificate of authority or a renewal or amendment thereof; or

(2) The certificate of authority to transact business in this state or any amendment thereof was procured through fraud; or(3) The foreign limited liability company has continued to transact business beyond the scope of the purpose or purposes expressed in its certificate of authority to transact business in this state; or

(4) A misrepresentation has been made of any material matter in any application, report, affidavit, or other document submitted by such foreign limited liability company as required by law.

B. The certificate of authority of a foreign limited liability company to transact business in this state may be revoked by order of the Secretary of State when it is established that it is in default in any of the following particulars:

(1) The foreign limited liability company has failed to file any report within the time required by law, or has failed to pay any fees, taxes, or penalties prescribed by law when the same have become due and payable; or

(2) The foreign limited liability company has failed to maintain a registered agent in this state as required by law; or

(3) The foreign limited liability company has changed its name and has failed to file with the Secretary of State within thirty days after such change of name became effective, an application for an amended certificate of authority, or that the foreign limited liability company has changed its foreign limited liability company name and that the newly adopted name is not available for use in this state; or

(4) The foreign limited liability company has failed to pay the filing fee for the foreign limited liability company certificate of authority or any required tax deposit, or the fee or any tax was paid by an instrument that was dishonored when presented by the state for payment.

C. (1) No foreign limited liability company shall have its certificate of authority to transact business in this state revoked under Subsection (1), (2), or (3) of Section B hereof unless the Secretary of State, or other state agency to which such report, taxes, fees, penalties is required to be made, gives the foreign limited liability company not less than 90 days notice of its neglect, delinquency, or omission by certified mail addressed to its registered office or to its principal place of business, or to the last known address of one of its managers, or to any other known place of business of said foreign limited liability company, and the foreign limited liability company has failed prior to such revocation to correct the neglect, omission or delinquency.

(2) When the certificate of authority of a foreign limited liability company to transact business in this state is revoked under Subsection (4) of Section B of this article, the Secretary of State shall give the foreign limited liability company notice of the revocation by regular mail addressed to its registered office, its principal place of business, the last known address of one of its managers or members or any other known place of business of the foreign limited liability company.

D. Whenever a foreign limited liability company has given cause for revocation of its certificate of authority and has failed to correct the neglect, omission or delinquency as provided in Sections B and C, the Secretary of State shall thereupon revoke the certificate of authority of the foreign limited liability company by issuing a certificate of revocation which shall include the fact of such revocation and the date and cause thereof. The original of such certificate shall be placed in the Secretary of State's office and a copy thereof mailed to the foreign limited liability company at its registered office or to its principal place of business, or to the last known address of one of its managers, or to any other known place of business of said foreign limited liability com-

pany. Upon the issuance of such certificate of revocation, the authority to transact business in this state shall cease.

E. Any foreign limited liability company whose certificate of authority has been revoked by the Secretary of State under the provisions of Section B of this article may be reinstated by the Secretary of State at any time within a period of 36 months from the date of revocation, upon approval of an application for reinstatement signed by a manager or member of the foreign limited liability company. Such application shall be filed by the Secretary of State whenever it is established to the Secretary of State's satisfaction that in fact there was no cause for the revocation, or whenever the neglect, omission or delinquency resulting in revocation has been corrected and payment made of all fees, taxes, penalties and interest due thereon which accrued before the revocation plus an amount equal to the total taxes from the date of revocation to the date of reinstatement which would have been payable had the foreign limited liability company certificate not been revoked. A reinstatement filing fee of $50 shall accompany the application for reinstatement.

Reinstatement shall not be authorized if the foreign limited liability company name is the same as or deceptively similar to a foreign limited liability company, corporation or limited partnership name already on file or reserved or registered, unless the foreign limited liability company being reinstated contemporaneously amends its certificate of authority to change its name.

When the application for reinstatement is approved and filed by the Secretary of State, the foreign limited liability company's authority to do business in Texas shall be deemed to have continued without interruption from the date of revocation, except that reinstatement shall have no effect upon any issue of personal liability of the manager or member, or agents of the foreign limited liability company during the period between revocation and reinstatement.

F. When a foreign limited liability company is convicted of a felony, or when a high managerial agent is convicted of a felony committed in the conduct of the affairs of the foreign limited liability company, the Attorney General may file an action to revoke the certificate of authority of the foreign limited liability company to transact business in this State in a district court of the county in which the registered office of the foreign limited liability company in this State is situated or in a district court of Travis County. The court may revoke the foreign limited liability company's certificate of authority if it is established that:

(1) The foreign limited liability company, or a high managerial agent acting in behalf of the foreign limited liability company has engaged in a persistent course of felonious conduct; and

(2) To prevent future felonious conduct of the same character, the public interest requires such revocation.

Filing of Decree of Revocation

Art. 7.12. A. In case a court shall enter a decree revoking the certificate of authority of a foreign limited liability company to transact business in this State, it shall be the duty of the clerk of such court to cause a certified copy of the decree to be filed with the Secretary of State. No fee shall be charged by the Secretary of State for the filing thereof.

Transacting Business Without Certificate of Authority

Art. 7.13. A. No foreign limited liability company which is transacting, or has transacted, business in this State without a certificate of authority shall be permitted to maintain any action, suit, or proceeding in any court of this State (whether brought directly by the foreign limited liability company or in the form of a derivative action by a member) on any cause of action arising out of the transaction of business in this State, until such foreign limited liability company shall have obtained a certificate of authority. Nor shall any action, suit, or proceeding on any such cause of action be maintained in any court of this State by a successor, assignee, or legal representative of such foreign limited liability company until a certificate of authority shall have been obtained by such foreign limited liability company or by a foreign limited liability company on which has acquired all or substantially all of its assets. It is expressly provided, however, that the provisions of this article shall not affect the rights of any assignee of the foreign limited liability company as the holder in due course of a negotiable promissory note, check or bill of exchange, or as the bona fide purchaser for value of a warehouse receipt, stock certificate, or other instrument made negotiable by law.

B. The failure of a foreign limited liability company to obtain a certificate of authority to transact business in this State shall not impair the validity of any contract or act of such foreign limited liability company, shall not cause any member or manager of such foreign limited liability company to become liable for the debts, obligations, or liabilities of such foreign limited liability company, and shall not prevent such foreign limited liability company from defending any action, suit or proceeding in any court of this State.

C. A foreign limited liability company which transacts business in this State without a certificate of authority shall be liable to this State, for the years or parts thereof during which it transacted business in this State without a certificate of authority, in an amount equal to all fees any taxes which would have been imposed by law upon such foreign limited liability company had it duly applied for and received a certificate of authority to transact business in this State as required by law and thereafter filed all reports required by law, plus all penalties imposed by law for failure to pay such fees and taxes. In addition to the penalties and payments thus prescribed, such foreign limited liability company shall forfeit to this State an amount not less than One Hundred Dollars ($100) nor more than Five Thousand Dollars ($5,000) for each month or fraction thereof it shall have transacted business in this State without a certificate. The Attorney General shall bring suit to recover all amounts due this State under the provisions of this section.

PART EIGHT

Interrogatories by Secretary of State

Art. 8.01. A. The Secretary of State may propound to any limited liability company, domestic or foreign, subject to the provisions of this Act, and to any manager thereof, such interrogatories as may be reasonably necessary and proper to enable the Secretary of State to ascertain whether such limited liability company has complied with all the provisions of this Act. Such interrogatories shall be answered within thirty days after the mailing thereof, or within such additional time as shall be fixed by the Secretary of State, and the answers thereto shall be full and complete and shall be made in writing and under oath. If such interrogatories be directed to an individual, they shall be answered by such individual, and if directed to a limited liability company, they shall be answered by an authorized manager or member of the limited liability company. The Secretary of State need not file any document to which such interrogatories relate until such interrogatories be answered as herein provided, and not then if the answers thereto disclose that such document is not in conformity with the provisions of this Act. The Secretary of State shall certify to the

Attorney General, for such action as the Attorney General may deem appropriate, all interrogatories and answers thereto which disclose a violation of the provisions of this Act.

Information Disclosed by Interrogatories

Art. 8.02. A. Interrogatories propounded by the Secretary of State and the answers thereto shall not be open to public inspection nor shall the Secretary of State disclose any facts or information obtained therefrom except insofar as official duty may require the same to be made public or in the event such interrogatories or the answers thereto are required for evidence in any criminal proceedings or in any other action by this State.

Powers of Secretary of State

Art. 8.03. A. The Secretary of State shall have the power and authority reasonably necessary to enable the Secretary of State to administer this Act efficiently and to perform the duties therein imposed upon the Secretary of State.

Appeals from Secretary of State

Art. 8.04. A. If the Secretary of State shall fail to approve any articles of organization, application for certificate of authority to transact business in this State, amendment, merger, consolidation, or dissolution, or any other document required by this Act to be approved by the Secretary of State before the same shall be filed in the office of the Secretary of State, the Secretary of State shall, within ten days after the delivery thereof to the Secretary of State, give written notice of disapproval to the person or limited liability company, domestic or foreign, delivering the same, specifying in such notice the reasons therefor. From such disapproval, such person or limited liability company may appeal to any district court of Travis County by filing with the clerk of such court a petition setting forth a copy of the articles or other document sought to be filed and a copy of the written disapproval thereof by the Secretary of State; whereupon the matter shall be tried de novo by the court, and the court shall either sustain the action of the Secretary of State or direct the Secretary of State to take such action as the court may deem proper.

B. Appeals from all final orders and judgments entered by the district court under this Article in review of any ruling or decision of the Secretary of State may be taken as in other civil actions.

Certificates and Certified Copies to be Received in Evidence

Art. 8.05. A. All certificates issued by the Secretary of State in accordance with the provisions of this Act, and all copies of documents filed in the office of the Secretary of State in accordance with the provisions of this Act, when certified by the Secretary of State, shall be taken and received in all courts, public offices, and official bodies as prima facie evidence of the facts therein stated, and shall be subject to recordation. A certificate by the Secretary of State, under the great seal of this State, as to the existence or non-existence of the facts relating to limited liability companies which would not appear from a certified copy of any of the foregoing documents or certificates shall be taken and received in all courts, public offices, and official bodies as prima facie evidence of the existence or non-existence of the facts therein stated.

Forms Promulgated by Secretary of State

Art. 8.06. A. Forms may be promulgated by the Secretary of State for all reports and all other documents required to be filed in the office of the Secretary of State. The use of such forms, however, shall not be mandatory, except in instances in which the law may specifically so provide.

Time for Filing Documents in the Office of the Secretary of State
Art. 8.07. A. Whenever any document is required to be filed in the office of the Secretary of State by any provision of this Act, the requirement of the statute shall be construed to involve the requirement that same be so filed with reasonable promptness.

Waiver of Notice
Art. 8.08. A. Whenever any notice is required to be given to any managers or members of a limited liability company under the provisions of this Act or under the provisions of the articles of organization or regulations of the limited liability company, a waiver thereof in writing signed by the person or persons entitled to such notice, whether before or after the time stated therein, shall be equivalent to the giving of such notice.

Application to Foreign and Interstate Commerce
Art. 8.09. A. The provisions of this Act shall apply to commerce with foreign nations and among the several states only insofar as the same may be permitted under the provisions of the Constitution of the United States.

Reservation of Power
Art. 8.10. A. The Legislature shall at all times have power to prescribe such regulations, provisions, and limitations as it may deem advisable, which regulations, provisions, and limitations shall be binding upon any and all limited liability companies subject to the provisions of this Act, and the Legislature shall have power to amend, repeal, or modify this Act.

Effect of Invalidity of Part of This Act
Art. 8.11. A. If a court of competent jurisdiction shall adjudge to be invalid or unconstitutional any clause, sentence, subsection, section, or Article of this Act, such judgment or decree shall not affect, impair, invalidate, or nullify the remainder of this Act, but the effect thereof shall be confined to the clause, sentence, subsection, section, or Article of this Act so adjudged to be invalid or unconstitutional.

Applicability of Other Statutes
Art. 8.12. A. Subject to Section C of this Article, Articles 2.07, 2.08, 4.14, and 5.14 and Part Seven of the TBCA apply to a limited liability company and its members, managers, and officers.B. Subject to Section C of this Article, Articles 2.03 through 2.06, 2.09, 2.09A, 3.01, 7.01 through 7.05, and 7.07, Texas Miscellaneous Corporation Laws Act (Article 1302-1.01 et seq., Vernon's Texas Civil Statutes), as amended, apply to a limited liability company and its members, managers, and officers.
C. For purposes of the application of the articles of the TBCA and the Texas Miscellaneous Corporation Laws Act as provided by Sections A and B of this Article, as context requires:
(1) a reference to a corporation includes a limited liability company;
(2) a reference to a share includes a membership interest;
(3) a reference to a shareholder includes a member;
(4) a reference to a director includes a manager or, to the extent that the management of the limited liability company is reserved in whole or in part to the members, a member who manages the limited liability company;
(5) a reference to articles of incorporation includes articles of organization; and
(6) a reference to bylaws includes regulations.

Applicability; Expiration
Art. 8.13. A. Except as provided by Title 8, Business Organizations Code, this Act does not apply to a limited liability company to which the Business Organizations Code applies.
B. This Act expires January 1, 2010.

PART NINE
Filing and Filing Fees
Art. 9.01. A. The Secretary of State is authorized and required to collect for the use of the State the following fees:
(1) Filing articles of organization of a domestic limited liability company and issuing the certificate of organization, Two Hundred Dollars ($200.00).
(2) Filing articles of amendment of a domestic limited liability company and issuing the certificate of amendment, One Hundred Dollars ($100.00).
(3) Filing articles of merger or articles of conversion involving one or more domestic or foreign limited liability companies, Two Hundred Dollars ($200.00), provided that any other filing fee paid under the corporation, partnership, or other entity statutes of this State for the filing of articles of merger or articles of conversion with respect to entities organized under those statutes shall be credited against the filing fee provided by this subsection.
(4) Filing an application of a foreign limited liability company for certificate of authority to transact business in this state and issuing such a certificate of authority, Five Hundred Dollars ($500.00).
(5) Filing an application of a foreign limited liability company for an amended certificate of authority to transact business in this state and issuing such an amended certificate of authority, One Hundred Dollars ($100.00).
(6) Filing restated articles of organization of a domestic limited liability company, Two Hundred Dollars ($200.00).
(7) Filing application for reservations of a limited liability company name and issuing certificate thereof, Twenty-Five Dollars ($25.00).
(8) Filing notice of transfer of reserved limited liability company name and issuing a certificate therefor, Ten Dollars ($10.00).
(9) Filing statement of change of registered office or registered agent, or both, Ten Dollars ($10.00).
(10) Filing statement of change of address of registered agent, Ten Dollars ($10.00); provided, however, that the maximum fee for simultaneous filings by a registered agent for more than one limited liability company shall not exceed Five Hundred Dollars ($500.00).
(11) Filing articles of dissolution and issuing certificate therefor, Twenty-Five Dollars ($25.00).
(12) Filing application for withdrawal and issuing certificate therefor, Ten Dollars ($10.00).
(13) Filing certificate from home state that foreign limited liability company is no longer existent in said state, Ten Dollars ($10.00).
(14) Filing any instrument pursuant to this act not expressly provided for above, Ten Dollars ($10.00).
(15) [Blank].
(16) Filing an application for reinstatement of the limited liability company charter or certificate of authority following forfeiture under the Tax Code, Seventy-Five Dollars ($75.00).
B. Except as otherwise expressly provided in this act, any instrument to be filed pursuant to this act shall be signed on behalf of the limited liability company by an authorized manager or member, and the orig-

inal and a copy of the instrument shall be delivered to the Secretary of State with copies attached thereto of any document incorporated by reference in or otherwise made a part of such instrument, or to be filed by means of such instrument. If the Secretary of State finds that such instrument conforms to law, the Secretary of State shall, when all taxes and fees, if any, have been paid as prescribed by law:

(1) endorse on the original and the copy of the word "filed", and the month, day, and year of the filing thereof;

(2) file the original in his office;

(3) issue any certificate required by this act relating to the subject matter of the filed instrument;

(4) return the copy, affixed to any certificate required to be issued by the Secretary of State, to the limited liability company or its representatives.

Penalty for Signing False Documents

Art. 9.02. A. A person commits an offense if such person signs a document such person knows to be false in any material respect with intent that the document be delivered on behalf of a limited liability company to the Secretary of State for filing.

B. An offense under this article is a Class A misdemeanor.

Delayed Effectiveness of Certain Filings

Art. 9.03. A. (1) For purposes of this Article, "permitted act" means a filing with the Secretary of State under this Act for:

(a) the articles of organization of a limited liability company under this Act;

(b) an amendment to or restatement of the articles of organization;

(c) a merger or conversion;

(d) the application of a foreign limited liability company to procure a certificate of authority to transact business in this state or to withdraw from doing business in this state;

(e) an amendment to the certificate of authority of a foreign limited liability company to transact business in this state;

(f) a change in registered office or registered agent;

(g) a change of address of a registered agent; or

(h) a voluntary dissolution.

(2) A permitted act may be made effective as of a time and date after the time and date otherwise provided in this Act or may be made effective on the occurrence of events or facts that may occur in the future. Those events or facts may include future acts of any person if the articles of organization, articles of amendment or restatement, articles of merger, application, or other document required by this Act to be filed with the Secretary of State to make the permitted act effective clearly and expressly states, in addition to any other statement or information required:

(a) a time and date certain on which the permitted act is to become effective; or

(b) if the permitted act is to become effective on the occurrence of events or facts that may occur in the future:

(i) the manner in which the events or facts cause the permitted act to become effective; and

(ii) the date of the 90th day after the date of the filing of the articles of organization, articles of amendment or restatement, articles of merger, application, or other document.

(3) A permitted act becoming effective as of a time or date certain that is after the time and date otherwise provided in this Act must specify a subsequent effective time and date that is not more than 90 days after the date of the filing of the articles of organization, articles of amendment or restatement, articles of merger, application, or other

document required by this Act. The time certain on which the permitted act is to become effective may not be midnight or 12 p.m.

(4) Within 90 days after the date of filing of the articles of organization, articles of amendment or restatement, articles of merger, application, or other document for a permitted act becoming effective on the occurrence of events or facts that may occur in the future, other than the mere passage of time, a statement must be filed with the Secretary of State confirming that all the events or facts on which the effectiveness of the permitted act is conditioned have been satisfied or waived and the date on which the condition was satisfied or waived.

B. A statement required by Section A of this Article must be executed on behalf of each domestic or foreign limited liability company or other person required to execute the articles of organization, articles of amendment or restatement, articles of merger, application, or other document required by this Act to be filed with the Secretary of State to make the permitted act effective by a member, manager, officer, or other duly authorized representative, including a member, manager, officer, or duly authorized representative of any successor domestic or foreign limited liability company or other entity. An original and a copy of the statement must be filed with the Secretary of State.

C. Notwithstanding any other provision of this Act to the contrary, a permitted act that is to become effective as of a time or date after the time and date otherwise provided in this Act, to the extent permitted by this Article, shall become effective as of the subsequent time and date. Any certificate issued by the Secretary of State on the filing of the articles of organization, articles of amendment or restatement, articles of merger, application, or other document otherwise required by this Act for the permitted act to become effective shall expressly set forth the time and date on which the permitted act is to become effective.

D. (1) A permitted act to be made effective on the occurrence of events or facts that may occur in the future, other than the mere passage of time, and for which the statement required by Subsection (4) of Section A of this Article is filed with the Secretary of State within the prescribed time becomes effective as of the time and date on which the latest specified event or fact occurred or the time and date on which the condition is otherwise satisfied or waived. Any certificate issued or notation, acknowledgment, or other statement made by the Secretary of State on the filing of the articles of organization, articles of amendment or restatement, articles of merger, application, or other document otherwise required by this Act for the permitted act to become effective must:

(a) state that "The effectiveness of the action to which this instrument relates is conditioned on the occurrence of certain facts or events described in the filing to which this instrument relates"; or

(b) make reference in any manner approved by the Secretary of State to the fact that the effectiveness of the action is so conditioned.

(2) The time and date on which a condition to the effectiveness of a permitted act is satisfied or waived as set forth in a statement filed with the Secretary of State pursuant to Subsection (4) of Section A of this Article shall be conclusively regarded as the time and date on which the condition was satisfied or waived for purposes of this section.

E. If the effectiveness of any permitted act is conditioned on the occurrence of events or facts that may occur in the future, other than the mere passage of time, and the statement required by Subsection (4) of Section A of this Article is not filed with the Secretary of State within the prescribed time, the permitted act does not become effective unless there is subsequently filed with the Secretary of State the articles of organization, articles of amendment or restatement, articles of merger, application, or other document required by this Act to be filed with the Secretary of State to make the permitted act effective.

F. If articles of organization, articles of amendment or restatement, articles of merger, articles of conversion, an application, or any other document permitted to be filed pursuant to this Act with the Secretary of State have been filed but the event or transaction evidenced by the filing has not become effective, the filing may be abandoned in accordance with the agreement of the parties to the filing by filing a certificate of abandonment with the Secretary of State before the effectiveness of the event or transaction in accordance with the terms of the document so filed. The certificate of abandonment must be signed on behalf of each domestic or foreign limited liability company or other entity that is a party to the event or transaction by a member, manager, officer, or other authorized representative and must state the nature of the filing to be abandoned, the date of the filing to be abandoned, the parties to the filing to be abandoned, and that the event or transaction has been abandoned in accordance with the agreement of the parties. On the filing of the certificate of abandonment with the Secretary of State, the event or transaction evidenced by the original filing shall be considered abandoned and may not become effective.

PART TEN
Merger

Art. 10.01. A. A domestic limited liability company may adopt a plan of merger and one or more domestic limited liability companies may merge with one or more domestic or foreign limited liability companies or other entities if:

(1) each constituent entity enters into a written plan of merger containing the provisions set forth in Article 10.02 of this Act for which:

(a) approval exists by all domestic limited liability companies by the vote of a majority of their respective members, unless the respective regulations or articles of organization of each limited liability company provide otherwise; and

(b) if one or more foreign limited liability companies or other entities is a party to the merger or is to be created by the terms of the plan of merger:

(i) the merger is permitted by the laws under which each foreign limited liability company and each other entity that is a party to the merger is formed or organized or by the organizational documents or other constituent documents of the foreign limited liability company or other entity that are not inconsistent with those laws; and

(ii) each foreign limited liability company or other entity that is a party to the merger complies with those laws or documents in effecting the merger; and

(2) a member of a domestic limited liability company that is a party to the merger, as a result of the merger, will not become personally liable for the liabilities or obligations of any other person unless the member consents to becoming personally liable by action taken in connection with the specific plan of merger approved by the domestic limited liability company.

Plan of Merger

Art. 10.02. A. A plan of merger must include:

(1) the name and state of domicile of each domestic or foreign limited liability company or other entity that is a party to the merger;

(2) the name of each domestic or foreign limited liability company or other entity, if any, that will survive the merger, which may be one or more of the domestic or foreign limited companies or other entities party to the merger;

(3) the name and state of domicile of each new domestic or foreign limited liability company or other entity, if any, that may be created by the terms of the plan of merger;

(4) the terms and conditions of the merger, including, if more than one domestic or foreign limited liability company or other entity is to survive or to be created by the terms of the plan of merger, the manner and basis of allocating and vesting:

(a) real estate and other property of each domestic or foreign limited liability company and of each other entity that is a party to the merger among one or more of the surviving or new domestic or foreign limited liability companies and other entities; and

(b) all liabilities and obligations of each domestic or foreign limited liability company and other entity that is a party to the merger among one or more of the surviving or new domestic or foreign limited liability companies and other entities or making adequate provision for the payment and discharge of the liabilities and obligations;

(5) the manner and basis of converting any of the limited liability company interests or other evidences of ownership of each domestic or foreign limited liability company or other entity that is a party to the merger into:

(a) limited liability company interests, shares, obligations, evidences of ownership, rights to purchase securities, or other securities of one or more of the surviving or new domestic or foreign limited liability company or other entities;

(b) cash or other property, including shares, obligations, evidences of ownership, rights to purchase securities, or other securities of any other person or entity; or

(c) any combination of the items described in Subdivisions (a) and (b) of this Subsection;

(6) the articles of organization of any new domestic limited liability company to be created by the terms of the plan of merger; and

(7) the articles of organization or other organizational documents of each other entity that is a party to the merger and that is to be created by the terms of the plan of merger.

B. The plan of merger may include:

(1) any amendments to the articles of organization or regulations of any surviving domestic limited liability company or to the organizational documents or other constituent documents of any other surviving entity; and

(2) any other provision relating to the merger.

Articles of Merger

Art. 10.03. A. After a plan of merger has been approved by each of the limited liability companies or other entities that is a party to the plan of merger, articles of merger shall be executed on behalf of each domestic limited liability company that is a party to the plan of merger by at least one member, manager, officer, or other agent or representative of the limited liability company who is authorized to execute articles of merger by the articles of organization or regulations or shall be approved by authorizing resolutions adopted by the act of the members. At least one authorized representative of each other foreign limited liability company or other entity that is a party to the plan of merger shall also execute the articles of merger. The articles of merger must include:

(1) the plan of merger or statement certifying the following:

(a) the name and state of incorporation or organization of each domestic or foreign limited liability company or other entity that is a party to the plan of merger or that is to be created thereby;

(b) that a plan of merger has been approved;

(c) such amendments or changes in the articles of organization of each domestic surviving limited liability company, or if no such amendments are desired to be effected by the merger, a statement to that effect;

(d) that the articles of organization of each new domestic limited liability company to be created pursuant to the terms of the plan of merger are being filed with the Secretary of State with the articles of merger;

(e) that an executed plan of merger is on file at the principal place of business of each surviving or new domestic or foreign limited liability company or other entity, stating the address thereof; and

(f) that a copy of the plan of merger will be furnished by each surviving or new domestic or foreign limited liability company or other entity, on written request and without cost, to any member of each domestic limited liability company that is a party to or created by the plan of merger and, in the case of a merger with multiple surviving domestic or foreign limited liability companies or other entities, to any creditor or obligee of the parties to the merger at the time of the merger if such obligation is then outstanding; and

(2) as to each domestic or foreign limited liability company or other entity that is a party to the plan of merger, a statement that the plan of merger was authorized by all action required by the laws under which it was formed or organized or by its constituent documents.

B. The original of the articles of merger and a number of copies equal to the number of surviving and new domestic or foreign limited liability companies and other entities that are a party to the plan of merger or that will be created by its terms shall be delivered to the Secretary of State. Unless the Secretary of State finds that the articles of merger do not conform to law, on receipt of all applicable filing fees and franchise taxes, if any, required by law or if the plan of merger provides that one or more of the surviving, new, or acquiring domestic or foreign limited liability companies or other entities will be responsible for the payment of all of such fees and franchise taxes and that all of such surviving, new, or acquiring domestic or foreign limited liability companies and other entities will be obligated to pay such fees and franchise taxes if the same are not timely paid, the Secretary of State shall:

(1) certify that the articles of merger have been filed in the Secretary of State's office by endorsing on the original the word "Filed" and the date of the filing;

(2) file and index the endorsed articles of merger; and

(3) issue a certificate of merger, together with a copy of the articles affixed to the certificate, to each surviving or new domestic or foreign limited liability company or other entity that is a party to the plan of merger or that is created by the merger, or to its respective representatives.

C. Except as provided by Article 9.03 of this Act, the merger is effective on the issuance of the certificate of merger by the Secretary of State.

Effect of Merger

Art. 10.04. A. When a merger takes effect:

(1) the separate existence of every domestic or foreign limited liability company or other entity that is a party to the merger, except any surviving or new domestic or foreign limited liability company or other entity, ceases;

(2) all rights, title, and interests to all real estate and other property owned by each domestic or foreign limited liability company and by each other entity that is a party to the merger shall be allocated to and vested in one or more of the surviving or resulting entities as provided in the plan of merger without reversion or impairment, without further act or deed, and without any transfer or assignment having occurred, but subject to any existing liens or other encumbrances on the property;

(3) all liabilities and obligations of each domestic or foreign limited liability company and each other entity that is a party to the merger shall be allocated to one or more of the surviving or new domestic or foreign limited liability companies and other entities in the manner provided by the plan of merger, and each surviving or new domestic or foreign limited liability company or other entity to which a liability or obligation has been allocated under the plan of merger becomes the primary obligor for the liability or obligation, and, except as otherwise provided by the plan of merger, law, or contract, a party to the merger other than a surviving domestic or foreign limited liability company or other entity liable at the time of the merger or another new domestic or foreign limited liability company or other entity created is not liable for the liability or obligation;

(4) a proceeding pending by or against a domestic or foreign limited liability company or another entity that is a party to the merger may be continued as if the merger did not occur, or the surviving or new domestic or foreign limited liability company or limited liability companies or the surviving or new other entity or other entities the liability, obligation, asset, or right associated with the proceeding is allocated to and vested in under the plan of merger may be substituted in the proceeding;

(5) the articles of organization and regulations of each surviving domestic limited liability company and the organizational documents and other constituent documents of each surviving foreign limited liability company and other entity shall be amended to the extent provided in the plan of merger;

(6) each new domestic limited liability company, the articles of organization of which are included in the plan of merger under Article 10.02 of this Act, shall be formed as a limited liability company under this Act, and each other entity to be formed or organized under the laws of this state, the organizational documents of which are included in the plan of merger, on an executed copy of the certificate of merger being delivered to or filed with any required governmental entity with which organizational documents of the other entity are required to be delivered or filed and on meeting additional requirements, if any, of law for its formation or organization, shall be formed or organized as provided in the plan of merger;

(7) the limited liability company interests of each domestic or foreign limited liability company and the interests, shares, or evidences of ownership in each other entity that is a party to the merger that are to be converted or exchanged, in whole or in part, into limited liability company interests, shares, obligations, evidences of ownership, rights to purchase securities, or other securities of one or more of the surviving or new domestic or foreign limited liability companies or other entities, into cash or other property, including shares, obligations, evidences of ownership, rights to purchase securities, or other securities of any other person or entity, or into a combination of those items, shall be so converted and exchanged, and the former members of each domestic limited liability company that is a party to the merger shall be entitled only to the rights provided in the plan of merger; and

(8) if the plan of merger does not provide for the allocation and vesting of the right, title, and interest in a particular item of real estate or

other property or for the allocation of a liability or obligation of a party to the merger, the item of real estate or other property shall be owned in undivided interests by, or the liability or obligation shall be a joint and several liability and obligation of, each of the surviving and new domestic and foreign limited liability companies and other entities, pro rata to the total number of surviving and new domestic and foreign limited liability companies and other entities resulting from the merger.

Merger Involving Subsidiary Entities

Art. 10.05. A. (1) This article applies to a merger if:

(a) at least 90 per cent of the outstanding membership interests, shares of stock, or other ownership interests of one or more domestic or foreign limited liability companies or other entities is owned by another domestic or foreign limited liability company or other entity;

(b) at least one of the parent or subsidiary entities is a domestic limited liability company; and

(c) for each parent or subsidiary entity that is not a domestic limited liability company:

(i) the merger of the entity with or into a domestic limited liability company is permitted by the laws under which that entity is formed or organized or by the organizational documents or other constituent documents of the entity that are not inconsistent with those laws; and (ii) the entity complies with those laws or documents in effectuating the merger.

(2) A parent entity described in Subsection (1) of this Section having at least 90 percent ownership may:

(a) merge the other entity or entities into itself;

(b) merge itself into the other entity or entities; or

(c) merge any one or more of the entities, including itself, into one or more of the other entities.

(3) If the parent entity having at least 90 percent ownership is a surviving entity in the merger, the parent entity must execute and file articles of merger as provided by Section B of this Article. If the parent entity having at least 90 percent ownership is not a surviving entity in the merger, the parent entity must:

(a) adopt a plan of merger in the manner required by Article 10.01 of this Act, except that an action under Article 10.01 is not required by the entity or entities whose membership interests, shares of stock, or other ownership interests are so owned; and

(b) execute and file articles of merger as provided by Section B of this Article.

B. The articles of merger must be signed on behalf of the parent entity by a member, manager, officer, or other agent or representative authorized by

(i) the organizational or other constituent documents of the parent entity, or

(ii) resolutions adopted by the parent entity in accordance with the laws of its jurisdiction of organization or formation and the documents. The articles of merger must include:

(1) the name of the parent entity and the name of each respective subsidiary entity;

(2) for each entity listed in Subsection (1) of this Section, the type of entity and the respective jurisdiction under which the entity is formed or organized;

(3) the total number or percentage of membership interests, shares, or other ownership interests in each subsidiary entity, identified by class, series, or group, and the number or percentage of membership inter-

ests, shares, or other ownership interests in each class, series, or group owned by the parent entity;

(4) a copy of the resolution of merger adopted by the parent entity in accordance with the laws of its jurisdiction of organization or formation and its organizational or other constituent documents, together with a statement that the resolution was so adopted and the date of adoption;

(5) if the parent entity does not own all of the outstanding membership interest, shares, or other ownership interests of each subsidiary entity party to the merger, the resolution described in Subsection (4) of this Section must state the terms and conditions of the merger, including the securities, cash, or other property to be used, paid, or delivered by the surviving corporation on surrender of each membership interest, share, or other ownership interest of the subsidiary entity or entities not owned by the parent entity;

(6) if the surviving entity is a foreign limited liability company or other entity, the address, including street number, if any, of its registered or principal office in the jurisdiction under whose laws it is governed; and

(7) if a plan of merger is required by Section A of this Article to be adopted in the manner required by Article 10.01 of this Act, the information required by Section A of Article 10.03 of this Act.

C. The articles of merger shall be filed as provided by Section B of Article 10.03 of this Act, become effective as provided by Section C of Article 10.03 of this Act, and have the effect stated in Article 10.04 of this Act.

Interest Exchange

Art. 10.06. A. One or more domestic or foreign limited liability companies or other entities may adopt a plan of exchange by which an entity acquires all of the outstanding limited liability company interests of one or more domestic limited liability companies or all of the outstanding interests, stock, partnership interests, or other ownership interests in one or more other entities in exchange for cash or securities of the acquiring entity if:

(1) each domestic limited liability company, the interests of which are to be acquired under the plan of exchange, approves the plan of exchange by majority vote or consent of its members or in a manner prescribed in its regulations; and

(2) each acquiring domestic or foreign limited liability company or other entity takes all action that may be required by the laws of the state or country under which it was formed and as required by its constituent documents to effect the exchange.

B. A filing with the Secretary of State is not necessary to evidence or effect the interest exchange with respect to a domestic limited liability company that is a party to the interest exchange. When an interest exchange takes effect as provided in the plan of exchange:

(1) the limited liability company interests of each domestic limited liability company that are to be acquired under the plan of exchange are considered exchanged as provided in the plan of exchange;

(2) the former holders of the limited liability company interests exchanged under the plan of exchange are entitled only to the exchange rights provided in the plan of exchange; and

(3) the acquiring domestic or foreign limited liability company or other entity or entities are entitled to all rights, title, and interests with respect to the interests so acquired and exchanged, subject to the provisions in the plan of exchange.

Definition of "Other Entity"

Art. 10.07. A. For purposes of this Part, "other entity" means any entity, whether organized for profit or not, that is a corporation, limited partnership, general partnership, joint venture, joint stock company, cooperative, association, bank, insurance company, or other legal entity organized under the laws of this state or any other state or country to the extent the laws or the constituent documents of that entity, not inconsistent with law, permit that entity to enter into a merger or interest exchange as permitted by this Part.

Conversion

Art. 10.08. A. A domestic limited liability company may adopt a plan of conversion and convert to a foreign limited liability company or any other entity if:

(1) the converting entity acts on and its members approve a plan of conversion in the manner prescribed by Article 10.01 of this Act as if the conversion were a merger to which the converting entity were a party and not the survivor;

(2) the conversion is permitted by, or not inconsistent with, the laws of the state or country in which the converted entity is to be incorporated, formed, or organized, and the incorporation, formation, or organization of the converted entity is effected in compliance with such laws;

(3) at the time the conversion becomes effective, each member of the converting entity will, unless otherwise agreed to by that member, own an equity interest or other ownership or security interest in, and be a shareholder, partner, member, owner, or other security holder of, the converted entity;

(4) no member of the domestic limited liability company will, as a result of the conversion, become personally liable, without the member's consent, for the liabilities or obligations of the converted entity; and

(5) the converted entity shall be incorporated, formed, or organized as part of or pursuant to the plan of conversion.

B. Any foreign limited liability company or other entity may adopt a plan of conversion and convert to a domestic limited liability company if:

(1) the conversion is permitted by the laws of the state or country in which the foreign limited liability company is incorporated, formed, or organized, if a foreign limited liability company is converting;

(2) the conversion is either permitted by the laws under which the other entity is incorporated, formed, or organized or by the constituent documents of the other entity that are not inconsistent with the laws of the state or country in which the other entity is incorporated, formed, or organized, if another entity is converting; and

(3) the converting entity takes all action that may be required by the laws of the state or country under which it is incorporated, formed, or organized and by its constituent documents to effect the conversion.

C. A plan of conversion shall set forth:

(1) the name of the converting entity and the converted entity;

(2) a statement that the converting entity is continuing its existence in the organizational form of the converted entity;

(3) a statement as to the type of entity that the converted entity is to be and the state or country under the laws of which the converted entity is to be incorporated, formed, or organized;

(4) the manner and basis of converting the membership interests or other evidences of ownership of the converting entity into membership interests or other evidences of ownership or securities of the converted entity, or any combination thereof;

(5) in an attachment or exhibit, the articles of organization of the domestic limited liability company, if the converted entity is a domestic limited liability company; and

(6) in an attachment or exhibit, the articles of organization or other organizational documents of the converted entity, if the converted entity is not a domestic limited liability company.

D. A plan of conversion may set forth such other provisions relating to the conversion not inconsistent with law, including the initial regulations of the converted entity.

Articles of Conversion

Art. 10.09. A. If a plan of conversion has been approved in accordance with Article 10.08 of this Act and has not been abandoned, articles of conversion shall be executed by the converting entity by a manager (or, if none, by a member) or other duly authorized representative thereof and shall set forth:

(1) the plan of conversion or a statement certifying the following:

(a) the name, the state of incorporation, formation, or organization of the converting entity, and the organizational form of the converting entity;

(b) that a plan of conversion has been approved;

(c) that an executed plan of conversion is on file at the principal place of business of the converting entity, stating the address thereof, and that an executed plan of conversion will be on file, from and after the conversion, at the principal place of business of the converted entity, stating the address thereof; and

(d) that a copy of the plan of conversion will be furnished by the converting entity (prior to the conversion) or the converted entity (after the conversion), on written request and without cost, to any shareholder, partner, or member of the converting entity or the converted entity;

(2) a statement that the approval of the plan of conversion was duly authorized by all action required by the laws under which the converting entity was incorporated, formed, or organized and by its constituent documents; and

(3) any other statements or information that may be required by any law or rule to which the converting entity or converted entity is subject or that the converting entity or the converted entity chooses to include in the articles.

B. The original and one copy of the articles of conversion shall be delivered to the Secretary of State. Two copies of the articles of organization of the domestic limited liability company, if the converted entity is a domestic limited liability company, shall also be delivered to the Secretary of State with the articles of conversion.

C. If the Secretary of State finds that the articles of conversion conform to law, has received all filings required to be received, and has issued all certificates required to be issued in connection with the incorporation, formation, or organization of the converted entity, if any, the Secretary of State shall, when all fees and franchise taxes have been paid as required by law or if the articles of conversion provide that the converted entity will be liable for the payment of all such fees and franchise taxes:

(1) Endorse on the original and each copy the word "Filed" and the month, day, and year of the filing.

(2) File the original in the office of the Secretary of State.

(3) Issue a certificate of conversion, together with a copy of the articles affixed thereto, to the converted entity or its representatives.

Effective Date of Conversion

Art. 10.10. A. Except as otherwise provided by Article 9.03 of this Act, on the issuance of the certificate of conversion by the Secretary of State, the conversion of a converting entity shall be effective.

Effect of Conversion

Art. 10.11. A. When a conversion of a converting entity takes effect:

(1) the converting entity shall continue to exist, without interruption, but in the organizational form of the converted entity rather than in its prior organizational form;

(2) all rights, title, and interests to all real estate and other property owned by the converting entity shall continue to be owned by the converted entity in its new organizational form without reversion or impairment, without further act or deed, and without any transfer or assignment having occurred, but subject to any existing liens or other encumbrances thereon;

(3) all liabilities and obligations of the converting entity shall continue to be liabilities and obligations of the converted entity in its new organizational form without impairment or diminution by reason of the conversion;

(4) all rights of creditors or other parties with respect to or against the prior interest holders or other owners of the converting entity in their capacities as such in existence as of the effective time of the conversion will continue in existence as to those liabilities and obligations and may be pursued by such creditors and obligees as if such conversion shall not have occurred;

(5) a proceeding pending by or against the converting entity or by or against any of the converting entity's interest holders or owners in their capacities as such may be continued by or against the converted entity in its new organizational form and by or against the prior interest holders or owners, as the case may be, without any need for substitution of parties;

(6) the membership interests and other evidences of ownership in the converting entity that are to be converted into membership interests, evidences of ownership, or other securities in the converted entity as provided in the plan of conversion shall be so converted, and if the converting entity is a domestic limited liability company, the former holders of membership interests in the domestic limited liability company shall be entitled only to the rights provided in the plan of conversion;

(7) if, after the effectiveness of the conversion, a shareholder, partner, member, or other owner of the converted entity would be liable under applicable law, in such capacity, for the debts or obligations of the converted entity, such shareholder, partner, member, or other owner of the converted entity shall be liable for the debts and obligations of the converting entity that existed before the conversion takes effect only to the extent that such shareholder, partner, member, or other owner:

(a) agreed in writing to be liable for such debts or obligations;

(b) was liable under applicable law, prior to the effectiveness of the conversion, for such debts or obligations; or

(c) by becoming a shareholder, partner, member, or other owner of the converted entity, becomes liable under applicable law for existing debts and obligations of the converted entity; and

(8) if the converted entity is a foreign limited liability company or other entity, such converted entity shall be deemed to appoint the Secretary of State in this state as its agent for service of process in a proceeding to enforce any obligation or the rights of dissenting members of the converting domestic limited liability company.

APPENDIX C: SAMPLE FILLED-IN FORMS

ARTICLES OF INCORPORATION

OF

<u>Xeron Corporation</u>

The undersigned, acting as the incorporator of a corporation under the Texas Business Corporation Act, hereby adopts the following Articles of Incorporation for such corporation:

ARTICLE ONE

The name of the corporation (the "Corporation") is ___Xeron Corporation___.

ARTICLE TWO

The period of the Corporation's duration is perpetual.

ARTICLE THREE

The purpose for which the Corporation is organized is to transact any or all lawful business for which corporations may be incorporated under the Texas Business Corporation Act.

ARTICLE FOUR

The Corporation shall have authority to issue_1,000,000_ shares of capital stock. All such shares shall be common stock, without par value/par value $_0.001_ per share, and shall have identical rights and privileges in every respect.

ARTICLE FIVE

The Corporation will not commence business until it has received for the issuance of its shares consideration the aggregate value of which is equal to at least $1,000.00, consisting of money, labor done or property actually received.

ARTICLE SIX

The address of the Corporation's initial registered office in the State of Texas is _____ __123 Main Street, Dallas TX 75222_____. The name of the Corporation's initial registered agent at such address is ___John Doe_____.

ARTICLE SEVEN

The initial Board of Directors of the Corporation shall consist of __2__ members who shall serve until the first annual meeting of shareholders and until their successors are elected and qualified. The names and mailing addresses of the persons who shall serve as the initial directors of the Corporation are as follows:

ARTICLE EIGHT

The name and mailing address of the incorporator of the Corporation is _____

__John Doe, 123 Main Street, Dallas, TX 75222_____

_____ .

IN WITNESS WHEREOF, the undersigned, a natural person of the age of eighteen years or more and the incorporator hereinafter named, does hereby execute these Articles of Incorporation this __12th__ day of __August__ , __2004__ .

_____*John Doe*_____
Incorporator

MINUTES OF THE ORGANIZATIONAL MEETING OF

INCORPORATORS AND DIRECTORS OF

Xeron Corporation

The organization meeting of the above corporation was held on _____ August 26 ___, _2004_ at ___123 Main Street, Dallas, TX_____ at _2_ o'clock _P_M.

The following persons were present:

_John Doe_____   _Jane Doe_____

_____   _____

_____   _____

The Waiver of notice of this meeting was signed by all directors and incorporators named in the Articles of Organization and filed in the minute book.

The meeting was called to order by _____John Doe_____ an Incorporator named in the Articles of Organization. _____John Doe_____ was nominated and elected Chairman and acted as such until relieved by the president. _____Jane Doe_____ was nominated and elected temporary secretary, and acted as such until relieved by the permanent secretary.

A copy of the Articles of Organization which was filed with the Secretary of State of the State of Texas on _August 12_____, _2004_ was examined by the Directors and Incorporators and filed in the minute book.

The election of officers for the coming year was then held and the following were duly nominated and elected by the Board of Directors to be the officers of the corporation, to serve until such time as their successors are elected and qualified:

President: _____John Doe_____
Vice President: _____Jane Doe_____
Secretary: _____Jane Doe_____
Treasurer: _____Jane Doe_____

The proposed Bylaws for the corporation were then presented to the meeting and discussed. Upon motion duly made, seconded and carried, the Bylaws were adopted and added to the minute book.

A corporate seal for the corporation was then presented to the meeting and upon motion duly made, seconded and carried, it was adopted as the seal of the corporation. An impression thereof was then made in the margin of these minutes.

The necessity of opening a bank account was then discussed and upon motion duly made, seconded and carried, the following resolution was adopted:

RESOLVED that the corporation open bank accounts with _____
_____Augustus Bank_____ and that the officers of the corporation are authorized to take such action as is necessary to open such accounts; that the bank's printed form of resolution is hereby adopted and incorporated into these minutes by reference and shall be placed in the minute book; that any ___1___ of the following persons shall have signature authority over the account:

_____John Doe_____   _____Jane Doe_____

_____   _____

_____   _____

Proposed stock certificates and stock transfer ledger were then presented to the meeting and examined. Upon motion duly made, seconded and carried the stock certificates and ledger were adopted as the certificates and transfer book to be used by the corporation. A sample stock certificate marked "VOID" and the stock transfer ledger were then added to the minute book. Upon motion duly made, seconded and carried, it was then resolved that the stock certificates, when issued, would be signed by the President and the Secretary of the corporation.

The tax status of the corporation was then discussed and it was moved, seconded and carried that the stock of the corporation be issued under § 1244 of the Internal Revenue Code and that the officers of the corporation take the necessary action to:

1.   Obtain an employer tax number by filing form SS-4,

2.   ☒   Become an S-Corporation for tax purposes,
        ☐   Remain a C-Corporation for tax purposes,

The expenses of organizing the corporation were then discussed and it was moved, seconded, and carried that the corporation pay in full from the corporate funds the expenses and reimburse any advances made by the incorporators upon proof of payment.

The Directors named in the Articles of Organization then tendered their resignations, effective upon the adjournment of this meeting. Upon motion duly made, seconded, and carried, the following named persons were elected as Directors of the corporation, each to hold office until the first annual meeting of shareholders, and until a successor of each shall have been elected and qualified.

_____John Doe_____
_____Jane Doe_____

_____

There were presented to the corporation, the following offer(s) to purchase shares of capital stock:

FROM	NO. OF SHARES	CONSIDERATION
John Doe and Jane Doe, his	1,000,000	$1,000
wife, as joint tenants with		
full rights of survivorship		

The offers were discussed and after motion duly made, seconded and carried were approved. It was further resolved that the Board of Directors has determined that the consideration was valued at least equal to the value of the shares to be issued and that upon tender of the consideration, fully paid non-assessable shares of the corporation be issued.

There being no further business before the meeting, on motion duly made, seconded, and carried, the meeting adjourned.

DATED: August 26, 2004

John Doe
President

Jane Doe
Secretary

Form **2553**	**Election by a Small Business Corporation**	
(Rev. December 2002)	(Under section 1362 of the Internal Revenue Code)	OMB No. 1545-0146
Department of the Treasury Internal Revenue Service	▶ See Parts II and III on back and the separate instructions. ▶ The corporation may either send or fax this form to the IRS. See page 2 of the instructions.	

Notes:
1. *Do not* file **Form 1120S**, *U.S. Income Tax Return for an S Corporation, for any tax year before the year the election takes effect.*
2. *This election to be an S corporation can be accepted only if all the tests are met under* **Who May Elect** *on page 1 of the instructions; all shareholders have signed the consent statement; and the exact name and address of the corporation and other required form information are provided.*
3. *If the corporation was in existence before the effective date of this election, see* **Taxes an S Corporation May Owe** *on page 1 of the instructions.*

Part I Election Information

Please Type or Print	Name of corporation (see instructions) **Xeron Corporation**	**A** Employer identification number 59 : 1234567
	Number, street, and room or suite no. (If a P.O. box, see instructions.) **123 Main Street**	**B** Date incorporated **01/29/05**
	City or town, state, and ZIP code **Dallas, TX 75222**	**C** State of incorporation **Texas**

D Check the applicable box(es) if the corporation, after applying for the EIN shown in **A** above, changed its name ☐ or address ☐

E Election is to be effective for tax year beginning (month, day, year) . . . . ▶ 01/ 29 / 05

F Name and title of officer or legal representative who the IRS may call for more information
John Doe, President

G Telephone number of officer or legal representative
(800)555-8000

H If this election takes effect for the first tax year the corporation exists, enter month, day, and year of the **earliest** of the following: (1) date the corporation first had shareholders, (2) date the corporation first had assets, or (3) date the corporation began doing business . . . . ▶ 01/ 29 / 05

I Selected tax year: Annual return will be filed for tax year ending (month and day) ▶ 12/31

If the tax year ends on any date other than December 31, except for a 52–53-week tax year ending with reference to the month of December, you **must** complete Part II on the back. If the date you enter is the ending date of a 52–53-week tax year, write "52–53-week year" to the right of the date.

J Name and address of each shareholder; shareholder's spouse having a community property interest in the corporation's stock; and each tenant in common, joint tenant, and tenant by the entirety. (A husband and wife (and their estates) are counted as one shareholder in determining the number of shareholders without regard to the manner in which the stock is owned.)	**K** Shareholders' Consent Statement. Under penalties of perjury, we declare that we consent to the election of the above-named corporation to be an S corporation under section 1362(a) and that we have examined this consent statement, including accompanying schedules and statements, and to the best of our knowledge and belief, it is true, correct, and complete. We understand our consent is binding and may not be withdrawn after the corporation has made a valid election. (Shareholders sign and date below.)		**L** Stock owned		**M** Social security number or employer identification number (see instructions)	**N** Share-holder's tax year ends (month and day)
	Signature	Date	Number of shares	Dates acquired		
John Doe 123 Main St. Dallas, TX 75222	*John Doe*	1/29/05	1,000,000	1/29/05	123-45-6789	12/31

Under penalties of perjury, I declare that I have examined this election, including accompanying schedules and statements, and to the best of my knowledge and belief, it is true, correct, and complete.

Signature of officer ▶ *John Doe* Title ▶ President Date ▶ 1/29/05

For Paperwork Reduction Act Notice, see page 4 of the instructions. Cat. No. 18629R Form **2553** (Rev. 12-2002)

Part II   **Selection of Fiscal Tax Year** (All corporations using this part must complete item O and item P, Q, or R.)

O   Check the applicable box to indicate whether the corporation is:

   1.   ☒   A new corporation adopting the tax year entered in item I, Part I.

   2.   ☐   An existing corporation retaining the tax year entered in item I, Part I.

   3.   ☐   An existing corporation changing to the tax year entered in item I, Part I.

P   Complete item P if the corporation is using the automatic approval provisions of Rev. Proc. 2002-38, 2002-22 I.R.B. 1037, to request **(1)** a natural business year (as defined in section 5.05 of Rev. Proc. 2002-38) or **(2)** a year that satisfies the ownership tax year test (as defined in section 5.06 of Rev. Proc. 2002-38). Check the applicable box below to indicate the representation statement the corporation is making.

   1. Natural Business Year ▶ ☐   I represent that the corporation is adopting, retaining, or changing to a tax year that qualifies as its natural business year as defined in section 5.05 of Rev. Proc. 2002-38 and has attached a statement verifying that it satisfies the 25% gross receipts test (see instructions for content of statement). I also represent that the corporation is not precluded by section 4.02 of Rev. Proc. 2002-38 from obtaining automatic approval of such adoption, retention, or change in tax year.

   2. Ownership Tax Year ▶ ☒   I represent that shareholders (as described in section 5.06 of Rev. Proc. 2002-38) holding more than half of the shares of the stock (as of the first day of the tax year to which the request relates) of the corporation have the same tax year or are concurrently changing to the tax year that the corporation adopts, retains, or changes to per item I, Part I, and that such tax year satisfies the requirement of section 4.01(3) of Rev. Proc. 2002-38. I also represent that the corporation is not precluded by section 4.02 of Rev. Proc. 2002-38 from obtaining automatic approval of such adoption, retention, or change in tax year.

Note: *If you do not use item P and the corporation wants a fiscal tax year, complete either item Q or R below. Item Q is used to request a fiscal tax year based on a business purpose and to make a back-up section 444 election. Item R is used to make a regular section 444 election.*

Q   Business Purpose- To request a fiscal tax year based on a business purpose, you must check box Q1. See instructions for details including payment of a user fee. You may also check box Q2 and/or box Q3.

   1. Check here ▶ ☐   if the fiscal year entered in item I, Part I, is requested under the prior approval provisions of Rev. Proc. 2002-39, 2002-22 I.R.B. 1046. Attach to Form 2553 a statement describing the relevant facts and circumstances and, if applicable, the gross receipts from sales and services necessary to establish a business purpose. See the instructions for details regarding the gross receipts from sales and services. If the IRS proposes to disapprove the requested fiscal year, do you want a conference with the IRS National Office?
   ☐ Yes   ☐ No

   2. Check here ▶ ☐   to show that the corporation intends to make a back-up section 444 election in the event the corporation's business purpose request is not approved by the IRS. (See instructions for more information.)

   3. Check here ▶ ☐   to show that the corporation agrees to adopt or change to a tax year ending December 31 if necessary for the IRS to accept this election for S corporation status in the event (1) the corporation's business purpose request is not approved and the corporation makes a back-up section 444 election, but is ultimately not qualified to make a section 444 election, or (2) the corporation's business purpose request is not approved and the corporation did not make a back-up section 444 election.

R   Section 444 Election- To make a section 444 election, you must check box R1 and you may also check box R2.

   1. Check here ▶ ☐   to show the corporation will make, if qualified, a section 444 election to have the fiscal tax year shown in item I, Part I. To make the election, you must complete **Form 8716,** Election To Have a Tax Year Other Than a Required Tax Year, and either attach it to Form 2553 or file it separately.

   2. Check here ▶ ☐   to show that the corporation agrees to adopt or change to a tax year ending December 31 if necessary for the IRS to accept this election for S corporation status in the event the corporation is ultimately not qualified to make a section 444 election.

Part III   **Qualified Subchapter S Trust (QSST) Election Under Section 1361(d)(2)***

Income beneficiary's name and address	Social security number
Trust's name and address	Employer identification number

Date on which stock of the corporation was transferred to the trust (month, day, year)   . . . . ▶   /   /

In order for the trust named above to be a QSST and thus a qualifying shareholder of the S corporation for which this Form 2553 is filed, I hereby make the election under section 1361(d)(2). Under penalties of perjury, I certify that the trust meets the definitional requirements of section 1361(d)(3) and that all other information provided in Part III is true, correct, and complete.

_____   _____
Signature of income beneficiary or signature and title of legal representative or other qualified person making the election   Date

*Use Part III to make the QSST election only if stock of the corporation has been transferred to the trust on or before the date on which the corporation makes its election to be an S corporation. The QSST election must be made and filed separately if stock of the corporation is transferred to the trust after the date on which the corporation makes the S election.

Form **SS-4**

(Rev. December 2001)

Department of the Treasury
Internal Revenue Service

Application for Employer Identification Number

(For use by employers, corporations, partnerships, trusts, estates, churches, government agencies, Indian tribal entities, certain individuals, and others.)

▶ See separate instructions for each line.   ▶ Keep a copy for your records.

EIN

OMB No. 1545-0003

1 Legal name of entity (or individual) for whom the EIN is being requested	
Xeron Corporation	

2 Trade name of business (if different from name on line 1)	**3** Executor, trustee, "care of" name

4a Mailing address (room, apt., suite no. and street, or P.O. box)	**5a** Street address (if different) (Do not enter a P.O. box.)
123 Main Street	
4b City, state, and ZIP code	**5b** City, state, and ZIP code
Dallas, TX 75222	

6 County and state where principal business is located
Dallas, Texas

7a Name of principal officer, general partner, grantor, owner, or trustor	**7b** SSN, ITIN, or EIN
John Doe	123-45-6789

8a **Type of entity** (check only one box)

☐ Sole proprietor (SSN) _____
☐ Partnership
☒ Corporation (enter form number to be filed) ▶ 12-3456789
☐ Personal service corp.
☐ Church or church-controlled organization
☐ Other nonprofit organization (specify) ▶ _____
☐ Other (specify) ▶

☐ Estate (SSN of decedent) _____
☐ Plan administrator (SSN) _____
☐ Trust (SSN of grantor) _____
☐ National Guard   ☐ State/local government
☐ Farmers' cooperative ☐ Federal government/military
☐ REMIC   ☐ Indian tribal governments/enterprises
Group Exemption Number (GEN) ▶ _____

8b If a corporation, name the state or foreign country (if applicable) where incorporated

State	Foreign country
Texas	

9 **Reason for applying** (check only one box)

☒ Started new business (specify type) ▶ _____
      clothing retailer

☐ Hired employees (Check the box and see line 12.)
☐ Compliance with IRS withholding regulations
☐ Other (specify) ▶

☐ Banking purpose (specify purpose) ▶ _____
☐ Changed type of organization (specify new type) ▶ _____
☐ Purchased going business
☐ Created a trust (specify type) ▶ _____
☐ Created a pension plan (specify type) ▶ _____

10 Date business started or acquired (month, day, year)	**11** Closing month of accounting year
01-29-05	12

12 First date wages or annuities were paid or will be paid (month, day, year). **Note:** If applicant is a withholding agent, enter date income will first be paid to nonresident alien. (month, day, year) . . . . ▶ 02-15-05

13 Highest number of employees expected in the next 12 months. **Note:** If the applicant does not expect to have any employees during the period, enter "-0-." . . . . ▶

Agricultural	Household	Other
		4

14 Check **one** box that best describes the principal activity of your business.

☐ Construction ☐ Rental & leasing ☐ Transportation & warehousing
☐ Real estate   ☐ Manufacturing   ☐ Finance & insurance

☐ Health care & social assistance ☐ Wholesale–agent/broker
☐ Accommodation & food service   ☐ Wholesale–other   ☒ Retail
☐ Other (specify)

15 Indicate principal line of merchandise sold; specific construction work done; products produced; or services provided.
clothing

16a Has the applicant ever applied for an employer identification number for this or any other business? . . . . . ☐ Yes ☒ No
Note: If "Yes," please complete lines 16b and 16c.

16b If you checked "Yes" on line 16a, give applicant's legal name and trade name shown on prior application if different from line 1 or 2 above.
Legal name ▶   Trade name ▶

16c Approximate date when, and city and state where, the application was filed. Enter previous employer identification number if known.

Approximate date when filed (mo., day, year)	City and state where filed	Previous EIN

Third Party Designee

Complete this section **only** if you want to authorize the named individual to receive the entity's EIN and answer questions about the completion of this form.

Designee's name	Designee's telephone number (include area code)
	( )
Address and ZIP code	Designee's fax number (include area code)
	( )

Under penalties of perjury, I declare that I have examined this application, and to the best of my knowledge and belief, it is true, correct, and complete.

	Applicant's telephone number (include area code)
Name and title (type or print clearly) ▶ John Doe	(800) 555-8000
	Applicant's fax number (include area code)
Signature ▶ *John Doe* Date ▶ 01-29-05	( )

For Privacy Act and Paperwork Reduction Act Notice, see separate instructions.   Cat. No. 16055N   Form **SS-4** (Rev. 12-2001)

Do I Need an EIN?

File Form SS-4 if the applicant entity does not already have an EIN but is required to show an EIN on any return, statement, or other document.[1] **See also the separate instructions for each line on Form SS-4.**

IF the applicant...	AND...	THEN...
Started a new business	Does not currently have (nor expect to have) employees	Complete lines 1, 2, 4a-6, 8a, and 9-16c.
Hired (or will hire) employees, including household employees	Does not already have an EIN	Complete lines 1, 2, 4a-6, 7a-b (if applicable), 8a, 8b (if applicable), and 9-16c.
Opened a bank account	Needs an EIN for banking purposes only	Complete lines 1-5b, 7a-b (if applicable), 8a, 9, and 16a-c.
Changed type of organization	Either the legal character of the organization or its ownership changed (e.g., you incorporate a sole proprietorship or form a partnership)[2]	Complete lines 1-16c (as applicable).
Purchased a going business[3]	Does not already have an EIN	Complete lines 1-16c (as applicable).
Created a trust	The trust is other than a grantor trust or an IRA trust[4]	Complete lines 1-16c (as applicable).
Created a pension plan as a plan administrator[5]	Needs an EIN for reporting purposes	Complete lines 1, 2, 4a-6, 8a, 9, and 16a-c.
Is a foreign person needing an EIN to comply with IRS withholding regulations	Needs an EIN to complete a Form W-8 (other than Form W-8ECI), avoid withholding on portfolio assets, or claim tax treaty benefits[6]	Complete lines 1-5b, 7a-b (SSN or ITIN optional), 8a-9, and 16a-c.
Is administering an estate	Needs an EIN to report estate income on Form 1041	Complete lines 1, 3, 4a-b, 8a, 9, and 16a-c.
Is a withholding agent for taxes on non-wage income paid to an alien (i.e., individual, corporation, or partnership, etc.)	Is an agent, broker, fiduciary, manager, tenant, or spouse who is required to file **Form 1042,** Annual Withholding Tax Return for U.S. Source Income of Foreign Persons	Complete lines 1, 2, 3 (if applicable), 4a-5b, 7a-b (if applicable), 8a, 9, and 16a-c.
Is a state or local agency	Serves as a tax reporting agent for public assistance recipients under Rev. Proc. 80-4, 1980-1 C.B. 581[7]	Complete lines 1, 2, 4a-5b, 8a, 9, and 16a-c.
Is a single-member LLC	Needs an EIN to file **Form 8832,** Classification Election, for filing employment tax returns, **or** for state reporting purposes[8]	Complete lines 1-16c (as applicable).
Is an S corporation	Needs an EIN to file **Form 2553,** Election by a Small Business Corporation[9]	Complete lines 1-16c (as applicable).

[1] For example, a sole proprietorship or self-employed farmer who establishes a qualified retirement plan, or is required to file excise, employment, alcohol, tobacco, or firearms returns, must have an EIN. **A partnership, corporation, REMIC (real estate mortgage investment conduit), nonprofit organization (church, club, etc.), or farmers' cooperative must use an EIN for any tax-related purpose even if the entity does not have employees.**

[2] However, **do not** apply for a new EIN if the existing entity only **(a)** changed its business name, **(b)** elected on Form 8832 to change the way it is taxed (or is covered by the default rules), or **(c)** terminated its partnership status because at least 50% of the total interests in partnership capital and profits were sold or exchanged within a 12-month period. (The EIN of the terminated partnership should continue to be used. See Regulations section 301.6109-1(d)(2)(iii).)

[3] Do not use the EIN of the prior business unless you became the "owner" of a corporation by acquiring its stock.

[4] However, IRA trusts that are required to file **Form 990-T,** Exempt Organization Business Income Tax Return, must have an EIN.

[5] A plan administrator is the person or group of persons specified as the administrator by the instrument under which the plan is operated.

[6] Entities applying to be a Qualified Intermediary (QI) need a QI-EIN even if they already have an EIN. **See Rev. Proc. 2000-12.**

[7] See also *Household employer* on page 4. (**Note:** State or local agencies may need an EIN for other reasons, e.g., hired employees.)

[8] Most LLCs **do not** need to file Form 8832. See **Limited liability company (LLC)** on page 4 for details on completing Form SS-4 for an LLC.

[9] An existing corporation that is electing or revoking S corporation status should use its previously-assigned EIN.

✪

<u>Offer to Purchase Stock</u>

Date: __01/29/05__

To the Board of Directors of

__Xeron Corporation__

The undersigned, hereby offers to purchase _____1,000,000_____ shares of the __common_____ stock of your corporation at a total purchase price of _____one thousand dollars in cash_____.

Very truly yours,

_____John Doe_____

- -

<u>Offer to Sell Stock</u>
Pursuant to Sec. 1244 I.R.C.

Date: __01/29/05_____

To: _____John Doe_____

Dear

The corporation hereby offers to sell to you __1,000,000__ shares of its common stock at a price of $__0.001____ per share. These shares are issued pursuant to Section 1244 of the Internal Revenue Code.

Your signature below shall constitute an acceptance of our offer as of the date it is received by the corporation.

Very truly yours,

_____Xeron Corporation_____

By:_____

Accepted:

ARTICLES OF ORGANIZATION
OF
<u>Bobbie's Flowers, LLC</u>

I, the undersigned natural person of the age of eighteen (18) years or more, acting pursuant to the provisions of the Texas Limited Liability Company Act as organizer of _____ (the "Company"), hereby adopt the following Articles of Organization for the Company.

ARTICLE I

The name of the Company is <u>Bobbie's Flowers, LLC</u>.

ARTICLE II

The period of duration of the Company is perpetual or until earlier dissolved in accordance with the regulations of the Company.

ARTICLE III

The Company is organized for the purpose of transacting any and all lawful business for which limited liability companies may be organized under the Texas Limited Liability Company Act.

ARTICLE IV

The street address of the initial registered office of the Company is <u>123 Main Street</u>, <u>Dallas</u>, <u>Texas</u>, <u>75021</u>, and the name of its initial registered agent at such address is <u>Bobbie Smith</u>.

ARTICLE V

The Company is to be managed by Managers. The name and address of the initial Managers are as follows:

INITIAL MANAGERS	**ADDRESS**
<u>Bobbie Smith</u>	<u>123 Main St</u> <u>Dallas TX, 75021</u>
<u>John Smith</u>	<u>123 Main St</u> <u>Dallas TX, 75021</u>

ARTICLE VI

A Manager of the Company shall not be personally liable to the Company or to any Member of the Company for monetary damages for an act or omission in the Manager's capacity as Manager of the Company, except for liability for any of the following:

(1)   A breach of the Manager's duty of loyalty to the Company or the Members of the Company;

(2)   An act or omission not in good faith that constitutes a breach of duty of the Manager to the Company or an act or omission that involves intentional misconduct or knowing violation of the law;

(3)   A transaction from which the Manager received an improper benefit, whether or not the benefit resulted from an action taken within the scope of the Manager's office; or

(4)   An act or omission for which the liability of a Manager is expressly provided by an applicable statute.

If the Texas Limited Liability Company Act or the Texas Miscellaneous Corporation Laws is amended to authorize Company action further eliminating or limiting the personal liability of managers, then the liability of a Manager of the Company shall be eliminated or limited to the fullest extent permitted by such Acts, as so amended.

Any repeal or modification of this Article by the Members of the Company shall not adversely affect any right or protection of a Managers of the Company existing at the time of such repeal or modification. Any repeal or modification of those provisions of the Texas Limited Liability Company Act or Texas Miscellaneous Corporation Laws Act that concern the limitation of manager liability shall not be construed to adversely affect any right or protection of a Manager of the Company existing at the time of such repeal or modification unless such adverse construction is required by law.

ARTICLE VII

The name of the organizer of the Company __Bobbie Smith__ , whose address is __123 Main Street__ , __Dallas__ , __Texas__ , __75021__ .
(Street Address)   (City)   (State)   (Zip Code)

IN WITNESS WHEREOF, I have hereunto set my hand this __4th__ day of __May__ , 20 __04__ .

Bobbie Smith
(Name)

MINUTES OF ACTION
WITHOUT A MEETING BY THE
MANAGERS OF
Bobbie's Flowers, LLC

Dated: __May 25__, 2005

The Managers of __Bobbie's Flowers, LLC__, a Texas limited liability company (the "Company"), acting pursuant to Article 2.23B of the Texas Limited Liability Company Act, by the signatures and with the approval and consent of the undersigned, who are the Managers of the Company, hereby take the following actions:

RESOLVED, that the minute book presented is hereby adopted as the minute book of the Company, and that the Managers authorize and direct to file in such minute book the minutes of meetings and minutes of actions taken without meetings of the Managers and Members;

RESOLVED FURTHER, that the form, terms, and provisions of the Articles of Organization of the Company approved and filed in the Office of the Secretary of State of Texas on the __5th__ day of __May__, 20__04__, are hereby in all respects approved and is filed in the Company's minute book the Company's Certificate of Organization, together with the duly certified duplicate original of the Articles of Organization;

RESOLVED FURTHER, that the Regulations executed by the initial Managers and initial Members of the Company as of the date hereof and filed in the Company's minute book are hereby acknowledged as the Regulations of this Company;

RESOLVED FURTHER, that the fiscal year of the Company shall end on December 31;

RESOLVED FURTHER, that the Managers are authorized and directed to open an account in the name of the Company with a bank selected by the Managers;

RESOLVED FURTHER, that the Managers of the Company are authorized and directed to execute such signature cards and other documents in connection with such account as may be necessary or advisable and to certify to the adoption of resolutions relating to such account, such resolutions being hereby adopted;

RESOLVED FURTHER, that, to the extent permitted by law, the organizer of this Company and the initial Managers of the Company, acting merely to adopt Regulations, admit members to the Company, and to form the Company, be indemnified and held harmless by the Company for all loss, cost or expense in connection with formation of this Company, the filing of its Articles of Organization, the adoption of Regulations, the admission of members and in connection with all activities of the Company, its managers, and employees, up to the time of the adoption of this resolution and that all acts and deeds taken by the initial Managers of the Company for and on behalf of the Company prior to the time of the adoption of this resolution be, and they hereby are, adopted, ratified and confirmed.

MANAGERS:

Bobbie Smith
(Name)

John Smith
(Name)

Appendix D:
Blank Corporate Forms

This page intentionally blank.

TRANSMITTAL LETTER

Corporations Section
Statutory Filings Division
Office of the Secretary of State
P.O. Box 13697
Austin, TX 78711-3697

SUBJECT: _____

(Proposed corporate name—must include suffix)

Enclosed is an original and one (1) copy of the articles of incorporation and a check for:

☐ $300.00   ☐ $325.00   ☐ $312.00
Filing Fee   Filing Fee   Filing Fee
                    & Special   & Certified Copy
                    Handling

Please return the photocopy to me with the filing date stamped on it.

FROM: _____

          Name (printed or typed)

          _____

          Address

          _____

          City, State & Zip

          _____

          Daytime Telephone Number

This page intentionally blank.

ARTICLES OF INCORPORATION
OF

_____

The undersigned, acting as the incorporator of a corporation under the Texas Business Corporation Act, hereby adopts the following Articles of Incorporation for such corporation:

ARTICLE ONE

The name of the corporation (the "Corporation") is

_____

ARTICLE TWO

The period of the Corporation's duration is perpetual.

ARTICLE THREE

The purpose for which the Corporation is organized is to transact any or all lawful business for which corporations may be incorporated under the Texas Business Corporation Act.

ARTICLE FOUR

The Corporation shall have authority to issue_____ shares of capital stock. All such shares shall be common stock, without par value/par value $_____ per share, and shall have identical rights and privileges in every respect.

ARTICLE FIVE

The Corporation will not commence business until it has received for the issuance of its shares consideration the aggregate value of which is equal to at least $1,000.00, consisting of money, labor done or property actually received.

ARTICLE SIX

The address of the Corporation's initial registered office in the State of Texas is _____
_____. The name of the Corporation's initial registered agent at such address is _____.

ARTICLE SEVEN

The initial Board of Directors of the Corporation shall consist of _____ members who shall serve until the first annual meeting of shareholders and until their successors are elected and qualified. The names and mailing addresses of the persons who shall serve as the initial directors of the Corporation are as follows:

ARTICLE EIGHT

The name and mailing address of the incorporator of the Corporation is _____
_____
_____.

IN WITNESS WHEREOF, the undersigned, a natural person of the age of eighteen years or more and the incorporator hereinafter named, does hereby execute these Articles of Incorporation this _____ day of _____, _____.

_____

Incorporator

ARTICLES OF INCORPORATION

OF

_____

_____

The undersigned, acting as the incorporator of a corporation under the Texas Business Corporation Act, hereby adopts the following Articles of Incorporation for such corporation:

ARTICLE ONE

The name of the corporation (the "Corporation") is

_____

ARTICLE TWO

The Corporation is a professional corporation.

ARTICLE THREE

The period of the Corporation's duration is perpetual.

ARTICLE FOUR

The purpose for which the Corporation is organized is _____

_____

ARTICLE FIVE

The Corporation shall have authority to issue_____ shares of capital stock. All such shares shall be common stock, without par value/par value $_____ per share, and shall have identical rights and privileges in every respect.

ARTICLE SIX

The Corporation will not commence business until it has received for the issuance of its shares consideration the aggregate value of which is equal to at least $1,000.00, consisting of money, labor done or property actually received.

ARTICLE SEVEN

The address of the Corporation's initial registered office in the State of Texas is _____
_____. The name of the Corporation's
initial registered agent at such address is _____.

ARTICLE EIGHT

The initial Board of Directors of the Corporation shall consist of _____ members who shall serve until the first
annual meeting of shareholders and until their successors are elected and qualified. The names and mailing addresses
of the persons who shall serve as the initial directors of the Corporation are as follows:

ARTICLE NINE

The name and mailing address of the incorporator of the Corporation is _____
_____
_____.

IN WITNESS WHEREOF, the undersigned, a natural person of the age of eighteen years or more and the
incorporator hereinafter named, does hereby execute these Articles of Incorporation this _____ day of
_____, _____.

_____
Incorporator

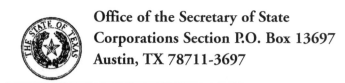

Office of the Secretary of State
Corporations Section P.O. Box 13697
Austin, TX 78711-3697

ARTICLES/CERTIFICATE OF CORRECTION

This correction by the undersigned corporation, limited liability company, or out-of-state financial institution is submitted pursuant to article 1302-7.01, Texas Miscellaneous Corporation Laws Act. In the case of a limited partnership, this certificate of correction is made pursuant to section 2.13, Texas Revised Limited Partnership Act. The undersigned entity seeks to correct a document which is an inaccurate record of the entity action, contains an inaccurate or erroneous statement, or was defectively or erroneously executed, sealed, acknowledged or verified, and for this purpose states the following:

ARTICLE ONE

The name of the entity is _____

ARTICLE TWO

The document to be corrected is the _____

ARTICLE THREE

The inaccuracy, error, or defect to be corrected is:

_____

_____

_____

ARTICLE FOUR

As corrected, the inaccurate, erroneous, or defective portion of the document reads as follows:

_____

_____

_____

_____
Name of Entity

By: _____
(A person authorized to sign on behalf of the entity.)

INSTRUCTIONS

Articles of correction or a certificate of correction are appropriate whenever an entity files an instrument which is an inaccurate record of the entity action referred to in the instrument, or which contains an inaccurate or erroneous statement, or which was defectively or erroneously executed, sealed, acknowledged, or verified. A correction may be used only to correct a previously filed document; it many not be used to negate or cancel a filing. If the entity chooses to make a change in its formation or qualification document (e.g. articles of incorporation), it may not use a correction. Instead, an amendment filing made pursuant to the law applicable to the type of entity must be filed.

The foregoing form promulgated by the secretary of state is designed to meet minimum statutory filing requirements; no warranty is made regarding the suitability of this form for any particular purpose. This form and the information provided are not substitutes for the advice of an attorney and it is recommended that the services of an attorney be obtained before preparation of the articles/certificate of correction.

1. Provide the current mane of the entity as it appears in the records of this office in article one of this form. If the error to be corrected is in the name of the entity, the entity name must be the name as it appears on the records of the secretary of state.

2. Identify the document to be corrected in article two of the form. For example, if the error was contained in articles of amendment, then article two of this form should state "articles of amendment." The date on which the document was filed also should be listed. This date is the date stamped on the upper right-hand corner of the acknowledge copy.

3. Article three should identify the error to be corrected. For example, if the article of incorporation misspelled the entity name, then article three of this form should state that it is correcting the misspelling of the entity name that appeared in article one of the articles of incorporation.

4. Article four should include only the corrected portion of the document. For example, if the error was a misspelling of the entity name which appeared in article one of the articles of incorporation, set forth in article four of this form a reference to the corrected article and its text as corrected.

The articles/certificate of correction must be signed by an officer or director of a corporation or out-of-state financial institution. In the case of a limited liability company, a member or manager must sign the document. A general partner of a limited partnership must sign on behalf of the limited partnership. The person signing should indicate the capacity in which the person signs next to the signature. Prior to signing, please read the statements on this form carefully. A person commits an offense under the Texas Business Corporation Act, the Texas Limited Liability Company Act or the Texas Non-profit Corporation Act if the person signs a document the person knows is false in any material with the intent that the document be delivered to the secretary of state for filing. The offense is a Class A misdemeanor.

The filing fee for a corporation, limited liability company, or out-of-state financial institution is $15. The fee for a limited partnership is $200. Personal checks and Mastercard®, Visa®, and Discover® are accepted in payment of filing fees. Fees paid by credit card are subject to a statutorily authorized processing cost of 2.1% of the total fees.

Two copies of the articles of correction together with the applicable fee should be submitted to the address shown on the heading of this form. We will place one document on record and return a file stamped copy, if a duplicate copy was provided for such purpose. The delivery address is James Earl Rudder office Building, 1019 Brazos, Austin , Texas 78701. The telephone number is (512) 463-5555, TDD: (800) 735-2989, FAX: (512) 463-5709.

Form No. 403
Revised 8/99

Office of the Secretary of State
Corporations Section P.O. Box 13697
Austin, TX 78711-3697

APPLICATION FOR AMENDED
CERTIFICATE OF AUTHORITY

Pursuant to the law governing the undersigned corporation or limited liability company, the entity makes this application to amend its certificate of authority to transact business in Texas and provides the following information:

1. The name of the entity as it currently appears on the records of the secretary of state of Texas is

    _____

2. (If the entity's name was previously unavailable and the entity elected to use an assumed name in Texas, complete the following.) The assumed name of the entity as it currently appears on the records of the secretary of state is _____

3. A certificate of authority was issued to the entity on the following date:_____

4. The name has been changed to _____

    ☐ The entity name has not been changed.

5. If applicable, the name that it elects to use hereafter in the state of Texas is

    _____

6. It desires to pursue in Texas purposes other than, or in addition to, those authorized by its certificate of authority, as follows: _____

    _____

    _____ It is authorized to pursue such purpose or purposes in the state or county under the laws of which it is organized.

7. It desires to change the statement(s) contained in item(s) number _____ of the original or amended certificate of authority to read as follows:

    _____
    _____
    _____

                         _____
                                      Name of Entity

                    By _____

                    Its _____
                              Authorized Officer of Corporation
                              Authorized Manager or Member of LLC

INSTRUCTIONS

1. This form is designed for use by a foreign corporation or a foreign limited liability company seeking to amend its certificate of authority. A foreign limited partnership seeking to amend its application for registration must utilize form number 412. A registered out-of-state financial institution should utilize form number 411.

2. An application for an amended certificate of authority must be submitted when a foreign corporation or limited liability company authorized to transact business in Texas changes its name, desires to pursue purposes other than, or in addition to, those authorized by its existing certificate of authority, or if such entity desires to change ant statement in its original application for certificate of authority. The attached form promulgated by the secretary of state is designed to meet minimum statutory filing requirements and no warranty is made regarding the suitability of this form for any particular purpose. This form and the information provided are not substitutes for the advice of an attorney and it it recommended that the services of an attorney be obtained before preparation of the application for amended certificate of authority.

3. An application for an amended certificate of authority submitted to record a name change must be accompanied by a certificate from the proper filing officer in the jurisdiction of organization evidencing the name change. In the event the new name is not available for use in Texas, the entity must adopt an assumed name and the assumed name must meet the same requirements of name availability as do entity names. The assumed name is to be set forth in item five of the application and, in addition, the entity is required to file an assumed name certificate in compliance with chapter 36 of the Texas Business and Commerce Code. The assumed name certificate is to be filed with the secretary of state and with the county clerk in the county in which the registered office is located and the county in which the principal office is located. The form promulgated by the secretary of state for making the assumed name filing is form 503. This forms is not acceptable for filing in the county clerk's office.

4. Applications submitted to show a change in the assumed name which the entity previously elected to use in Texas should be accompanied by a new assumed name certificate in accordance with Chapter 36 of the Texas Business & Commerce Code.

5. The application must be signed by an authorized officer of a corporation or an authorized manager or member of a limited liability company. <u>Prior to signing, please read the statements on this form carefully. A person commits an offense under the Texas Business Corporation Act, the Texas Limited Liability Company Act or the Texas Non-Profit Corporation Act if the person signs a document the person knows is false in any material respect with the intent that the document be delivered to the secretary of state for filing. The offense is a Class A misdemeanor.</u>

6. The filing fee for an amended certificate of authority is: business corporation, $150.00; non-profit corporations, $25.00; limited liability company, $100.00. Personal checks and MasterCard®, Visa®, and Discover® are accepted in payment of the filing fee. Checks or money orders must be payable through a U.S. bank or other financial institution and made payable to the secretary of state. Fees paid by a credit card are subject to a statutorily authorized processing cost of 2.1% of the total fees.

7. Two copies of the document along with the filing fee should be mailed to the address shown in the heading of this form. We will place one document on record and return a file stamped copy, if a duplicate copy was provided for such purpose. The delivery address is: Secretary of State, Statutory Filing Division, Corporations Section, James Earl Rudder Office Building, 1019 Brazos, Austin, Texas 78701. The telephone number is (512) 463-5582, TDD: (800) 735-2989, FAX: (512) 463-5709.

Form **SS-4**
(Rev. December 2001)
Department of the Treasury
Internal Revenue Service

Application for Employer Identification Number

(For use by employers, corporations, partnerships, trusts, estates, churches, government agencies, Indian tribal entities, certain individuals, and others.)

▶ See separate instructions for each line.　　▶ Keep a copy for your records.

EIN

OMB No. 1545-0003

Type or print clearly.

1 Legal name of entity (or individual) for whom the EIN is being requested

2 Trade name of business (if different from name on line 1)

3 Executor, trustee, "care of" name

4a Mailing address (room, apt., suite no. and street, or P.O. box)

5a Street address (if different) (Do not enter a P.O. box.)

4b City, state, and ZIP code

5b City, state, and ZIP code

6 County and state where principal business is located

7a Name of principal officer, general partner, grantor, owner, or trustor

7b SSN, ITIN, or EIN

8a **Type of entity** (check only one box)
- ☐ Sole proprietor (SSN) _____
- ☐ Partnership
- ☐ Corporation (enter form number to be filed) ▶ _____
- ☐ Personal service corp.
- ☐ Church or church-controlled organization
- ☐ Other nonprofit organization (specify) ▶ _____
- ☐ Other (specify) ▶
- ☐ Estate (SSN of decedent) _____
- ☐ Plan administrator (SSN) _____
- ☐ Trust (SSN of grantor) _____
- ☐ National Guard　　☐ State/local government
- ☐ Farmers' cooperative　　☐ Federal government/military
- ☐ REMIC　　☐ Indian tribal governments/enterprises
- Group Exemption Number (GEN) ▶ _____

8b If a corporation, name the state or foreign country (if applicable) where incorporated

State

Foreign country

9 **Reason for applying** (check only one box)
- ☐ Started new business (specify type) ▶ _____
- ☐ Hired employees (Check the box and see line 12.)
- ☐ Compliance with IRS withholding regulations
- ☐ Other (specify) ▶
- ☐ Banking purpose (specify purpose) ▶ _____
- ☐ Changed type of organization (specify new type) ▶ _____
- ☐ Purchased going business
- ☐ Created a trust (specify type) ▶ _____
- ☐ Created a pension plan (specify type) ▶ _____

10 Date business started or acquired (month, day, year)

11 Closing month of accounting year

12 First date wages or annuities were paid or will be paid (month, day, year). **Note:** *If applicant is a withholding agent, enter date income will first be paid to nonresident alien. (month, day, year)* . . . . ▶

13 Highest number of employees expected in the next 12 months. **Note:** *If the applicant does not expect to have any employees during the period, enter "-0-."* . . . . ▶

	Agricultural	Household	Other

14 Check **one** box that best describes the principal activity of your business.
- ☐ Construction
- ☐ Rental & leasing
- ☐ Transportation & warehousing
- ☐ Real estate
- ☐ Manufacturing
- ☐ Finance & insurance
- ☐ Health care & social assistance
- ☐ Accommodation & food service
- ☐ Other (specify)
- ☐ Wholesale–agent/broker
- ☐ Wholesale–other
- ☐ Retail

15 Indicate principal line of merchandise sold; specific construction work done; products produced; or services provided.

16a Has the applicant ever applied for an employer identification number for this or any other business? . . . . . ☐ **Yes**　☐ **No**
Note: *If "Yes," please complete lines 16b and 16c.*

16b If you checked "Yes" on line 16a, give applicant's legal name and trade name shown on prior application if different from line 1 or 2 above.
Legal name ▶　　　　　Trade name ▶

16c Approximate date when, and city and state where, the application was filed. Enter previous employer identification number if known.

Approximate date when filed (mo., day, year)	City and state where filed	Previous EIN

Third Party Designee

Complete this section **only** if you want to authorize the named individual to receive the entity's EIN and answer questions about the completion of this form.

Designee's name

Designee's telephone number (include area code)
(　　　)

Address and ZIP code

Designee's fax number (include area code)
(　　　)

Under penalties of perjury, I declare that I have examined this application, and to the best of my knowledge and belief, it is true, correct, and complete.

Applicant's telephone number (include area code)
(　　　)

Name and title (type or print clearly) ▶

Applicant's fax number (include area code)
(　　　)

Signature ▶　　　　　Date ▶

For Privacy Act and Paperwork Reduction Act Notice, see separate instructions.　　Cat. No. 16055N　　Form **SS-4** (Rev. 12-2001)

Do I Need an EIN?

File Form SS-4 if the applicant entity does not already have an EIN but is required to show an EIN on any return, statement, or other document.[1] **See also the separate instructions for each line on Form SS-4.**

IF the applicant...	AND...	THEN...
Started a new business	Does not currently have (nor expect to have) employees	Complete lines 1, 2, 4a-6, 8a, and 9-16c.
Hired (or will hire) employees, including household employees	Does not already have an EIN	Complete lines 1, 2, 4a-6, 7a-b (if applicable), 8a, 8b (if applicable), and 9-16c.
Opened a bank account	Needs an EIN for banking purposes only	Complete lines 1-5b, 7a-b (if applicable), 8a, 9, and 16a-c.
Changed type of organization	Either the legal character of the organization or its ownership changed (e.g., you incorporate a sole proprietorship or form a partnership)[2]	Complete lines 1-16c (as applicable).
Purchased a going business[3]	Does not already have an EIN	Complete lines 1-16c (as applicable).
Created a trust	The trust is other than a grantor trust or an IRA trust[4]	Complete lines 1-16c (as applicable).
Created a pension plan as a plan administrator[5]	Needs an EIN for reporting purposes	Complete lines 1, 2, 4a-6, 8a, 9, and 16a-c.
Is a foreign person needing an EIN to comply with IRS withholding regulations	Needs an EIN to complete a Form W-8 (other than Form W-8ECI), avoid withholding on portfolio assets, or claim tax treaty benefits[6]	Complete lines 1-5b, 7a-b (SSN or ITIN optional), 8a-9, and 16a-c.
Is administering an estate	Needs an EIN to report estate income on Form 1041	Complete lines 1, 3, 4a-b, 8a, 9, and 16a-c.
Is a withholding agent for taxes on non-wage income paid to an alien (i.e., individual, corporation, or partnership, etc.)	Is an agent, broker, fiduciary, manager, tenant, or spouse who is required to file **Form 1042,** Annual Withholding Tax Return for U.S. Source Income of Foreign Persons	Complete lines 1, 2, 3 (if applicable), 4a-5b, 7a-b (if applicable), 8a, 9, and 16a-c.
Is a state or local agency	Serves as a tax reporting agent for public assistance recipients under Rev. Proc. 80-4, 1980-1 C.B. 581[7]	Complete lines 1, 2, 4a-5b, 8a, 9, and 16a-c.
Is a single-member LLC	Needs an EIN to file **Form 8832,** Classification Election, for filing employment tax returns, **or** for state reporting purposes[8]	Complete lines 1-16c (as applicable).
Is an S corporation	Needs an EIN to file **Form 2553,** Election by a Small Business Corporation[9]	Complete lines 1-16c (as applicable).

[1] For example, a sole proprietorship or self-employed farmer who establishes a qualified retirement plan, or is required to file excise, employment, alcohol, tobacco, or firearms returns, must have an EIN. **A partnership, corporation, REMIC (real estate mortgage investment conduit), nonprofit organization (church, club, etc.), or farmers' cooperative must use an EIN for any tax-related purpose even if the entity does not have employees.**

[2] However, **do not** apply for a new EIN if the existing entity only **(a)** changed its business name, **(b)** elected on Form 8832 to change the way it is taxed (or is covered by the default rules), or **(c)** terminated its partnership status because at least 50% of the total interests in partnership capital and profits were sold or exchanged within a 12-month period. (The EIN of the terminated partnership should continue to be used. See Regulations section 301.6109-1(d)(2)(iii).)

[3] Do not use the EIN of the prior business unless you became the "owner" of a corporation by acquiring its stock.

[4] However, IRA trusts that are required to file **Form 990-T,** Exempt Organization Business Income Tax Return, must have an EIN.

[5] A plan administrator is the person or group of persons specified as the administrator by the instrument under which the plan is operated.

[6] Entities applying to be a Qualified Intermediary (QI) need a QI-EIN even if they already have an EIN. **See Rev. Proc. 2000-12.**

[7] See also *Household employer* on page 4. (**Note:** State or local agencies may need an EIN for other reasons, e.g., hired employees.)

[8] Most LLCs **do not** need to file Form 8832. See **Limited liability company (LLC)** on page 4 for details on completing Form SS-4 for an LLC.

[9] An existing corporation that is electing or revoking S corporation status should use its previously-assigned EIN.

✪

Instructions for Form SS-4

Department of the Treasury
Internal Revenue Service

(Rev. September 2003)

For use with Form SS-4 (Rev. December 2001)
Application for Employer Identification Number.

Section references are to the Internal Revenue Code unless otherwise noted.

General Instructions

Use these instructions to complete **Form SS-4,** Application for Employer Identification Number. Also see **Do I Need an EIN?** on page 2 of Form SS-4.

Purpose of Form

Use Form SS-4 to apply for an employer identification number (EIN). An EIN is a nine-digit number (for example, 12-3456789) assigned to sole proprietors, corporations, partnerships, estates, trusts, and other entities for tax filing and reporting purposes. The information you provide on this form will establish your business tax account.

*An EIN is for use in connection with your business activities only. Do **not** use your EIN in place of your social security number (SSN).*

Items To Note

Apply online. You can now apply for and receive an EIN online using the internet. See **How To Apply** below.

File only one Form SS-4. Generally, a sole proprietor should file only one Form SS-4 and needs only one EIN, regardless of the number of businesses operated as a sole proprietorship or trade names under which a business operates. However, if the proprietorship incorporates or enters into a partnership, a new EIN is required. Also, each corporation in an affiliated group must have its own EIN.

EIN applied for, but not received. If you do not have an EIN by the time a return is due, write "Applied For" and the date you applied in the space shown for the number. **Do not** show your SSN as an EIN on returns.

If you do not have an EIN by the time a tax deposit is due, send your payment to the Internal Revenue Service Center for your filing area as shown in the instructions for the form that you are filing. Make your check or money order payable to the "United States Treasury" and show your name (as shown on Form SS-4), address, type of tax, period covered, and date you applied for an EIN.

How To Apply

You can apply for an EIN online, by telephone, by fax, or by mail depending on how soon you need to use the EIN. Use only one method for each entity so you do not receive more than one EIN for an entity.

Online. You can receive your EIN by internet and use it immediately to file a return or make a payment. Go to the

IRS website at **www.irs.gov/businesses** and click on **Employer ID Numbers** under **topics.**

Telephone. You can receive your EIN by telephone and use it immediately to file a return or make a payment. Call the IRS at **1-800-829-4933.** (International applicants must call 215-516-6999.) The hours of operation are 7:00 a.m. to 10:00 p.m. The person making the call must be authorized to sign the form or be an authorized designee. See **Signature** and **Third Party Designee** on page 6. Also see the **TIP** below.

If you are applying by telephone, it will be helpful to complete Form SS-4 before contacting the IRS. An IRS representative will use the information from the Form SS-4 to establish your account and assign you an EIN. Write the number you are given on the upper right corner of the form and sign and date it. Keep this copy for your records.

If requested by an IRS representative, mail or fax (facsimile) the signed Form SS-4 (including any Third Party Designee authorization) within 24 hours to the IRS address provided by the IRS representative.

*Taxpayer representatives can apply for an EIN on behalf of their client and request that the EIN be faxed to their **client** on the same day. **Note:** By using this procedure, you are authorizing the IRS to fax the EIN without a cover sheet.*

Fax. Under the Fax-TIN program, you can receive your EIN by fax within 4 business days. Complete and fax Form SS-4 to the IRS using the Fax-TIN number listed on page 2 for your state. A long-distance charge to callers outside of the local calling area will apply. Fax-TIN numbers can only be used to apply for an EIN. **The numbers may change without notice.** Fax-TIN is available 24 hours a day, 7 days a week.

Be sure to provide your fax number so the IRS can fax the EIN back to you. **Note:** By using this procedure, you are authorizing the IRS to fax the EIN without a cover sheet.

Mail. Complete Form SS-4 at least 4 to 5 weeks before you will need an EIN. Sign and date the application and mail it to the service center address for your state. You will receive your EIN in the mail in approximately 4 weeks. See also **Third Party Designee** on page 6.

Call 1-800-829-4933 to verify a number or to ask about the status of an application by mail.

Where To Fax or File

If your principal business, office or agency, or legal residence in the case of an individual, is located in:	Call the Fax-TIN number shown or file with the "Internal Revenue Service Center" at:
Connecticut, Delaware, District of Columbia, Florida, Georgia, Maine, Maryland, Massachusetts, New Hampshire, New Jersey, New York, North Carolina, Ohio, Pennsylvania, Rhode Island, South Carolina, Vermont, Virginia, West Virginia	Attn: EIN Operation P. O. Box 9003 Holtsville, NY 11742-9003 Fax-TIN 631-447-8960
Illinois, Indiana, Kentucky, Michigan	Attn: EIN Operation Cincinnati, OH 45999 Fax-TIN 859-669-5760
Alabama, Alaska, Arizona, Arkansas, California, Colorado, Hawaii, Idaho, Iowa, Kansas, Louisiana, Minnesota, Mississippi, Missouri, Montana, Nebraska, Nevada, New Mexico, North Dakota, Oklahoma, Oregon, Puerto Rico, South Dakota, Tennessee, Texas, Utah, Washington, Wisconsin, Wyoming	Attn: EIN Operation Philadelphia, PA 19255 Fax-TIN 215-516-3990
If you have no legal residence, principal place of business, or principal office or agency in any state:	Attn: EIN Operation Philadelphia, PA 19255 Telephone 215-516-6999 Fax-TIN 215-516-3990

How To Get Forms and Publications

Phone. You can order forms, instructions, and publications by phone 24 hours a day, 7 days a week. Call 1-800-TAX-FORM (1-800-829-3676). You should receive your order or notification of its status within 10 workdays.

Personal computer. With your personal computer and modem, you can get the forms and information you need using the IRS website at **www.irs.gov** or File Transfer Protocol at **ftp.irs.gov.**

CD-ROM. For small businesses, return preparers, or others who may frequently need tax forms or publications, a CD-ROM containing over 2,000 tax products (including many prior year forms) can be purchased from the National Technical Information Service (NTIS).

To order **Pub. 1796,** Federal Tax Products on CD-ROM, call **1-877-CDFORMS** (1-877-233-6767) toll free or connect to **www.irs.gov/cdorders.**

Tax Help for Your Business

IRS-sponsored Small Business Workshops provide information about your Federal and state tax obligations.

For information about workshops in your area, call 1-800-829-4933.

Related Forms and Publications

The following **forms** and **instructions** may be useful to filers of Form SS-4:
- **Form 990-T,** Exempt Organization Business Income Tax Return
- **Instructions for Form 990-T**
- **Schedule C (Form 1040),** Profit or Loss From Business
- **Schedule F (Form 1040),** Profit or Loss From Farming
- **Instructions for Form 1041 and Schedules A, B, D, G, I, J, and K-1,** U.S. Income Tax Return for Estates and Trusts
- **Form 1042,** Annual Withholding Tax Return for U.S. Source Income of Foreign Persons
- **Instructions for Form 1065,** U.S. Return of Partnership Income
- **Instructions for Form 1066,** U.S. Real Estate Mortgage Investment Conduit (REMIC) Income Tax Return
- **Instructions for Forms 1120 and 1120-A**
- **Form 2553,** Election by a Small Business Corporation
- **Form 2848,** Power of Attorney and Declaration of Representative
- **Form 8821,** Tax Information Authorization
- **Form 8832,** Entity Classification Election
  For more **information** about filing Form SS-4 and related issues, see:
- **Circular A,** Agricultural Employer's Tax Guide (Pub. 51)
- **Circular E,** Employer's Tax Guide (Pub. 15)
- **Pub. 538,** Accounting Periods and Methods
- **Pub. 542,** Corporations
- **Pub. 557,** Exempt Status for Your Organization
- **Pub. 583,** Starting a Business and Keeping Records
- **Pub. 966,** Electronic Choices for Paying ALL Your Federal Taxes
- **Pub. 1635,** Understanding Your EIN
- **Package 1023,** Application for Recognition of Exemption Under Section 501(c)(3) of the Internal Revenue Code
- **Package 1024,** Application for Recognition of Exemption Under Section 501(a)

Specific Instructions

Print or type all entries on Form SS-4. Follow the instructions for each line to expedite processing and to avoid unnecessary IRS requests for additional information. Enter "N/A" (nonapplicable) on the lines that do not apply.

Line 1—Legal name of entity (or individual) for whom the EIN is being requested. Enter the legal name of the entity (or individual) applying for the EIN exactly as it appears on the social security card, charter, or other applicable legal document.

Individuals. Enter your first name, middle initial, and last name. If you are a sole proprietor, enter your individual name, not your business name. Enter your business name on line 2. Do not use abbreviations or nicknames on line 1.

Trusts. Enter the name of the trust.

Estate of a decedent. Enter the name of the estate.

Partnerships. Enter the legal name of the partnership as it appears in the partnership agreement.

Corporations. Enter the corporate name as it appears in the corporation charter or other legal document creating it.

Plan administrators. Enter the name of the plan administrator. A plan administrator who already has an EIN should use that number.

Line 2—Trade name of business. Enter the trade name of the business if different from the legal name. The trade name is the "doing business as " (DBA) name.

*Use the full legal name shown on line 1 on all tax returns filed for the entity. (However, if you enter a trade name on line 2 and choose to use the trade name instead of the legal name, enter the trade name on **all returns** you file.) To prevent processing delays and errors, **always** use the legal name only (or the trade name only) on **all** tax returns.*

Line 3—Executor, trustee, "care of" name. Trusts enter the name of the trustee. Estates enter the name of the executor, administrator, or other fiduciary. If the entity applying has a designated person to receive tax information, enter that person's name as the "care of" person. Enter the individual's first name, middle initial, and last name.

Lines 4a-b—Mailing address. Enter the mailing address for the entity's correspondence. If line 3 is completed, enter the address for the executor, trustee or "care of" person. Generally, this address will be used on all tax returns.

*File **Form 8822**, Change of Address, to report any subsequent changes to the entity's mailing address.*

Lines 5a-b—Street address. Provide the entity's physical address **only** if different from its mailing address shown in lines 4a-b. **Do not** enter a P.O. box number here.

Line 6—County and state where principal business is located. Enter the entity's primary **physical** location.

Lines 7a-b—Name of principal officer, general partner, grantor, owner, or trustor. Enter the first name, middle initial, last name, and SSN of **(a)** the principal officer if the business is a corporation, **(b)** a general partner if a partnership, **(c)** the owner of an entity that is disregarded as separate from its owner (disregarded entities owned by a corporation enter the corporation's name and EIN), or **(d)** a grantor, owner, or trustor if a trust.

If the person in question is an **alien individual** with a previously assigned individual taxpayer identification number (ITIN), enter the ITIN in the space provided and submit a copy of an official identifying document. If

necessary, complete **Form W-7**, Application for IRS Individual Taxpayer Identification Number, to obtain an ITIN.

You are **required** to enter an SSN, ITIN, or EIN unless the only reason you are applying for an EIN is to make an entity classification election (see Regulations sections 301.7701-1 through 301.7701-3) and you are a nonresident alien with no effectively connected income from sources within the United States.

Line 8a—Type of entity. Check the box that best describes the type of entity applying for the EIN. If you are an alien individual with an ITIN previously assigned to you, enter the ITIN in place of a requested SSN.

*This is not an election for a tax classification of an entity. See **Limited liability company (LLC)** on page 4.*

Other. If not specifically listed, check the "Other" box, enter the type of entity and the type of return, if any, that will be filed (for example, "Common Trust Fund, Form 1065" or "Created a Pension Plan"). Do not enter "N/A." If you are an alien individual applying for an EIN, see the **Lines 7a-b** instructions above.

● **Household employer.** If you are an individual, check the "Other" box and enter "Household Employer" and your SSN. If you are a state or local agency serving as a tax reporting agent for public assistance recipients who become household employers, check the "Other" box and enter "Household Employer Agent." If you are a trust that qualifies as a household employer, you do not need a separate EIN for reporting tax information relating to household employees; use the EIN of the trust.

● **QSub.** For a qualified subchapter S subsidiary (QSub) check the "Other" box and specify "QSub."

● **Withholding agent.** If you are a withholding agent required to file Form 1042, check the "Other" box and enter "Withholding Agent."

Sole proprietor. Check this box if you file Schedule C, C-EZ, or F (Form 1040) and have a qualified plan, or are required to file excise, employment, alcohol, tobacco, or firearms returns, or are a payer of gambling winnings. Enter your SSN (or ITIN) in the space provided. If you are a nonresident alien with no effectively connected income from sources within the United States, you do not need to enter an SSN or ITIN.

Corporation. This box is for any corporation **other than a personal service corporation.** If you check this box, enter the income tax form number to be filed by the entity in the space provided.

*If you entered "1120S" after the "Corporation" checkbox, the corporation **must** file Form 2553 **no later than the 15th day of the 3rd month of the tax year the election is to take effect.** Until Form 2553 has been received and approved, you will be considered a Form 1120 filer. See the Instructions for Form 2553.*

Personal service corp. Check this box if the entity is a personal service corporation. An entity is a personal service corporation for a tax year only if:

• The principal activity of the entity during the testing period (prior tax year) for the tax year is the performance of personal services substantially by employee-owners, and

• The employee-owners own at least 10% of the fair market value of the outstanding stock in the entity on the last day of the testing period.

Personal services include performance of services in such fields as health, law, accounting, or consulting. For more information about personal service corporations, see the Instructions for Forms 1120 and 1120-A and Pub. 542.

Other nonprofit organization. Check this box if the nonprofit organization is other than a church or church-controlled organization and specify the type of nonprofit organization (for example, an educational organization).

 *If the organization also seeks tax-exempt status, you **must** file either Package 1023 or Package 1024. See Pub. 557 for more information.*

If the organization is covered by a group exemption letter, enter the four-digit **group exemption number (GEN).** (Do not confuse the GEN with the nine-digit EIN.) If you do not know the GEN, contact the parent organization. Get Pub. 557 for more information about group exemption numbers.

Plan administrator. If the plan administrator is an individual, enter the plan administrator's SSN in the space provided.

REMIC. Check this box if the entity has elected to be treated as a real estate mortgage investment conduit (REMIC). See the Instructions for Form 1066 for more information.

Limited liability company (LLC). An LLC is an entity organized under the laws of a state or foreign country as a limited liability company. For Federal tax purposes, an LLC may be treated as a partnership or corporation or be disregarded as an entity separate from its owner.

By **default,** a domestic LLC with only one member is **disregarded** as an entity separate from its owner and must include all of its income and expenses on the owner's tax return (e.g., **Schedule C (Form 1040)**). Also by default, a domestic LLC with two or more members is treated as a partnership. A domestic LLC may file Form 8832 to avoid either default classification and elect to be classified as an association taxable as a corporation. For more information on entity classifications (including the rules for foreign entities), see the instructions for Form 8832.

 Do not** file Form 8832 if the LLC accepts the default classifications above. **However, if the LLC will be electing S Corporation status, it must timely file both Form 8832 and Form 2553.

Complete Form SS-4 for LLCs as follows:
• A single-member domestic LLC that accepts the default classification (above) does not need an EIN and generally should not file Form SS-4. Generally, the LLC

should use the name and EIN of its **owner** for all Federal tax purposes. However, the reporting and payment of employment taxes for employees of the LLC may be made using the name and EIN of **either** the owner or the LLC as explained in Notice 99-6. You can find Notice 99-6 on page 12 of Internal Revenue Bulletin 1999-3 at **www.irs.gov/pub/irs-irbs/irb99-03.pdf. (Note:** If the LLC applicant indicates in box 13 that it has employees or expects to have employees, the owner (whether an individual or other entity) of a single-member domestic LLC will also be assigned its own EIN (if it does not already have one) even if the LLC will be filing the employment tax returns.)
• A single-member, domestic LLC that accepts the default classification (above) and wants an EIN for filing employment tax returns (see above) or non-Federal purposes, such as a state requirement, must check the "Other" box and write "Disregarded Entity" or, when applicable, "Disregarded Entity—Sole Proprietorship" in the space provided.
• A multi-member, domestic LLC that accepts the default classification (above) must check the "Partnership" box.
• A domestic LLC that will be filing Form 8832 to elect corporate status must check the "Corporation" box and write in "Single-Member" or "Multi-Member" immediately below the "form number" entry line.

Line 9—Reason for applying. Check only **one** box. Do not enter "N/A."

Started new business. Check this box if you are starting a new business that requires an EIN. If you check this box, enter the type of business being started. **Do not** apply if you already have an EIN and are only adding another place of business.

Hired employees. Check this box if the existing business is requesting an EIN because it has hired or is hiring employees and is therefore required to file employment tax returns. **Do not** apply if you already have an EIN and are only hiring employees. For information on employment taxes (e.g., for family members), see Circular E.

 You may be required to make electronic deposits of all depository taxes (such as employment tax, excise tax, and corporate income tax) using the Electronic Federal Tax Payment System (EFTPS). See section 11, Depositing Taxes, of Circular E and Pub. 966.

Created a pension plan. Check this box if you have created a pension plan and need an EIN for reporting purposes. Also, enter the type of plan in the space provided.

 Check this box if you are applying for a trust EIN when a new pension plan is established. In addition, check the "Other" box in line 8a and write "Created a Pension Plan" in the space provided.

Banking purpose. Check this box if you are requesting an EIN for banking purposes only, and enter the banking purpose (for example, a bowling league for depositing dues or an investment club for dividend and interest reporting).

Changed type of organization. Check this box if the business is changing its type of organization. For example, the business was a sole proprietorship and has been incorporated or has become a partnership. If you check this box, specify in the space provided (including available space immediately below) the type of change made. For example, "From Sole Proprietorship to Partnership."

Purchased going business. Check this box if you purchased an existing business. **Do not** use the former owner's EIN unless you became the "owner" of a corporation by acquiring its stock.

Created a trust. Check this box if you created a trust, and enter the type of trust created. For example, indicate if the trust is a nonexempt charitable trust or a split-interest trust.

Exception. Do **not** file this form for certain grantor-type trusts. The trustee does not need an EIN for the trust if the trustee furnishes the name and TIN of the grantor/owner and the address of the trust to all payors. See the Instructions for Form 1041 for more information.

 Do not check this box if you are applying for a trust EIN when a new pension plan is established. Check "Created a pension plan."

Other. Check this box if you are requesting an EIN for any other reason; and enter the reason. For example, a newly-formed state government entity should enter "Newly-Formed State Government Entity" in the space provided.

Line 10—Date business started or acquired. If you are starting a new business, enter the starting date of the business. If the business you acquired is already operating, enter the date you acquired the business. If you are changing the form of ownership of your business, enter the date the new ownership entity began. Trusts should enter the date the trust was legally created. Estates should enter the date of death of the decedent whose name appears on line 1 or the date when the estate was legally funded.

Line 11—Closing month of accounting year. Enter the last month of your accounting year or tax year. An accounting or tax year is usually 12 consecutive months, either a calendar year or a fiscal year (including a period of 52 or 53 weeks). A calendar year is 12 consecutive months ending on December 31. A fiscal year is either 12 consecutive months ending on the last day of any month other than December or a 52-53 week year. For more information on accounting periods, see Pub. 538.

Individuals. Your tax year generally will be a calendar year.

Partnerships. Partnerships must adopt one of the following tax years:
- The tax year of the majority of its partners,
- The tax year common to all of its principal partners,
- The tax year that results in the least aggregate deferral of income, or
- In certain cases, some other tax year.

See the Instructions for Form 1065 for more information.

REMICs. REMICs must have a calendar year as their tax year.

Personal service corporations. A personal service corporation generally must adopt a calendar year unless:
- It can establish a business purpose for having a different tax year, or
- It elects under section 444 to have a tax year other than a calendar year.

Trusts. Generally, a trust must adopt a calendar year except for the following:
- Tax-exempt trusts,
- Charitable trusts, and
- Grantor-owned trusts.

Line 12—First date wages or annuities were paid or will be paid. If the business has or will have employees, enter the date on which the business began or will begin to pay wages. If the business does not plan to have employees, enter "N/A."

Withholding agent. Enter the date you began or will begin to pay income (including annuities) to a nonresident alien. This also applies to individuals who are required to file Form 1042 to report alimony paid to a nonresident alien.

Line 13—Highest number of employees expected in the next 12 months. Complete each box by entering the number (including zero ("-0-")) of "Agricultural," "Household," or "Other" employees expected by the applicant in the next 12 months. For a definition of agricultural labor (farmwork), see Circular A.

Lines 14 and 15. Check the **one** box in line 14 that best describes the principal activity of the applicant's business. Check the "Other" box (and specify the applicant's principal activity) if none of the listed boxes applies.

Use line 15 to describe the applicant's principal line of business in more detail. For example, if you checked the "Construction" box in line 14, enter additional detail such as "General contractor for residential buildings" in line 15.

Construction. Check this box if the applicant is engaged in erecting buildings or other structures, (e.g., streets, highways, bridges, tunnels). The term "Construction" also includes special trade contractors, (e.g., plumbing, HVAC, electrical, carpentry, concrete, excavation, etc. contractors).

Real estate. Check this box if the applicant is engaged in renting or leasing real estate to others; managing, selling, buying or renting real estate for others; or providing related real estate services (e.g., appraisal services).

Rental and leasing. Check this box if the applicant is engaged in providing tangible goods such as autos, computers, consumer goods, or industrial machinery and equipment to customers in return for a periodic rental or lease payment.

Manufacturing. Check this box if the applicant is engaged in the mechanical, physical, or chemical transformation of materials, substances, or components into new products. The assembling of component parts of manufactured products is also considered to be manufacturing.

Transportation & warehousing. Check this box if the applicant provides transportation of passengers or cargo; warehousing or storage of goods; scenic or sight-seeing transportation; or support activities related to these modes of transportation.

Finance & insurance. Check this box if the applicant is engaged in transactions involving the creation, liquidation, or change of ownership of financial assets and/or facilitating such financial transactions; underwriting annuities/insurance policies; facilitating such underwriting by selling insurance policies; or by providing other insurance or employee-benefit related services.

Health care and social assistance. Check this box if the applicant is engaged in providing physical, medical, or psychiatric care using licensed health care professionals or providing social assistance activities such as youth centers, adoption agencies, individual/family services, temporary shelters, etc.

Accommodation & food services. Check this box if the applicant is engaged in providing customers with lodging, meal preparation, snacks, or beverages for immediate consumption.

Wholesale–agent/broker. Check this box if the applicant is engaged in arranging for the purchase or sale of goods owned by others or purchasing goods on a commission basis for goods traded in the wholesale market, usually between businesses.

Wholesale–other. Check this box if the applicant is engaged in selling goods in the wholesale market generally to other businesses for resale on their own account.

Retail. Check this box if the applicant is engaged in selling merchandise to the general public from a fixed store; by direct, mail-order, or electronic sales; or by using vending machines.

Other. Check this box if the applicant is engaged in an activity not described above. Describe the applicant's principal business activity in the space provided.

Lines 16a-c. Check the applicable box in line 16a to indicate whether or not the entity (or individual) applying for an EIN was issued one previously. Complete lines 16b and 16c **only** if the "Yes" box in line 16a is checked. If the applicant previously applied for **more than one** EIN, write "See Attached" in the empty space in line 16a and attach a separate sheet providing the line 16b and 16c information for each EIN previously requested.

Third Party Designee. Complete this section **only** if you want to authorize the named individual to receive the entity's EIN and answer questions about the completion of Form SS-4. The designee's authority terminates at the time the EIN is assigned and released to the designee. **You must complete the signature area for the authorization to be valid.**

Signature. When required, the application must be signed by **(a)** the individual, if the applicant is an individual, **(b)** the president, vice president, or other principal officer, if the applicant is a corporation, **(c)** a responsible and duly authorized member or officer having knowledge of its affairs, if the applicant is a partnership, government entity, or other unincorporated organization, or **(d)** the fiduciary, if the applicant is a trust or an estate. Foreign applicants may have any duly-authorized person, (e.g., division manager), sign Form SS-4.

Privacy Act and Paperwork Reduction Act Notice. We ask for the information on this form to carry out the Internal Revenue laws of the United States. We need it to comply with section 6109 and the regulations thereunder which generally require the inclusion of an employer identification number (EIN) on certain returns, statements, or other documents filed with the Internal Revenue Service. If your entity is required to obtain an EIN, you are required to provide all of the information requested on this form. Information on this form may be used to determine which Federal tax returns you are required to file and to provide you with related forms and publications.

We disclose this form to the Social Security Administration for their use in determining compliance with applicable laws. We may give this information to the Department of Justice for use in civil and criminal litigation, and to the cities, states, and the District of Columbia for use in administering their tax laws. We may also disclose this information to Federal and state agencies to enforce Federal nontax criminal laws and to combat terrorism.

We will be unable to issue an EIN to you unless you provide all of the requested information which applies to your entity. Providing false information could subject you to penalties.

You are not required to provide the information requested on a form that is subject to the Paperwork Reduction Act unless the form displays a valid OMB control number. Books or records relating to a form or its instructions must be retained as long as their contents may become material in the administration of any Internal Revenue law. Generally, tax returns and return information are confidential, as required by section 6103.

The time needed to complete and file this form will vary depending on individual circumstances. The estimated average time is:

Recordkeeping	6 min.
Learning about the law or the form	22 min.
Preparing the form	46 min.
Copying, assembling, and sending the form to the IRS	20 min.

If you have comments concerning the accuracy of these time estimates or suggestions for making this form simpler, we would be happy to hear from you. You can write to the Tax Products Coordinating Committee, Western Area Distribution Center, Rancho Cordova, CA 95743-0001. **Do not** send the form to this address. Instead, see **How To Apply** on page 1.

Form 501 **(revised 9/03)**		This space reserved for office use.
Return in Duplicate to: Secretary of State P.O. Box 13697 Austin, TX 78711-3697 FAX: 512/463-5709		
Filing Fees: Corporations and Professional Associations ($40); Limited Liability Companies ($25), and Limited Partnerships ($50)	**APPLICATION FOR RESERVATION OF AN ENTITY NAME**	

ENTITY NAME TYPE

Pursuant to the applicable statutory provision for reservation of an entity name, the undersigned applicant hereby applies for reservation of an entity name to be used for the following type of entity (choose only one)

☐ Domestic Business Corporation	☐ Domestic Professional Corporation	☐ Foreign Limited Liability Co.
☐ Foreign Business Corporation	☐ Foreign Professional Corporation	☐ Domestic Limited Partnership
☐ Domestic Non-Profit Corporation	☐ Professional Association	☐ Foreign Limited Partnership
☐ Foreign Non-Profit Corporation	☐ Domestic Limited Liability Co.	

Please choose carefully. Note that name reservations filed under one statute cannot be used for, or transferred to, filings made under another statute.

ENTITY NAME TO BE RESERVED

The name must contain an appropriate organizational ending for the type of entity for which the name is to be reserved (See instructions.) The name must not be the same as, deceptively similar to or similar to that of an existing corporate, limited liability company, or limited partnership name on file with the secretary of state. A preliminary check for "name availability" is recommended.

The applicant requests that the following entity name be reserved for a period of one hundred twenty (120) days:

APPLICANT NAME (Choose and complete either A or B.)

☐   A. The applicant is an organized entity by the name set forth below:

OR

☐   B. The applicant is an individual by the name set forth below:

First Name	M. I.	Last Name	Suffix

APPLICANT ADDRESS

Street Address	City	State	Zip Code

EXECUTION

The undersigned signs this document subject to the penalties imposed by law for the submission of a false or fraudulent document.

Signature of applicant, applicant's attorney or agent

Form 501—General Information
(Application for Reservation of Entity Name)

> **The attached form is a standardized form designed to meet minimal statutory filing requirements pursuant to the relevant statutory provisions.** *This form and the information provided are not substitutes for the advice and services of an attorney and tax specialist.*

The name of a corporation, professional association, limited liability company, or limited partnership may be reserved for a period of 120 days. There is no provision for renewal of a name reservation. Consequently, a subsequent application for reservation of the same entity name will not be accepted for filing until the original reservation period has expired.

Item 1—Entity Type: A name may be reserved only by a person intending to organize a Texas business or non-profit corporation, limited liability company or limited partnership, or a person intending to qualify a foreign (out-of-state) corporation, foreign limited liability company or foreign limited partnership to transact business in Texas, or any such entity that intends to change its name. Although this form is designed to be used by different types of entities, you must specify the type of entity to which the name reservation is to apply **since a name reservation filed under one statute cannot be used for, or transferred to, filings made under another statute.**

Item 2—Entity Name: Set forth the entity name to be reserved together with the appropriate organizational ending. Appropriate organizational endings are shown in the table below:

Entity Type	Appropriate Organizational Terms					
Business Corporation	Corporation	Incorporated	Company	Corp.	Inc.	Co.
Non-Profit Corporation	**Use of an organizational ending is not required for a domestic non-profit corporation.**					
Professional Corporation	**The same as business corporations. However, may also use Professional Corporation or abbreviation PC.**					
Professional Association	Professional Association	Association	Associated	and Associates	Assoc.	P.A.
Limited Liability Company	Limited Liability Company	Limited Company	LLC or L.L.C.	LC or L.C.	Ltd. Co.	
Professional Limited Liability Company	Professional Limited Liability Company	PLLC or P.L.L.C.				
Limited Partnership	Limited Partnership	Limited	L.P. or LP	Ltd.		

The applicable statutes and the secretary of state's name availability rules provide that a proposed name cannot be the same as, deceptively similar to, or similar to (without a letter of consent) that of any existing domestic or foreign corporation, limited partnership, limited liability company or any name reservation or registration filed with the secretary of state. The administrative rules adopted for determining entity name availability (Texas Administrative Code, Title 1, Part 4, Chapter 79, Subchapter C) may be viewed at www.sos.state.tx.us/tac/index.html. If you wish the secretary of state to provide a preliminary determination on "name availability," you may call (512) 463-5555 or e-mail your name inquiry to *corpinfo@sos.state.tx.us*. **Warning:** This is only an initial clearance and should not be relied upon as final approval of the name. The final decision regarding name availability will be made when the document is submitted for filing.

Items 3 and 4—Applicant Name and Address: Specify the name of the person for whom the reservation is made. If the name is being reserved by a corporation, limited partnership, limited liability company or other organized legal entity, select and complete option A. If an individual is reserving the name, please select and complete option B. Once the application for reservation is filed, the name reservation will be recorded exclusively in the name of the applicant or the applicant's transferee if a notice of transfer is filed with the appropriate fee.

Item 5—Execution: The applicant or applicant's attorney or agent must sign the application for name reservation. Prior to signing, please read the statements on this form carefully. A person commits an offense under the Texas Business Corporation Act, the Texas Limited Liability Company Act or the Texas Non-Profit Corporation Act if the person signs a document the person knows is false in any material respect with the intent that the document be delivered to the secretary of state for filing. The offense is a Class A misdemeanor.

Termination: A registrant may terminate the reservation of a name prior to the expiration of the reservation period by filing an application to cancel the name reservation; no form is provided for this purpose. The filing fee for cancellation of a corporate or professional association name reservation is $15, cancellation of a limited partnership name reservation is $25, and cancellation of a limited liability company name reservation is $10.

Fees and Delivery Instructions:

Entity Type	Fee
Domestic or foreign business corporation, non-profit corporation, professional corporation or professional association	$40
Domestic or foreign limited liability company	$25
Domestic or foreign limited partnership	$50

Mail the completed form along with the correct filing fee to the address shown in the heading of this form. The delivery address is James Earl Rudder Office Building, 1019 Brazos, Austin, Texas 78701. Upon filing the reservation the secretary of state will issue a certificate of name reservation and return it to the submitter. The telephone number is (512) 463-5555, TDD: (800) 735-2989, FAX: (512) 463-5709.

This page intentionally blank.

Office of the Secretary of State
Corporations Section P.O. Box 13697
Austin, TX 78711-3697

ASSUMED NAME CERTIFICATE
FOR FILING WITH THE SECRETARY OF STATE

1. The name of the corporation, limited liability company, limited partnership, or registered limited liability partnership as stated in its articles of incorporation, articles or organization, certificate of limited partnership, application for certificate of authority or comparable document is _____

2. The assumed name under which the business or professional service is or is not to be conducted or rendered is _____

3. The state, county, or other jurisdiction under the laws of which it was incorporated, organized or associated is _____ and the address of its registered or similar office in that jurisdiction is _____

4. The period, not to exceed 10 years, during which the assumed name will be used   is

   _____

5. The entity is a (check one):

   A.

   ☐ Business Corporation   ☐ Non-Profit Corporation
   ☐ Professional Corporation   ☐ Professional Association
   ☐ Limited Liability Company   ☐ Limited Partnership
   ☐ Registered Limited Liability Partnership

   B.   If the entity is some other type of business, professional or other association that is incorporated, please specify below (e.g. bank, savings and loan associations, etc.)

6. If the entity is required to maintain a registered office in Texas, the address of the registered office is _____

   _____ and the name of its registered agent at such address is _____

   The address of the principal office (if not the same as the registered office) is

   _____

7. If the entity is not required to or does not maintain a registered office in Texas, the office address in Texas is _____

   _____ and if the entity is not incorporated, organized or associated under the laws of Texas, the address of its place of business in Texas is _____

   _____ and the office address elsewhere is _____

   _____

8. The county or counties where business or professional services are being or are to be conducted or rendered under such assumed name are (if applicable, use the designation "ALL" or "ALL EXCEPT")

   _____

   _____

9. The undersigned, if acting in the capacity of an attorney-in-fact of the entity, certifies that the entity has duly authorized the attorney-in-fact in writing to execute this document.

By _____
   Signature of officer, general partner, manager, representative or attorney-in-fact of the entity

<u>NOTE</u>

This form is designed to meet statutory requirements for fling with the secretary of state and in not designed to meet filing requirements on the county level. Filing requirements for assumed name documents to be filed with the county clerk differ. Assumed name documents filed with the county clerk are to executed and acknowledged by the filing party, which requires that the document be notarized.

Form No. 503
Revised 9/99

INSTRUCTIONS

1. A corporation, limited liability company, limited partnership or registered limited liability partnership which regularly conducts business or renders a professional service in this state under a name other than its true name, must file an assumed name certificate with the secretary of state. In addition, an assumed name certificate must be filed with the county clerk in the county in which the registered office is located and with the county clerk in the county which the principal office is located if these are not in the same county.

2. This form is designed to meet minimum statutory filing requirements for filing with the secretary of state; no warranty is made regarding the suitability of this form fro any particular purpose. This form and the information provided are not substitutes for the advice of an attorney. Prior to signing, please review carefully the statements set forth in the document. A person commits an offense under section 36.27 of the Business & Commerce Code if the person signs a document the person knows is false in any material respect with the intent that the document be delivered to the secretary of state for filing. The offense is punishable as if it were an offense under section 37.10 of the Penal Code.

3. Send the executed certificate accompanied by the filing fee of $25 to the Secretary of State, Statutory Filings Division, Corporations Section, P.O. 13697, Austin, Texas 78711-3697. The delivery address is 1019 Brazos, Austin, Texas 78701. The telephone number is (512) 463-5555, TDD: (800) 735-2989, FAX: (512) 463-5709. Upon filing, the certificate will be placed on record. If a duplicate file-stamped copy is desired, you must submit a duplicate copy of the document for this purpose.

4. Personal checks and MasterCard®, Visa®, and Discover® are accepted in payment of the filing fee. Fees paid by credit card are subject to a statutorily authorized cost of 2.1% of the total fees.

5. The information provided in paragraph 6 regarding the registered agent and registered office address in Texas must match the information on file in this office. To verify the information on file, you may contact our Public Information Team at (512) 463-5555 or email at corpinfo@sos.state.tx.us.

6. Whenever an event occurs that causes information in the assumed name certificate to become materially misleading (e.g. change of registered agent/office or a change of name), a new certificate must be filed within 60 days after the occurrence of the event which necessitates the filing.

7. A registrant that ceases to transact business or render professional services under an assumed name for which a certificate has been filed may file an abandonment of use pursuant to the Texas Business & Commerce Code, section 36.14. (Form 504)

8. Assumed name certificates to be filed with the county clerk must be notarized and contain original signatures; this form does not satisfy county filing requirements. An assumed name certificate to be filed with the county clerk must be sent directly to the appropriate county clerk and not to the secretary of state.

Form No. 503
Revised 9/99

This page intentionally blank.

WAIVER OF NOTICE

OF THE ORGANIZATION MEETING

OF

_____

We, the undersigned incorporators named in the certificate of incorporation of the above-named corporation hereby agree and consent that the organization meeting of the corporation be held on the date and time and place stated below and hereby waive all notice of such meeting and of any adjournment thereof.

Place of meeting: _____

Date of Meeting: _____

Time of meeting: _____

Dated: _____

_____
Incorporator

_____
Incorporator

_____
Incorporator

This page intentionally blank.

MINUTES OF THE ORGANIZATIONAL MEETING OF

INCORPORATORS AND DIRECTORS OF

_____

The organization meeting of the above corporation was held on _____,
_____ at _____
at _____ o'clock ___M.

The following persons were present:

_____   _____
_____   _____
_____   _____

The Waiver of notice of this meeting was signed by all directors and incorporators named in the Articles of Incorporation and filed in the minute book.

The meeting was called to order by _____ an Incorporator named in the Articles of Incorporation. _____ was nominated and elected Chairman and acted as such until relieved by the president. _____ was nominated and elected temporary secretary, and acted as such until relieved by the permanent secretary.

A copy of the Articles of Incorporation which was filed with the Secretary of State of the State of Texas on _____, _____ was examined by the Directors and Incorporators and filed in the minute book.

The election of officers for the coming year was then held and the following were duly nominated and elected by the Board of Directors to be the officers of the corporation, to serve until such time as their successors are elected and qualified:

President: _____
Vice President: _____
Secretary: _____
Treasurer: _____

The proposed Bylaws for the corporation were then presented to the meeting and discussed. Upon motion duly made, seconded, and carried, the Bylaws were adopted and added to the minute book.

A corporate seal for the corporation was then presented to the meeting and upon motion duly made, seconded and carried, it was adopted as the seal of the corporation. An impression thereof was then made in the margin of these minutes.

The necessity of opening a bank account was then discussed and upon motion duly made, seconded, and carried, the following resolution was adopted:

RESOLVED that the corporation open bank accounts with _____
_____ and that the officers of the corporation are authorized to take
such action as is necessary to open such accounts; that the bank's printed form of resolution is hereby adopted
and incorporated into these minutes by reference and shall be placed in the minute book; that any _____
of the following persons shall have signature authority over the account:

_____ _____

_____ _____

_____ _____

Proposed stock certificates and stock transfer ledger were then presented to the meeting and examined. Upon
motion duly made, seconded and carried the stock certificates and ledger were adopted as the certificates and transfer
book to be used by the corporation. A sample stock certificate marked "VOID" and the stock transfer ledger were
then added to the minute book. Upon motion duly made, seconded and carried, it was then resolved that the stock certificates, when issued, would be signed by the President and the Secretary of the corporation.

The tax status of the corporation was then discussed and it was moved, seconded and carried that the stock of
the corporation be issued under § 1244 of the Internal Revenue Code and that the officers of the corporation take the
necessary action to:

1.   Obtain an employer tax number by filing form SS-4,

2.   ☐   Become an S-Corporation for tax purposes,
      ☐   Remain a C-Corporation for tax purposes,

The expenses of organizing the corporation were then discussed and it was moved, seconded, and carried that
the corporation pay in full from the corporate funds the expenses and reimburse any advances made by the incorporators upon proof of payment.

The Directors named in the Articles of Incorporation then tendered their resignations, effective upon the
adjournment of this meeting. Upon motion duly made, seconded, and carried, the following named persons were
elected as Directors of the corporation, each to hold office until the first annual meeting of shareholders, and until a
successor of each shall have been elected and qualified.

_____

_____

_____

There were presented to the corporation, the following offer(s) to purchase shares of capital stock:

	NO. OF	
FROM	SHARES	CONSIDERATION
_____	_____	_____
_____	_____	_____
_____	_____	_____
_____	_____	_____

The offers were discussed and after motion duly made, seconded, and carried were approved. It was further resolved that the Board of Directors has determined that the consideration was valued at least equal to the value of the shares to be issued and that upon tender of the consideration, fully paid non-assessable shares of the corporation be issued.

There being no further business before the meeting, on motion duly made, seconded, and carried, the meeting adjourned.

DATED: _____

_____
President

_____
Secretary

This page intentionally blank.

BYLAWS OF

_____

A TEXAS CORPORATION

ARTICLE I - OFFICES

The principal office of the Corporation shall be located in the City of _____ and the State of Texas. The Corporation may also maintain offices at such other places as the Board of Directors may, from time to time, determine.

ARTICLE II - SHAREHOLDERS

<u>Section 1 - Annual Meetings</u>: The annual meeting of the shareholders of the Corporation shall be held each year on _____ at ____M. at the principal office of the Corporation or at such other places, within or without the State of Texas, as the Board may authorize, for the purpose of electing directors, and transacting such other business as may properly come before the meeting.

<u>Section 2 - Special Meetings</u>: Special meetings of the shareholders may be called at any time by the Board, the President, or by the holders of twenty-five percent (25%) of the shares then outstanding and entitled to vote.

<u>Section 3 - Place of Meetings</u>: All meetings of shareholders shall be held at the principal office of the Corporation, or at such other places as the board shall designate in the notice of such meetings.

<u>Section 4 - Notice of Meetings</u>: Written or printed notice stating the place, day, and hour of the meeting and, in the case of a special meeting, the purpose of the meeting, shall be delivered personally or by mail not less than ten days, nor more than sixty days, before the date of the meeting. Notice shall be given to each Member of record entitled to vote at the meeting. If mailed, such notice shall be deemed to have been delivered when deposited in the United States Mail with postage paid and addressed to the Member at his address as it appears on the records of the Corporation.

<u>Section 5 - Waiver of Notice</u>: A written waiver of notice signed by a Member, whether before or after a meeting, shall be equivalent to the giving of such notice. Attendance of a Member at a meeting shall constitute a waiver of notice of such meeting, except when the Member attends for the express purpose of objecting, at the beginning of the meeting, to the transaction of any business because the meeting is not lawfully called or convened.

<u>Section 6 - Quorum</u>: Except as otherwise provided by Statute, or the Articles of Incorporation, at all meetings of shareholders of the Corporation, the presence at the commencement of such meetings in person or by proxy of shareholders of record holding a majority of the total number of shares of the Corporation then issued and outstanding and entitled to vote, but in no event less than one-third of the shares entitled to vote at the meeting, shall constitute a quorum for the transaction of any business. If any shareholder leaves after the commencement of a meeting, this shall have no effect on the existence of a quorum, after a quorum has been established at such meeting.

Despite the absence of a quorum at any annual or special meeting of shareholders, the shareholders, by a majority of the votes cast by the holders of shares entitled to vote thereon, may adjourn the meeting. At any such adjourned meeting at which a quorum is present, any business may be transacted at the meeting as originally called as if a quorum had been present.

<u>Section 7 - Voting</u>: Except as otherwise provided by Statute or by the Articles of Incorporation, any corporate action, other than the election of directors, to be taken by vote of the shareholders, shall be authorized by a majority of votes cast at a meeting of shareholders by the holders of shares entitled to vote thereon.

Except as otherwise provided by Statute or by the Articles of Incorporation, at each meeting of shareholders, each holder of record of stock of the Corporation entitled to vote thereat, shall be entitled to one vote for each share of stock registered in his name on the stock transfer books of the corporation.

Each shareholder entitled to vote may do so by proxy; provided, however, that the instrument authorizing such proxy to act shall have been executed in writing by the shareholder himself. No proxy shall be valid after the expiration of eleven months from the date of its execution, unless the person executing it shall have specified therein, the length of time it is to continue in force. Such instrument shall be exhibited to the Secretary at the meeting and shall be filed with the records of the corporation.

Any resolution in writing, signed by all of the shareholders entitled to vote thereon, shall be and constitute action by such shareholders to the effect therein expressed, with the same force and effect as if the same had been duly passed by unanimous vote at a duly called meeting of shareholders and such resolution so signed shall be inserted in the Minute Book of the Corporation under its proper date.

ARTICLE III - BOARD OF DIRECTORS

Section 1 - Number, Election and Term of Office: The number of the directors of the Corporation shall be (_____) This number may be increased or decreased by the amendment of these bylaws by the Board but shall in no case be less than _____ director(s). The members of the Board, who need not be shareholders, shall be elected by a majority of the votes cast at a meeting of shareholders entitled to vote in the election. Each director shall hold office until the annual meeting of the shareholders next succeeding his election, and until his successor is elected and qualified, or until his prior death, resignation or removal.

Section 2 - Vacancies: Any vacancy in the Board shall be filled for the unexpired portion of the term by a majority vote of the remaining directors, though less than a quorum, at any regular meeting or special meeting of the Board called for that purpose. Any such director so elected may be replaced by the shareholders at a regular or special meeting of shareholders.

Section 3 - Duties and Powers: The Board shall be responsible for the control and management of the affairs, property and interests of the Corporation, and may exercise all powers of the Corporation, except as limited by statute.

Section 4 - Annual Meetings: An annual meeting of the Board shall be held immediately following the annual meeting of the shareholders, at the place of such annual meeting of shareholders. The Board from time to time, may provide by resolution for the holding of other meetings of the Board, and may fix the time and place thereof.

Section 5 - Special Meetings: Special meetings of the Board shall be held whenever called by the President or by one of the directors, at such time and place as may be specified in the respective notice or waivers of notice thereof.

Section 6 - Notice and Waiver: Notice of any special meeting shall be given at least five days prior thereto by written notice delivered personally, by mail or by telegram to each Director at his address. If mailed, such notice shall be deemed to be delivered when deposited in the United States Mail with postage prepaid. If notice is given by telegram, such notice shall be deemed to be delivered when the telegram is delivered to the telegraph company.

Any Director may waive notice of any meeting, either before, at, or after such meeting, by signing a waiver of notice. The attendance of a Director at a meeting shall constitute a waiver of notice of such meeting and a waiver of any and all objections to the place of such meeting, or the manner in which it has been called or convened, except when a Director states at the beginning of the meeting any objection to the transaction of business because the meeting is not lawfully called or convened.

Section 7 - Chairman: The Board may, at its discretion, elect a Chairman. At all meetings of the Board, the Chairman of the Board, if any and if present, shall preside. If there is no Chairman, or he is absent, then the President shall preside, and in his absence, a Chairman chosen by the directors shall preside.

Section 8 - Quorum and Adjournments: At all meetings of the Board, the presence of a majority of the entire Board shall be necessary and sufficient to constitute a quorum for the transaction of business, except as otherwise provided by law, by the Articles of Incorporation, or by these bylaws. A majority of the directors present at the time and place of any regular or special meeting, although less than a quorum, may adjourn the same from time to time without notice, until a quorum shall be present.

Section 9 - Board Action: At all meetings of the Board, each director present shall have one vote, irrespective of the number of shares of stock, if any, which he may hold. Except as otherwise provided by Statute, the action of a majority of the directors present at any meeting at which a quorum is present shall be the act of the Board. Any action authorized, in writing, by all of the Directors entitled to vote thereon and filed with the minutes of the Corporation shall be the act of the Board with the same force and effect as if the same had been passed by unanimous vote at a duly called meeting of the Board. Any action taken by the Board may be taken without a meeting if agreed to in writing by all members before or after the action is taken and if a record of such action is filed in the minute book.

Section 10 - Telephone Meetings: Directors may participate in meetings of the Board through use of a telephone if such can be arranged so that all Board members can hear all other members. The use of a telephone for participation shall constitute presence in person.

Section 11 - Resignation and Removal: Any director may resign at any time by giving written notice to another Board member, the President or the Secretary of the Corporation. Unless otherwise specified in such written notice, such resignation shall take effect upon receipt thereof by the Board or by such officer, and the acceptance of such resignation shall not be necessary to make it effective. Any director may be removed with or without cause at any time by the affirmative vote of shareholders holding of record in the aggregate at least a majority of the outstanding shares of the Corporation at a special meeting of the shareholders called for that purpose, and may be removed for cause by action of the Board.

Section 12 - Compensation: No stated salary shall be paid to directors, as such for their services, but by resolution of the Board a fixed sum and/or expenses of attendance, if any, may be allowed for attendance at each regular or special meeting of the Board. Nothing herein contained shall be construed to preclude any director from serving the Corporation in any other capacity and receiving compensation therefor.

ARTICLE IV - OFFICERS

Section 1 - Number, Qualification, Election and Term: The officers of the Corporation shall consist of a President, a Secretary, a Treasurer, and such other officers, as the Board may from time to time deem advisable. Any officer may be, but is not required to be, a director of the Corporation. The officers of the Corporation shall be elected by the Board at the regular annual meeting of the Board. Each officer shall hold office until the annual meeting of the Board next succeeding his election, and until his successor shall have been elected and qualified, or until his death, resignation or removal.

Section 2 - Resignation and Removal: Any officer may resign at any time by giving written notice of such resignation to the President or the Secretary of the Corporation or to a member of the Board. Unless otherwise specified in such written notice, such resignation shall take effect upon receipt thereof by the Board member or by such officer, and the acceptance of such resignation shall not be necessary to make it effective. Any officer may be removed, either with or without cause, and a successor elected by a majority vote of the Board at any time.

Section 3 - Vacancies: A vacancy in any office may at any time be filled for the unexpired portion of the term by a majority vote of the Board.

Section 4 - Duties of Officers: Officers of the Corporation shall, unless otherwise provided by the Board, each have such powers and duties as generally pertain to their respective offices as well as such powers and duties as may from time to time be specifically decided by the Board. The President shall be the chief executive officer of the Corporation.

Section 5 - Compensation: The officers of the Corporation shall be entitled to such compensation as the Board shall from time to time determine.

Section 6 - Delegation of Duties: In the absence or disability of any Officer of the Corporation or for any other reason deemed sufficient by the Board of Directors, the Board may delegate his powers or duties to any other Officer or to any other Director.

Section 7 - Shares of Other Corporations: Whenever the Corporation is the holder of shares of any other Corporation, any right or power of the Corporation as such shareholder (including the attendance, acting and voting at shareholders' meetings and execution of waivers, consents, proxies or other instruments) may be exercised on behalf of the Corporation by the President, any Vice President, or such other person as the Board may authorize.

ARTICLE V - COMMITTEES

The Board of Directors may, by resolution, designate an Executive Committee and one or more other committees. Such committees shall have such functions and may exercise such power of the Board of Directors as can be lawfully delegated, and to the extent provided in the resolution or resolutions creating such committee or committees. Meetings of committees may be held without notice at such time and at such place as shall from time to time be determined by the committees. The committees of the corporation shall keep regular minutes of their proceedings, and report these minutes to the Board of Directors when required.

ARTICLE VI - BOOKS, RECORDS AND REPORTS

Section 1 - Annual Report: The Corporation shall send an annual report to the Members of the Corporation not later than _____ months after the close of each fiscal year of the Corporation. Such report shall include a balance sheet as of the close of the fiscal year of the Corporation and a revenue and disbursement statement for the year ending on such closing date. Such financial statements shall be prepared from and in accordance with the books of the Corporation, and in conformity with generally accepted accounting principles applied on a consistent basis.

Section 2 - Permanent Records: The corporation shall keep current and correct records of the accounts, minutes of the meetings and proceedings and membership records of the corporation. Such records shall be kept at the registered office or the principal place of business of the corporation. Any such records shall be in written form or in a form capable of being converted into written form.

Section 3 - Inspection of Corporate Records: Any person who is a Voting Member of the Corporation shall have the right at any reasonable time, and on written demand stating the purpose thereof, to examine and make copies from the relevant books and records of accounts, minutes, and records of the Corporation. Upon the written request of any Voting Member, the Corporation shall mail to such Member a copy of the most recent balance sheet and revenue and disbursement statement.

ARTICLE VII- SHARES OF STOCK

Section 1 - Certificates: Each shareholder of the corporation shall be entitled to have a certificate representing all shares which he or she owns. The form of such certificate shall be adopted by a majority vote of the Board of Directors and shall be signed by the President and Secretary of the Corporation and sealed with the seal of the corporation. No certificate representing shares shall be issued until the full amount of consideration therefore has been paid.

Section 2 - Stock Ledger: The corporation shall maintain a ledger of the stock records of the Corporation. Transfers of shares of the Corporation shall be made on the stock ledger of the Corporation only at the direction of the holder of record upon surrender of the outstanding certificate(s). The Corporation shall be entitled to treat the holder of record of any share or shares as the absolute owner thereof for all purposes and, accordingly, shall not be bound to recognize any legal, equitable or other claim to, or interest in, such share or shares on the part of any other person, whether or not it shall have express or other notice thereof, except as otherwise expressly provided by law.

ARTICLE VIII - DIVIDENDS

Upon approval by the Board of Directors the corporation may pay dividends on its shares in the form of cash, property or additional shares at any time that the corporation is solvent and if such dividends would not render the corporation insolvent.

ARTICLE IX - FISCAL YEAR

The fiscal year of the Corporation shall be the period selected by the Board of Directors as the tax year of the Corporation for federal income tax purposes.

ARTICLE X - CORPORATE SEAL

The Board of Directors may adopt, use and modify a corporate seal. Failure to affix the seal to corporate documents shall not affect the validity of such document.

ARTICLE XI - AMENDMENTS

The Articles of Incorporation may be amended by the Shareholders as provided by Texas statutes. These Bylaws may be altered, amended, or replaced by the Board of Directors; provided, however, that any Bylaws or amendments thereto as adopted by the Board of Directors may be altered, amended, or repealed by vote of the Shareholders. Bylaws adopted by the Members may not be amended or repealed by the Board.

ARTICLE XII - INDEMNIFICATION

Any officer, director or employee of the Corporation shall be indemnified to the full extent allowed by the laws of the State of Texas.

Certified to be the Bylaws of the corporation adopted by the Board of Directors on _____, _____.

_____
Secretary

BYLAWS OF

_____

A TEXAS PROFESSIONAL CORPORATION

<u>ARTICLE I - OFFICES</u>

The principal office of the Corporation shall be located in the City of _____ and the State of Texas. The Corporation may also maintain offices at such other places as the Board of Directors may, from time to time, determine.

<u>ARTICLE II - PURPOSES</u>

The business purpose of the Corporation shall be to engage in all aspects of the practice of _____ and its fields of specialization. The Corporation shall render professional services only through its legally authorized officers, agents and employees.

<u>ARTICLE III - SHAREHOLDERS</u>

<u>Section 1 - Qualifications</u>: Only persons who are duly licensed and in good standing in the profession by the State of Texas may be shareholders of the Corporation. Neither the Corporation nor the shareholders may transfer any shares to persons who are not duly licensed. All share certificates of the corporation shall contain a notice that the transfer is restricted by the bylaws of the Corporation. If any shareholder shall become disqualified to practice the profession, he or she shall immediately make arrangements to transfer his or her shares to a qualified person or to the Corporation and shall no longer participate in the profits of the Corporation related to the profession.

<u>Section 2 - Annual Meetings</u>: The annual meeting of the shareholders of the Corporation shall be held each year on _____ at _____M. at the principal office of the Corporation or at such other places, within or without the State of Texas, as the Board may authorize, for the purpose of electing directors, and transacting such other business as may properly come before the meeting.

<u>Section 3 - Special Meetings</u>: Special meetings of the shareholders may be called at any time by the Board, the President, or by the holders of twenty-five percent (25%) of the shares then outstanding and entitled to vote.

<u>Section 4 - Place of Meetings</u>: All meetings of shareholders shall be held at the principal office of the Corporation, or at such other places as the Board shall designate in the notice of such meetings.

<u>Section 5 - Notice of Meetings</u>: Written or printed notice stating the place, day, and hour of the meeting and, in the case of a special meeting, the purpose of the meeting, shall be delivered personally or by mail not less than ten days, nor more than sixty days, before the date of the meeting. Notice shall be given to each Member of record entitled to vote at the meeting. If mailed, such notice shall be deemed to have been delivered when deposited in the United States Mail with postage paid and addressed to the Member at his address as it appears on the records of the Corporation.

<u>Section 6 - Waiver of Notice</u>: A written waiver of notice signed by a Member, whether before or after a meeting, shall be equivalent to the giving of such notice. Attendance of a Member at a meeting shall constitute a waiver of notice of such meeting, except when the Member attends for the express purpose of objecting, at the beginning of the meeting, to the transaction of any business because the meeting is not lawfully called or convened.

<u>Section 7 - Quorum</u>: Except as otherwise provided by Statute, or the by Articles of Incorporation, at all meetings of shareholders of the Corporation, the presence at the commencement of such meetings of shareholders of record holding a majority of the total number of shares of the Corporation then issued and outstanding and entitled to vote, but in no event less than one-third of the shares entitled to vote at the meeting, shall constitute a quorum for the transaction of any business. If any shareholder leaves after the commencement of a meeting, this shall have no effect on the existence of a quorum, after a quorum has been established at such meeting.

Despite the absence of a quorum at any annual or special meeting of shareholders, the shareholders, by a majority of the votes cast by the holders of shares entitled to vote thereon, may adjourn the meeting. At any such adjourned meeting at which a quorum is present, any business may be transacted at the meeting as originally called as if a quorum had been present.

Section 8 - Voting: Except as otherwise provided by Statute or by the Articles of Incorporation, any corporate action, other than the election of directors, to be taken by vote of the shareholders, shall be authorized by a majority of votes cast at a meeting of shareholders by the holders of shares entitled to vote thereon.

Except as otherwise provided by Statute or by the Articles of Incorporation, at each meeting of shareholders, each holder of record of stock of the Corporation entitled to vote thereat, shall be entitled to one vote for each share of stock registered in his name on the stock transfer books of the corporation.

Any resolution in writing, signed by all of the shareholders entitled to vote thereon, shall be and constitute action by such shareholders to the effect therein expressed, with the same force and effect as if the same had been duly passed by unanimous vote at a duly called meeting of shareholders and such resolution so signed shall be inserted in the Minute Book of the Corporation under its proper date.

Section 9 - Proxies: Shareholders may not at any time vote by proxy or enter into any voting trust or other agreement vesting another person with the voting power of his stock.

ARTICLE IV - BOARD OF DIRECTORS

Section 1 Qualifications: Only persons who are duly licensed and in good standing in the profession by the State of Texas may be directors of the Corporation. If any director shall become disqualified from practicing the profession, he or she shall immediately resign his or her directorship and any other employment with the Corporation.

Section 2 - Number, Election and Term of Office: The number of the directors of the Corporation shall be (____) This number may be increased or decreased by the amendment of these bylaws by the Board but shall in no case be less than one director. The members of the Board, who need not be shareholders, shall be elected by a majority of the votes cast at a meeting of shareholders entitled to vote in the election. Each director shall hold office until the annual meeting of the shareholders next succeeding his election, and until his successor is elected and qualified, or until his prior death, resignation or removal.

Section 3 - Vacancies: Any vacancy in the Board shall be filled for the unexpired portion of the term by a majority vote of the remaining directors, though less than a quorum, at any regular meeting or special meeting of the Board called for that purpose. Any such director so elected may be replaced by the shareholders at a regular or special meeting of shareholders.

Section 4 - Duties and Powers: The Board shall be responsible for the control and management of the affairs, property and interests of the Corporation, and may exercise all powers of the Corporation, except as limited by statute.

Section 5 - Annual Meetings: An annual meeting of the Board shall be held immediately following the annual meeting of the shareholders, at the place of such annual meeting of shareholders. The Board, from time to time, may provide by resolution for the holding of other meetings of the Board, and may fix the time and place thereof.

Section 6 - Special Meetings: Special meetings of the Board shall be held whenever called by the President or by one of the directors, at such time and place as may be specified in the respective notice or waivers of notice thereof.

Section 7 - Notice and Waiver: Notice of any special meeting shall be given at least five days prior thereto by written notice delivered personally, by mail or by telegram to each director at his address. If mailed, such notice shall be deemed to be delivered when deposited in the United States Mail with postage prepaid. If notice is given by telegram, such notice shall be deemed to be delivered when the telegram is delivered to the telegraph company.

Any director may waive notice of any meeting, either before, at, or after such meeting, by signing a waiver of notice. The attendance of a director at a meeting shall constitute a waiver of notice of such meeting and a waiver of any and all objections to the place of such meeting, or the manner in which it has been called or convened, except when a director states at the beginning of the meeting any objection to the transaction of business because the meeting is not lawfully called or convened.

Section 8 - Chairman: The Board may, at its discretion, elect a Chairman. At all meetings of the Board, the Chairman of the Board, if any and if present, shall preside. If there is no Chairman, or he is absent, then the President shall preside, and in his absence, a Chairman chosen by the directors shall preside.

Section 9 - Quorum and Adjournments: At all meetings of the Board, the presence of a majority of the entire Board shall be necessary and sufficient to constitute a quorum for the transaction of business, except as otherwise provided by law, by the Articles of Incorporation, or by these bylaws. A majority of the directors present at the time and place of any regular or special meeting, although less than a quorum, may adjourn the same from time to time without notice, until a quorum shall be present.

Section 10 - Board Action: At all meetings of the Board, each director present shall have one vote, irrespective of the number of shares of stock, if any, which he may hold. Except as otherwise provided by Statute, the action of a majority of the directors present at any meeting at which a quorum is present shall be the act of the Board. Any action authorized, in writing, by all of the Directors entitled to vote thereon and filed with the minutes of the Corporation shall be the act of the Board with the same force and effect as if the same had been passed by unanimous vote at a duly called meeting of the Board. Any action taken by the Board may be taken without a meeting if agreed to in writing by all members before or after the action is taken and if a record of such action is filed in the Minute Book.

Section 11 - Telephone Meetings: Directors may participate in meetings of the Board through use of a telephone if such can be arranged so that all Board members can hear all other members. The use of a telephone for participation shall constitute presence in person.

Section 12 - Resignation and Removal: Any director may resign at any time by giving written notice to another Board member, the President or the Secretary of the Corporation. Unless otherwise specified in such written notice, such resignation shall take effect upon receipt thereof by the Board or by such officer, and the acceptance of such resignation shall not be necessary to make it effective. Any director may be removed with or without cause at any time by the affirmative vote of shareholders holding of record in the aggregate at least a majority of the outstanding shares of the Corporation at a special meeting of the shareholders called for that purpose, and may be removed for cause by action of the Board.

Section 13 - Compensation: No stated salary shall be paid to directors, as such for their services, but by resolution of the Board a fixed sum and/or expenses of attendance, if any, may be allowed for attendance at each regular or special meeting of the Board. Nothing herein contained shall be construed to preclude any director from serving the Corporation in any other capacity and receiving compensation therefor.

ARTICLE V - OFFICERS

Section 1 Qualifications: Only persons who are duly licensed and in good standing in the profession by the State of Texas may be officers of the Corporation. If any director shall become disqualified from practicing the profession, he or she shall immediately resign his or her directorship and any other employment with the corporation.

Section 2 - Number, Election and Term: The officers of the Corporation shall consist of a President, a Secretary, a Treasurer, and such other officers, as the Board may from time to time deem advisable. Any officer may be, but is not required to be, a director of the Corporation. Any two or more offices may be held by the same person. The officers of the Corporation shall be elected by the Board at the regular annual meeting of the Board. Each officer shall hold office until the annual meeting of the Board next succeeding his election, and until his successor shall have been elected and qualified, or until his death, resignation or removal.

Section 3 - Resignation and Removal: Any officer may resign at any time by giving written notice of such resignation to the President or the Secretary of the Corporation or to a member of the Board. Unless otherwise specified in such written notice, such resignation shall take effect upon receipt thereof by the Board member or by such officer, and the acceptance of such resignation shall not be necessary to make it effective. Any officer may be removed, either with or without cause, and a successor elected by a majority vote of the Board at any time.

Section 4 - Vacancies: A vacancy in any office may at any time be filled for the unexpired portion of the term by a majority vote of the Board.

Section 5 - Duties of Officers: The officers of the Corporation shall, unless otherwise provided by the Board, each have such powers and duties as generally pertain to their respective offices as well as such powers and duties as may from time to time be specifically decided by the Board. The President shall be the chief executive officer of the Corporation.

Section 6 - Compensation: The officers of the Corporation shall be entitled to such compensation as the Board shall from time to time determine.

Section 7 - Delegation of Duties: In the absence or disability of any Officer of the Corporation or for any other reason deemed sufficient by the Board of Directors, the Board may delegate his powers or duties to any other Officer or to any other director.

Section 8 - Shares of Other Corporations: Whenever the Corporation is the holder of shares of any other Corporation, any right or power of the Corporation as such shareholder (including the attendance, acting and voting at shareholders' meetings and execution of waivers, consents, proxies or other instruments) may be exercised on behalf of the Corporation by the President, any Vice President, or such other person as the Board may authorize.

ARTICLE VI - COMMITTEES

The Board of Directors may, by resolution, designate an Executive Committee and one or more other committees. Such committees shall have such functions and may exercise such power of the Board of Directors as can be lawfully delegated, and to the extent provided in the resolution or resolutions creating such committee or committees. Meetings of committees may be held without notice at such time and at such place as shall from time to time be determined by the committees. The committees of the corporation shall keep regular minutes of their proceedings, and report these minutes to the Board of Directors when required.

ARTICLE VII - BOOKS, RECORDS AND REPORTS

Section 1 - Annual Report: The Corporation shall send an annual report to the Members of the Corporation not later than four months after the close of each fiscal year of the Corporation. Such report shall include a balance sheet as of the close of the fiscal year of the Corporation and a revenue and disbursement statement for the year ending on such closing date. Such financial statements shall be prepared from and in accordance with the books of the Corporation, and in conformity with generally accepted accounting principles applied on a consistent basis.

Section 2 - Permanent Records: The Corporation shall keep current and correct records of the accounts, minutes of the meetings and proceedings and membership records of the Corporation. Such records shall be kept at the registered office or the principal place of business of the Corporation. Any such records shall be in written form or in a form capable of being converted into written form.

Section 3 - Inspection of Corporate Records: Any person who is a Voting Member of the Corporation shall have the right at any reasonable time, and on written demand stating the purpose thereof, to examine and make copies from the relevant books and records of accounts, minutes, and records of the Corporation. Upon the written request of any Voting Member, the Corporation shall mail to such Member a copy of the most recent balance sheet and revenue and disbursement statement.

ARTICLE VIII- SHARES OF STOCK

Section 1 - Authorized shares: The Corporation shall be authorized to issue _____ shares of stock in one class only, each with a par value of $_____.

Section 2 - Certificates: Each shareholder of the Corporation shall be entitled to have a certificate representing all shares which he or she owns. The form of such certificate shall be adopted by a majority vote of the Board of Directors and shall be signed by the President and Secretary of the Corporation and sealed with the seal of the Corporation. No certificate representing shares shall be issued until the full amount of consideration therefore has been paid.

Section 3 - Stock Ledger: The Corporation shall maintain a ledger of the stock records of the Corporation. Transfers of shares of the Corporation shall be made on the stock ledger of the Corporation only at the direction of the holder of record upon surrender of the outstanding certificate(s). The Corporation shall be entitled to treat the holder of record of any share or shares as the absolute owner thereof for all purposes and, accordingly, shall not be bound to recognize any legal, equitable or other claim to, or interest in, such share or shares on the part of any other person, whether or not it shall have express or other notice thereof, except as otherwise expressly provided by law.

ARTICLE IX - DIVIDENDS

Upon approval by the Board of Directors the corporation may pay dividends on its shares in the form of cash, property or additional shares at any time that the Corporation is solvent and if such dividends would not render the Corporation insolvent.

ARTICLE X - FISCAL YEAR

The fiscal year of the Corporation shall be the period selected by the Board of Directors as the tax year of the Corporation for federal income tax purposes.

ARTICLE XI - CORPORATE SEAL

The Board of Directors may adopt, use and modify a corporate seal. Failure to affix the seal to corporate documents shall not affect the validity of such document.

ARTICLE XII - AMENDMENTS

The Articles of Incorporation may be amended by the shareholders as provided by Texas statutes. These bylaws may be altered, amended, or replaced by the Board of Directors; provided, however, that any bylaws or amendments thereto as adopted by the Board of Directors may be altered, amended, or repealed by vote of the shareholders. Bylaws adopted by the Members may not be amended or repealed by the Board.

ARTICLE XIII - INDEMNIFICATION

Any officer, director or employee of the Corporation shall be indemnified to the full extent allowed by the laws of the State of Texas.

Certified to be the bylaws of the corporation adopted by the Board of Directors on _____, _____.

_____

Secretary

This page intentionally blank.

BANKING RESOLUTION
OF

_____

The undersigned, being the corporate secretary of the above corporation, hereby certifies that on the _____ day of _____, _____ the Board of Directors of the corporation adopted the following resolution:

RESOLVED that the corporation open bank accounts with _____ and that the officers of the corporation are authorized to take such action as is necessary to open such accounts; that the bank's printed form of resolution is hereby adopted and incorporated into these minutes by reference and shall be placed in the minute book; that any ____ of the following persons shall have signature authority over the account:

_____   _____

_____   _____

and that said resolution has not been modified or rescinded.

Date: _____

_____
Corporate Secretary

(Seal)

This page intentionally blank.

<u>Offer to Purchase Stock</u>

Date: _____

To the Board of Directors of

_____

The undersigned, hereby offers to purchase _____ shares of the
_____ stock of your corporation at a total purchase price of
_____

Very truly yours,

_____

- -

<u>Offer to Sell Stock</u>
Pursuant to Sec. 1244 I.R.C.

Date: _____

To: _____

Dear

The corporation hereby offers to sell to you _____ shares of its common stock at a price of
$_____ per share. These shares are issued pursuant to Section 1244 of the Internal Revenue Code.

Your signature below shall constitute an acceptance of our offer as of the date it is received by the corporation.

Very truly yours,

_____

By:_____

Accepted:

_____

This page intentionally blank.

RESOLUTION
of

_____

a Texas Corporation

RESOLVED that the corporation shall reimburse the following parties for the organizational expenses of the organizers of this corporation and that the corporation shall amortize these expenses as allowed by IRS regulations.

Name	Expense	Amount
_____	_____	$_____
_____	_____	$_____
_____	_____	$_____
_____	_____	$_____
_____	_____	$_____

Date:_____

_____

_____

_____

_____

_____

This page intentionally blank.

BILL OF SALE

The undersigned, in consideration of the issuance of _____ shares of common stock of

_____, a Texas corporation, hereby grants, bargains, sells, transfers

and delivers unto said corporation the following goods and chattels:

To have and to hold the same forever.

And the undersigned, their heirs, successors and administrators, covenant and warrant that they are the lawful own-

ers of the said goods and chattels and that they are free from all encumbrances. That the undersigned have the right to

sell this property and that they will warrant and defend the sale of said property against the lawful claims and demands of

all persons.

IN WITNESS whereof the undersigned have executed this Bill of Sale this _____ day of _____, _____.

_____

_____

_____

This page intentionally blank.

Form **2553**
(Rev. December 2002)

Department of the Treasury
Internal Revenue Service

Election by a Small Business Corporation
(Under section 1362 of the Internal Revenue Code)
▶ See Parts II and III on back and the separate instructions.
▶ The corporation may either send or fax this form to the IRS. See page 2 of the instructions.

OMB No. 1545-0146

Notes: 1. ***Do not* file *Form 1120S,*** *U.S. Income Tax Return for an S Corporation, for any tax year before the year the election takes effect.*

2. *This election to be an S corporation can be accepted only if all the tests are met under **Who May Elect** on page 1 of the instructions; all shareholders have signed the consent statement; and the exact name and address of the corporation and other required form information are provided.*

3. *If the corporation was in existence before the effective date of this election, see **Taxes an S Corporation May Owe** on page 1 of the instructions.*

Part I	**Election Information**		
Please Type or Print	Name of corporation (see instructions)	**A** Employer identification number	
	Number, street, and room or suite no. (If a P.O. box, see instructions.)	**B** Date incorporated	
	City or town, state, and ZIP code	**C** State of incorporation	

D Check the applicable box(es) if the corporation, after applying for the EIN shown in **A** above, changed its name ☐ or address ☐

E Election is to be effective for tax year beginning (month, day, year) . . . . ▶ / /

F Name and title of officer or legal representative who the IRS may call for more information

G Telephone number of officer or legal representative

( )

H If this election takes effect for the first tax year the corporation exists, enter month, day, and year of the **earliest** of the following: (1) date the corporation first had shareholders, (2) date the corporation first had assets, or (3) date the corporation began doing business . . . . ▶ / /

I Selected tax year: Annual return will be filed for tax year ending (month and day) ▶ . . . .

If the tax year ends on any date other than December 31, except for a 52–53-week tax year ending with reference to the month of December, you **must** complete Part II on the back. If the date you enter is the ending date of a 52–53-week tax year, write "52–53-week year" to the right of the date.

J Name and address of each shareholder; shareholder's spouse having a community property interest in the corporation's stock; and each tenant in common, joint tenant, and tenant by the entirety. (A husband and wife (and their estates) are counted as one shareholder in determining the number of shareholders without regard to the manner in which the stock is owned.)	**K** Shareholders' Consent Statement. Under penalties of perjury, we declare that we consent to the election of the above-named corporation to be an S corporation under section 1362(a) and that we have examined this consent statement, including accompanying schedules and statements, and to the best of our knowledge and belief, it is true, correct, and complete. We understand our consent is binding and may not be withdrawn after the corporation has made a valid election. (Shareholders sign and date below.)		**L** Stock owned		**M** Social security number or employer identification number (see instructions)	**N** Shareholder's tax year ends (month and day)
	Signature	Date	Number of shares	Dates acquired		

Under penalties of perjury, I declare that I have examined this election, including accompanying schedules and statements, and to the best of my knowledge and belief, it is true, correct, and complete.

Signature of officer ▶   Title ▶   Date ▶

For Paperwork Reduction Act Notice, see page 4 of the instructions.   Cat. No. 18629R   Form **2553** (Rev. 12-2002)

| **Part II** | Selection of Fiscal Tax Year (All corporations using this part must complete item O and item P, Q, or R.) |

O Check the applicable box to indicate whether the corporation is:

1. ☐ A new corporation adopting the tax year entered in item I, Part I.

2. ☐ An existing corporation retaining the tax year entered in item I, Part I.

3. ☐ An existing corporation changing to the tax year entered in item I, Part I.

P Complete item P if the corporation is using the automatic approval provisions of Rev. Proc. 2002-38, 2002-22 I.R.B. 1037, to request **(1)** a natural business year (as defined in section 5.05 of Rev. Proc. 2002-38) or **(2)** a year that satisfies the ownership tax year test (as defined in section 5.06 of Rev. Proc. 2002-38). Check the applicable box below to indicate the representation statement the corporation is making.

1. Natural Business Year ▶ ☐ I represent that the corporation is adopting, retaining, or changing to a tax year that qualifies as its natural business year as defined in section 5.05 of Rev. Proc. 2002-38 and has attached a statement verifying that it satisfies the 25% gross receipts test (see instructions for content of statement). I also represent that the corporation is not precluded by section 4.02 of Rev. Proc. 2002-38 from obtaining automatic approval of such adoption, retention, or change in tax year.

2. Ownership Tax Year ▶ ☐ I represent that shareholders (as described in section 5.06 of Rev. Proc. 2002-38) holding more than half of the shares of the stock (as of the first day of the tax year to which the request relates) of the corporation have the same tax year or are concurrently changing to the tax year that the corporation adopts, retains, or changes to per item I, Part I, and that such tax year satisfies the requirement of section 4.01(3) of Rev. Proc. 2002-38. I also represent that the corporation is not precluded by section 4.02 of Rev. Proc. 2002-38 from obtaining automatic approval of such adoption, retention, or change in tax year.

Note: *If you do not use item P and the corporation wants a fiscal tax year, complete either item Q or R below. Item Q is used to request a fiscal tax year based on a business purpose and to make a back-up section 444 election. Item R is used to make a regular section 444 election.*

Q Business Purpose- To request a fiscal tax year based on a business purpose, you must check box Q1. See instructions for details including payment of a user fee. You may also check box Q2 and/or box Q3.

1. Check here ▶ ☐ if the fiscal year entered in item I, Part I, is requested under the prior approval provisions of Rev. Proc. 2002-39, 2002-22 I.R.B. 1046. Attach to Form 2553 a statement describing the relevant facts and circumstances and, if applicable, the gross receipts from sales and services necessary to establish a business purpose. See the instructions for details regarding the gross receipts from sales and services. If the IRS proposes to disapprove the requested fiscal year, do you want a conference with the IRS National Office?
☐ Yes   ☐ No

2. Check here ▶ ☐ to show that the corporation intends to make a back-up section 444 election in the event the corporation's business purpose request is not approved by the IRS. (See instructions for more information.)

3. Check here ▶ ☐ to show that the corporation agrees to adopt or change to a tax year ending December 31 if necessary for the IRS to accept this election for S corporation status in the event (1) the corporation's business purpose request is not approved and the corporation makes a back-up section 444 election, but is ultimately not qualified to make a section 444 election, or (2) the corporation's business purpose request is not approved and the corporation did not make a back-up section 444 election.

R Section 444 Election- To make a section 444 election, you must check box R1 and you may also check box R2.

1. Check here ▶ ☐ to show the corporation will make, if qualified, a section 444 election to have the fiscal tax year shown in item I, Part I. To make the election, you must complete **Form 8716,** Election To Have a Tax Year Other Than a Required Tax Year, and either attach it to Form 2553 or file it separately.

2. Check here ▶ ☐ to show that the corporation agrees to adopt or change to a tax year ending December 31 if necessary for the IRS to accept this election for S corporation status in the event the corporation is ultimately not qualified to make a section 444 election.

| **Part III** | Qualified Subchapter S Trust (QSST) Election Under Section 1361(d)(2)* |

Income beneficiary's name and address	Social security number
Trust's name and address	Employer identification number

Date on which stock of the corporation was transferred to the trust (month, day, year) . . . . ▶   /   /

In order for the trust named above to be a QSST and thus a qualifying shareholder of the S corporation for which this Form 2553 is filed, I hereby make the election under section 1361(d)(2). Under penalties of perjury, I certify that the trust meets the definitional requirements of section 1361(d)(3) and that all other information provided in Part III is true, correct, and complete.

_____   _____
Signature of income beneficiary or signature and title of legal representative or other qualified person making the election   Date

*Use Part III to make the QSST election only if stock of the corporation has been transferred to the trust on or before the date on which the corporation makes its election to be an S corporation. The QSST election must be made and filed separately if stock of the corporation is transferred to the trust after the date on which the corporation makes the S election.

Instructions for Form 2553
(Rev. December 2002)

Election by a Small Business Corporation

Section references are to the Internal Revenue Code unless otherwise noted.

Department of the Treasury
Internal Revenue Service

General Instructions

Purpose

To elect to be an S corporation, a corporation must file Form 2553. The election permits the income of the S corporation to be taxed to the shareholders of the corporation rather than to the corporation itself, except as noted below under **Taxes an S Corporation May Owe.**

Who May Elect

A corporation may elect to be an S corporation only if it meets all of the following tests:

1. It is a domestic corporation.

Note: *A limited liability company (LLC) **must** file **Form 8832,** Entity Classification Election, to elect to be treated as an association taxable as a corporation in order to elect to be an S corporation.*

2. It has no more than 75 shareholders. A husband and wife (and their estates) are treated as one shareholder for this requirement. All other persons are treated as separate shareholders.

3. Its only shareholders are individuals, estates, exempt organizations described in section 401(a) or 501(c)(3), or certain trusts described in section 1361(c)(2)(A). See the instructions for Part III regarding qualified subchapter S trusts (QSSTs).

A trustee of a trust wanting to make an election under section 1361(e)(3) to be an electing small business trust (ESBT) should see Notice 97-12, 1997-1 C.B. 385. However, in general, for tax years beginning after May 13, 2002, Notice 97-12 is superseded by Regulations section 1.1361-1(c)(1). Also see Rev. Proc. 98-23, 1998-1 C.B. 662, for guidance on how to convert a QSST to an ESBT. However, in general, for tax years beginning after May 13, 2002, Rev. Proc. 98-23 is superseded by Regulations section 1.1361-1(j)(12). If there was an inadvertent failure to timely file an ESBT election, see the relief provisions under Rev. Proc. 98-55, 1998-2 C.B. 643.

4. It has no nonresident alien shareholders.

5. It has only one class of stock (disregarding differences in voting rights). Generally, a corporation is treated as having only one class of stock if all outstanding shares of the corporation's stock confer identical rights to distribution and liquidation proceeds. See Regulations section 1.1361-1(l) for details.

6. It is not one of the following ineligible corporations:

a. A bank or thrift institution that uses the reserve method of accounting for bad debts under section 585,

b. An insurance company subject to tax under the rules of subchapter L of the Code,

c. A corporation that has elected to be treated as a possessions corporation under section 936, or

d. A domestic international sales corporation (DISC) or former DISC.

7. It has a permitted tax year as required by section 1378 or makes a section 444 election to have a tax year other than a permitted tax year. Section 1378 defines a permitted tax year as a tax year ending December 31, or any other tax year for which the corporation establishes a business purpose to the satisfaction of the IRS. See Part II for details on requesting a fiscal tax year based on a business purpose or on making a section 444 election.

8. Each shareholder consents as explained in the instructions for column K.

See sections 1361, 1362, and 1378 for additional information on the above tests.

A parent S corporation can elect to treat an eligible wholly-owned subsidiary as a qualified subchapter S subsidiary (QSub). If the election is made, the assets, liabilities, and items of income, deduction, and credit of the QSub are treated as those of the parent. To make the election, get **Form 8869,** Qualified Subchapter S Subsidiary Election. If the QSub election was not timely filed, the corporation may be entitled to relief under Rev. Proc. 98-55.

Taxes an S Corporation May Owe

An S corporation may owe income tax in the following instances:

1. If, at the end of any tax year, the corporation had accumulated earnings and profits, and its passive investment income under section 1362(d)(3) is more than 25% of its gross receipts, the corporation may owe tax on its excess net passive income.

2. A corporation with net recognized built-in gain (as defined in section 1374(d)(2)) may owe tax on its built-in gains.

3. A corporation that claimed investment credit before its first year as an S corporation will be liable for any investment credit recapture tax.

4. A corporation that used the LIFO inventory method for the year immediately preceding its first year as an S corporation may owe an additional tax due to LIFO recapture. The tax is paid in four equal installments, the first of which must be paid by the due date (not including extensions) of the corporation's income tax return for its last tax year as a C corporation.

For more details on these taxes, see the Instructions for Form 1120S.

Where To File

Send the original election (no photocopies) or fax it to the Internal Revenue Service Center listed below. If the corporation files this election by fax, keep the original Form 2553 with the corporation's permanent records.

If the corporation's principal business, office, or agency is located in	Use the following Internal Revenue Service Center address or fax number ▼
Connecticut, Delaware, District of Columbia, Illinois, Indiana, Kentucky, Maine, Maryland, Massachusetts, Michigan, New Hampshire, New Jersey, New York, North Carolina, Ohio, Pennsylvania, Rhode Island, South Carolina, Vermont, Virginia, West Virginia, Wisconsin	Cincinnati, OH 45999 (859) 669-5748
Alabama, Alaska, Arizona, Arkansas, California, Colorado, Florida, Georgia, Hawaii, Idaho, Iowa, Kansas, Louisiana, Minnesota, Mississippi, Missouri, Montana, Nebraska, Nevada, New Mexico, North Dakota, Oklahoma, Oregon, South Dakota, Tennessee, Texas, Utah, Washington, Wyoming	Ogden, UT 84201 (801) 620-7116

When To Make the Election

Complete and file Form 2553 **(a)** at any time before the 16th day of the 3rd month of the tax year, if filed during the tax year the election is to take effect, or **(b)** at any time during the preceding tax year. An election made no later than 2 months and 15 days after the beginning of a tax year that is less than 2½ months long is treated as timely made for that tax year. **An election made after the 15th day of the 3rd month but before the end of the tax year is effective for the next year.** For example, if a calendar tax year corporation makes the election in April 2002, it is effective for the corporation's 2003 calendar tax year.

However, an election made after the due date will be accepted as timely filed if the corporation can show that the failure to file on time was due to reasonable cause. To request relief for a late election, the corporation generally must request a private letter ruling and pay a user fee in accordance with Rev. Proc. 2002-1, 2002-1 I.R.B. 1 (or its successor). But if the election is filed within 12 months of its due date and the original due date for filing the corporation's initial Form 1120S has not passed, the ruling and user fee requirements do not apply. To

request relief in this case, write "FILED PURSUANT TO REV. PROC. 98-55" at the top of page 1 of Form 2553, attach a statement explaining the reason for failing to file the election on time, and file Form 2553 as otherwise instructed. See Rev. Proc. 98-55 for more details.

See Regulations section 1.1362-6(b)(3)(iii) for how to obtain relief for an inadvertent invalid election if the corporation filed a timely election, but one or more shareholders did not file a timely consent.

Acceptance or Nonacceptance of Election

The service center will notify the corporation if its election is accepted and when it will take effect. The corporation will also be notified if its election is not accepted. The corporation should generally receive a determination on its election within 60 days after it has filed Form 2553. If box Q1 in Part II is checked on page 2, the corporation will receive a ruling letter from the IRS in Washington, DC, that either approves or denies the selected tax year. When box Q1 is checked, it will generally take an additional 90 days for the Form 2553 to be accepted.

Care should be exercised to ensure that the IRS receives the election. If the corporation is not notified of acceptance or nonacceptance of its election within 3 months of the date of filing (date mailed), or within 6 months if box Q1 is checked, take follow-up action by corresponding with the service center where the corporation filed the election.

If the IRS questions whether Form 2553 was filed, an acceptable proof of filing is **(a)** certified or registered mail receipt (timely postmarked) from the U.S. Postal Service, or its equivalent from a designated private delivery service (see Notice 2002-62, 2002-39 I.R.B. 574 (or its successor)); **(b)** Form 2553 with accepted stamp; **(c)** Form 2553 with stamped IRS received date; or **(d)** IRS letter stating that Form 2553 has been accepted.

 Do not file Form 1120S for any tax year before the year the election takes effect. If the corporation is now required to file **Form 1120,** *U.S. Corporation Income Tax Return, or any other applicable tax return, continue filing it until the election takes effect.*

End of Election

Once the election is made, it stays in effect until it is terminated. If the election is terminated in a tax year beginning after 1996, IRS consent is generally required for another election by the corporation (or a successor corporation) on Form 2553 for any tax year before the 5th tax year after the first tax year in which the termination took effect. See Regulations section 1.1362-5 for details.

Specific Instructions

Part I (*All corporations must complete.*)

Name and Address of Corporation

Enter the true corporate name as stated in the corporate charter or other legal document creating it. If the corporation's mailing address is the same as someone else's, such as a shareholder's, enter "c/o" and this person's name following the name of the corporation. Include the suite, room, or other unit number after the street address. If the Post Office does not deliver to the street address and the corporation has a P.O. box, show the box number instead of the street address. If the corporation changed its name or address after applying for its employer identification number, be sure to check the box in item D of Part I.

Item A. Employer Identification Number (EIN)

If the corporation has applied for an EIN but has not received it, enter "applied for." If the corporation does not have an EIN, it should apply for one on **Form SS-4,** Application for Employer Identification Number. You can order Form SS-4 by calling 1-800-TAX-FORM (1-800-829-3676) or by accessing the IRS Web Site **www.irs.gov**.

Item E. Effective Date of Election

Enter the beginning effective date (month, day, year) of the tax year requested for the S corporation. Generally, this will be the beginning date of the tax year for which the ending effective date is required to be shown in item I, Part I. For a new corporation (first year the corporation exists) it will generally be the date required to be shown in item H, Part I. The tax year of a new corporation starts on the date that it has shareholders, acquires assets, or begins doing business, whichever happens first. If the effective date for item E for a newly formed corporation is later than the date in item H, the corporation should file Form 1120 or Form 1120-A for the tax period between these dates.

Column K. Shareholders' Consent Statement

Each shareholder who owns (or is deemed to own) stock at the time the election is made must consent to the election. If the election is made during the corporation's tax year for which it first takes effect, any person who held stock at any time during the part of that year that occurs before the election is made, must consent to the election, even though the person may have sold or transferred his or her stock before the election is made.

An election made during the first 2$\frac{1}{2}$ months of the tax year is effective for the following tax year if any person who held stock in the corporation during the part of the tax year before the election was made, and who did not hold stock at the time the election was made, did not consent to the election.

Note: *Once the election is made, a new shareholder is not required to consent to the election; a new Form 2553 will not be required.*

Each shareholder consents by signing and dating in column K or signing and dating a separate consent statement described below. The following special rules apply in determining who must sign the consent statement.
- If a husband and wife have a community interest in the stock or in the income from it, both must consent.
- Each tenant in common, joint tenant, and tenant by the entirety must consent.
- A minor's consent is made by the minor, legal representative of the minor, or a natural or adoptive parent of the minor if no legal representative has been appointed.
- The consent of an estate is made by the executor or administrator.
- The consent of an electing small business trust is made by the trustee.
- If the stock is owned by a trust (other than an electing small business trust), the deemed owner of the trust must consent. See section 1361(c)(2) for details regarding trusts that are permitted to be shareholders and rules for determining who is the deemed owner.

Continuation sheet or separate consent statement. If you need a continuation sheet or use a separate consent statement, attach it to Form 2553. The separate consent statement must contain the name, address, and EIN of the corporation and the shareholder information requested in columns J through N of Part I. If you want, you may combine all the shareholders' consents in one statement.

Column L

Enter the number of shares of stock each shareholder owns and the dates the stock was acquired. If the election is made during the corporation's tax year for which it first takes effect, do not list the shares of stock for those shareholders who sold or transferred all of their stock before the election was made. However, these shareholders must still consent to the election for it to be effective for the tax year.

Column M

Enter the social security number of each shareholder who is an individual. Enter the EIN of each shareholder that is an estate, a qualified trust, or an exempt organization.

Column N

Enter the month and day that each shareholder's tax year ends. If a shareholder is changing his or her tax year, enter the tax year the shareholder is changing to, and attach an explanation indicating the present tax year and the basis for the change (e.g., automatic revenue procedure or letter ruling request).

Signature

Form 2553 must be signed by the president, treasurer, assistant treasurer, chief accounting officer, or other corporate officer (such as tax officer) authorized to sign.

Part II

Complete Part II if you selected a tax year ending on any date other than December 31 (other than a 52-53-week tax year ending with reference to the month of December).

Note: *In certain circumstances the corporation may not obtain automatic approval of a fiscal year under the natural business year (Box P1) or ownership tax year (Box P2) provisions if it is under examination, before an area office, or before a federal court with respect to any income tax issue and the annual accounting period is under consideration. For details, see section 4.02 of Rev. Proc. 2002-38, 2002-22 I.R.B. 1037.*

Box P1

Attach a statement showing separately for each month the amount of gross receipts for the most recent 47 months. A corporation that does not have a 47-month period of gross receipts cannot automatically establish a natural business year.

Box Q1

For examples of an acceptable business purpose for requesting a fiscal tax year, see section 5.02 of Rev. Proc. 2002-39, 2002-22 I.R.B. 1046, and Rev. Rul. 87-57, 1987-2 C.B. 117.

Attach a statement showing the relevant facts and circumstances to establish a business purpose for the requested fiscal year. For details on what is sufficient to establish a business purpose, see section 5.02 of Rev. Proc. 2002-39.

If your business purpose is based on one of the natural business year tests provided in section 5.03 of Rev. Proc. 2002-39, identify if you are using the 25% gross receipts, annual business cycle, or seasonal business test. For the 25% gross receipts test, provide a schedule showing the amount of gross receipts for each month for the most recent 47 months. For either the annual business cycle or seasonal business test, provide the gross receipts from sales and services (and inventory costs, if applicable) for each month of the short period, if any, and the three immediately preceding tax years. If the corporation has been in existence for less than three tax years, submit figures for the period of existence.

If you check box Q1, you will be charged a user fee of up to $600 (subject to change—see Rev. Proc. 2002-1 or its successor). Do not pay the fee when filing Form 2553. The service center will send Form 2553 to the IRS in Washington, DC, who, in turn, will notify the corporation that the fee is due.

Box Q2

If the corporation makes a back-up section 444 election for which it is qualified, then the election will take effect in the event the business purpose request is not approved. In some cases, the tax year requested under the back-up section 444 election may be different than the tax year requested under business purpose. See **Form 8716,** Election To Have a Tax Year Other Than a Required Tax Year, for details on making a back-up section 444 election.

Boxes Q2 and R2

If the corporation is not qualified to make the section 444 election after making the item Q2 back-up section 444 election or indicating its intention to make the election in item R1, and therefore it later files a calendar year return, it should write "Section 444 Election Not Made" in the top left corner of the first calendar year Form 1120S it files.

Part III

Certain qualified subchapter S trusts (QSSTs) may make the QSST election required by section 1361(d)(2) in Part III. Part III may be used to make the QSST election only if corporate stock has been transferred to the trust on or before the date on which the corporation makes its election to be an S corporation. However, a statement can be used instead of Part III to make the election. If there was an inadvertent failure to timely file a QSST election, see the relief provisions under Rev. Proc. 98-55.

Note: *Use Part III only if you make the election in Part I (i.e., Form 2553 cannot be filed with only Part III completed).*

The deemed owner of the QSST must also consent to the S corporation election in column K, page 1, of Form 2553. See section 1361(c)(2).

Paperwork Reduction Act Notice. We ask for the information on this form to carry out the Internal Revenue laws of the United States. You are required to give us the information. We need it to ensure that you are complying with these laws and to allow us to figure and collect the right amount of tax.

You are not required to provide the information requested on a form that is subject to the Paperwork Reduction Act unless the form displays a valid OMB control number. Books or records relating to a form or its instructions must be retained as long as their contents may become material in the administration of any Internal Revenue law. Generally, tax returns and return information are confidential, as required by section 6103.

The time needed to complete and file this form will depend on individual circumstances. The estimated average time is:

Recordkeeping	9 hr., 34 min.
Learning about the law or the form	3 hr., 28 min.
Preparing, copying, assembling, and sending the form to the IRS	3 hr., 47 min.

If you have comments concerning the accuracy of these time estimates or suggestions for making this form simpler, we would be happy to hear from you. You can write to the Tax Forms Committee, Western Area Distribution Center, Rancho Cordova, CA 95743-0001. **Do not** send the form to this address. Instead, see **Where To File** on page 2.

RESOLUTION
of

_____

a Texas Corporation

RESOLVED that the corporation elects "S-Corporation" status for tax purposes under the Internal Revenue Code and that the officers of the corporation are directed to file IRS Form 2553 and to take any further action necessary for the corporation to qualify for S-corporation status.

Shareholders' Consent

The undersigned shareholders being all of the shareholders of the above corporation, a _____ corporation hereby consent to the election of the corporation to obtain S-corporation status

Name and Address of Shareholder	Shares Owned	Date Acquired
_____	_____	_____
_____	_____	_____
_____	_____	_____

Date:_____

_____

_____

_____

_____

_____

This page intentionally blank.

WAIVER OF NOTICE OF THE ANNUAL MEETING OF THE BOARD OF DIRECTORS OF

_____

The undersigned, being all the Directors of the Corporation, hereby agree and consent that an annual meeting of the Board of Directors of the Corporation be held on the _____ day of _____, _____ at _____ o'clock ____M. at _____ and do hereby waive all notice whatsoever of such meeting and of any adjournment or adjournments thereof.

We do further agree and consent that any and all lawful business may be transacted at such meeting or at any adjournment or adjournments thereof as may be deemed advisable by the Directors present. Any business transacted at such meeting or at any adjournment or adjournments thereof shall be as valid and legal as if such meeting or adjourned meeting were held after notice.

Date: _____

_____
Director

_____
Director

_____
Director

_____
Director

This page intentionally blank.

MINUTES OF THE ANNUAL MEETING OF
THE BOARD OF DIRECTORS OF

_____

The annual meeting of the Board of Directors of the Corporation was held on the date and at the time and place set forth in the written waiver of notice signed by the directors, and attached to the minutes of this meeting.

The following were present, being all the directors of the Corporation:

_____   _____

_____   _____

The meeting was called to order and it was moved, seconded and unanimously carried that _____ act as Chairman and that _____ act as Secretary.

The minutes of the last meeting of the Board of Directors which was held on _____, _____ were read and approved by the Board.

Upon motion duly made, seconded and carried, the following were elected officers for the following year and until their successors are elected and qualify:

President:
Vice President:
Secretary
Treasurer:

There being no further business to come before the meeting, upon motion duly made, seconded, and unanimously carried, it was adjourned.

_____
Secretary

Directors:

_____

_____

_____

_____

This page intentionally blank.

WAIVER OF NOTICE OF THE ANNUAL MEETING OF
THE SHAREHOLDERS OF

_____

The undersigned, being all the shareholders of the Corporation, hereby agree and consent that an annual meeting of the shareholders of the Corporation be held on the _____ day of _____, _____ at _____ o'clock ____M. at _____ and do hereby waive all notice whatsoever of such meeting and of any adjournment or adjournments thereof.

We do further agree and consent that any and all lawful business may be transacted at such meeting or at any adjournment or adjournments thereof. Any business transacted at such meeting or at any adjournment or adjournments thereof shall be as valid and legal as if such meeting or adjourned meeting were held after notice.

Date: _____

_____
Shareholder

_____
Shareholder

_____
Shareholder

_____
Shareholder

This page intentionally blank.

MINUTES OF THE ANNUAL MEETING OF
SHAREHOLDERS OF

_____

The annual meeting of Shareholders of the Corporation was held on the date and at the time and place set forth in the written waiver of notice signed by the shareholders, and attached to the minutes of this meeting.

There were present the following shareholders:

Shareholder   No. of Shares

_____   _____

_____   _____

_____   _____

_____   _____

The meeting was called to order and it was moved, seconded, and unanimously carried that _____ act as Chairman and that _____ act as Secretary.

A roll call was taken and the Chairman noted that all of the outstanding shares of the Corporation were represented in person or by proxy. Any proxies were attached to these minutes.

The minutes of the last meeting of the shareholders which was held on _____, _____ were read and approved by the shareholders.

Upon motion duly made, seconded and carried, the following were elected directors for the following year:

_____   _____

_____   _____

There being no further business to come before the meeting, upon motion duly made, seconded, and unanimously carried, it was adjourned.

_____
Secretary

Shareholders:

_____

_____

_____

_____

This page intentionally blank.

WAIVER OF NOTICE OF SPECIAL MEETING OF
THE BOARD OF DIRECTORS OF

_____

The undersigned, being all the Directors of the Corporation, hereby agree and consent that a special meeting of the Board of Directors of the Corporation be held on the _____ day of _____, _____ at ____ o'clock ___M. at _____ and do hereby waive all notice whatsoever of such meeting and of any adjournment or adjournments thereof.

The purpose of the meeting is:

We do further agree and consent that any and all lawful business may be transacted at such meeting or at any adjournment or adjournments thereof as may be deemed advisable by the Directors present. Any business transacted at such meeting or at any adjournment or adjournments thereof shall be as valid and legal as if such meeting or adjourned meeting were held after notice.

Date: _____

_____
Director

_____
Director

_____
Director

_____
Director

This page intentionally blank.

MINUTES OF SPECIAL MEETING OF
THE BOARD OF DIRECTORS OF

_____

A special meeting of the Board of Directors of the Corporation was held on the date and at the time and place set forth in the written waiver of notice signed by the directors, and attached to the minutes of this meeting.

The following were present, being all the directors of the Corporation:

_____   _____

_____   _____

The meeting was called to order and it was moved, seconded and unanimously carried that _____ act as Chairman and that _____ act as Secretary.

The minutes of the last meeting of the Board of Directors which was held on _____, _____ were read and approved by the Board.

Upon motion duly made, seconded and carried, the following resolution was adopted:

There being no further business to come before the meeting, upon motion duly made, seconded, and unanimously carried, it was adjourned.

_____
Secretary

Directors:

_____

_____

_____

_____

This page intentionally blank.

WAIVER OF NOTICE OF SPECIAL MEETING OF
THE SHAREHOLDERS OF

_____

The undersigned, being all the shareholders of the Corporation, hereby agree and consent that a special meeting of the shareholders of the Corporation be held on the _____ day of _____, _____ at ____ o'clock ___M. at _____ and do hereby waive all notice whatsoever of such meeting and of any adjournment or adjournments thereof.

The purpose of the meeting is

We do further agree and consent that any and all lawful business may be transacted at such meeting or at any adjournment or adjournments thereof. Any business transacted at such meeting or at any adjournment or adjournments thereof shall be as valid and legal as if such meeting or adjourned meeting were held after notice.

Date: _____

_____
Shareholder

_____
Shareholder

_____
Shareholder

_____
Shareholder

This page intentionally blank.

MINUTES OF SPECIAL MEETING OF
SHAREHOLDERS OF

_____

A special meeting of Shareholders of the Corporation was held on the date and at the time and place set forth in the written waiver of notice signed by the shareholders, and attached to the minutes of this meeting.

There were present the following shareholders:

Shareholder   No. of Shares

_____   _____

_____   _____

_____   _____

_____   _____

The meeting was called to order and it was moved, seconded and unanimously carried that _____ act as Chairman and that _____ act as Secretary.

A roll call was taken and the Chairman noted that all of the outstanding shares of the Corporation were represented in person or by proxy. Any proxies were attached to these minutes.

The minutes of the last meeting of the shareholders which was held on _____, _____ were read and approved by the shareholders.

Upon motion duly made, seconded and carried, the following resolution was adopted:

There being no further business to come before the meeting, upon motion duly made, seconded, and unanimously carried, it was adjourned.

_____
Secretary

Shareholders:

_____

_____

_____

This page intentionally blank.

Office of the Secretary of State
Corporations Section P.O. Box 13697
Austin, TX 78711-3697

ARTICLES OF DISSOLUTION
BY INCORPORATORS OR DIRECTORS
(Article 6.01)

1. The name of the corporation is _____

    The file number is _____

2. The date of issuance of its certificate of incorporation was_____

3. None of its shares have been issues.

4. The corporation has not commenced business

5. The amount if any, actually paid on subscriptions for the corporation's shares (if any), less the amount paid for necessary expenses, has been returned to those entitled to receive it.

6. No debts of the corporation remain unpaid.

7. Check either A or B below; do not check both:

4. ☐   A. A majority of the directors elect that the corporation be dissolved. (A director is a person authorized to manage and direct the activities of the corporation).

    or

    ☐   B. A majority of the incorporators elect that the corporation be dissolved (An incorporator is a person who signed the articles of incorporation)

    _____

    _____

    _____

    _____

(Must be signed by a majority of directors if 7A is checked or by a majority of incorporators if 7B is checked)

INSTRUCTIONS FOR FILING ARTICLES OF DISSOLUTION
WHEN NO SHARES HAVE BEEN ISSUED
AND THE CORPORATION HAS NOT COMMENCED BUSINESS

1. If the corporation has been issued shares <u>or</u> commenced business, obtain and file an article 6.06 dissolution form; DO NOT FILE THIS FORM.

2. Attach certificate #05-305 or #05-329 from the Comptroller of Public Accounts indicating that all franchise taxes have been paid and the corporation is in good standing for all purposes of dissolution. <u>The articles of dissolution cannot be filed without a current certificate.</u> Requests for certificates or questions on tax status should be directed to the Comptroller of Public Accounts, Tax Assistance Section, Austin, Texas 78774-0100. The phone number is (512) 463-4600 or (800) 252-1381. TDD: (800) 248-4099 or (512) 463-4621.

    NOTE: The franchise tax year ends on December 31st. The corporation must be in good standing through the date of receipt of the articles of dissolution by the secretary of state. A post mark date will not be considered as the date of receipt.

    Documents are not received on Saturdays, Sundays or legal holidays. If December 31st falls on a Saturday, Sunday, or legal holiday, the documents must be received no later than the last business day before December 31st. It is suggested that corporations attempting to dissolve prior to the end of the franchise tax year on December 31st, make their submissions well in advance of such tax deadline. Corporations not dissolved on or before December 31st will automatically be subject to the new franchise tax year's requirements as of January 1st.

    Submissions which are incorrect or incomplete in any manner cannot be filed and will be returned. The effective date of filing is the date of receipt of the re-submission of a document which conforms to law.

3. Enclose $40.00 remittance for the filing fee for the articles of dissolution. The check should be made payable to the secretary of state.

4. Two copies of this form along with the filing fee should be mailed to the address shown in the heading of this form. The delivery address is James Earl Rudder Office Building, 1019 Brazos, Austin, Texas 78701. We will place one document on record and return a file stamped copy. The telephone number is (512) 463-5555, TDD: (800) 735-2989, FAX: (512) 463-5709.

5. Under article 10.03 of the Texas Business Corporation Act, a business may choose to make the filing of certain documents effective as of a date within 90 days of the date of submission. This can be accomplished by stating either a future date or describing a future event within the document submitted for filing. Please refer to article 10.03 of the TBCA for the specific requirements necessary for filing documents with a future effective date.

Form No. 601
Revised 9/96

Office of the Secretary of State
Corporations Section P.O. Box 13697
Austin, TX 78711-3697

ARTICLES OF DISSOLUTION
BUSINESS CORPORATION

Pursuant to the provisions of article 6.06 of the Texas Business Corporation Act, the undersigned corporation adopts the following articles of dissolution:

1. The name of the corporation is _____

2. The file number is _____

NAME	OFFICE HELD	ADDRESS
_____	_____	_____
_____	_____	_____
_____	_____	_____

3. The names and respective addresses of its directors are as follows:

NAME	ADDRESS
_____	_____
_____	_____
_____	_____

YOU MUST CHECK EITHER BOX A OR B IN ITEMS FOUR THROUGH SIX

4. ☐ A. A written consent to dissolve was signed by all shareholders of the corporation or was signed in their names by their attorneys thereunto duly authorized.

or

☐ B. A resolution to dissolve was adopted by not less than a two-thirds vote of the shareholders of the corporation on the following date:_____

The number of shares outstanding and entitled to vote, and voting for and against the dissolution were as follows:

CLASS	SERIES	OUTSTANDING AND ENTITLED TO VOTE	TOTAL VOTED FOR	TOTAL VOTED AGAINST
_____	_____	_____	_____	_____
_____	_____	_____	_____	_____

5. ☐ A. All debts, liabilities and obligations of the corporation have been paid, satisfied, or discharged or adequate provision has been made for payment, satisfaction, or discharge thereof.

or

☐ B. The properties and assets of the corporation were not sufficient to pay, satisfy, or discharge all of the corporation's debts, liabilities, and obligations. All properties and assets of the corporation have been applied so far as they would go to the just and equitable payment of those debts, liabilities, and obligations or adequate provision has been made for such application.

6. ☐ A. The remainder of the properties and assets of the corporation have been distributed to its shareholders according to their respective rights and interests.

or

☐ B. No properties or assets of the corporation remained for distribution to shareholders after applying the properties and assets of the corporation so far as they would go to the just and equitable payment of the debts, liabilities, and obligations of the corporation or making adequate provision for such application.

By _____ Officer   Title: _____

INSTRUCTIONS

1. Attach certificate #05-305 from the comptroller of public accounts indicating that all taxes have been paid and the corporation is in good standing for the purpose of dissolution. Requests for certificates or questions on tax status should be directed to the Tax Assistance Section, Comptroller of Public Accounts, Austin, Texas 78774-0100; (512) 463-4600; toll-free (800) 252-1381; TDD: (800) 248-4099.

2. The franchise tax year ends on December 31st. The corporation must be in good standing through the date of receipt of the article of dissolution by the secretary of state. A post mark date will not be considered as the date of receipt. If December 31st falls on a Saturday, Sunday, or legal holiday, the documents must be received no later than the last business day before December 31st. It is suggested that corporations attempting to dissolve prior to the end of the franchise tax year make their submissions well in advance of such tax deadline. Corporations not dissolved on or before December 31st will be subject to the new franchise tax year's requirements as of January 1st. Submissions which are incorrect or incomplete in any manner cannot be filed and will be returned. The effective date of filing is the date of receipt of the resubmission of a complete document which conforms to law.

3. Send a $40 payment for the filing fee along with two copies of the articles of dissolution, and the certificate from the Comptroller of public accounts to the Secretary of State, Statutory Filings Division, Corporations Section, P.O. Box 13697, Austin, Texas 78711-3697. The delivery address is 1019 Brazos, Austin, Texas 78701. We will place one document on record and, *if a duplicate copy has been provided for such purpose,* return a file stamped copy. The telephone number is (512) 463-5555, TDD: (800) 735-2989, FAX: (512) 463-5709.

4. The attached form promulgated by the secretary of state is designed to meet minimum statutory filing requirements and no warranty is made regarding the suitability of this form for any particular purpose. This form and the information provided are not substitutes for the advice of an attorney and it is recommended that the services of an attorney be obtained before preparation of the articles of dissolution.

Form No. 602
Revised 9/99

WRITTEN CONSENT OF SHAREHOLDERS
of

_____

a Texas Corporation

The undersigned shareholders, being all of the shareholders of the above corporation, a Texas Corporation, hereby consent to the dissolution of the corporation and authorize the officers of the corporation to take all steps necessary to liquidate the corporation in accordance with article 6.06 of the Texas Business Corporation Act.

Name and Address of Shareholder   Shares Owned

_____   _____
_____   _____
_____   _____
_____   _____

Date:_____   SHAREHOLDERS SIGNATURES

This page intentionally blank.

RESOLUTION OF DIRECTORS
of

_____

a Texas Corporation

RESOLVED, the undersigned, being all of the directors of the corporation have deemed that it is in the best interests of the corporation and its shareholders that the corporation be dissolved pursuant to article 6.06 of the Texas Business Corporation Act and that the corporation be liquidated, the directors hereby adopt the following resolution to be voted upon by the shareholders of the corporation at a special meeting of shareholders to be held _____,_____.

      RESOLVED, that the corporation be dissolved in accordance with article 6.06 of the Texas Business Corporation Act on or before _____, _____;

      RESOLVED FURTHER, that the officers of the corporation will take necessary and normal steps required to liquidate the assets and properties of the corporation, pay, satisfy or discharge all of the corporation's debts, liabilities and obligations, and distribute any remaining assets appropriately.

Signed this _____ day of _____, _____ by the undersigned directors.

DIRECTORS:

This page intentionally blank.

VOTE OF SHAREHOLDERS
of

_____

a Texas corporation

The attached RESOLUTION of the Directors of _____, a Texas corporation, for the dissolution of the corporation, being presented to the Shareholders at a special meeting of the Shareholders on _____, was voted upon by the Shareholders present at the meeting, by proxy, whether written or through an authorized attorney.

The Resolution was adopted by not less than two-thirds of the Shareholders of the corporation. The results of the vote are recorded as follows:

CLASS	OUTSTANDING AND ENTITLED TO VOTE	TOTAL VOTED FOR	TOTAL VOTED AGAINST
_____	_____	_____	_____
_____	_____	_____	_____

Signed this_____ day of_____, _____.

By:_____
             Secretary

This page intentionally blank.

Office of the Secretary of State
Corporations Section P.O. Box 13697
Austin, TX 78711-3697

CHANGE OF REGISTERED AGENT/REGISTERED OFFICE

1. The name of the entity is _____ and the file number issued to the entity by the secretary of state is _____

2. The entity is: (Check one.)

   ☐ a *business corporation*, which has authorized the changes indicated below through its board of directors or by an officer of the corporation so authorized by its board of directors, as provided by the Texas Business Corporation Act.

   ☐ a *non-profit corporation*, which has authorized the changes indicate below through its board of directors or by an officer of the corporation so authorized by its board of directors, or through its members in whom management of the corporation is vested pursuant to article 2.14C, as provided by the Texas Non-Profit Corporation Act.

   ☐ a *limited liability company*, which has authorized the changes indicated below through its members or managers, as provided by the Texas Limited Liability Company Act.

   ☐ a *limited partnership*, which has authorized the changes indicated below through its partners, as provided by the Texas Revised Limited Partnership Act.

   ☐ an *out-of-state financial institution*, which has authorized the changes indicated below in the manner provided under the laws governing its formation.

3. The registered office address is PRESENTLY shown in the records of the Texas secretary of state is _____

4. ☐ **A.** The address of the NEW registered office is: (Please provide street address, city, state and zip code. The address must be in Texas.)

   _____

   or

   ☐ **B.** The registered office address will not change.

5. The name of the registered agent as PRESENTLY shown in the records of the Texas secretary of state is _____

6. ☐ **A.** The name of the NEW registered agent is _____

   or

   ☐ **B.** The registered agent will not change.

7. Following the changes shown above, the address of the registered office and the address of the office of the registered agent will continue to be identical, as required by law.

By: _____

(A person authorized to sign
on behalf of the entity)

INSTRUCTIONS

1. it is recommended that you call (512) 463-5555 to verify the information in items 3 and 5 as it currently appears on the records of the secretary of state before submitting the statement for filing. You also may e-mail an inquiry to *corpinfo@sos.state.tx.us*. As information on out-of-state financial institutions is maintained on a separate database, a financial institution must call (512) 463-5701 to verify registered agent and registered office information. If the information on the form is inconsistent with the records of this office, the statement will be returned.

2. You are required by law to provide a street address in item 4 unless the registered office is located in a city with a population of 5,000 or less. The purpose of this requirement is to provide the public with notice of a physical location at which process may be served on the registered agent. A statement submitted with a post office box address or a lock box address will not be filed.

3. An authorized officer of the corporation or financial institution must sign the statement. In the case of a limited liability company, an authorized member or manager of a limited liability company must sign eh statement. A general partner must sign the statement on behalf of a limited partnership. A person commits an offense under the Texas Business Corporation Act, the Texas Non-Profit Corporation Act or the Texas Limited Liability Company Act if the person signs a document the person knows is false in any material respect with the intent that the document be delivered to the secretary of state for filing. The offense is a Class A misdemeanor.

4. Please attach the appropriate fee:

Business Corporation	$15.00
Financial Institution, other than Credit Unions	$15.00
Financial Institution that is a Credit Union	$ 5.00
Non-Profit Corporation	$ 5.00
Limited Liability Company	$10.00
Limited Partnership	$50.00

    Personal checks and MasterCard®, Visa®, and Discover® are accepted in payment of the filing fee. Checks or money orders must be payable through a U.S. bank or other financial institution and made payable to the secretary of state. Fees paid by credit card are subject to a statutorily authorized processing cost 2.1% of the total fees.

5. Two copies of the form along with the filing fee should be mailed to the address shown in the heading on this form. The delivery address is: Secretary of State, Statutory Filings Division, Corporations Section, James Earl Rudder Building, 1019 Brazos, Austin, Texas 78701. We will place one document on record and return a file stamped copy, if a duplicate is provided for such purpose. The telephone number is (512) 463-5555, TDD: (800) 735-2989, FAX: (512) 463-5709.

Form No. 401
Revised 9/99

Stock Transfer Ledger

Certificates Issued

Transfer of Shares

Cert. No.	No. of Shares	Date of Acquisition	Shareholder Name and Address	From Whom Transferred	Amount Paid	Date of Transfer	To Whom Transferred	Cert. No. Surrendered	No. of Shares Transferred	Cert. No.

This page intentionally blank.

Certificate No.
No. of shares
Dated
Issued to:

☐ Original issue
Documentary stamp tax paid:
$
(Attach stamps to this stub.)

☐ Transferred from:
Date:

Original Cert. No.	Original No. Shares	No. of Shares Transferred

Received Cert. No.
No. of shares
New certificates issued:

Cert. No.	No. of Shares

Certificate No.
No. of shares
Dated
Issued to:

☐ Original issue
Documentary stamp tax paid:
$
(Attach stamps to this stub.)

☐ Transferred from:
Date:

Original Cert. No.	Original No. Shares	No. of Shares Transferred

Received Cert. No.
No. of shares
New certificates issued:

Cert. No.	No. of Shares

Certificate No.
No. of shares
Dated
Issued to:

☐ Original issue
Documentary stamp tax paid:
$
(Attach stamps to this stub.)

☐ Transferred from:
Date:

Original Cert. No.	Original No. Shares	No. of Shares Transferred

Received Cert. No.
No. of shares
New certificates issued:

Cert. No.	No. of Shares

This page intentionally blank.

Certificate No. _____
No. of shares _____
Dated _____
Issued to: _____
_____

□ Original issue
Documentary stamp tax paid:
$ _____
(Attach stamps to this stub.)

□ Transferred from: _____
_____

Date: _____

Original Cert. No.	Original No. Shares	No. of Shares Transferred
_____	_____	_____

Received Cert. No. _____
No. of shares _____
New certificates issued:

Cert. No.	No. of Shares
_____	_____
_____	_____

Certificate No. _____
No. of shares _____
Dated _____
Issued to: _____
_____

□ Original issue
Documentary stamp tax paid:
$ _____
(Attach stamps to this stub.)

□ Transferred from: _____
_____

Date: _____

Original Cert. No.	Original No. Shares	No. of Shares Transferred
_____	_____	_____

Received Cert. No. _____
No. of shares _____
New certificates issued:

Cert. No.	No. of Shares
_____	_____
_____	_____

Certificate No. _____
No. of shares _____
Dated _____
Issued to: _____
_____

□ Original issue
Documentary stamp tax paid:
$ _____
(Attach stamps to this stub.)

□ Transferred from: _____
_____

Date: _____

Original Cert. No.	Original No. Shares	No. of Shares Transferred
_____	_____	_____

Received Cert. No. _____
No. of shares _____
New certificates issued:

Cert. No.	No. of Shares
_____	_____
_____	_____

This page intentionally blank.

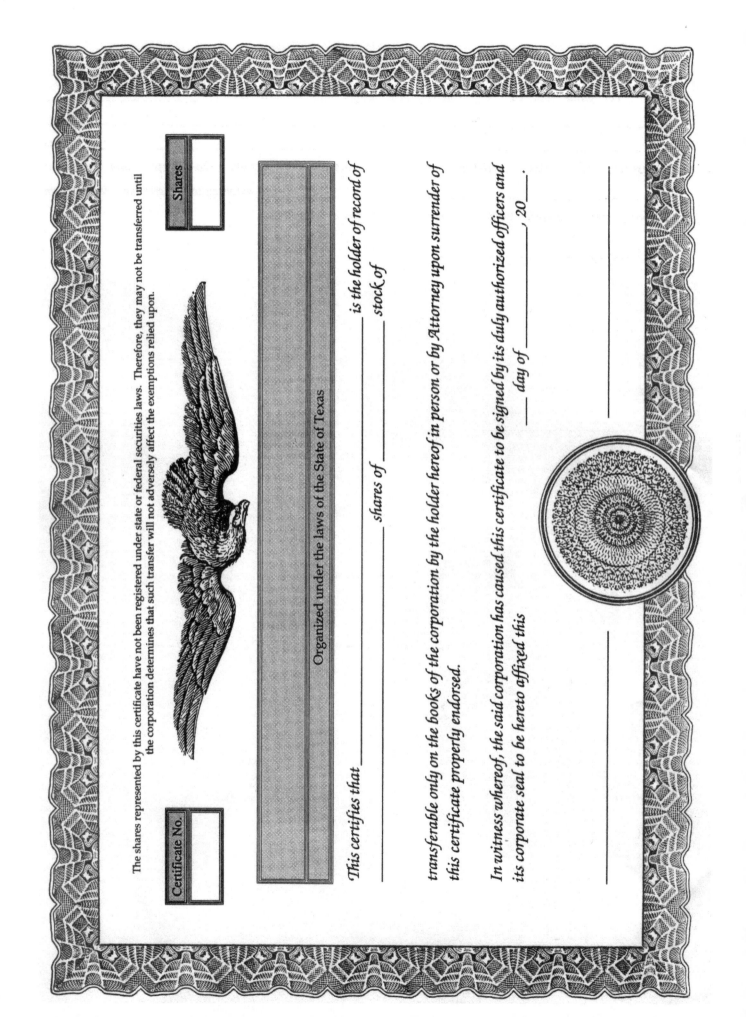

The shares represented by this certificate have not been registered under state or federal securities laws. Therefore, they may not be transferred until the corporation determines that such transfer will not adversely affect the exemptions relied upon.

Certificate No.

Shares

Organized under the laws of the State of Texas

This certifies that _____

is the holder of record of _____

_____ shares of _____ stock of

transferable only on the books of the corporation by the holder hereof in person or by Attorney upon surrender of this certificate properly endorsed.

In witness whereof, the said corporation has caused this certificate to be signed by its duly authorized officers and its corporate seal to be hereto affixed this _____ day of _____, 20____.

_____

_____

For value received, _____ hereby sell, assign and transfer unto _____
_____,
_____ shares represented by
this certificate and do hereby irrevocably constitute and appoint _____
attorney to transfer the said shares on the books of the corporation with full power of substitution in the premises.

Dated _____

_____

Witness:

_____

The shares represented by this certificate have not been registered under state or federal securities laws. Therefore, they may not be transferred until the corporation determines that such transfer will not adversely affect the exemptions relied upon.

Certificate No.

Shares

Organized under the laws of the State of Texas

This certifies that

is the holder of record of

_____ shares of _____ stock of

transferable only on the books of the corporation by the holder hereof in person or by Attorney upon surrender of this certificate properly endorsed.

In witness whereof, the said corporation has caused this certificate to be signed by its duly authorized officers and its corporate seal to be hereto affixed this _____ day of _____, 20 _____.

For value received, _____ hereby sell, assign and transfer unto _____

_____,

_____ shares represented by

this certificate and do hereby irrevocably constitute and appoint _____

attorney to transfer the said shares on the books of the corporation with full power of substitution in the premises.

Dated _____

_____

Witness:

_____

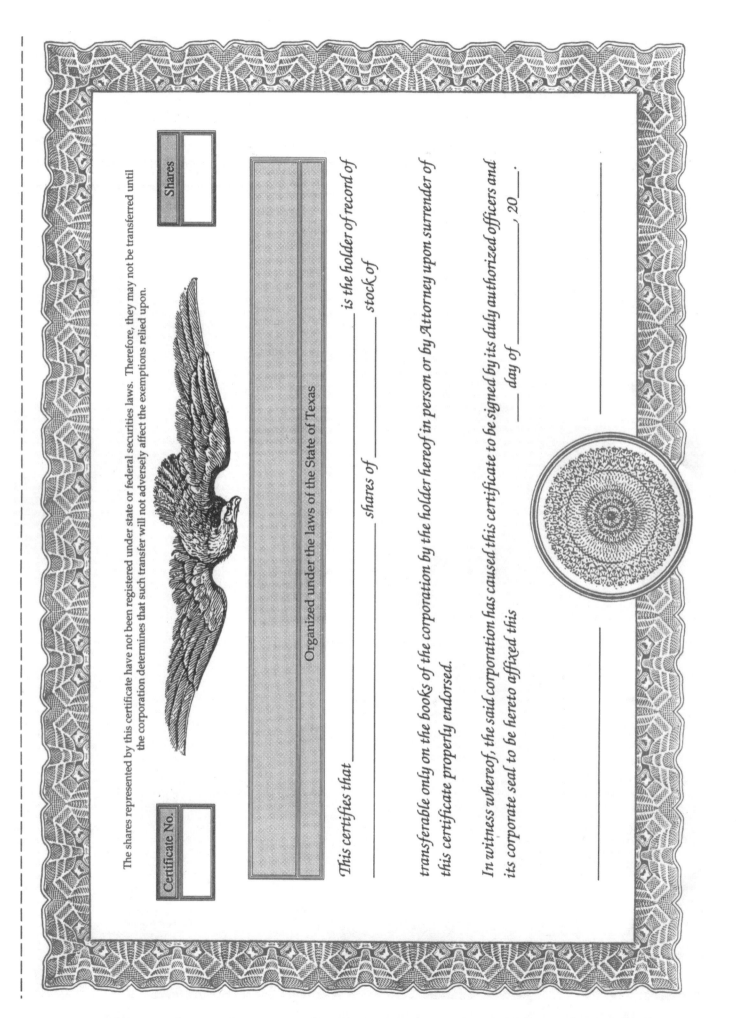

The shares represented by this certificate have not been registered under state or federal securities laws. Therefore, they may not be transferred until the corporation determines that such transfer will not adversely affect the exemptions relied upon.

Certificate No.

Shares

Organized under the laws of the State of Texas

This certifies that _____

is the holder of record of _____ shares of _____ stock of

transferable only on the books of the corporation by the holder hereof in person or by Attorney upon surrender of this certificate properly endorsed.

In witness whereof, the said corporation has caused this certificate to be signed by its duly authorized officers and its corporate seal to be hereto affixed this _____ day of _____, 20____.

For value received, _____ hereby sell, assign and transfer unto _____

_____,

_____ shares represented by

this certificate and do hereby irrevocably constitute and appoint _____

attorney to transfer the said shares on the books of the corporation with full power of substitution in the premises.

Dated _____

_____

Witness:

_____

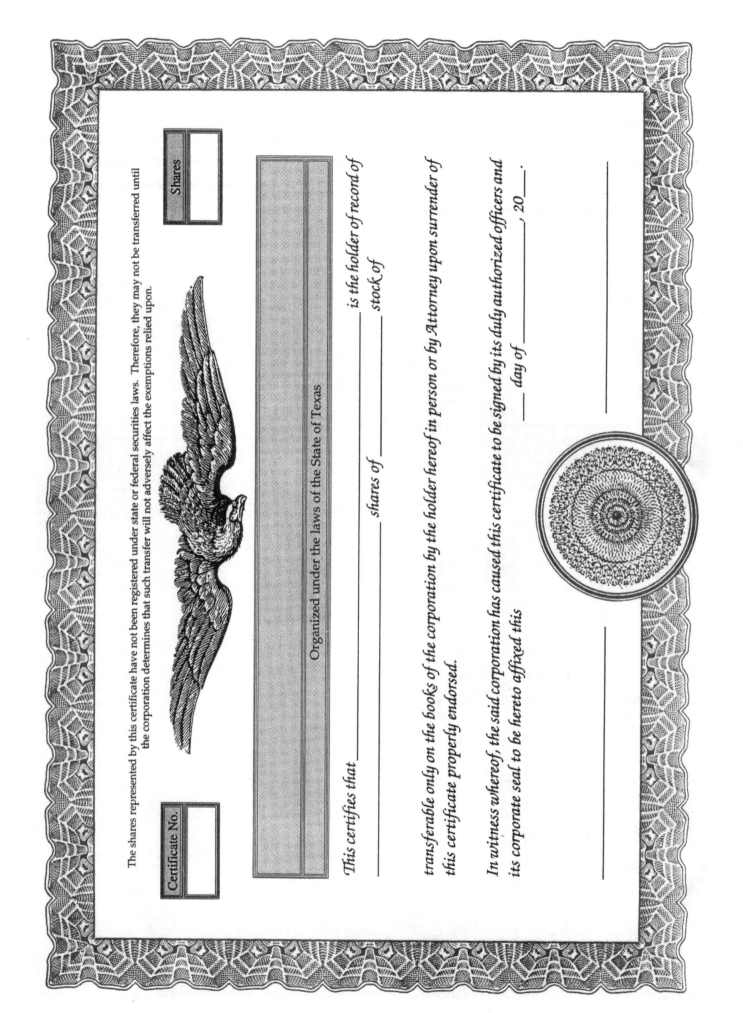

The shares represented by this certificate have not been registered under state or federal securities laws. Therefore, they may not be transferred until the corporation determines that such transfer will not adversely affect the exemptions relied upon.

Certificate No.

Shares

Organized under the laws of the State of Texas

This certifies that _____ is the holder of record of
_____ shares of _____
_____ stock of

transferable only on the books of the corporation by the holder hereof in person or by Attorney upon surrender of this certificate properly endorsed.

In witness whereof, the said corporation has caused this certificate to be signed by its duly authorized officers and its corporate seal to be hereto affixed this _____ day of _____, 20____.

_____

_____

For value received, _____ *hereby sell, assign and transfer unto* _____
_____,
_____ *shares represented by*
this certificate and do hereby irrevocably constitute and appoint _____
attorney to transfer the said shares on the books of the corporation with full power of substitution in the premises.

Dated _____

_____

Witness:

_____

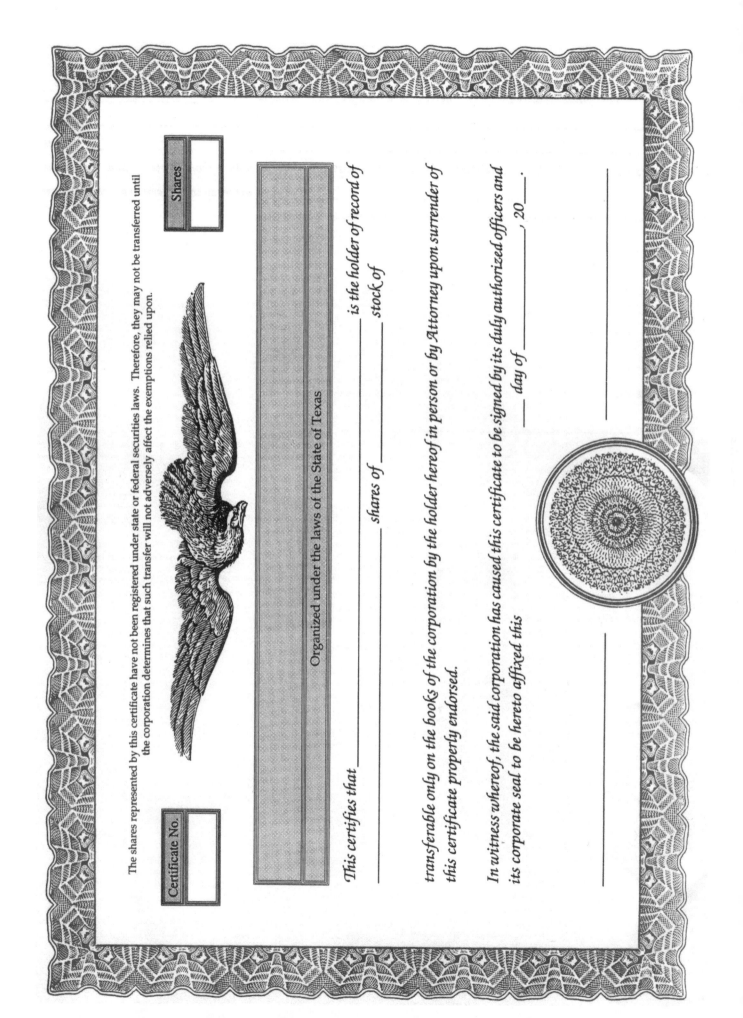

The shares represented by this certificate have not been registered under state or federal securities laws. Therefore, they may not be transferred until the corporation determines that such transfer will not adversely affect the exemptions relied upon.

Shares

Certificate No.

Organized under the laws of the State of Texas

This certifies that

is the holder of record of

shares of

stock of

transferable only on the books of the corporation by the holder hereof in person or by Attorney upon surrender of this certificate properly endorsed.

In witness whereof, the said corporation has caused this certificate to be signed by its duly authorized officers and its corporate seal to be hereto affixed this

day of

, 20   .

For value received, _____ hereby sell, assign and transfer unto _____

_____,

_____ shares represented by

this certificate and do hereby irrevocably constitute and appoint _____

attorney to transfer the said shares on the books of the corporation with full power of substitution in the premises.

Dated _____

_____

Witness:

_____

ARTICLES OF ORGANIZATION
OF

_____

I, the undersigned natural person of the age of eighteen (18) years or more, acting pursuant to the provisions of the Texas Limited Liability Company Act as organizer of _____ (the "Company"), hereby adopt the following Articles of Organization for the Company.

ARTICLE I

The name of the Company is _____.

ARTICLE II

The period of duration of the Company is perpetual or until earlier dissolved in accordance with the regulations of the Company.

ARTICLE III

The Company is organized for the purpose of transacting any and all lawful business for which limited liability companies may be organized under the Texas Limited Liability Company Act.

ARTICLE IV

The street address of the initial registered office of the Company is _____,
_____, _____, _____, _____
(Street Address)   (City)   (State)   (Zip Code)
and the name of its initial registered agent at such address is _____.

ARTICLE V

The Company is to be managed by Managers. The name and address of the initial Managers are as follows:

INITIAL MANAGERS   **ADDRESS**

_____   _____
                                       _____

_____   _____
                                       _____

ARTICLE VI

A Manager of the Company shall not be personally liable to the Company or to any Member of the Company for monetary damages for an act or omission in the Manager's capacity as Manager of the Company, except for liability for any of the following:

(1) A breach of the Manager's duty of loyalty to the Company or the Members of the Company;

(2) An act or omission not in good faith that constitutes a breach of duty of the Manager to the Company or an act or omission that involves intentional misconduct or knowing violation of the law;

(3) A transaction from which the Manager received an improper benefit, whether or not the benefit resulted from an action taken within the scope of the Manager's office; or

(4) An act or omission for which the liability of a Manager is expressly provided by an applicable statute.

If the Texas Limited Liability Company Act or the Texas Miscellaneous Corporation Laws is amended to authorize Company action further eliminating or limiting the personal liability of managers, then the liability of a Manager of the Company shall be eliminated or limited to the fullest extent permitted by such Acts, as so amended.

Any repeal or modification of this Article by the Members of the Company shall not adversely affect any right or protection of a Managers of the Company existing at the time of such repeal or modification. Any repeal or modification of those provisions of the Texas Limited Liability Company Act or Texas Miscellaneous Corporation Laws Act that concern the limitation of manager liability shall not be construed to adversely affect any right or protection of a Manager of the Company existing at the time of such repeal or modification unless such adverse construction is required by law.

ARTICLE VII

The name of the organizer of the Company _____, whose address is _____, _____, _____, _____.
(Street Address)   (City)   (State)   (Zip Code)

IN WITNESS WHEREOF, I have hereunto set my hand this _____ day of _____, 20_____.

_____
(Name)

REGULATIONS
OF

_____

A TEXAS LIMITED LIABILITY COMPANY

These Regulations of _____, a Texas limited liability company, dated as of _____, 20_____, are executed by _____ and _____, as the initial Members of the Company and as the initial Managers of the Company.

ARTICLE 1
DEFINED TERMS

1.01   **Definitions.**   As used in these Regulations, each of the following terms has the meaning given to it below:

"*Act*" means the Texas Limited Liability Company Act, as amended from time to time.

"*Articles*" means the Articles of Organization of the Company as filed with the Secretary of State of Texas on _____, 20_____, together with such amendments made thereto from time to time in accordance with applicable law.

"*Capital Contributions*" has the meaning assigned to it in Section 4.01.

"*Capital Account*" has the meaning assigned to it in Section 4.03.

"*Change in Control*" means, with respect to any Shares, a change in the ultimate control of those Shares.

"*Code*" means the Internal Revenue Code of 1986, as amended from time to time.

"*Company*" means _____, a Texas limited liability company.

"*Indemnitee*" has the meaning assigned to it in Section 6.12.

"*Initial Members*" means _____ and _____.

"*Majority Interest*" has the meaning assigned to it in Section 6.08.

"*Manager*" has the meaning assigned to it in Section 6.03.

"*Members*" means the Initial Members and each other Person that is hereafter admitted to the Company as a Member in accordance with these Regulations.

"*Membership Interest*" means a Member's limited liability company interest (as defined in the Act).

"*Person*" includes any individual, partnership, limited partnership, joint venture, corporation, limited liability company, trust, estate, custodian, trustee, executor, administrator, nominee, representative, unincorporated organization, sole proprietorship, trust, employee benefit plan, tribunal, governmental entity, department, or agency, or other entity.

"*Regulations*" means these regulations of the Company, as amended from time to time.

"*Sharing Ratio*" means the ratio, expressed as a percentage, obtained for a Member by dividing each Member's Membership Interest by the total of all of the Members' Membership Interests. The initial Sharing Ratio of each Initial Member is shown on Exhibit A attached hereto.

"*Sole Discretion*" of a Person means such Person's sole and absolute discretion, with or without cause, and subject to such conditions as such Person shall deem appropriate.

"*Transfer*" means (i) any sale, transfer, encumbrance, gift, donation, assignment, pledge, hypothecation, a Change in Control, or other transfer of Shares (or any of the membership interest in the Company represented thereby), whether voluntary or involuntary, and whether during the transferor's lifetime or upon or after the transferee's death, including, but not limited to, any transfer by operation of law, by court order, by judicial process, or by foreclosure, levy, or attachment; or (ii) the act of making any of the foregoing.

1.02 **Other Definitions.** Other terms defined herein have the meanings so given them.

1.03 **Headings.** The headings and subheadings in these Regulations are included for convenience and identification only and are in no way intended to describe, interpret, define or limit the scope, extent or intent of these Regulations or any provisions hereof.

ARTICLE 2
ORGANIZATION

2.01 **Formation.** The Company has been organized as a Texas limited liability company by the filing of Articles of Organization with the Texas Secretary of State.

2.02 **Name.** The name of the Company is "_____" and all Company business must be conducted in that name or such other names as may be selected by the Manager and as comply with applicable law.

2.03 **Registered Office; Registered Agent; Offices.** The registered office and registered agent of the Company in the State of Texas shall be as specified in the Articles or as designated by the Manager in the manner provided by applicable law. The business office of the Company shall be in _____, Texas or such other location as the Manager may deem appropriate.

2.04 **Purpose.** The purpose of the Company shall be to engage in any and all lawful business for which limited liability companies may be organized under the Act.

2.05 **Foreign Qualification.** The Company shall comply with all requirements necessary to qualify as a foreign limited liability company in any foreign jurisdiction in which such qualification is necessary under applicable law.

2.06 **Term.** The Company commenced on the effective date of the Articles and shall have a perpetual existence, unless and until it is dissolved in accordance with Article 9.

2.07   Partnership. The Member intends that the Company shall be treated as or construed to be a partnership for purposes of the laws of any state and for any purposes from and after such date. For federal income tax purposes, as of the date hereof and until such time as the Company becomes owned by only one Member, the Company and the Members desire and intend that the Company be treated as a partnership pursuant to Treasury Regulation Sec. 301.7701-3(b)(1)(i).

ARTICLE 3
MEMBERSHIP

3.01   Members. The Initial Members of the Company, as of the date hereof, are_____ and _____. From and after the date hereof, the Manager may admit additional Persons as Members of the Company on such terms and subject to such conditions as the Manager may deem appropriate.

3.02   Resignation. A Member does not have the right to resign from the Company; provided, however, a Member shall have the power to resign at any time in violation of these Regulations. If a Member exercises such power in violation of these Regulations, (a) such resigning Member shall be liable to the Company and the other Members, if any, for all monetary damages suffered by them as a result of such resignation; and (b) such resigning Member shall not have any rights under Article 5.06 of the Act. In no event shall the Company or any Member have the right, through specific performance or otherwise, to prevent a Member from resigning in violation of these Regulations.

3.03   Information. In addition to the other rights specifically set forth in these Regulations, each Member and each transferee is entitled to all information to which that Member or transferee is entitled to have access pursuant to Article 2.22 of the Act under the circumstances and subject to the conditions therein stated.

3.04   Liability to Third Parties. No Member shall be liable for the debts, obligations, or liabilities of the Company or of any other Member.

ARTICLE 4
CAPITAL CONTRIBUTIONS

4.01   Capital Contributions. Each Member shall, from time to time, make the cash contributions to the capital of the Company (***"Capital Contributions"***), on or before the date specified as hereinafter described, in such amounts that in the judgment of a Majority Interest (as defined in Section 6.08) are desirable to enable the Company to cause the assets of the Company to be properly operated and maintained and to discharge its costs, expenses, obligations, and liabilities. Such Capital Contributions shall be made within five days after receipt of written notice from the Manager so authorized as provided in Section 6.01 specifying the amount of such Capital Contribution. If a Member does not contribute, on or before the due date thereof, all or any portion of a Capital Contribution that Member is required to make as provided in these Regulations, the Company may exercise, on notice to that Member, any right or remedy available at law or in equity for such breach. Each Member may also contribute to the capital of the Company such non-cash property as such Member and a Majority Interest may agree.

4.02   Return of Contributions. A Member is not entitled to the return of any part of its Capital Contributions or to be paid interest in respect of either its Capital Account (as defined below), if applicable, or its Capital Contributions. An unrepaid Capital Contribution is not a liability of the Company or of any Member. A Member is not required to contribute or to lend any cash or property to the Company to enable the Company to return any Member's Capital Contributions.

4.03   Capital Accounts. A capital account (*"Capital Account"*) shall be established and maintained for each Member. Each Member's Capital Account (a) shall be increased by (i) the amount of money contributed by that Member to the Company, (ii) the fair market value of property contributed by that Member to the Company (net of liabilities secured by the contributed property that the Company is considered to assume or take subject to under section 752 of the Code), and (iii) allocations to that Member of Company income and gain (or items of income and gain), including income and gain exempt from tax and income and gain described in Treas. Reg. Sec. 1.704-1(b)(2)(iv)(*g*), but excluding income and gain described in Treas. Reg. Sec. 1.704-1(b)(4)(i), and (b) shall be decreased by (i) the amount of money distributed to that Member by the Company, (ii) the fair market value of property distributed to that Member by the Company (net of liabilities secured by the distributed property that the Member is considered to assume or take subject to under section 752 of the Code), (iii) allocations to that Member of expenditures of the Company described in section 705(a)(2)(B) of the Code, and (iv) allocations of Company loss and deduction (or items of loss and deduction), including loss and deduction described in Treas. Reg. Sec. 1.704-1(b)(2)(iv)(*g*), but excluding items described in clause (b)(iii) above and loss or deduction described in Treas. Reg. Sec. 1.704-1(b)(4)(i) or Sec. 1.704-1(b)(4)(iii). The Members' Capital Accounts also shall be maintained and adjusted as permitted by the provisions of Treas. Reg. Sec. 1.704-1(b)(2)(iv)(f) and as required by the other provisions of Treas. Reg. Secs. 1.704-1(b)(2)(iv) and 1.704-1(b)(4), including adjustments to reflect the allocations to the Members of depreciation, depletion, amortization, and gain or loss as computed for book purposes rather than the allocation of the corresponding items as computed for tax purposes, as required by Treas. Reg. Sec. 1.704-1(b)(2)(iv)(*g*). A Member that has more than one Membership Interest shall have a single Capital Account that reflects all its Membership Interests, regardless of the class of Membership Interests owned by that Member and regardless of the time or manner in which those Membership Interests were acquired. On the transfer of all or part of a Membership Interest, the Capital Account of the transferor that is attributable to the transferred Membership Interest or part of a Membership Interest shall carry over to the transferee Member in accordance with the provisions of Treas. Reg. Sec. 1.704-1(b)(2)(iv)(*l*).

ARTICLE 5
DISTRIBUTIONS AND ALLOCATIONS

5.01   Distributions. Distributions, if any, shall be made from time to time as determined by the Manager in accordance with Section 6.01 to the Member(s) pro rata in accordance with their Sharing Ratios.

5.02   Allocations. For purposes of maintaining the books of the Company, all items of income, gain, loss and deduction of the Company shall be allocated to the Members in accordance with their Sharing Ratios. For United States federal income tax and all other United States tax purposes, (a) all items of income, gain, loss and deduction of the Company shall be allocated in the same manner as its correlative book item is allocated; (b) all tax credits shall be allocated in the same manner as the receipt, income, expenditure, or deduction giving rise thereto is allocated; and (c) notwithstanding clause (a) hereof, the allocations, if any, required by section 704(c) of the Code and sections 1.704-1(b)(2)(iv)(d)(3) and 1.704-1(b)(2)(iv)(f) of the Treasury Regulations promulgated thereunder shall be effected.

ARTICLE 6
MANAGEMENT

6.01   Management by Managers.

(a)   Subject to the provisions of Section 6.03, the powers of the Company shall be exercised by or under the authority of, and the business and affairs of the Company shall be managed under the direction of one or more Managers. No Member in its capacity as a Member has the right, power or authority to act for or on behalf of the Company, to do any act that would be binding on the Company, or to incur any expenditures on behalf of the Company.

(b)   In managing the business and affairs of the Company and exercising its powers, the Managers shall act (i) collectively through resolutions adopted at meetings and in written consents pursuant to Sections 6.05, 6.08 and 6.09; and (ii) through committees and individual Managers (as defined in Section 6.03) to which authorities and duties have been delegated pursuant to Section 6.06. Neither the Managers nor any Committee thereof has the right, power or authority to act for or on behalf of the Company, to do any act that would be binding on the Company, or to incur any expenditures on behalf of the Company, except in accordance with the immediately preceding sentence. Decisions or actions taken by the Managers in accordance with these Regulations (including this Section 6.01 and Section 6.02) shall constitute decisions or actions by the Company and shall be binding on the Managers, each Member and employee of the Company.

6.02   Decisions Requiring Member Consent. Notwithstanding any power or authority granted the Managers under the Act, the Articles or these Regulations, (a) the Managers may not make any decision or take any action for which the consent of a Majority Interest or other consent of the Member(s) is expressly required by the Articles or these Regulations, without first obtaining such consent, and (b) the Managers may not make any of the following decisions or actions without first obtaining the consent of a Majority Interest:

(i)   causing or permitting the Company to be a party to a merger, consolidation, share exchange or to convert into any other type of entity;

(ii)   causing or permitting the Company to dispose of or encumber all or substantially all of its assets;

(iii)   causing or permitting the Company to enter into or engage in any transaction, contract, agreement or arrangement that (A) is unrelated to the Company's purpose (as set forth in the Articles and in Section 1.04 hereof), (B) otherwise contravenes the Articles or these Regulations, or (C) would make it impossible to carry on the ordinary business of the Company; and

(iv)   performing any other act that is prohibited by Article 2.18B of the Act from being performed by the Managers.

Each Member may, with respect to any vote, consent or approval that it is entitled to grant pursuant to these Regulations, grant or withhold such vote, consent or approval in its Sole Discretion.

6.03   Management of the Company. The Members hereby establish that the management of the Company shall be vested in of _____ (____) managers (*"Managers"*) to be elected by the vote of a majority, in interest and not in number, of the Members. The initial Managers shall consist of _____ and _____.

6.04   Designation of Managers. Each Member who is entitled to vote in the election of Managers shall promptly notify the other Members of the names and addresses of the persons it wishes to nominate for election as a Manager.

6.05   Meetings of Managers. Regular meetings of the Managers may be held on such dates and at such times as shall be determined by the Managers, with notice of the establishment of such regular meeting schedule being given to each Managers that was not present at the meeting at which it was adopted. Special meetings of the Manager may be called by any Manager by notice thereof (specifying the place and time of such meeting) that is delivered to each other Manager at least 24 hours prior to such meeting. Neither the business to be transacted at, nor the purpose of, such special meeting need be specified in the notice (or waiver of notice) thereof. Unless otherwise expressly provided in these Regulations, at any meeting of the Managers, a majority of the Managers shall constitute a quorum for the transaction of business, and an act of a majority of the Managers who are present at such a meeting at which a quorum is present shall be the act of the Managers.

6.06 <u>**Committees of Managers, Delegation of Authority to Individual Managers**</u>. The Managers may designate one or more committees, each of which shall be comprised of one or more of the Managers, and may designate one or more of the Managers as alternate members of any committee. Any such committee, to the extent provided in the resolution establishing it, shall have and may exercise all of the authority that may be exercised by the Managers. Regular and special meetings of such committee shall be held in the manner designated by the Managers or, if not so designated, by such committee. The Managers may dissolve any committee at any time.

6.07 <u>**Compensation.**</u> The Managers shall not receive any compensation for their services. The Managers shall be entitled to be reimbursed for out-of-pocket costs and expenses incurred in the course of their service hereunder.

6.08 <u>**Meetings of Members**</u>. An annual meeting of the Members for the transaction of such business as may properly come before the meeting shall be held on such date and at such time as the Managers shall specify in the notice of the meeting, which shall be delivered to each Member at least 20 days prior to such meeting. Special meetings of the Members may be called by the Managers or by one or more Members owning, in the aggregate, at least ten percent of the Sharing Ratios of all Members. Any such meeting shall be held on such date and at such time as the Person calling such meeting shall specify in the notice of the meeting, which shall be delivered to each Member at least ten days prior to such meeting. Only business within the purpose or purposes described in the notice (or waiver thereof) for such meeting may be conducted at such meeting. Unless otherwise expressly provided in these Regulations, at any meeting of the Members, Members holding among them at least a majority of all Sharing Ratios (a *"Majority Interest"*), represented either in person or by proxy, shall constitute a quorum for the transaction of business, and an act of a Majority Interest shall be the act of the Members.

6.09 <u>**Provisions Applicable to All Meetings**</u>. In connection with any meeting of the Managers, Members or any committee designated by the Managers, the following provisions shall apply:

(a) <u>**Place of Meeting**</u>. Any such meeting shall be held at the principal place of business of the Company, unless the notice of such meeting (or resolution by the Managers or committee thereof, as applicable) specifies a different place, which need not be in the State of Texas.

(b) <u>**Waiver of Notice Through Attendance**</u>. Attendance of a Person at such meeting (including pursuant to Section 6.09(e)) shall constitute a waiver of notice of such meeting, except where such Person attends the meeting for the express purpose of objecting to the transaction of any business on the ground that the meeting is not lawfully called or convened.

(c) <u>**Proxies**</u>. A Person may vote at such meeting by a written proxy executed by that Person and delivered to another Manager or Member, as applicable. A proxy shall be revocable unless it is stated to be irrevocable.

(d) <u>**Action by Written Consent**</u>. Any action required or permitted to be taken at such a meeting may be taken without a meeting, without prior notice, and without a vote if a consent or consents in writing, setting forth the action so taken, is signed by the Managers, Members or members of a committee, as applicable, having not fewer than the minimum number of Sharing Ratios or votes that would be necessary to take the action at a meeting at which all Managers, Members or members of a committee, as applicable, entitled to vote on the action were present and voted.

(e) <u>**Meetings by Telephone**</u>. Managers, Members or members of a committee, as applicable, may participate in and hold such meeting by means of conference telephone, video conference or similar communications equipment by means of which all Persons participating in the meeting can hear each other.

6.10 <u>**Limitations on Liability of Managers**</u>. Except as provided otherwise in these Regulations, the Managers shall conduct the affairs of the Company in good faith toward the best interests of the Company. The Managers shall be liable for errors or omissions in performing their duties with respect to the Company only in the case of gross negligence, willful misconduct, bad faith or breach of the provisions of these Regulations, but not otherwise. The Managers shall devote such time and effort to the Company's business and operations as is necessary to promote fully the interests of the Company; however, no Manager must devote full time to Company business.

6.11 <u>**Conflicts of Interest**</u>. Subject to the other express provisions of these Regulations, each Member, Manager, or affiliate thereof may engage in and possess interests in other business ventures of any and every type and description, independently or with others, including ones in competition with the Company, with no obligation to offer to the Company or any other Member or Manager the right to participate therein. The Company may transact business with any Member, Manager or affiliate thereof, provided the terms of those transactions are no less favorable than those the Company could obtain from unrelated third parties.

6.12 <u>**Indemnification; Reimbursement of Expenses; Insurance**</u>. In consideration of a person (*"**Indemnitee**"*) serving as a Manager of the Company, and subject to the further provisions and exceptions hereof, the Company, to the extent permitted by Article 2.20 of the Act and the Texas Business Corporation Act, (i) may indemnify and advance expenses to an Indemnitee who was, is, or is threatened to be made a named defendant or respondent in a proceeding, because the Indemnitee is or was a Manager of the Company, and (ii) shall indemnify an Indemnitee against reasonable expenses incurred by the Indemnitee in connection with the proceeding in which the Indemnitee is a named defendant or respondent, because the Indemnitee is or was a Manager, if the Indemnitee has been wholly successful on the merits or otherwise in the defense of the proceeding.

ARTICLE 7

TAXES

7.01 <u>**Tax Matters Member**</u>. _____, ("the Tax Manager") shall be the "tax matters partner" of the Company pursuant to Code Section 6231(a)(7). Any cost or expense incurred by the Tax Manager in connection with its duties, including the preparation for or pursuance of administrative or judicial proceedings, shall be paid by the Company.

7.02 <u>**Tax Returns**</u>. The Tax Manager, as the "tax matters partner" under the Code, shall prepare and timely file all federal, state and local and foreign tax returns required to be filed by the Company. Each Member shall furnish to the Tax Manager all pertinent information in its possession relating to the Company's operations that is necessary to enable the Company's tax returns to be timely prepared and filed. The Tax Manager shall deliver a copy of each such return to the Members on or before ten days prior to the due date of any such return, together with such additional information as may be required by the Members in order for the Members to file their individual returns reflecting the Company's operations. The Company shall bear the costs of the preparation and filing of its returns.

7.03 <u>**Tax Elections.**</u> The Company shall make such elections as the Tax Manager, as the "tax matters partner" under the Code, deems appropriate after consultation with the Members with respect to tax returns required to be filed by the Company. Neither the Company nor any Member may make an election for the Company to be excluded from the application of the provisions of subchapter K of chapter 1 of subtitle A of the Code or any similar provisions of applicable state law and no provision of these Regulations (including Section 2.07) shall be construed to sanction or approve such an election.

ARTICLE 8
BOOKS, RECORDS AND BANK ACCOUNTS

8.01 **Maintenance of Books.** Complete and accurate books and records of the Company shall be kept at the principal office of the Company which shall include, without limitation, supporting documentation of the transactions with respect to the conduct of the Company's business and minutes of the proceedings of its Members. The books and records shall be maintained with respect to accounting matters in accordance with sound accounting practices. All books and records shall be available at the Company's principal office for examination by any Member or the Member's duly authorized representative at any and all reasonable times during normal business hours.

8.02 **Accounts**. The Company shall establish one or more separate bank and investment accounts and arrangements for the Company.

ARTICLE 9
DISSOLUTION, WINDING-UP AND TERMINATION

9.01 **Dissolution**. The Company shall dissolve and its affairs shall be wound up on the first to occur of the following events:

(a) the consent of Members holding among them at least _____ % of all Sharing Ratios; or

(b) entry of a decree of judicial dissolution of the Company under Article 6.02 of the Act.

9.02 **Winding-Up and Termination**.

(a) On the occurrence of an event described in Section 9.01, the initial Members shall act as liquidators. Until final distribution, the liquidators shall continue to operate the Company properties. The costs of winding up shall be borne as a Company expense.

(b) Any assets of the Company remaining at the conclusion of the winding-up process shall be distributed among the Members in accordance with their Sharing Ratios. All distributions in kind to the Members shall be made subject to the liability of each distributee for costs, expenses, and liabilities theretofore incurred or for which the Company has committed prior to the date of termination. The distribution of cash and/or property to a Member in accordance with the provisions of this Section 9.01 constitutes a complete return to the Member of its Capital Contributions and a complete distribution to the Member of its membership interest and all the Company's property, and the Members acknowledge that such distribution complies with Article 6.04 of the Act and discharges any rights the Members may have as creditors of the Company under Article 5.08 of the Act.

(c) On completion of such final distribution, the initial Members, in their capacity as liquidator, shall file Articles of Dissolution with the Secretary of State of Texas, cancel any other filings made pursuant to Section 2.05, and take such other actions as may be necessary to terminate the existence of the Company.

9.03 **No Restoration of Deficit Capital Accounts**. No Member shall be required to pay to the Company, to any other Member or to any third party any deficit balance that may exist from time to time in such Member's Capital Account.

ARTICLE 10
GENERAL PROVISIONS

10.01 Offset. Whenever the Company is to pay any sum to any Member, any amounts that Member owes the Company may be deducted from that sum before payment.

10.02 Notices. All notices, requests or consents under these Regulations shall be (a) in writing, (b) delivered to the recipient in person, by courier or mail or by facsimile, telegram, telex, cablegram or similar transmission, (c) if to an initial Member or the Company, delivered to such initial Member or the Company at the applicable address on Exhibit A or such other address as that Member or the Company may specify by notice to the other Members, (d) if to any other Member, delivered to the last known address of such Member as maintained in the books and records of the Company, and (e) effective only upon actual receipt by such Person. Whenever any notice is required to be given by applicable law, the Articles or these Regulations, a written waiver thereof, signed by the Person entitled to notice, whether before or after the time stated therein, shall be deemed equivalent to the giving of such notice.

10.03 Effect of Waiver or Consent. A waiver or consent, express or implied, to or of any breach or default by any Person in the performance by that Person of its obligations with respect to the Company is not a consent or waiver to or of any other breach or default in the performance by that Person of the same or any other obligations of that Person with respect to the Company.

10.04 Amendments to Articles and Agreement. The Articles and these Regulations may be amended or restated only with the approval of Members holding among them at least 75% of all Sharing Ratios.

10.05 Binding Effect. Subject to the restrictions on Transfer set forth in these Regulations, these Regulations are binding on and shall inure to the benefit of the Members and their respective heirs, representatives, successors, and assigns.

10.06 Governing Law; Severability. These Regulations are governed by and shall be construed in accordance with the laws of the State of Texas (excluding its conflict-of-laws rules). If any provision of these Regulations or the application thereof to any Person or circumstance is held invalid or unenforceable to any extent, the remainder of these Regulations and the application of that provision to other Persons or circumstances shall not be affected thereby and that provision shall be enforced to the greatest extent permitted by applicable law.

10.07 Construction. Unless the context requires otherwise:

(a)   the gender (or lack of gender) of all words used in these Regulations includes the masculine, feminine, and neuter;

(b)   the word "including" means "including, without limitation,";

(c)   references to Articles and Sections refer to Articles and Sections of these Regulations; and

(d)   references to Exhibits are to the Exhibits attached to these Regulations, each of which is made a part hereof for all purposes.

10.08 Further Assurances. In connection with the performance of these Regulations and the transactions contemplated hereby, each Member shall execute and deliver any additional documents and instruments and perform any additional acts that may be necessary or appropriate to effectuate and perform the provisions of these Regulations and those transactions.

10.09 <u>Counterparts</u>. These Regulations may be executed via facsimile signature and in multiple counterparts, each of which shall be deemed to be an original, and all of which together shall constitute one and the same Regulations.

IN WITNESS WHEREOF, the initial Managers and initial Members have adopted and executed these Regulations as of the date first set forth above.

INITIAL MANAGERS: **INITIAL MEMBERS:**

_____   _____

(Name)   (Name)

_____   _____

(Name)   (Name)

Exhibit A

Initial Contributions; Address for Notice; Sharing Ratios

Name/Address	Initial Contribution	Sharing Ratios

This page intentionally blank.

MINUTES OF ACTION
WITHOUT A MEETING BY THE
MANAGERS OF

_____

Dated: _____, _____

The Managers of _____, a Texas limited liability company (the "Company"), acting pursuant to Article 2.23B of the Texas Limited Liability Company Act, by the signatures and with the approval and consent of the undersigned, who are the Managers of the Company, hereby take the following actions:

RESOLVED, that the minute book presented is hereby adopted as the minute book of the Company, and that the Managers authorize and direct to file in such minute book the minutes of meetings and minutes of actions taken without meetings of the Managers and Members;

RESOLVED FURTHER, that the form, terms, and provisions of the Articles of Organization of the Company approved and filed in the Office of the Secretary of State of Texas on the _____ day of _____, 20_____, are hereby in all respects approved and is filed in the Company's minute book the Company's Certificate of Organization, together with the duly certified duplicate original of the Articles of Organization;

RESOLVED FURTHER, that the Regulations executed by the initial Managers and initial Members of the Company as of the date hereof and filed in the Company's minute book are hereby acknowledged as the Regulations of this Company;

RESOLVED FURTHER, that the fiscal year of the Company shall end on December 31;

RESOLVED FURTHER, that the Managers are authorized and directed to open an account in the name of the Company with a bank selected by the Managers;

RESOLVED FURTHER, that the Managers of the Company are authorized and directed to execute such signature cards and other documents in connection with such account as may be necessary or advisable and to certify to the adoption of resolutions relating to such account, such resolutions being hereby adopted;

RESOLVED FURTHER, that, to the extent permitted by law, the organizer of this Company and the initial Managers of the Company, acting merely to adopt Regulations, admit members to the Company, and to form the Company, be indemnified and held harmless by the Company for all loss, cost or expense in connection with formation of this Company, the filing of its Articles of Organization, the adoption of Regulations, the admission of members and in connection with all activities of the Company, its managers, and employees, up to the time of the adoption of this resolution and that all acts and deeds taken by the initial Managers of the Company for and on behalf of the Company prior to the time of the adoption of this resolution be, and they hereby are, adopted, ratified and confirmed.

MANAGERS:

_____
(Name)

_____
(Name)

This page intentionally blank.

MINUTES OF THE ANNUAL MEETING OF
THE MEMBERS OF

_____

The annual meeting of the Members of _____Texas limited liability company, ("Company") was held on the date and place set forth in the written waiver of notice signed by the Members and attached to the minutes of this meeting.

The following Members were present:

_____

_____

The meeting was called to order and it was moved, seconded and unanimously carried that _____ act as Chairman and that _____ act as Secretary.

A roll call was taken and the Chairman noted that all of the outstanding shares of the Company were represented in person or by proxy. Any proxies were attached to these minutes.

The minutes of the last meeting of the Members which was held on the _____ day of _____, 20_____, were read and approved by the Members.

Upon motion duly made, seconded and carried, the following were elected Managers for the following year and until their successors are elected and qualify:

_____

_____

There being no further business to come before the meeting, upon motion duly made, seconded and unanimously carried, the meeting was adjourned.

_____
Secretary

MEMBERS:

_____
(Name)

_____
(Name)

This page intentionally blank.

MINUTES OF THE ANNUAL MEETING OF
THE MANAGERS OF

_____

The annual meeting of the Managers of _____, a Texas limited liability company, ("Company") was held on the date and place set forth in the written waiver of notice signed by the Managers and attached to the minutes of this meeting.

The following were present, being all of the Managers of the Company:

_____

_____

The meeting was called to order and it was moved, seconded and unanimously carried that _____ act as Chairman and that _____ act as Secretary.

The minutes of the last meeting of the Managers which was held on the _____ day of _____, 20_____, were read and approved by the Board.

Upon motion duly made, seconded and carried, the following were elected officers for the following year and until their successors are elected and qualify:

President - _____

Treasurer & Secretary - _____

There being no further business to come before the meeting, upon motion duly made, seconded and unanimously carried, the meeting was adjourned.

_____
Secretary

MANAGERS:

_____
(Name)

_____
(Name)

INDEX

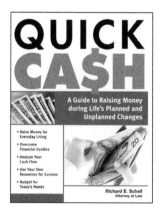
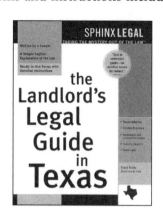

Sphinx® Publishing's National Titles
Valid in All 50 States

LEGAL SURVIVAL IN BUSINESS

The Complete Book of Corporate Forms	$24.95
The Complete Partnership Book	$24.95
The Complete Patent Book	$26.95
Employees' Rights	$18.95
Employer's Rights	$24.95
The Entrepreneur's Internet Handbook	$21.95
The Entrepreneur's Legal Guide	$26.95
How to Form a Limited Liability Company (2E)	$24.95
How to Form a Nonprofit Corporation (2E)	$24.95
How to Form Your Own Corporation (4E)	$26.95
How to Register Your Own Copyright (5E)	$24.95
How to Register Your Own Trademark (3E)	$21.95
Incorporate in Delaware from Any State	$26.95
Incorporate in Nevada from Any State	$24.95
The Law (In Plain English)® for Small Business	$19.95
Most Valuable Business Legal Forms You'll Ever Need (3E)	$21.95
Profit from Intellectual Property	$28.95
Protect Your Patent	$24.95
The Small Business Owner's Guide to Bankruptcy	$21.95
Tax Smarts for Small Business	$21.95

LEGAL SURVIVAL IN COURT

Attorney Responsibilities & Client Rights	$19.95
Crime Victim's Guide to Justice (2E)	$21.95
Grandparents' Rights (3E)	$24.95
Help Your Lawyer Win Your Case (2E)	$14.95
Legal Research Made Easy (3E)	$21.95
Winning Your Personal Injury Claim (2E)	$24.95

LEGAL SURVIVAL IN REAL ESTATE

The Complete Kit to Selling Your Own Home	$18.95
Essential Guide to Real Estate Contracts (2E)	$18.95
Essential Guide to Real Estate Leases	$18.95
Homeowner's Rights	$19.95
How to Buy a Condominium or Townhome (2E)	$19.95
How to Buy Your First Home	$18.95
Working with Your Homeowners Association	$19.95

LEGAL SURVIVAL IN SPANISH

Cómo Hacer su Propio Testamento	$16.95
Cómo Restablecer su propio Crédito y Renegociar sus Deudas	$21.95
Cómo Solicitar su Propio Divorcio	$24.95
Guía de Inmigración a Estados Unidos (3E)	$24.95
Guía de Justicia para Víctimas del Crimen	$21.95
Guía Esencial para los Contratos de Arrendamiento de Bienes Raices	$22.95
Inmigración a los EE. UU. Paso a Paso	$22.95
Inmigración y Ciudadanía en los EE. UU. Preguntas y Respuestas	$16.95
Manual de Beneficios para el Seguro Social	$18.95
El Seguro Social Preguntas y Respuestas	$16.95

LEGAL SURVIVAL IN PERSONAL AFFAIRS

101 Complaint Letters That Get Results	$18.95
The 529 College Savings Plan (2E)	$18.95
The Antique and Art Collector's Legal Guide	$24.95
The Complete Legal Guide to Senior Care	$21.95
Credit Smart	$18.95
Family Limited Partnership	$26.95
Gay & Lesbian Rights	$26.95
How to File Your Own Bankruptcy (5E)	$21.95
How to File Your Own Divorce (5E)	$26.95
How to Make Your Own Simple Will (3E)	$18.95
How to Write Your Own Living Will (4E)	$18.95
How to Write Your Own Premarital Agreement (3E)	$24.95
Law School 101	$16.95
Living Trusts and Other Ways to Avoid Probate (3E)	$24.95
Mastering the MBE	$16.95
Most Valuable Personal Legal Forms You'll Ever Need (2E)	$26.95
The Power of Attorney Handbook (5E)	$22.95
Quick Cash	$14.95
Repair Your Own Credit and Deal with Debt (2E)	$18.95
Sexual Harassment:Your Guide to Legal Action	$18.95
The Social Security Benefits Handbook (3E)	$18.95
Social Security Q&A	$12.95
Teen Rights	$22.95
Traveler's Rights	$21.95
Unmarried Parents' Rights (2E)	$19.95
U.S. Immigration and Citizenship Q&A	$18.95
U.S. Immigration Step by Step (2E)	$24.95
U.S.A. Immigration Guide (5E)	$26.95
The Visitation Handbook	$18.95
The Wills, Estate Planning and Trusts Legal Kit	$26.95
Win Your Unemployment Compensation Claim (2E)	$21.95
Your Right to Child Custody, Visitation and Support (3E)	$24.95

SPHINX® PUBLISHING ORDER FORM

BILL TO:		SHIP TO:	
Phone #	Terms	F.O.B. Chicago, IL	Ship Date

Charge my: ☐ VISA ☐ MasterCard ☐ American Express

☐ **Money Order or Personal Check**

Credit Card Number

Expiration Date

Qty	ISBN	Title	Retail	Ext.	Qty	ISBN	Title	Retail	Ext.
		SPHINX PUBLISHING NATIONAL TITLES				1-57248-374-1	Law School 101	$16.95	
	1-57248-363-6	101 Complaint Letters That Get Results	$18.95			1-57248-377-6	The Law (In Plain English)® for Small Business	$19.95	
	1-57248-361-X	The 529 College Savings Plan (2E)	$18.95			1-57248-223-0	Legal Research Made Easy (3E)	$21.95	
	1-57248-349-0	The Antique and Art Collector's Legal Guide	$24.95			1-57248-165-X	Living Trusts and Other Ways to Avoid Probate (3E)	$24.95	
	1-57248-347-4	Attorney Responsibilities & Client Rights	$19.95			1-57248-186-2	Manual de Beneficios para el Seguro Social	$18.95	
	1-57248-148-X	Cómo Hacer su Propio Testamento	$16.95			1-57248-220-6	Mastering the MBE	$16.95	
	1-57248-226-5	Cómo Restablecer su propio Crédito y Renegociar sus Deudas	$21.95			1-57248-167-6	Most Val. Business Legal Forms You'll Ever Need (3E)	$21.95	
	1-57248-147-1	Cómo Solicitar su Propio Divorcio	$24.95			1-57248-360-1	Most Val. Personal Legal Forms You'll Ever Need (2E)	$26.95	
	1-57248-166-8	The Complete Book of Corporate Forms	$24.95			1-57248-388-1	The Power of Attorney Handbook (5E)	$22.95	
	1-57248-353-9	The Complete Kit to Selling Your Own Home	$18.95			1-57248-332-6	Profit from Intellectual Property	$28.95	
	1-57248-229-X	The Complete Legal Guide to Senior Care	$21.95			1-57248-329-6	Protect Your Patent	$24.95	
	1-57248-391-1	The Complete Partnership Book	$24.95			1-57248-385-7	Quick Cash	$14.95	
	1-57248-201-X	The Complete Patent Book	$26.95			1-57248-344-X	Repair Your Own Credit and Deal with Debt (2E)	$18.95	
	1-57248-369-5	Credit Smart	$18.95			1-57248-350-4	El Seguro Social Preguntas y Respuestas	$16.95	
	1-57248-163-3	Crime Victim's Guide to Justice (2E)	$21.95			1-57248-217-6	Sexual Harassment: Your Guide to Legal Action	$18.95	
	1-57248-367-9	Employees' Rights	$18.95			1-57248-219-2	The Small Business Owner's Guide to Bankruptcy	$21.95	
	1-57248-365-2	Employer's Rights	$24.95			1-57248-168-4	The Social Security Benefits Handbook (3E)	$18.95	
	1-57248-251-6	The Entrepreneur's Internet Handbook	$21.95			1-57248-216-8	Social Security Q&A	$12.95	
	1-57248-235-4	The Entrepreneur's Legal Guide	$26.95			1-57248-221-4	Teen Rights	$22.95	
	1-57248-346-6	Essential Guide to Real Estate Contracts (2E)	$18.95			1-57248-366-0	Tax Smarts for Small Business	$21.95	
	1-57248-160-9	Essential Guide to Real Estate Leases	$18.95			1-57248-335-0	Traveler's Rights	$21.95	
	1-57248-254-0	Family Limited Partnership	$26.95			1-57248-236-2	Unmarried Parents' Rights (2E)	$19.95	
	1-57248-331-8	Gay & Lesbian Rights	$26.95			1-57248-362-8	U.S. Immigration and Citizenship Q&A	$18.95	
	1-57248-139-0	Grandparents' Rights (3E)	$24.95			1-57248-387-3	U.S. Immigration Step by Step (2E)	$24.95	
	1-57248-188-9	Guía de Inmigración a Estados Unidos (3E)	$24.95			1-57248-392-X	U.S.A. Immigration Guide (5E)	$26.95	
	1-57248-187-0	Guía de Justicia para Víctimas del Crimen	$21.95			1-57248-192-7	The Visitation Handbook	$18.95	
	1-57248-253-2	Guía Esencial para los Contratos de Arrendamiento de Bienes Raices	$22.95			1-57248-225-7	Win Your Unemployment Compensation Claim (2E)	$21.95	
	1-57248-103-X	Help Your Lawyer Win Your Case (2E)	$14.95			1-57248-330-X	The Wills, Estate Planning and Trusts Legal Kit	&26.95	
	1-57248-334-2	Homeowner's Rights	$19.95			1-57248-138-2	Winning Your Personal Injury Claim (2E)	$24.95	
	1-57248-164-1	How to Buy a Condominium or Townhome (2E)	$19.95			1-57248-333-4	Working with Your Homeowners Association	$19.95	
	1-57248-328-8	How to Buy Your First Home	$18.95			1-57248-380-6	Your Right to Child Custody, Visitation and Support (3E)	$24.95	
	1-57248-191-9	How to File Your Own Bankruptcy (5E)	$21.95				**CALIFORNIA TITLES**		
	1-57248-343-1	How to File Your Own Divorce (5E)	$26.95			1-57248-150-1	CA Power of Attorney Handbook (2E)	$18.95	
	1-57248-222-2	How to Form a Limited Liability Company (2E)	$24.95			1-57248-337-7	How to File for Divorce in CA (4E)	$26.95	
	1-57248-231-1	How to Form a Nonprofit Corporation (2E)	$24.95			1-57248-145-5	How to Probate and Settle an Estate in CA	$26.95	
	1-57248-345-8	How to Form Your Own Corporation (4E)	$26.95			1-57248-336-9	How to Start a Business in CA (2E)	$21.95	
	1-57248-232-X	How to Make Your Own Simple Will (3E)	$18.95			1-57248-194-3	How to Win in Small Claims Court in CA (2E)	$18.95	
	1-57248-379-2	How to Register Your Own Copyright (5E)	$24.95			1-57248-246-X	Make Your Own CA Will	$18.95	
	1-57248-104-8	How to Register Your Own Trademark (3E)	$21.95			1-57248-397-0	The Landlord's Legal Guide in CA (2E)	$24.95	
	1-57248-394-6	How to Write Your Own Living Will (4E)	$18.95			1-57248-241-9	Tenants' Rights in CA	$21.95	
	1-57248-156-0	How to Write Your Own Premarital Agreement (3E)	$24.95			**Form Continued on Following Page**		**SubTotal**	
	1-57248-230-3	Incorporate in Delaware from Any State	$26.95						
	1-57248-158-7	Incorporate in Nevada from Any State	$24.95						
	1-57248-250-8	Inmigración a los EE.UU. Paso a Paso	$22.95						
	1-57248-400-4	Inmigración y Ciudadanía en los EE.UU. Preguntas y Respuestas	$16.95						

To order, call Sourcebooks at 1-800-432-7444 or FAX (630) 961-2168 (Bookstores, libraries, wholesalers—please call for discount)

Prices are subject to change without notice.

Find more legal information at: **www.SphinxLegal.com**

SPHINX® PUBLISHING ORDER FORM

Qty	ISBN	Title	Retail	Ext.
		FLORIDA TITLES		
___	1-57071-363-4	Florida Power of Attorney Handbook (2E)	$16.95	___
___	1-57248-396-2	How to File for Divorce in FL (8E)	$28.95	___
___	1-57248-356-3	How to Form a Corporation in FL (6E)	$24.95	___
___	1-57248-203-6	How to Form a Limited Liability Co. in FL (2E)	$24.95	___
___	1-57071-401-0	How to Form a Partnership in FL	$22.95	___
___	1-57248-113-7	How to Make a FL Will (6E)	$16.95	___
___	1-57248-088-2	How to Modify Your FL Divorce Judgment (4E)	$24.95	___
___	1-57248-354-7	How to Probate and Settle an Estate in FL (5E)	$26.95	___
___	1-57248-339-3	How to Start a Business in FL (7E)	$21.95	___
___	1-57248-204-4	How to Win in Small Claims Court in FL (7E)	$18.95	___
___	1-57248-381-4	Land Trusts in Florida (7E)	$29.95	___
___	1-57248-338-5	Landlords' Rights and Duties in FL (9E)	$22.95	___
		GEORGIA TITLES		
___	1-57248-340-7	How to File for Divorce in GA (5E)	$21.95	___
___	1-57248-180-3	How to Make a GA Will (4E)	$16.95	___
___	1-57248-341-5	How to Start a Business in Georgia (3E)	$21.95	___
		ILLINOIS TITLES		
___	1-57248-244-3	Child Custody, Visitation, and Support in IL	$24.95	___
___	1-57248-206-0	How to File for Divorce in IL (3E)	$24.95	___
___	1-57248-170-6	How to Make an IL Will (3E)	$16.95	___
___	1-57248-247-8	How to Start a Business in IL (3E)	$21.95	___
___	1-57248-252-4	The Landlord's Legal Guide in IL	$24.95	___
		MARYLAND, VIRGINIA AND THE DISTRICT OF COLUMBIA		
___	1-57248-240-0	How to File for Divorce in MD, VA and DC	$28.95	___
___	1-57248-359-8	How to Start a Business in MD, VA or DC	$21.95	___
		MASSACHUSETTS TITLES		
___	1-57248-128-5	How to File for Divorce in MA (3E)	$24.95	___
___	1-57248-115-3	How to Form a Corporation in MA	$24.95	___
___	1-57248-108-0	How to Make a MA Will (2E)	$16.95	___
___	1-57248-248-6	How to Start a Business in MA (3E)	$21.95	___
___	1-57248-398-9	The Landlord's Legal Guide in MA (2E)	$24.95	___
		MICHIGAN TITLES		
___	1-57248-215-X	How to File for Divorce in MI (3E)	$24.95	___
___	1-57248-182-X	How to Make a MI Will (3E)	$16.95	___
___	1-57248-183-8	How to Start a Business in MI (3E)	$18.95	___
		MINNESOTA TITLES		
___	1-57248-142-0	How to File for Divorce in MN	$21.95	___
___	1-57248-179-X	How to Form a Corporation in MN	$24.95	___
___	1-57248-178-1	How to Make a MN Will (2E)	$16.95	___
		NEW JERSEY TITLES		
___	1-57248-239-7	How to File for Divorce in NJ	$24.95	___
___	1-57248-448-9	How to Start a Business in NJ	$21.95	___
		NEW YORK TITLES		
___	1-57248-193-5	Child Custody, Visitation and Support in NY	$26.95	___
___	1-57248-351-2	File for Divorce in NY	$26.95	___
___	1-57248-249-4	How to Form a Corporation in NY (2E)	$24.95	___
___	1-57248-401-2	How to Make a NY Will (3E)	$16.95	___
___	1-57248-199-4	How to Start a Business in NY (2E)	$18.95	___
___	1-57248-198-6	How to Win in Small Claims Court in NY (2E)	$18.95	___
___	1-57248-197-8	Landlords' Legal Guide in NY	$24.95	___
___	1-57071-188-7	New York Power of Attorney Handbook	$19.95	___

Qty	ISBN	Title	Retail	Ext.
___	1-57248-122-6	Tenants' Rights in NY	$21.95	___
		NORTH CAROLINA TITLES		
___	1-57248-185-4	How to File for Divorce in NC (3E)	$22.95	___
___	1-57248-129-3	How to Make a NC Will (3E)	$16.95	___
___	1-57248-184-6	How to Start a Business in NC (3E)	$18.95	___
___	1-57248-091-2	Landlords' Rights & Duties in NC	$21.95	___
		NORTH CAROLINA AND SOUTH CAROLINA TITLES		
___	1-57248-371-7	How to Start a Business in NC or SC	$24.95	___
		OHIO TITLES		
___	1-57248-190-0	How to File for Divorce in OH (2E)	$24.95	___
___	1-57248-174-9	How to Form a Corporation in OH	$24.95	___
___	1-57248-173-0	How to Make an OH Will	$16.95	___
		PENNSYLVANIA TITLES		
___	1-57248-242-7	Child Custody, Visitation and Support in PA	$26.95	___
___	1-57248-211-7	How to File for Divorce in PA (3E)	$26.95	___
___	1-57248-358-X	How to Form a Cooporation in PA	$24.95	___
___	1-57248-094-7	How to Make a PA Will (2E)	$16.95	___
___	1-57248-357-1	How to Start a Business in PA (3E)	$21.95	___
___	1-57248-245-1	The Landlord's Legal Guide in PA	$24.95	___
		TEXAS TITLES		
___	1-57248-171-4	Child Custody, Visitation, and Support in TX	$22.95	___
___	1-57248-399-7	How to File for Divorce in TX (4E)	$24.95	___
___	1-57248-114-5	How to Form a Corporation in TX (2E)	$24.95	___
___	1-57248-255-9	How to Make a TX Will (3E)	$16.95	___
___	1-57248-214-1	How to Probate and Settle an Estate in TX (3E)	$26.95	___
___	1-57248-228-1	How to Start a Business in TX (3E)	$18.95	___
___	1-57248-111-0	How to Win in Small Claims Court in TX (2E)	$16.95	___
___	1-57248-355-5	The Landlord's Legal Guide in TX	$24.95	___

SubTotal This page   ___

SubTotal previous page   ___

Shipping — $5.00 for 1st book, $1.00 each additional   ___

Illinois residents add 6.75% sales tax   ___

Connecticut residents add 6.00% sales tax   ___

Total   ___

To order, call Sourcebooks at 1-800-432-7444 or FAX (630) 961-2168 (Bookstores, libraries, wholesalers—please call for discount)

Prices are subject to change without notice.

Find more legal information at: **www.SphinxLegal.com**